# VIRAGO
## CLASSIC NON-FICTION

*Kathleen Jones*

Kathleen Jones was born and brought up on a hill farm in the Lake District. After spending some years in Africa and the Middle East, where she worked in English broadcasting, she returned to Cumbria where she now lives with sculptor Neil Ferber. She has four children and writes full-time, working occasionally as a creative writing tutor. Her published work includes three biographies, *Glorious Fame: The Life of Margaret Cavendish, Duchess of Newcastle* (Bloomsbury 1988), *Learning not to be First: The Life of Christina Rossetti* (Oxford University Press 1991) and *Catherine Cookson: The Biography* (Constable and Robinson 1999), short fiction (for which she has received a number of awards), journalism and a collection of poetry entitled *Unwritten Lives* (Redbeck Press 1995).

# A PASSIONATE SISTERHOOD

*The Sisters, Wives and Daughters
of the Lake Poets*

## Kathleen Jones

Virago

VIRAGO

Published by Virago Press 1998
Reprinted 2000, 2002, 2005, 2006

First published in Great Britain by Constable and Company Ltd, 1997

Copyright © Kathleen Jones 1997

The moral right of the author has been asserted

A CIP catalogue record for this book
is available from the British Library

ISBN-13: 978-1-86049-492-5
ISBN-10: 1-86049-492-7

Typeset by Hewer Text Ltd, Edinburgh
Printed and bound in Great Britain by Clays Ltd, St Ives plc

Virago Press
An imprint of
Little, Brown Book Group
Brettenham House
Lancaster Place
London WC2E 7EN

A member of the Hachette Livre Group of Companies

www.virago.co.uk

# Contents

## PART THREE: THE TRIAD

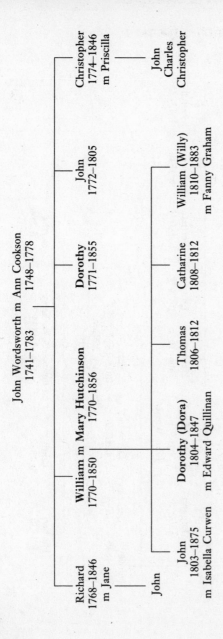
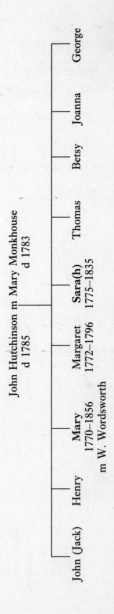

John Wordsworth m Ann Cookson
1741–1783    1748–1778

Richard
1768–1846
m Jane

John

William m Mary Hutchinson
1770–1850    1770–1856

Dorothy
1771–1855

John
1772–1805

Christopher
1774–1846
m Priscilla

John
Charles
Christopher

John
1803–1875
m Isabella Curwen

Dorothy (Dora)
1804–1847
m Edward Quillinan

Thomas
1806–1812

Catharine
1808–1812

William (Willy)
1810–1883
m Fanny Graham

John Hutchinson m Mary Monkhouse
d 1783

John (Jack)

Henry

Mary
1770–1856
m W. Wordsworth

Margaret
1772–1796

Sara(h)
1775–1835

Thomas

Betsy

Joanna

George

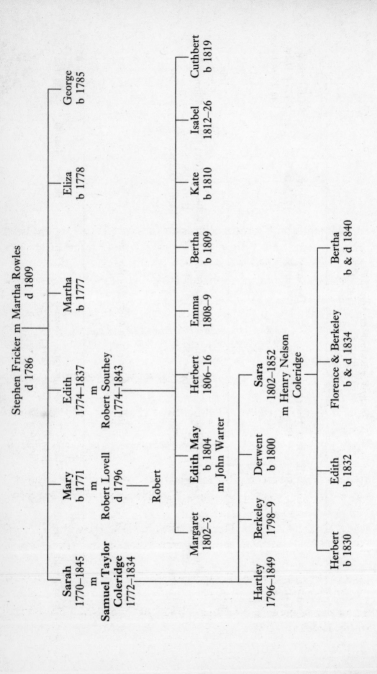

Stephen Fricker m Martha Rowles
d 1786              d 1809

**Sarah**          **Mary**         Edith          Martha      Eliza      George
1770–1845         b 1771         1774–1837       b 1777      b 1778     b 1785
m                 m              m
**Samuel Taylor   Robert Lovell  Robert Southey**
Coleridge**       d 1796         1774–1843
1772–1834

                  Robert

Margaret   **Edith May**   Derwent   Herbert    Emma      Bertha   Kate     Isabel    Cuthbert
1802–3     b 1804          b 1800    1806–16    1808–9    b 1809   b 1810   1812–26   b 1819
           m John Warter

Hartley    Berkeley                  **Sara**
1796–1849  1798–9                    1802–1852
                                     m Henry Nelson
                                     Coleridge

Herbert    Edith      Florence & Berkeley   Bertha
b 1830     b 1832     b & d 1834            b & d 1840

## Illustrations

Sara Hutchinson, Dorothy Wordsworth, Mary Wordsworth, Kate Southey, Edith May Southey, Bertha Southey. Silhouettes *circa* 1815 (*The Wordsworth Trust*)

Coleridge's Cottage and Alfoxden Park (from *Line Drawings of the Quantock Area* by Edmund New, 1914)

Sarah Coleridge by Mathilda Betham, 1809 (*Hulton Deutsch Collection. By kind permission of Mrs A.H.B. Coleridge*)

Samuel Taylor Coleridge by Robert Hancock, 1796 (*National Portrait Gallery*)

Edith Southey, aged 35, by Mathilda Betham, 1809 (*Fitzpatrick Museum, Keswick*)

Robert Southey at Greta Hall by Robert Hancock, 1804 (*National Portrait Gallery*)

Young Dorothy Wordsworth (*by kind permission of Mrs A.H.B. Coleridge, photo Tony Riley*)

William Wordsworth by Robert Hancock (*National Portrait Gallery*)

Dove Cottage, sketch by Dora Wordsworth (*The Wordsworth Trust*)

Rydal Mount, sketch by Dora Wordsworth (*The Wordsworth Trust*)

Greta Hall, floor plan (*by kind permission of the Governors of Keswick School*)

Greta Hall and Keswick Bridge with Latrigg Fell behind (*Cumbria County Library*)

The Rock of Names, Thirlmere, by Henry Goodwin (*The Wordsworth Trust*)

## *Acknowledgements*

The author acknowledges with gratitude the financial assistance of the Society of Authors and the Authors' Foundation in order to complete her research. Many individuals and organisations have given invaluable assistance to the author, supplied illustrations and granted permission to quote from manuscripts and books. Particular thanks must go to the staff of Penrith Library, Jeff Cowton and the staff of the Wordsworth Trust Library at Dove Cottage, the Dove Cottage Trustees, Mr and Mrs Peter Elkington and the Trustees of Rydal Mount, the Governors of Keswick School, Mrs A.H.B. Coleridge, Mrs Priscilla Coleridge Cassam, the research librarian of the Harry Ransom Humanities Research Centre at the University of Texas at Austin, the staff of Coleridge Cottage, Richard Holmes, Molly Lefebure, Neil Ferber, Tony Riley, Richard Gollner and Carol O'Brien.

Every effort has been made by the author to contact the copyright holders of manuscripts and other published material, but in some cases no replies were ever received to communications sent. The author therefore apologises to anyone whose name has been omitted due to inadequate or out-of-date information. The source material has been fully acknowledged in every case.

## On the Other Side of the Glass

> Winter rain looked at
> through the windows of great men
> is still only rain.[1]

To an eighteenth-century sensibility, the Lake District was not necessarily a desirable place to live in. Its wild, mountainous prospects and great beauty excited the romantic imagination. But the privations of life in so remote and barbaric a region – its rocks and 'torrents roaring' – could also induce a shudder of horror and offered little to the sophisticated tourist who required both bodily comfort and elegant diversion. It was these extremes that drew Wordsworth, Coleridge and Southey north; their friend Charles Lamb preferred to remain in the civilised surroundings of a London street.

The Wordsworths lived at Grasmere, the Coleridges and Southeys 12 miles away at Keswick. The two households, linked initially by the friendship of the poets, remained close even after relations between the men deteriorated – bound together by the extraordinary tenacity of their wives and sisters. These six women, two groups of sisters, connected by blood and marriage, formed a series of passionate, triangular relationships. The three Fricker sisters, Sarah Coleridge, Edith Southey and Mary Lovell at Greta Hall, near Keswick, Dorothy Wordsworth and her childhood friends Mary (who married William) and Sara Hutchinson at Dove Cottage in Grasmere created a kind of extended family that kept the Lake Poets together long after they had ceased to be friends.

Inevitably their daughters – Dora Wordsworth, Sara Coleridge and Edith May Southey – thrown so much upon each others' company, formed close friendships and perpetuated the links.

The modern reader will be astonished by the distances they travelled, often on foot. Coleridge and the Wordsworths thought nothing of walking the 12 or 13 miles between Grasmere and Keswick to visit each other, sometimes in the dark. The roads were rough and often unmetalled. They were shod either in clogs – wooden soles with a leather shoe upper for rough walking – or stout shoes with a double leather sole. The cobbler's bill was one of their biggest expenses.

Sarah Coleridge and her sisters were city girls. Unlike Dorothy and Mary Wordsworth, they had little relish for vigorous exercise and the outdoor hazards of wind, rain and mud. Both Sarah and her sister Mary Lovell became very stout in middle age and found it an effort to walk even short distances. Visits to Grasmere were made either in a borrowed carriage or a 'returned chaise'.

Sara Hutchinson, too, had little fondness for long walks. A stroll along the garden terraces or the margins of the lake should, she felt, be enough exercise for anyone. Longer journeys were undertaken by coach or on horseback – sometimes on a 'double horse', a sturdy mount with a double saddle for riders in tandem. Only the rich had their own carriages. For long journeys the better off hired a chaise with post horses and post boys. Others bought a seat on a mail coach, travelling in cramped conditions and much discomfort. Cheaper seats were to be had outside on the roof exposed to the elements. For the poor there were slow rides in a carrier's cart sometimes pulled by oxen.

Horse travel was not without its hazards. Both William and Mary Wordsworth narrowly escaped serious injury when their carriages were overturned, and William was thrown from his horse more than once. Mary's cousin was permanently paralysed by just such an accident, and Sara Hutchinson was almost killed when the horse in front of her was struck by lightning.

It was perhaps inevitable that Wordsworth, Coleridge and Southey should meet. They were of a similar age and inclination, aspiring poets and ardent democrats. They were introduced by mutual friends at university. All three men had been orphaned at an early age, and so were the women they married. This sense of loss and abandonment was another common bond. They clung together, not because of youthful ideals of community, but because they sought to recreate the security of family life. Their lives were financially precarious – all were dependent on the charity of friends to free them from the burden of earning a living in order to write. Wordsworth was left a legacy from his school friend Raisley Calvert to sustain himself and Dorothy; Southey was given an annuity by an Oxford contemporary, Wynn, and Coleridge was given a similar annuity by the benevolent Wedgwood brothers, whom he had met in the West Country.

To their families and more conventional acquaintances they were spongers – unwilling to take proper jobs to support themselves, scribbling the odd line of poetry, which paid little or nothing, lying in bed till lunchtime and wandering about the countryside like gypsies at all hours of the day and night, returning with torn, dirty clothes and broken shoes. The women they married had to take their share of the general atmosphere of disapproval.

Drawn together initially by marriage and friendship, forced on each others' society by geographical proximity, the women's relationships were far from harmonious. There was intense jealousy between Sarah Coleridge and Dorothy Wordsworth, the pivotal figures in the group. They had conflicting personalities. Dorothy was tall, lean, 'all fire and ardour', eyes 'wild and startling in a face of Egyptian brown'. Heedless of appearances, she transmitted intellectual energy to everyone around her and was credited by William with having awakened his senses to the beauties of nature. But this vivid creature, whose neighbours long remembered both her eccentricity and her kindness, had another side to her which she tried very hard to suppress. Her gentleness was paralleled by a ruthless streak that bordered on cruelty, a trait her brother described in an early draft of the poem 'Nutting', where he describes her slashing down the hazels: 'in truth/If I had met thee here with that keen look/Half cruel in its eagerness, those cheeks/Thus . . . flushed with a tempestuous bloom,/I might have almost deem'd that I had pass'd/A houseless being in a human shape,/ An enemy of nature'.[2] Dorothy's love affair with her brother is one of the great literary relationships.

Sarah Coleridge was plump, 'in person full and rather below the common height', but always elegantly dressed, something Dorothy scoffed at behind her back. But Sarah was far from the domestic cipher often portrayed. She and her sister Edith were well educated and followers of Mary Wollstonecraft. It was their emancipated behaviour that caused Byron to remark sarcastically that Coleridge and Southey had 'married two milliners from Bath' – milliner being a contemporary euphemism for an immoral woman. Byron was also referring unkindly to the Fricker sisters' unfortunate circumstances, which had forced them to earn their own livings as seamstresses before they married.

Marriage was virtually the only career open to a respectable middle-class woman. It was extremely difficult to earn an independent living. As Mary Wollstonecraft pointed out, 'Few are the modes of earning a subsistence, and those very humiliating.' The poor worked on the land or in factories, or went into service. For the single middle-class woman lucky enough to have some education, the only careers were those of needlewoman or governess – or the more limited possibilities of the female author. There was little formal education, and universities and professions were barred to women until the latter part of the nineteenth century.

This situation often trapped women into positions of dependency, either on their husbands or on their families if they failed to marry. For those whose marriages did not turn out well there was no escape. Divorce and separation were rare, expensive and socially ruinous for women, who were usually forced to stay in unhappy, sometimes abusive relationships. It is not surprising to find that such claustrophobic emotional conditions caused considerable stress and adversely affected their general health. The Coleridge, Southey and Wordsworth women were no exceptions.

Reading their diaries and letters, you begin to realise how much the issue of health dominated their lives. Minor ailments, meriting no more than a course of antibiotics or a couple of paracetamol today, confined them to bed and left them weak and ill. Childhood illnesses such as whooping cough and measles often killed both children and adults. Immunisation was in its infancy. Public hygiene was primitive and cholera and typhoid were realities of everyday British life.

Medical practice killed as often as it cured. Patients, already weakened by disease, were often bled to death. Another supposedly beneficial torture was 'blistering', where hot cups were applied to the skin producing a superficial burn. The pain and irritation of the wound distracted the patient from whatever other affliction they were suffering and gave them the illusion that the condition had improved.

The only pain-killers available were opiates, whose addictive properties were little understood. The most commonly used was laudanum – a distillation of opium in alcohol available in a number of different strengths. Large numbers of people became addicted to laudanum, including Coleridge, his daughter Sara, De Quincey and Dorothy Wordsworth.

By far the greatest scourge for adults and children alike was toothache. Modern dentistry was far in the future and most people suffered torture as their teeth decayed. The only solution was to have the tooth pulled, without anaesthetic, by the feared 'tooth drawer'. By the time she was thirty Dorothy Wordsworth had lost most of her teeth and paid large sums of money to have the remaining stumps drawn. Sarah Coleridge and her sisters had rather stronger enamel – perhaps as a result of having been brought up in a hard-water area – but even so by the time Sarah was forty-five her irrepressible smile had a number of gaps in it.

Sara Hutchinson was reduced to only one good tooth, which she wrenched eating a pear, and had to masticate her food on the roof of her mouth with her tongue. She debated for quite a while on the pros and cons of false teeth made from porcelain. 'There is nothing of disgust can attach to them as there does to the human teeth when set in bone – the very sight makes your flesh creep – which was one of the reasons of my reluctance to have anything to do with them . . . the price is *awful*, two G[uinea]'s!! But they will last longer than I shall . . .'[3] Apparently Dorothy had already had three sets. Some did not fit and Sara feared that she would be unable to wear them, but thought it worth the risk.

What is striking about the group is the amount of mental illness suffered by the women. Of them all, only Sarah Coleridge, Mary Wordsworth and her sister Sara Hutchinson were largely free of it, though they too were ill with nervous exhaustion or what we would now refer to as 'stress' at certain times of their lives.

Depression and 'hysteria' were a prominent feature of nineteenth-century women's lives, a phenomenon lucidly discussed in Elaine Showalter's book *The Female Malady*. Intelligent, creative, full of potential, the women of the Wordsworth, Coleridge and Southey families led stifling lives within the four walls of their houses – their lives bounded by child-rearing and domestic concerns without any prospect of escape. Dorothy Wordsworth found relief in long solitary walks on the hills, but her mind finally gave way under the emotional stresses of her life, the corrosion of opium and a lack of personal fulfilment that left her feeling barren and useless.

For Edith Southey, a fearful, pessimistic disposition and a miserable marriage made her depressed and the victim of eating disorders. Her grief at losing four of her children finally eroded the last shreds of her sanity. She became increasingly hostile towards her sisters, her husband and even her remaining children. She was often violent towards them and had to be restrained. When Edith was taken to the Quaker Retreat at York, she showed no desire to go back home at all.

Mary Lovell – possessed of a fine intellect grounded in the classics and a lively, extrovert disposition that had taken her on to the Bristol stage – was literally bored out of her mind in the back room at Greta Hall. The knowledge that the future held nothing for her except more of the same kept her prostrated on the sofa with only hartshorn and lavender water for alleviation.

This blight affected the younger generation too. The beautiful, wilful Dora Wordsworth, whose literary and artistic talents are apparent in her journals, letters and drawings, remained dutifully silent for most of her life. She formed romantic attachments with both men and women, the most intense and significant being with the novelist Maria Jane Jewsbury. After Jane died she married a lifelong friend, Edward Quillinan – a poet thirteen years her senior – against her father's wishes. William disliked losing what Coleridge called 'his petticoats'. Despite further family opposition, Dora travelled to Portugal with Quillinan and on her return published an account of her experiences which violated yet another family taboo. Dora died at home the following year, an emaciated skeleton whose tubercular bones protruded through her pressure sores. She withstood the agony with the stoicism that had kept her smiling through all her earlier discouragements and disappointments.

Dora's best friend, Edith May Southey, escaped the family net into a fashionable marriage, bearing the burden of guilt that her departure had precipitated the final crumbling of her mother's mind. Edith May's cousin, Sara Coleridge, determined not to be caught in the same trap, found herself in the double bind of a woman trying to lead two lives. The roles of wife and mother did not fit neatly with those of scholar and author. In the conflict between the demands of her body and those of her mind, both were almost wrecked. As Adrienne Rich put it, 'trying to fulfil traditional female functions in a traditional way is in direct conflict with the subversive function of the imagination'.[4] In order to conform to society's notions of what women were supposed to be, much of a woman's real personality – particularly her longings and expectations – was suppressed.

The Wordsworth, Coleridge and Southey women were very familiar with this subversive female 'other' – a truculent, disobedient, independently minded, creative, sexual being, whose face rose towards them every time they looked in the mirror. It was a vision perfectly evoked by Sara Coleridge's second cousin Mary Coleridge.

I sat before my glass one day,
  And conjured up a vision bare,
Unlike the aspects glad and gay,
  That erst were found reflected there –
The vision of a woman wild
  With more than womanly despair . . .

Her lips were open – not a sound
  Came through the parted lines of red.
Whate'er it was, the hideous wound
  In silence and in secret bled.
No sigh relieved her speechless woe,
  She had no voice to speak her dread . . .

Shade of a shadow in the glass,
  O set the crystal surface free!
Pass – as the fairer visions pass –
  Nor ever more return, to be
The ghost of a distracted hour,
  That heard me whisper, 'I am she!'[5]

Writing a group biography has the advantage of allowing a multi-faceted view of each individual, seen from a number of different perspectives. As the young Sara Coleridge wrote, 'Poor is the portrait that one look pourtrays/It mocks the face on which we loved to gaze'.[6] But it also poses a number of technical problems and, with so many people in focus at the same time, the duplication of names can be very confusing to the reader. There are three Saras, two Dorothys, two Marys and two Ediths. In order to simplify, I have adopted the practice of distinguishing one Sara from another by keeping the 'h' for Sarah Coleridge and dropping it for her daughter Sara and – as Coleridge wished – for Sara Hutchinson (his beloved Asra). Sarah's sister Mary Lovell is usually referred to by first and second names to distinguish her from Mary Hutchinson (subsequently Wordsworth). Edith Southey is referred to as Edith and her daughter as Edith May, which was the usual practice of the family. Dorothy Wordsworth shared the same name as her niece, who was usually known to family and friends as Dora.

It was usual at this date for men to refer to their peers by their surnames only – their wives and female relatives would also do this when talking about their husbands and fathers outside the family. Christian names were only used between husband and wife, brother and sister or very close friends. Mary would talk about William within the family but to others he would be 'Wordsworth' or 'Mr Wordsworth'. Coleridge preferred to be known by his surname or his initials STC (Esteesi), even by his family circle, since he hated his Christian name. This practice has, where practicable, been followed in the book.

# PART ONE

_Brothers and Sisters_

# 1

## *Three Milliners from Bath*

If the Fricker sisters' life story was a fairy-tale their extraordinary history would begin something like this: 'Once upon a time there were three sisters, all rich, beautiful and clever . . .' Sarah, Edith and Mary were destined to marry three friends – three of the most brilliant and creative men of their generation – and spend not only their childhood, but most of their adult lives under the same roof. Obedient to the ancient traditions of folk-tale construction, their story contains conflicts and rivalries and great reverses of fortune.

It begins in Bristol and Bath. During the period of the Regency, until the death of George III in 1820, Bath was at its zenith as a fashionable resort for those exhausted by the dissipation of the London Season, or bored witless by the dullness of life on their country estates. In strict contrast, 9 miles away in Bristol, there was a thriving, independently minded, progressive merchant-venturer community. For the middle classes, to which the Fricker family belonged, the two cities together provided not only a good living from service industries, but a unique opportunity to visit the Pump Rooms and assemblies and mingle with the aristocracy. This was the lively, prosperous and upwardly mobile context in which Sarah Fricker and her sisters grew up.

The Frickers were typical of many middle-class families leaving behind their rural yeoman roots for a life in the city, money earned from trade rather than the soil, and the opportunity to enjoy more fashionable and cultured pursuits. The girls' grandfather had been a farmer and maltster in Somerset. Their father Stephen, a younger son, decided to move to Bristol to set up as a wine and spirit merchant, though his personal input into the business was somewhat reluctant, since he thought himself 'too much of a gentleman for business'. Mrs Fricker was the daughter of a radical, merchant-venturer family who owned a large iron foundry. She had been well educated at a girls' boarding school, brought her own money into the marriage and reared her daughters in an aura of claustrophobic gentility.

Their childhood was divided between a smart house in Bath and a villa at Westbury, just outside Bristol, which had its own kitchen garden and dairies. There was a series of failed businesses. At one time or another Stephen Fricker's holdings included a tavern, a pottery, a coal yard and a liquor vault. But his own reluctance to involve himself in the business, extravagant living standards and general incompetence with money meant that he got through his own and his wife's money very quickly. The girls' childhood was punctuated by financial crises, usually resolved by an application to relatives for financial assistance.

Sarah was the eldest child in the family, born on 10 September 1770. Her sister Mary followed in 1771, Edith in 1774 and then three younger children – Martha, Elizabeth and George. Four other children died in infancy. The three older girls were all very different in appearance and temperament. Sarah was friendly, outgoing, quick-tempered, impulsive and had a natural sensuality. Mary was apparently the liveliest and most academic of the three, while Edith, the most elegant, was prone to depression, self-effacing to a fault and fearful of anything new or strange.

Bristol was the home of Hannah More, a great advocate of female education, and the girls were all educated rather above the normal standards of the day – probably at the school run by Hannah More. Sarah read widely in both English and French and was particularly proficient in maths. Mary learned Latin and Greek. They were also progressive in their outlook, brought up in liberal, Unitarian surroundings – the girls apparently read Mary Wollstonecraft's *Vindication of the Rights of Woman* almost as soon as it was published in 1792. For Sarah its ideals of sexual equality accorded with her own passionate nature. She had no intention of being 'the toy of man, his rattle', willing to 'jingle in his ears whenever . . . he chooses to be amused'. The idea of being a loving friend to your husband rather than a 'humble dependent' was very attractive, and what Wollstonecraft wrote about female independence and self-reliance had become so evidently necessary by the time Sarah read the book, it seemed a fundamental truth.

In 1786 Stephen Fricker's financial difficulties reached a point where they could no longer be shored up by household economies or family charity. In any case, both his own family and that of his wife had long since lost patience with Stephen's financial incompetence and were no longer willing to put their hands in their pockets. When he went bankrupt in 1786 the girls were pitched violently into a very different world. They lost houses, furniture, everything but the clothes they stood up in and, as the family of a bankrupt, their social credibility. Without a roof over their heads, the family was broken up. Sarah, just sixteen years old, went with her father to stay at a friend's house outside Bristol, her mother and the youngest children were taken in by another friend, while Edith and Mary (twelve and fourteen respectively) were lodged elsewhere. A few months later Stephen Fricker died aged forty-eight, leaving a widow and six children aged between one and sixteen without any means of support.

Mrs Fricker rented lodgings on Redcliffe Hill in Bristol, ran a small private school for a while and then a dress shop. Neither enterprise was very successful, so Sarah, Mary and Edith went out to work as needlewomen. The fashionable society in which they had been consumers suddenly became their livelihood. It was obligatory for the wealthy women who frequented Bristol and Bath to be dressed in the latest kick of fashion, so dressmaking and millinery trades flourished, and Bath modistes were noted for their skills, being second only to London. The Fricker girls, trained in female accomplishments, were all skilled needlewomen and had no difficulty earning their livings from their needles. But it was a profession with a dubious reputation. It was Byron who made the sarcastic remark about Coleridge and Southey marrying 'two milliners from Bath', gossip repeated by Thomas De Quincey, who added, 'Everybody knows what is meant to be conveyed in that expression.'[1]

This fragmentation of a close family unit, the sudden loss of social standing and of prospects, and the inevitable isolation affected the girls deeply. The shame and the disgrace of it stayed with Sarah all her life but she was by nature a fighter, determined to come through it all successfully. To the end of her life she persisted in using a particular motto to seal her letters with the optimistic words '*Toujours gai!*' printed on it. Her sister Edith, already inclined to gloom, always expecting the worst, became paranoid about money – convinced even when she was comfortably off that she was on the brink of ruin. For Mary it created a sense of helplessness – that whatever she did, she was powerless to alter her ultimate fate.

Many of the people who gave the girls work were old friends of the family and one of the people Sarah went out to sew for was Mrs Margaret Southey, mother of Robert. The Southey and Fricker families had known each other since the children were small and went to dame school together. Their circumstances were very similar, Mr Southey senior having come up from the country, where his parents were woollen manufacturers, to go into business in Bristol as a linen draper. Like Stephen Fricker, he paid others to manage the business for him while he adopted a style of living inappropriate to his income and expectations. He married the daughter of a Bristol tradesman, whose half-sister, Miss Elizabeth Tyler, led a fashionable life in Bath.

Robert Southey, the eldest son, was born in 1774, 'a great red creature covered in rolls of fat' and initially rejected by his mother, who thought she would never be able to love such an ugly creature. Thereafter he lived mainly with his aunt in Bath. She was beautiful, but possessed of a violent temper and used to having her own way. She also had a private income left to her by an uncle and aspired to climb the social ladder. Rich and wilful; 'Tyrannical and Indulgent'; clever and spendthrift – her personality was a litany of antitheses.

She insisted that Robert should sleep in her bed. As she didn't get up until about eleven – quite a reasonable hour for a fashion-able lady – and he was awake by six, he was forced to lie unnaturally still and quiet for several hours. She had an obsession about dirt and dust so he was not allowed to play in the garden in case he tore or dirtied his clothes. If someone she classed as 'unclean' came into the house the cup and saucer they used had to be buried in the garden for six weeks before they could be used again. Her portrait, painted by Gainsborough, was covered by a curtain to keep it free from dust and flies. She also had a phobia about marriage, and her servants were turned out if they married. But she did take Southey to the theatre to see Mrs Siddons and introduced him to literature through the Bath circulating library. This lonely, rather boring childhood schooled Southey in self-control, self-reliance, concealment of real feeling and a dedication to duty.

Not surprisingly Southey had little affection for Miss Tyler and became rebellious. This wore her patience thin, as the adorable precocious baby became a boy. On one occasion, when Southey's father came to see him, he 'found me pale and thin. I had just recovered from a fever and have not yet forgotten the tea-cup in which the bark was given me, and a foul sweet medicine. He returned home in a rage – swore my Aunt would kill "the boy" and in consequence I was transported to Bristol.' Starved of love, Southey was overjoyed to be at home again with his nursemaid Pat: 'I loved her dearly, she had neither temperance soberness or chastity – but she was fond of me.' He was sent to school to a Mrs Powell, which he hated so much that at six he was taken away, and very soon he was back in Bath living with his aunt again.[2] Even after he was sent to boarding school he found that he was expected to spend the holidays with his aunt, in Bath, Bristol and the various fashionable watering-places she frequented.

Sarah Fricker, four years older, first saw him as 'a little boy in frocks'. Miss Tyler used to dress him up in 'A fantastic costume of nankeen . . . trimmed with green fringe; a vest and tunic outfit known as a *jam*' (ancestor of the pyjama!).[3] According to Sarah, the Fricker girls thought Miss Tyler 'elegant, handsome and fashionable', a social example whose dress and manners could be emulated, but 'very haughty'.[4] She was an egotistical snob, but she took the Fricker girls under her wing, employing Edith and finding work for the others among her wealthy friends. She used her connections to find a place for Mary, who had a beautiful singing voice, in the theatre. So Mary became an actress – a profession with as many immodest associations as millinery.

Sarah Fricker and Robert Southey were very good friends, despite Sarah's four-year seniority. When Robert's father also went bankrupt in 1792 and died a few months later, probably from consumption, they found themselves in almost identical circumstances. Southey found the humiliation of having to apply to his father's wealthy relatives and expose himself to rejection almost too much to bear. He also felt keenly the responsibility of his position as the head of the family with two younger brothers and a sister to provide for. Sarah Fricker, having been through the same experience, provided a sympathetic ear for Southey's difficulties.

He had recently been expelled from Westminster school for writing a provocative article on flogging in a radical news-sheet. Southey had been deeply affected by the French Revolution, writing later: 'Few persons but those who have lived in it can conceive or comprehend what the memory of the French Revolution was, nor what a visionary world seemed to open upon those who were just entering it. Old things seemed passing away, and nothing was dreamt of but the regeneration of the human race.'[5] Southey recalled that he 'left Westminster in a perilous state – a heart full of poetry and feeling, a head full of Rousseau and Werther, and my religious principles shaken by Gibbon.' He had also discovered Epictetus. 'I carried Epictetus in my pocket till my very heart was ingrained with it . . . And the longer I live, and the more I learn, the more am I convinced that Stoicism, properly understood, is the best and noblest of systems.'[6]

Sarah was also one of the few people with whom Southey could discuss his radical ideas, and when he went up to Balliol College, Oxford in 1792, funded by his maternal uncle, he corresponded with her. For two young single people to write to each other at this date was usually evidence of a close attachment, either an engagement or a blood relationship. Their close friendship lasted for the rest of their lives, but it may well have begun as a romantic attachment. One of Southey's letters, written before his involvement with Edith, mentions an occasion when 'In the evening I walked round Bath in hopes of meeting one whom I earnestly wished to see – my hopes were raised to the highest pitch when I thought I recognised the dress, but disappointment soon checked them and the rest of the evening passed heavily and sadly.'[7] Miss Tyler was worried enough to forbid Robert to have anything to do with the Fricker girls, whom she considered his social inferiors. If he married at all, she wanted him to make a 'good match' to restore the family fortunes and was presumably confident that with her money and connections it could be achieved. But Southey resisted her attempts at matchmaking. 'The only society that could please me here is that of some young women, sisters, with whom I was partly educated and whose histories are as melancholy as my own. The ill-grounded fears of my Aunt forbid it. I see them seldom, but they know my motives and pity me. Other society I have none. This city is peopled with rich fools . . .'[8]

Miss Tyler's disapproval of the Fricker girls was problematic since it was Miss Tyler's fortune that was helping to support both the Southey and the Fricker families. Not only was she using her connections to find employment for the girls, she had also lent Mrs Southey money to purchase a lease on a house in Bath in order to rent out rooms. Mrs Southey was ill with consumption and hardly in a position to help herself.

Southey was an attractive, willowy figure, described by De Quincey as being 'somewhat taller than Wordsworth, being about five feet eleven in height, or a trifle more'; his slender limbs made him seem taller than he was. He had a quiet air of elegance, though he did not dress in a particularly fashionable manner, wearing a short jacket and pantaloons which gave him the appearance 'of a Tyrolese mountaineer'. He had black, curly hair, but a very fair complexion, a strong, aquiline nose and large hazel eyes. Most people commented, like De Quincey, on the air of 'reserve and distance' which he had, the product of a shy and intensely private disposition in which all passionate emotion must be publicly suppressed. He was also very fastidious in sexual matters, stating emphatically: 'Nothing is more astonishing to me than that a virtue so rigidly demanded from women should be so despised among men.'[9] He remained a virgin until his marriage.

Southey was rapidly becoming a republican, embracing opposition to the established Church as part of his radical stance. He was not exactly an atheist – he always acknowledged the existence of some Deity, describing himself sometimes as a 'Deist'. This was extremely awkward because his uncle, the Rev. William Hill, was paying for his education at Oxford on the understanding that Southey would go into the Church. Southey was torn between his duty and principles. Writing to a friend, he declared that he would exchange every intellectual gift he had been blessed with if he could only have implicit faith in order to please his uncle and provide support for his mother and his siblings. But, he went on, 'My principles and practice are . . . democratic . . . the very existence of a priest is wrong. To obtain future support – to return the benefits I have received – I must become contemptible . . . and perjured.'[10] Southey – like Dorothy Wordsworth, educated to please – found it difficult to kick over the traces. The atmosphere of Balliol horrified him. He found himself with young men 'who were sent to Oxford in order that they might proceed through their course of shooting, horse-racing, whoring, and drinking, out of sight of their families and without injury to their characters.'[11]

Mary Fricker, through her work in the theatre, had met Robert Lovell, the twenty-two-year-old son of a wealthy Bristol Quaker. He led the life of a wealthy gentleman's son; like many young bucks of the day, he was interested in pugilism and blood sports and, on the face of it, had little in common with Southey. But he had similar democratic sympathies and poetic ambitions and when the Fricker sisters introduced the two men, they were instantly attracted to each other and became great friends. Four years older than Southey, Lovell too had been to Balliol, where a brilliant career had been predicted. His relationship with Mary met with considerable disapproval. She had no money, she was an actress, and she was not a Quaker: she was thus totally ineligible. Lovell, a 'birthright' Quaker who was expected to marry within the faith, was warned that his family would disinherit him if he married Mary Fricker.

Southey was still spending his time, when not up at Balliol, staying with Miss Tyler. This meant that he saw a great deal of Edith Fricker, now working for his aunt. Edith was a very shy girl, who took a great deal of getting to know, but her modest and retiring disposition was very attractive to Southey, himself a man of much reserve. He began to walk her home every evening when she finished work. It surprised most people (including Sarah) that Southey preferred Edith to her older sister, but perhaps Sarah was too much like Miss Tyler with her strong personality – outgoing, energetic, clever, quick-tempered – for Southey to choose her as a wife. There was also the four-year age gap.

The significant moment came in May 1794, 'playing with the lilacs' on a visit to the Old Market in Bristol. He wrote to his friend Grosvenor Bedford that Edith was 'my own age. Her face expresses the mildness of her disposition – and if her calm affection cannot render me happy I deserve to be wretched. She is mild and affectionate . . .'[12] To Sarah Fricker he wrote that Edith was like 'the lily of the valley lovely in humility but like that delicate and lowly flower she would bend before the storm of pride. If error can be amiable the error of too much humility is so. I wish Edith would think more highly of herself. Tis the only fault I have discovered in her, and that is almost a virtue!'[13]

1794 was a momentous year for the Fricker girls. On 20 January Mary married Robert Lovell, whose family promptly threw him out and withdrew their financial support. Edith became involved with Robert Southey, and in August, Samuel Taylor Coleridge walked into the dining-room of the Lovells' lodgings in College Street in the middle of a lively family party.

Predictably most of those present fell under the spell of

Coleridge's charismatic charm and irresistible enthusiasm. Sarah Fricker did not at first succumb. She looked at him objectively and recorded that he was 'brown as a berry . . . Plain, but eloquent and clever. His clothes were worn out; his hair wanted cutting. He was a dreadful figure.' He also had chronic sinus problems that meant he had to breathe through his mouth. Sarah couldn't help comparing him to Southey across the table, 'very neat, gay and smart'.[14] But her objectivity quickly failed to withstand the onslaught of Coleridge's devastating charm. She was also moved by the verbal portrait he drew of his childhood, conjuring images of a cold and unsympathetic family. Isolation and alienation were things that Sarah had herself experienced and she could empathise with his feelings; his 'lost child' act also appealed to her strong maternal instincts; and above all his sensuality and sheer joy at being alive brought out both those answering qualities in Sarah.

Coleridge told a very carefully edited and well-dramatised life story to the Frickers and Southeys. He always told romanticised apocryphal stories of his ancestry, sometimes a bastard grandfather, brought up on the parish, sometimes 'a weaver, half poet and half madman'. In fact, his father had been vicar at Ottery St Mary and also headmaster of King's Grammar School. An erudite man of many interests, he had published a variety of works, including religious studies and a Latin grammar, contributed to the *Gentleman's Magazine* and translated a play from the Latin entitled *The Fair Barbarian*.

Coleridge had been born in the vicarage of Ottery St Mary in Devon on 21 October 1772, the youngest of a family of ten (eight brothers and one sister as well as three older half-sisters). At the time of his birth his father was fifty-three, his mother forty-five. He was very spoilt, by his own admission, which he said made him miserable, because it made his siblings jealous. He hated his name, shortened in the family to Sam – he had been named for his godfather, a local gentleman – and preferred to be known by his initials, STC.

Like many creative artists, Coleridge professed to a sense of isolation and difference from an early age. William Wordsworth believed that he had had a revelation marking him out as a 'chosen son' and Coleridge had a similar sense of vocation. The older boys were all settled in traditional military, ecclesiastical or scholastic careers and were all high achievers in their fields. When John Coleridge died, Samuel was nine years old, but there was already a pressure to succeed in the conventional sense, as well as an implicit expectation of conformity.

Coleridge was precocious and from the first displayed a voracious appetite for books. He later characterised himself as 'a library cormorant'. There was a lot of rivalry at home. His brothers punished him for being their mother's favourite. As for his mother, after doting on him as a small child, she gradually found him more difficult and less appealing, and eventually a disappointment. Coleridge felt rejected by her. He became withdrawn and isolated and retreated into the world of books and the imagination. This rejection had a profound effect on Coleridge's adult relationships with women. He was always looking for absolute, unconditional love and commitment and, when he didn't get it, felt rejected and betrayed.

Amongst his siblings he was always closest to George, eight years his senior, whom he regarded as a second father. The rivalry was greatest with his brother Frank, the next youngest, and it was after being teased beyond endurance by him in 1779 that Samuel attacked him with a knife and then ran away, not being found until dawn on a cold, stormy October night. It was the first of many spectacular demands for attention, the first of many instances of running away from difficult situations he had caused himself.

Coleridge went to dame school until he was six and was allowed to read anything he could lay his hands on. The result was that he 'became a dreamer – and acquired an indisposition to all bodily activity – and I was fretful, and inordinately passionate, and as I could not play at any thing, and was slothful, I was despised & hated by the boys; and because I could read & spell & had, I may truly say, a memory & understanding forced into almost an unnatural ripeness, I was flattered & wondered at by all the old women.'[15]

His father then sent him to the King's School where he did exceptionally well, revealing a precocious intelligence. His father died in 1781 and Coleridge was sent as a charity boy to Christ's Hospital school, which had been founded for the children of poor clergy. He was sent off to his mother's brother John Bowden, an underwriter's clerk who also kept a tobacconist's, in London, where he also spent his school holidays. He rarely saw his mother again.

It is something more than coincidence that all the major players in this drama were orphans; the Wordsworths, the Hutchinson sisters, Robert Southey, Coleridge and the Fricker girls. All had not only lost one or both parents while still young, but had experienced a loss of social status and financial hardship as a result. All of them suffered the burdens of charity, and of being in a state of dependence. This shared experience was one of the things that bound them together as they sought – in their friendships – to recreate the loving, secure family relationships they had lost.

One of Coleridge's contemporaries at school was Charles Lamb, who became a lifelong friend. The atmosphere was one of humiliation – never being allowed to forget their charitable status – as well as the usual brutality, the physical and sexual abuse of boys' boarding schools. Coleridge was flogged for day-dreaming and carelessness. And there were many floggings – the headmaster was a famous sadist. Coleridge escaped on to the roof and lay on the tiles looking at the sky, dreaming of other landscapes, 'for, cloister'd in a city School/The Sky was all I knew of Beautiful'.[16] His experiences there as a child gave him nightmares as an adult.

He first began writing poetry at school, and in January 1791 won an exhibition to Jesus College, Cambridge. Much was expected of him. But he was already taking opium for the pains of rheumatic fever, spending much of the winter in the school sanatorium. And then came a series of family tragedies. In 1791 his sister Nancy died from consumption and his brother Luke (who had qualified as a doctor and was practising in Devon) died from fever; in 1792 his brother Frank shot himself out in India in a delirious fit.

In the autumn of 1791 Coleridge went up to Cambridge, and

while he was there he renewed his friendship with the Evans family – a mother and three daughters, Anne, Eliza and Mary – who had befriended him when he was at school with their brother. They became his surrogate family and he fell in love with Mary, a relationship which ended when she became involved with someone else. In his first year at Cambridge he won the Brown Gold Medal with a Greek sapphic 'Ode on the Slave Trade' – quite an achievement for a first-year student and George was delighted. Coleridge went home to visit his family and found it a very alien environment: he felt like a stranger. His mother treated him like a child and he was even forbidden to drink wine at table.

In his second year he continued to do extremely well, but probably set his sights too high; he was second in the Brown Medal and failed narrowly to get the Craven Scholarship. Coming second was not good enough for Coleridge and it intensified his sense of failure. He began running up enormous debts in the pursuit of what he called 'unchastities'. He went home and confessed to his family that he owed almost £150. After enduring their strictures he was given the money to pay the debts, most of which unfortunately was spent in much the same way. Unable to extricate himself from the predicament, he buried himself recklessly in a delirium of drink and pleasure. He disappeared for two months and reappeared on 2 December 1793 when he volunteered as a private in the 15th Light Dragoons, giving his name as Silas Tomkyn Comberbache.

When finally tracked down by George, he indulged in a melodramatic display of self-recrimination – probably genuine. 'I have been a fool even to madness . . . My mind is illegible to myself – I am lost in the labyrinth, the trackless wilderness of my own bosom . . . The shame and sorrow of those who loved me . . . They haunt my sleep – they enfever my Dreams!'[17] George finally managed to have him discharged as insane on 10 April 1794 for the payment of 25 guineas.

Initially gated by the college, as soon as his punishment was over he left on a walking tour, heading for the West Country and Wales accompanied by a friend. They left Cambridge on 15 June, intending to visit another friend from schooldays who was at Oxford. There on 17 June they met Robert Southey, already famous for his republicanism. He was in the process of writing an epic poem on Joan of Arc. Always prolific, he apparently burned 10,000 lines of it before publication.

Both Southey and Coleridge were disillusioned by university life, unsuited to traditional careers by virtue of their beliefs, and perplexed by the problem of maintaining themselves. From their 'metaphysical' and philosophical discussions, Pantisocracy was born. The word was created by Coleridge from the Greek *pan-socratia* which means an all-governing society. At its heart was the notion of a community of self-governing equals. There was to be no private ownership of land, which was regarded as a common heritage belonging to everyone. Man and nature would live in harmony. Even animals were to be sisters and brothers 'in the Fraternity of universal Nature'. Children had to be removed from the corruptions and prejudices of modern society and brought up as 'children of Nature'. It was to be a totally democratic society, in harmony with nature; a new beginning. Coleridge wrote: 'The Leading Idea of Pantisocracy is to make men necessarily virtuous by removing all Motives to Evil – all possible Temptations . . . It is each Individual's duty to be Just, because it is in his Interest . . . The Heart should have fed upon the truth, as Insects on a Leaf – till it be tinged with the colour, and show its food in every the minutest fibre.'[18]

Southey was fascinated by Coleridge, writing to a friend that he was 'of the most uncommon merit, – of the strongest genius, the clearest judgment, the best heart. My friend he already is, and must hereafter be yours. It is, I fear, impossible to keep him till you come, but my efforts shall not be wanting.'[19] Coleridge was similarly impressed, referring to Southey as 'a nightingale among owls . . . truly a man of *perpendicular virtue – a downright, upright Republican*!'[20] He was also much impressed with Southey's virginity. Richard Holmes, in his biography of Coleridge, points to a certain element of sexual attraction between the two men, though both were heterosexual. Southey had a little of the dandy in him –

he had once minced through Bristol dressed as a woman – and was, physically, the exact opposite of Coleridge. Southey was very fastidious, unlike his sensual companion, confessing distaste when he was forced to share a bed with Coleridge on a walking tour, something that perhaps had its origins in childhood memories of sharing a bed with Miss Tyler.

After his expedition to Wales, Coleridge arrived in Bristol on 5 August and presented himself at the Lovells' in order to renew his acquaintance with Southey and Robert Lovell. When he was introduced to the Fricker sisters, he was newly on the rebound from Mary Evans. He had seen her in the street as he passed through Wrexham a few days earlier and been so shaken by the encounter it made him physically ill. He admitted to Southey that 'her Image is in the Sanctuary of my Heart, and never can it be torn away'.[21]

Despite Sarah Fricker's initial reserve towards Coleridge, there was a strong sexual attraction between the two almost from the beginning. Sarah's ample figure, lustrous brown hair and 'speaking' eyes, full of fun, made an instant impression. Coleridge, despite his dishevelled appearance and long, unruly hair, was very attractive to women, perhaps because he gave the impression of being 'a very gentle bear'. His conversation, his intellectual accomplishments and extravagant manner dazzled most people who met him. Like a benevolent necromancer he cast a spell which soon bound the more pragmatic Sarah in its web.

The talk around the dinner table was all of Pantisocracy, the girls already being well grounded in democratic principles by Lovell and Southey. Any reservations they may have had about the scheme were erased by Coleridge's persuasive tongue. He talked, it was said, 'above singing'. Curiously, Pantisocracy seems to have been from the beginning more of a flight of fancy to Coleridge than a practical reality. Southey really believed that it could be achieved; Coleridge believed in the ideal and the principle with all the passion of his turbulent nature, but it was only a dream – what his publisher Cottle called 'an epidemic delusion'. To Southey it was a passionately longed-for reality, an escape from

[ 17 ]

the dilemmas that faced him. 'I look forward with impatience to the moment when I shall ascend the bark, and gaze on the lessening shore till it be for ever lost in distance. Like Adam I may "drop some natural tears – but dry them soon" . . . When Coleridge and I are sawing down a tree we shall discuss metaphysics; criticise poetry when hunting a buffalo, and write sonnets whilst following the plough. Our society will be of the most polished order . . . Our females are beautiful amiable and accomplished . . .'[22]

Pantisocracy was based on the philosophies of David Hartley and Spinoza, and the men were heavily influenced by the writings of Dr Joseph Priestley and William Godwin. The plan was that a community of twelve men and twelve women would emigrate to America – possibly Kentucky. A lot of time was spent drawing up the principles their community would be based on and the rules that would regulate it. According to a friend, 'The regulations relating to the females strike them as the most difficult . . .' Their intentions were admirable and worthy of any twentieth-century New Man, but the sheer unreality of their idea of domestic democracy is revealed by one of Coleridge's letters: 'Let the married Women do only what is absolutely convenient and customary for pregnant Women or nurses. – Let the Husbands do *all* the Rest – and what will that all be –? Washing with a Machine and cleaning the House. One Hour's addition to our daily Labor – and Pantisocracy in its most perfect Sense is practicable.' He added airily that the women's labours would be similarly light since 'An Infant is almost always sleeping – and during its slumbers the Mother may in the same Room perform the little offices of ironing Cloaths or making Shirts.'[23] The women, who might have been able to draw up a more realistic timetable, were never consulted. There were also unresolved difficulties about the whole question of marriage, and whether an unhappy union should be dissolved if both parties wished it.

Lovell introduced Southey and Coleridge to Joseph Cottle, the Bristol bookseller and publisher, and they discovered in him a willing patron who was as 'inexperienced and ardent' as themselves. Cottle remembered Southey as 'tall, dignified, possessing great suavity of manners; an eye piercing, with a countenance full of genius, kindliness, and intelligence, I gave him at once the right hand of fellowship, and to the moment of his decease, that cordiality was never withdrawn.'[24] His relationship with Coleridge was more turbulent but Cottle's friendship was vitally important to the group.

Coleridge and Southey went off to Somerset to visit Thomas Poole, a new acquaintance who was a radical sympathiser, returning at the end of August. They stayed with Mrs Southey in Bath and Coleridge discovered that she had invited Sarah Fricker to stay with her. In the few days before he went back to Cambridge, he converted them all to Pantisocracy. Even Mrs Southey felt inclined to join the emigration scheme. Miss Tyler's manservant Shadrach Weeks was also very keen to go. Miss Tyler was as yet totally ignorant of the project, Southey having not had the courage to tell her.

The attraction between Coleridge and Sarah was once more apparent, and deepened by their proximity under one roof. When Coleridge left he asked Sarah to write to him, and then precipitately to marry him and go to America. It appears to have been impulsive and unpremeditated. People have speculated since that he did so simply for Pantisocratic convenience, partly because Lovell and Southey were marrying her sisters, and also because 'passionless union', based on friendship rather than lust, was one of the ideals of Pantisocracy. But Coleridge's views on love would not have allowed him to contemplate marriage without emotional involvement – he regarded sex without love as extremely sordid, writing later to Southey that the idea of having sexual intercourse with Sarah without love, even within marriage, would have reduced her to the level of a common prostitute: 'to marry a woman whom I do *not* love – to degrade her, whom I call my Wife, by making her the Instrument of low Desire – and on the removal of a desultory Appetite, to be perhaps not displeased with her Absence! – Enough! These Refinements are the wildering Fires that lead me into Vice.'[25]

His first letter to Southey after his return to London was certainly written in the belief that his feelings were real. 'Well, my dear Southey! I am at last arrived at Jesus. My God! how tumultuous are the movements of my Heart – Since I quitted this room what and how important Events have been evolved! America! Southey! Miss Fricker! – Yes – Southey – you are right – Even Love is the creature of strong Motive – I certainly love her. I think of her incessantly & with unspeakable tenderness – with that inward melting away of Soul that symptomatizes it.'[26] He wrote a letter to Sarah, which has unfortunately not survived, in similar terms.

It is much more likely that Coleridge, on the rebound from Mary Evans, was carried away by the powerful physical attraction he felt for Sarah and the undeniable pleasure he found in her company. He was 'in love with love', and once alone in the cooler surroundings of his lodgings, came to his senses and believed that he had made a dreadful mistake. He bitterly regretted being carried away by 'an ebullient Fancy, a flowing Utterance, a light & dancing Heart, & a disposition to catch fire by the very rapidity of my own motion, & to speak vehemently from mere verbal association, choosing sentiments' which now induced 'Horror from the actions expressed in such sentences & sentiments'.[27]

He later confessed to Southey that his feelings for Sarah probably had their origins in lust: 'the sexual impulse, acting not openly in the excitement of conscious desire . . . but acting covertly and unconsciously in the imagination, and in that form contracting a temporary alliance with the best moral Feelings, may assume and counterfeit the appearance of exclusive *Love* . . .'[28]

He wrote a letter to Southey, hoping that he would extricate him from his predicament, explaining that he had been carried away by 'the ebullience of schematism (mistaking it) for affection . . . A moment's reflection might have told me, Love is not a plant of so mushroom a growth.'[29] His worst mistake had been to write Sarah a glowing love letter when he returned; this was 'the most criminal action of my life . . . I had worked myself to such a pitch, that I scarcely knew I was writing like an hypocrite.'[30] Southey was determined that if Coleridge was going to break the engagement, he would have to tell Sarah himself.

Meanwhile Edith was still wavering with regard to Southey's proposal. She wanted to marry him but was totally daunted by the idea of America with all its unknown terrors, and by the idea of leaving her mother. But in the end she capitulated. Southey wrote to his friend Grosvenor Bedford: 'The woman I love almost unmans me by looking with such exquisite affection and saying "I cannot leave my Mother without being unhappy – yet I will go with you – staying or going I must be miserable." Did I not know her strength of mind and how ardently I shall endeavour to make her happy this would drive me beyond the bounds of reason.'[31]

Mrs Fricker's decision to emigrate with her daughters made the decision easier. Edith was inclined to be timid and pessimistic – what her sister Sarah described as 'an uncheerful disposition'. She also hated writing letters, even to Southey. He was obliged to write to Sarah for news of her. 'She suffers me to write rather in compliance to my wishes than her own. I must not trespass on this sufferance by writing as often as my heart would dictate . . . Your sister is not fond of writing, and why indeed should I plague others with the emotion of this strange mind? . . . Let me hear from you. Do you tell me how your sister is. She dislikes writing herself, and I ought not to urge her against her inclination.'[32]

Southey's friend Burnett, who was also going to join the scheme, proposed to Edith's younger sister Martha, but she refused, as Sarah Fricker later recorded in her memoirs, 'scornfully, saying that he only wanted a wife in a hurry, not her individually of all the world.'[33] If Sarah had suspected for a moment that Coleridge had proposed to her simply for the Pantisocratic ideal, it is clear that she too would have refused.

On 17 October 1794, all their plans were thrown into doubt. Miss Tyler found out about the emigration plan and Southey's secret engagement to Edith, whom she referred to scathingly as 'a mere seamstress'. She turned Southey out of the house, without even an overcoat, though it was cold and pelting down with rain. She told him that she wished to have nothing more to do with him or with his family, and that, in future, she would not even open a letter from him. This was a terrible blow. Southey borrowed an overcoat from the Lovells and walked to his mother's house in Bath though the rain. Edith also found herself without employment.

Sarah, having read Coleridge's passionate letter, and the four or five that followed it, was totally ignorant of his change of heart. However, as time went on and he neither wrote to her again nor reappeared in Bristol, she must have suspected something. She was both proud and practical. She stopped writing to Coleridge, perhaps intuitively aware that he was the kind of person who runs away from emotional demands, and waited. Certain of her own feelings, even though she had known Coleridge for only a matter of weeks, she gave the appearance of being confident that Coleridge would return and marry her, long after friends and family had begun to have serious doubts.

Coleridge, meanwhile, once again in turmoil about his future and the conflicting demands of family, friends and his own inclinations, divided his time between Cambridge and London, lodging at the Salutation and Cat in Newgate Street, supposedly furthering the Pantisocratic project. Mary Wollstonecraft's former lover Gilbert Imlay was promoting the Susquehanna as a desirable location for their community, and Coleridge wrote enthusiastic letters to Southey about its suitability.

Coleridge was also suffering from guilt, not just about his conduct towards Sarah; he felt that he was letting his family down by planning to abandon his degree, get married and go off to America. They seriously thought that he had become insane and talked about 'restraint' and having him admitted to an asylum. Coleridge was also receiving a succession of letters from Southey urging him to do his duty by Sarah. Coleridge promised to come to Bristol several times; Lovell and Southey even walked to Marlborough to meet him on one occasion, but he failed to arrive. Coleridge was under pressure from both sides. It was a great mistake on Southey's part to try to influence Coleridge.

He had a brief affair with an actress and renewed contact with Mary Evans, who sent him a letter urging him to abandon such an 'absurd and extravagant' scheme. She commented perceptively: 'There is an Eagerness in your Nature which is ever hurrying you into the sad Extreme.'[34] She said enough in her letter to revive Coleridge's romantic hopes, even though she was still engaged to someone else. He was torn between her and Sarah, and panicking.

He wrote Mary a long letter at the beginning of November asking her to tell him once and for all whether her affections were irrevocably committed elsewhere and confessing the extent of his own passion to her. He asked her to tell him whether she was engaged to someone else, but gave no hint that he himself might be similarly attached. Such is the tone of the letter that it is clear that if she had written back willing to renew their relationship, Sarah Fricker would have been abandoned. Mary wrote back at the end of December, gently telling him that it was over. Coleridge was devastated, writing back to her that 'to love you Habit has made unalterable'.[35]

Although Coleridge had not written to Sarah for quite a while, he wrote to Edith – a curiously oblique system of communication, since he must have known that she would show the correspondence to her sister. His letters betray a longing for companionship and for a close family relationship. He talked about his dead sister in extravagant terms: 'I had a Sister – an only Sister. Most tenderly did I love her! Yea, I had woke at midnight, and wept – because she was not . . . My Sister, like you, was beautiful and accomplished – like you, she was lowly of Heart . . . I know, and feel, that I am your Brother.'[36] He admired the closeness of his friend Charles Lamb and his sister Mary, just as he would later idealise Wordsworth's relationship with Dorothy.

He spent the Christmas vacation either at the Lambs' or the Salutation and Cat in a confused and undecided state. Early in January Southey, having decided that things had gone on long enough, and unable to leave well alone, travelled to London to bring Coleridge back to Bristol.

Sarah had received two more proposals of marriage in Coleridge's absence, one of which was from a wealthy man able to provide the kind of financial security she longed to have. Her father's bankruptcy, and the hard years she and her sisters had shared, had left deep insecurities. But they had also given her confidence in her own strength of character and ability to survive. She disliked both her suitors, but left the more advantageous proposal open. It is very tempting to think that she did so in order to goad Coleridge into making a decision. It is obvious from the correspondence that neither side had finally settled the issue. Sarah was still considering her position with regard to Coleridge and her wealthy lover as late as February; Coleridge was still coming to terms with the end of his love affair with Mary Evans. He could quite easily have let the relationship with Sarah go.

In January Coleridge came back to Bristol and lodged at 25 College Street in a bachelor household with Southey and his friend Burnett. They talked of finding a farm in Wales where they could set up a small community until they could raise the £2000 needed to emigrate. They had abandoned their academic careers and all other conventional prospects, to the horror of their families.

Far from breaking off his engagement to Sarah, as everyone expected, Coleridge renewed the affair, this time, he told Southey, 'from Feeling & Principle' rather than principle alone. From Sarah he received 'a reward more than proportionate to the greatness of the Effort . . . I love and I am beloved, and I am happy'.[37] There was genuine passion on both sides which Coleridge later tried to repudiate. He told De Quincey that 'his marriage was . . . forced upon his sense of honour by the scrupulous Southey'. But De Quincey didn't believe him because 'a neutral spectator of the parties protested to me, that, if ever in his life he had seen a man under deep fascination, and what he would have called desperately in love, Coleridge, in relation to Miss F., was that man'.[38] Coleridge's contemporary letters, a series of richly sensual poems and the observations of his friends confirm this.

About this time Coleridge wrote Sarah 'The Kiss'.

> Too well those lovely lips disclose
> The triumphs of the opening Rose;
> O fair! O graceful! bid them prove

As passive to the breath of Love,
In tender accents, faint and low,
Well-pleased I hear the whisper'd 'No!'
The whispered 'No' – how little meant!
Sweet Falsehood that endears Consent!
For on those lovely lips the while
Dawns the soft relenting smile,
And tempts with feign'd dissuasion coy
The gentle violence of Joy.[39]

This was one of the happiest periods in the Fricker sisters' lives. They were either married or engaged to three brilliant and gifted young men who were close friends, and there was the exciting prospect of founding a new society in America. The only problem was the lack of money. How were they all to support themselves? Mary Lovell was already pregnant.

The men, particularly Coleridge, were full of schemes to earn money. Southey had his *Joan of Arc*, which Cottle was willing to publish, and Lovell and Coleridge were both working on literary projects – though Coleridge's failed to materialise. Southey, living in the same house as Coleridge, after initial euphoria, was beginning to suspect that Coleridge had a problem with laudanum, though the full extent of his addiction (the addictive properties of opium were not as well known then as now) would be concealed for years. De Quincey – something of an expert on the subject – observed, after conversations with Coleridge, that he had first begun to take opium for non-medicinal purposes 'as a source of luxurious sensations'. Coleridge wrote to his brother George on the effects of laudanum on the psyche, 'how divine that repose is – what a spot of inchantment, a green spot of fountains, & flowers & trees, in the very heart of a waste of Sands'.[40] The effects of the drug, generally referred to as 'indolence', were certainly noticed by Coleridge's fellow lodgers, one of whom, Burnett, was also to become an addict.

Southey was beginning to realise that Coleridge was not the 'shining soul' he had thought him, that he could be unreliable, untruthful and irresponsible. He lived by his own agenda and with little consideration for those around him.

One of the money-making ideas was to give a series of lectures in Bristol, which had a large, radical, free-thinking, Unitarian population. There were to be two 'Moral and Political' lectures a week in rooms above Bristol's Corn Market, half by Southey, the rest by Coleridge. These were a great success. Coleridge was a brilliant speaker who could hold audiences both public and private absolutely rapt. Southey was less charismatic, rather stiff and awkward in public, but incisive in debate. The content was controversial and revolutionary, arousing passionate sentiments in the listeners, who paid a shilling entrance fee for the privilege of being provoked – Coleridge even received death-threats afterwards.

Somewhere about this time one of the pivotal events of their lives occurred, scarcely mentioned in letters or diaries. William Wordsworth was in Bristol for about five weeks visiting a wealthy sugar merchant, John Pinney, whose country house in Dorset was to be lent to William and Dorothy as their first home. William, who had just published *An Evening Walk* and *Descriptive Sketches*, was drawn into the Bristol circle, meeting Cottle, Southey and Coleridge for the first time. There was initially more contact with Southey as Coleridge was away from Bristol for part of William's visit. William wrote to a friend that his meetings with Coleridge had been very brief. 'I saw but little of him. I wished indeed I had seen more – his talents appear to me very great, I met Southey also. His manners pleased me exceedingly and I have every reason to think very highly of his powers of mind. He is about publishing an epic poem on the subject of the Maid of Orleans. From the specimens I have seen I am inclined to think it will have many beauties. I recollect your mentioning you had met Southey and thought him a Coxcomb. This surprises me much, as I never saw a young man who seemed to have less of that character.'[41]

However, when Cottle sent William a copy of Southey's *Joan of Arc*, he revised his opinion, writing: 'You were right about Southey, he is certainly a coxcomb . . .' William thought the preface 'a very conceited performance' and the poem 'a very inferior execution'.[42] Coleridge was very impressed by Wordsworth, having known his brother Christopher at Cambridge and having read William's publications with admiration. He obtained his Dorset address and began a correspondence that was to have far-reaching consequences for them all.

On the domestic front, Sarah's family were urging her to make a decision in favour of her wealthy suitor. Even Robert Lovell counselled her not to marry Coleridge, whom he also had begun to distrust. In February Coleridge wrote to a friend: 'So commanding are the requests of her Relations, that a short time must decide whether she marries me whom she loves with an affection to the ardor of which my Deserts bear no proportion – or a man whom she strongly dislikes in spite of his fortune and solicitous attention to her.'[43] Pressure was also being put on Southey to abandon Edith. His family presumably hoped to regain Miss Tyler's patronage once the unfortunate engagement was broken off. Southey, aware of his family's intention to separate them, began to seek some means of marrying Edith secretly. He does not seem to have realised the incompatibility of his personal aims with the Pantisocratic plan. At the end of March he was still talking of a communal life and shared income. 'If Coleridge and I can get 150 pounds a year between us, we purpose marrying and retiring into the country, as our literary business can be carried on there, and practising agriculture till we can raise money for America – still the grand object in view.'[44] This seemed to recede further and further away. At times they had no money to buy food and had to borrow money from Cottle for the rent.

The girls, being all emancipated followers of Mary Wollstonecraft and Pantisocracy, dispensed with the eighteenth-century conventions thought proper for respectable young women. In particular they went out with young men without chaperones. Their unconventional behaviour led to gossip. They were believed to be 'immodest' and people were talking 'strangely' about them. The men were known to be 'Jacobins' and revolutionaries, dangerous radicals from whom the worst could be expected. The

Pantisocratic ideal of shared property was believed to extend to the women too and there were rumours that the formalities of marriage were to be dispensed with.[45] This gossip caused Sarah and Edith a great deal of distress. There were social slights that occasioned much pain, though Hannah More and other teachers at her school confirmed, when appealed to, that the girls 'had maintained an irreproachable character, though naturally exposed by their personal attractions to some peril, and to the malevolence of envy.'[46]

Southey at first advised the girls to ignore the malice. 'Can you not smile at the envy and absurdity of the many?' But he was unaware of the way in which society judged women by their conduct, how important virtue was to a woman's reputation, and what effects its loss – even suspected – could have on their lives.

Things were brought to a head by an expedition to Wales, organised in April by Joseph Cottle. Edith, Sarah, Southey and Coleridge were to accompany him to the Wye Valley and Tintern Abbey. This was morally a very risky venture, the girls being without the chaperonage of a married woman, staying overnight at an inn and as such 'technically compromised'. To make things worse, Southey and Coleridge quarrelled bitterly because Coleridge had failed to turn up to give his lecture the day before. Southey accused him of irresponsibility and other derelictions of duty. This argument was only a symptom of a deeper rift between the two men as their own interests pulled in different directions and the incompatibility of their natures became apparent. Southey was punctual, tidy and meticulous; Coleridge irresponsible, unpredictable and chaotic. Southey doubted whether Coleridge could be relied upon to see the scheme through; Coleridge had begun to doubt the sincerity of Southey's belief in Pantisocracy. He suspected an imminent betrayal.

The scene at the inn was painful. Southey left the table abruptly and went to stare out of the window. Coleridge joined him, 'greatly agitated', fearing that he was 'meditating a Separation'. Edith and Sarah found themselves having to take sides in the argument and the atmosphere at the Beaufort Arms was very uncomfortable. The following day they got lost as it was getting dark on the way to

Tintern in wet weather and, although Southey and Coleridge apologised and appeared to patch up their differences, there was a coolness. The girls found when they came back that, having defied convention so openly, they were generally believed to have been 'ruined'.

Edith's prospects improved a few weeks later when Southey's friend Wynn offered to pay him an annuity of £160 out of his inheritance when he came of age the following year. This would make it possible for them to marry and Southey decided to accept. He told Burnett at a strawberry party at Long Ashton, explaining that, although they had originally agreed that all income would go into a joint purse in line with their Pantisocratic beliefs, circumstances had changed and he would be using the annuity to support himself and Edith. It was in reality evidence that Southey, increasingly mistrustful of Coleridge, was withdrawing from the Pantisocratic scheme and Coleridge, when Burnett told him what Southey was planning to do, saw it as such. Coleridge exploded with rage and loathing, expressing sentiments of 'unutterable contempt'. Southey was a traitor. Coleridge wrote him a letter, the contents of which were difficult to forgive and impossible to forget. It began: 'You are lost to me, because you are lost to Virtue . . .'[47] They ceased to speak to each other and Sarah and Edith found themselves again forced to take sides.

After the Tintern episode, Sarah's family changed their minds. They still had reservations about her marrying Coleridge, but, watching the progress of their passionate relationship, Mrs Fricker was afraid that something worse might happen if she didn't. Current gossip of the day had it that 'the marriage was believed to have been rather hurried on, in consequence of some hostile breath of rumour that had arisen in connection with the Misses Fricker, caused partly by the unconventional manner in which they were constantly to be seen walking about Bristol with two such remarkable and well-known young men as Coleridge and Southey, and partly from the impression that pantisocracy meant a system of things that dispensed with the marriage-tie.'[48]

The problem for Coleridge, as it was for Southey, was how to support a wife. However, with the success of the lecture scheme, he had been offered a guinea and a half by Cottle for every hundred lines of poetry he wrote and it seemed likely that more money would flow in from his pen. His mind was full of literary schemes. On a wave of optimism he found a cottage in Clevedon, a small village on the coast about 12 miles from Bristol. It was tiny and in a poor state of decoration. But it was cheap, only £5 a year, and it was close to the sea and had roses and jasmine outside the door.

While he was down at Clevedon finalising arrangements, Coleridge took the opportunity to walk along the coast at Shurton Bars. Sarah, on her own in Bristol, was in very low spirits. She was being battered on all sides, by the opposition of family and friends to her intended marriage, the malicious gossip around her and, in particular, the estrangement from Edith. Even Southey, who had been her friend for so long, was frigid towards her. She wrote Samuel a long, unhappy letter.

In response he composed the 'Ode to Sara: Lines written at Shurton Bars, near Bridgwater, September 1795, in Answer to a Letter from Bristol'. It reveals something of the closeness and intensity of their relationship, and must have gone a long way to alleviating her distress.

> O ever present to my view!
> My wafted spirit is with you.
>    And soothes your boding fears:
> I see you all oppressed with gloom
> Sit lonely in that cheerless room –
>    Ah me! You are in tears!
>
> Beloved Woman! did you fly
> Chill'd Friendship's dark disliking eye,
>    Or Mirth's untimely din?
> With cruel weight these trifles press
> A temper sore with tenderness,
>    When aches the void within.

The poem goes on to assure her that 'When stormy Midnight' howls around their cottage, she need have no fears, since his arms will be there to comfort and protect her 'with a husband's care'.

Sarah Fricker was married to Samuel Taylor Coleridge on Sunday, 4 October 1795, at St Mary Redcliffe church. No one from Coleridge's family came to the ceremony; Mrs Fricker was there as a witness, and so was Josiah Wade, a radical Bristol merchant and friend of the bridegroom. Neither Southey nor Edith was there. But despite the family rifts that the relationship had produced, they were both happy. Coleridge wrote ecstatically to Thomas Poole: 'On Sunday morning I was *married* . . . united to the woman, whom I love best of all created Beings . . . Mrs Coleridge – MRS COLERIDGE!! – I like to *write* the name . . .'

# 2

## A State of Dependence

Dorothy Wordsworth was born on Christmas Day 1771 at Cockermouth, a small but attractive market town on the westernmost edge of the Lake District. Although she was only six when she left, all her life she vividly remembered the house she was born in – an imposing, though rather gloomy, eighteenth-century building fronting on to the main street, with a terrace and garden overlooking the River Derwent behind. Unquestionably a gentleman's residence, it became a symbol of all that she had lost, and in later years her memories of that early childhood spent in the company of her four brothers came to assume the character of an idyll.

The Wordsworths were part of that ambitious middle class portrayed so successfully by Jane Austen, a mixture of clergymen, lawyers, doctors, tradesmen and minor gentry. Their grandfather was an attorney who had originally come from Yorkshire to live near Penrith. Their father, John, had followed his father into the law, married Ann Cookson, the daughter of a well-connected draper in Penrith, and taken a post as agent to James Lowther, Lord Lonsdale – the largest landowner in the county. James Lowther, known as the 'Bad Earl', was both feared and hated and this ill-feeling was transferred to the Wordsworth family as his employees. John Wordsworth appears to have been a rather taciturn workaholic, ruthlessly pursuing his unpopular employer's interests. He was Coroner for the district of Millom, and was also responsible for making sure that all the tenants on the Lowther estates voted for their landlord's candidates. At one point James Lowther controlled nine Parliamentary seats. Dorothy later recalled, with some mortification, that their father had had no real friends. He seems to have had little time for his family either, in the welter of estate business, though it was from him that William later acknowledged his introduction to poetry.

William remembered Dorothy as a sensitive little girl who burst into tears at her first sight of the sea. It was the age of sensibility, of effusive emotion and the cultivation of sentiment. This was particularly encouraged in young women. While William was running around naked, catching butterflies, Dorothy was afraid that if she caught them she would brush the dust from their wings and they would not be able fly.

While her other brothers were quiet and well behaved, William was thought rather wild and uncontrollable – something of a 'young savage'. He later admitted that he had been 'stiff, moody, and violent tempered'. The children appear to have spent quite a lot of time with their grandparents in Penrith and Dorothy and William were the least liked of the five siblings. This childhood alienation later contributed to the closeness of their relationship. The Cooksons lived in well-proportioned rooms above their shop. The building still stands – a handsome red sandstone house with shopfronts on the ground floor and rooms above, still a draper's shop, at the top end of Devonshire Street at right angles to the George Hotel.

While in Penrith on these extended visits, they attended a dame school run by a local woman, and there they first met the Hutchinson sisters, Mary, Margaret and Sara, whose mother (also called Mary) was a close friend of Ann Wordsworth. The Hutchinsons came from north-eastern farming stock and kept a tobacco business in Penrith. Initially the Wordsworth children played with Mary and Margaret Hutchinson, who were almost exactly the same age as William and Dorothy. Sara was three years younger, still very much the baby of the family.

Dorothy and William remembered very little about their mother, except as a benign and loving presence who moved 'with them in tenderness and love,/A centre to the circle' of the family.[1] Her death was a tragedy. The circumstances of Ann Wordsworth's death pose a number of unanswered questions. In 1778, she left the children with her parents in Penrith and went to London alone, returning some time later very ill. William referred to an act of negligence and family rumour hinted at the fact that she had been allowed to sleep in damp sheets. But her reasons for making an unaccompanied trip to London, her illness and death at her parents', not her husband's home, invite futile speculation.

When she realised that she might die, Ann asked her cousin Elizabeth Threlkeld to care for Dorothy. Ann was buried in Penrith churchyard, only a few hundred yards from the house, on a bitterly cold day in March 1778. She was only thirty. After the funeral the children remembered Mary Hutchinson's mother sitting beside the kitchen fire to warm herself after the chill of the graveyard, weeping. The death of their mother and the resulting break-up of the family dislocated the young Words-worths' sibling relationships. From this point on, Dorothy and William would develop separately into adulthood, while still retaining at a deeper level of consciousness the memory of the close bond they had enjoyed in infancy.

On 13 June 1778 Elizabeth came from Halifax to collect six-year-old Dorothy from her grandparents. She was given 5 guineas for her travel and promised 10 guineas a year for Dorothy's keep. Elizabeth was the daughter of Mrs Cookson's brother, a congregational minister, who had moved to Halifax before Elizabeth was born. She was already caring for her dead sister's children, and after her brother-in-law died she managed his shop as well. She was a model of female selflessness and sacrifice. Dorothy found herself in a large family of six foster children, but had a very happy time there, making a lifelong friend of Jane Pollard, a girl of her own age who lived opposite. They 'wandered wild together' in the countryside – still accessible from the town. They attended the Unitarian Chapel on Sundays and Dorothy was brought up as a dissenter, in an atmosphere of liberal enlightenment. It was also a conspicuously female environment, family and business run by women.

Dorothy was sent to boarding school in 1781 at the age of nine but taken away for reasons of economy when her father died three years later. She had never seen her father or her brothers since the death of her mother – an interval of six years. 'I was never once at home, never was for a single moment under my Father's roof after her death, which I cannot think of without regret.'[2] This loss and rejection had a profound effect on Dorothy, throughout her life. Why her father should have been so reluctant to have contact with his children after the death of his wife is a puzzle. It may be that his grief was so great he couldn't bear to see them and to be reminded of her. Or perhaps there was some bitterness attached to her death which he preferred to shut out.

Dorothy's father died suddenly, from the effects of exposure, at the age of forty-two. He had ridden over to Millom to conduct an inquest just before Christmas and, instead of spending the night there, decided to return home in the dark. He got lost in bad weather on the high fell road and was forced to spend an icy December night in the open. He died on New Year's Eve, his affairs in total disorder and without a will. He was owed about £5000 by Lord Lonsdale. As a gentleman could live in London with one servant for about £200 a year at the time, this was a considerable sum. While Dorothy's uncles, who were her father's executors, took action to reclaim the debt, Dorothy went back to Elizabeth Threlkeld and joined her friend Jane at the local school. She was part of a group of girls who went to dances together, visited each others' houses, went on alfresco summer outings, and kept in touch with each other for the rest of their lives.

Dorothy was educated in line with Erasmus Darwin's *Plan for the Conduct of Female Education*. Aunt Elizabeth, dearly beloved, took the place of Dorothy's mother and was always referred to as 'my dear Aunt, my best friend'. Dorothy was a precocious reader and a member of the local lending library, devouring *Clarissa* at fourteen, reading Fielding, Milton and the *Iliad* – the latter being presents from her brothers, whose gifts also included Dr Gregory's *A Father's Legacy to His Daughters*, an improving Conduct Book for girls whose precepts had incensed Mary Wollstonecraft and provoked her into writing page after page of refutation in her

*Vindication.* The vexed subject of educating daughters had been vigorously debated throughout the seventeenth and eighteenth centuries and the result was a plethora of Conduct Books designed to make women fit for society. The only object of female education at that time, wrote Mary Wollstonecraft, was to train girls to be a 'fit companion for a man of sense' and to make them 'agreeable and useful'.

Most Conduct Books warned that girls should on no account be allowed to read romances since they would be 'astonished not to find in the World real persons, who may answer to these Romantick Heroes'. Nor were these the only disillusionments in store for her; parents were urged to 'begin early thus to harden her for disappointment, to moderate her Desires and Affections, and to render her easy to bear Refusals'. This was a lesson that Dorothy learned very early in her life. She suppressed her own desires and opinions – even her own personality – becoming one of those who by choice or necessity live life by proxy.

Dr Gregory's *Legacy to His Daughters* went even further. A woman's whole life was likely to be 'a life of suffering . . . You must bear your sorrows in silence, unknown and unpitied. You must often put on a face of serenity and cheerfulness, when your hearts are torn with anguish and sinking in despair'. He advocated religion as a woman's only comfort. It was a woman's God-given duty, according to Dr Gregory, to 'live under subjection'. That women found this difficult and unacceptable was the Curse of The Fall. In Paradise things would have been different; Adam's wishes 'would all have appeared so useful, so becoming, so necessary to their Good, that Women would have hastened with great Pleasure to perform them'. It was part of a woman's punishment for consumption of the apple that her husband would command her to do 'many Things that you dislike, and yet you shall obey. As unreasonable and extravagant as his Desire shall often appear to you, yet it shall govern you.'

When the financial situation of the Wordsworth children became apparent and her uncles realised that Lonsdale was not going to pay his debts, Dorothy, aged fifteen, was removed from what she regarded as her home and sent back to her inhospitable and unsympathetic grandparents in Penrith, a town described by her as 'this little petty place'. She wrote to Jane: 'One would imagine that a Grandmr would feel for her grandchild all the tenderness of a mother, particularly when that Grandchild had no other parent, but there is so little of tenderness in her manner or of anything affectionate, that while I am in her house I cannot at all consider myself as at home; I feel like a stranger. You cannot think how gravely and silently I sit with her and my Gfr . . . I sit for whole hours without saying anything.'[3] This was a considerable admission for someone noted for their 'quick tongue' and ability to do several things at once – all at top speed. She was dreadfully homesick. 'I would give anything to go to Halifax instead, to that dear place which I shall ever consider as my home . . . the loss of a Mother can only be made up by such a friend as my dear Aunt.'[4]

At the end of the summer term, Dorothy was impatient to be reunited with her brothers who were boarding at Hawkshead Grammar School. However, 'I was for a whole week kept in expectation of my Brothers, who staid at school all that time after the vacation begun owing to the ill-nature of my uncle who would not send horses for them . . . W[illiam], J[ohn], C[hristopher], and myself shed tears together, tears of the bitterest sorrow, we all of us, each day, feel more sensibly the loss we sustained when we were deprived of our parents, and each day do we receive fresh insults . . . the servants are every one of them so insolent to us as makes the kitchen as well as the parlour quite insupportable.'[5] They had a wonderful summer together before the boys went back. Although William had finished school, his grandparents were unwilling to have him with them any longer than they could help, so he was sent back to lodge in Hawkshead until his admission to Cambridge, where he was to go as a 'sizar' – a kind of charitable status for boys in 'reduced circumstances' who were given assistance with the fees.

When their father's affairs were sorted out – apart from the Lonsdale debt – the Wordsworth children were entitled to about £600 each out of what was left of the estate – an amount which would, if invested in a bank, yield about £20–£25 a year. This was a pitiful amount. It was generally reckoned that £60 a year was the minimum in order to live. William and Dorothy were obliged to become dependent on the charity of their relatives, and hope that one day Lord Lonsdale could be compelled to pay what was owed to them. In fact, they had to wait twenty years until he died.

Dorothy renewed old friendships in Penrith – notably with Mary Hutchinson, now also an orphan and living 'at the mercy of ill-natured and illiberal relations'. Mary's mother had died shortly after giving birth to her youngest brother, who survived only two years. Her father died at about the same time. Dorothy recalled that 'Mary and her sister Margaret and I used to steal to each other's houses, and when we had had our talk over the kitchen fire, to delay the moment of parting, paced up one street and down another by moon or starlight.'[6] Sara Hutchinson had been sent to live with relatives in Kendall who seem to have been more sympathetic and certainly provided her with an excellent education and love of literature.

At this time Dorothy's interests were much the same as those of any other teenage girl – hairstyles, hats and high heels, assemblies and the dearth of gentlemen to dance with. She wrote to Jane on 6 August 1787: 'My Grandmother is now gone to bed and I am quite alone. Imagine me sitting in my bed-gown, my hair out of curl and hanging about my face, with a small candle beside me, and my whole person the picture of poverty (as it always is in a bed-gown) and you will then see your friend Dorothy . . . You know not how forlorn and dull I find myself now that my Brs are gone . . . So, you have got high-heeled shoes [? I do not] think of having them yet a while, I am so little, and wish to appear as Girlish as possible. I wear my hair curled about my face in light curls friz'd at the bottom and turned at the ends. How have you yours?'[7]

Dorothy's grandfather, who had been an invalid for two years, died and was buried just before Christmas 1787. During the following summer, William came home from Cambridge and joined her in her outings with Mary and Margaret Hutchinson. He was attracted from the first by Mary's quietness and strength of character – a 'warm sweetness' at the centre of her nature. There may well have been a brief romance. In *The Prelude*, he describes a period before 1789 when he roamed 'alone or with the Maid/to whom were breathed my first fond vows' of love. This would have had to have been the summer of 1788, just before Mary went to live with her great-uncle at Sockburn-on-Tees near Darlington. The two girls vowed never to lose contact with each other and Mary gave Dorothy a seal for her letters as a mark of her regard. Dorothy's friend Jane speculated that it might be from a lover and was quickly disabused!

Dorothy, in this long vacation, had also been getting to know William and described his character quite acutely, observing to Jane that he had 'a sort of violence of Affection if I may so Term it which demonstrates itself every moment of the Day when the Objects of his affection are present with him, in a thousand almost imperceptible attentions to their wishes, in a sort of restless watchfulness which I know not how to describe, a Tenderness that never sleeps, and at the same Time such a Delicacy of Manners as I have observed in few Men.'[8] Her words reveal a deep attraction.

Dorothy found it even more insupportable in her grandmother's house without either William or Mary to alleviate its rigours. But shortly after their departure, the Rev. William Cookson, one of her uncles, came to stay and he befriended her. Unlike Dorothy he was allowed to have a fire in his room and sometimes invited her to come and sit there to write letters, or to read. He was a friend of William Wilberforce and supporter of his campaign to end the slave trade. In October 1788 he proposed marriage to a Penrith woman and asked Dorothy to come to his new parish in Norfolk to live with them. Dorothy was overjoyed. 'To live in the country and with such kind friends! . . . I was almost mad with joy; I cried and laughed alternately.'[9]

Forncett rectory was set in Forncett St Mary, a little village 'almost entirely inhabited by farmers, who seem very decent kind of people . . . my Uncle's house is now very comfortable . . . the gardens will be charming. I intend to be a great gardener and promise myself much pleasure in taking care of the poultry of which we are to have a great abundance . . . we have been introduced to some of the genteelest families in the place, but have visited very little on account of business . . . they are so ridiculous as to send invitations three weeks or a month beforehand. We had an invitation came on the 26th November for the 18th of December to tea and cards, can any thing be more absurd?'[10]

When Dorothy described their nearest neighbour, Mrs Dix, as being 2 miles away, she meant only that there were no other people in the same social class living nearer. It was not possible to be on reciprocal visiting terms with anyone else. 'She appears to be a sensible woman, but has a good many of the particularities, and some of the bad qualities ascribed to old maids; her appearance is rather remarkable as she always wears long ruffles and a common stuff gown; she is rich, but lives alone and in a very plain manner, I cannot say whether it proceeds from covetousness or not . . . her worst fault is censoriousness . . .'[11]

Two other visitors were Miss Burroughs and her sister, 'accomplished and agreeable girls', the daughters of an 'elegant and sensible woman' whose mind was, unfortunately, 'frequently deranged'. 'Miss Burroughs and I are very happy when we meet; but still we are not upon very intimate terms nor I think ever shall be, they are, however, very pleasant, good-tempered, unaffected girls.'[12] She later wrote that they improved with further knowledge. She missed Jane's friendship: 'I cannot help often regretting that I have not a more intimate friend near me; but I am convinced that I shall never form a friendship that will not appear trifling indeed compared with that I feel for you. You are the friend of my childhood, and Oh! how endearing a thought is that. You shared all my little distresses and were the partner of all my pleasures.'[13]

Dorothy's life at Forncett was structured by religion. Her mornings began with prayers, and were spent reading and writing and doing domestic duties. Afternoons were spent visiting sick and poor parishioners, until an early dinner at three. Afterwards the Rev. Cookson read to them from improving books. On Wednesdays and Saturdays, Dorothy taught some of the small girls reading and spelling, prayers, hymns and catechisms. She wrote to Jane that one small child who 'did not know a letter when she came to me . . . [after six months] is able to read exceedingly well in the testament and can repeat the catechism and a part of an explanation of it; five or six hymns, the Lord's prayer, the creed and a morning and evening prayer.'[14] It was a life of self-sacrifice and the strict, uncompromising morality of the evangelical creed.

When William Wilberforce came to stay, he was so impressed with Dorothy's enthusiasm for this work that he gave her 10 guineas to be distributed as she pleased. He also gave her Mrs Trimmer's *The Oeconomy of Charity* to read. Apart from good works, there was very little else to do. No balls, no plays, no concerts, or any of the other diversions of young people. It was also very difficult for Dorothy to have any of her friends or relatives to stay, since she would have imposed on the hospitality of her benefactors.

In the summer of 1790, her aunt, Elizabeth Threlkeld, accepted a proposal of marriage from a Halifax merchant, William Rawson. Dorothy could not afford to travel to the wedding, and was forced to apply to her friend Jane for details. Dorothy denied having any romantic attachments to anyone. Jane was rebuked when she suggested that she might have an interest in Wilberforce: '. . . no man I have seen has appeared to regard me with any degree of partiality; nor has anyone gained my affections, of this you need not doubt . . .'[15] There was a vacancy in her affections which was shortly to be filled by her brother William, a man she admired and loved so much there was no room for anyone else.

Mrs Cookson proceeded to have four children in three years, and Dorothy found herself in charge of the nursery, often sharing her aunt's bed in order to be useful. She was 'head nurse, housekeeper, tutoress of the little ones or rather superintendent of the nursery . . .' Dorothy was haunted by the fear that she might not be useful enough. She had the orphaned child's fear of not being loved or needed – 'a painful idea that one's existence is of very little use, which I really have always been obliged to feel'.[16]

Dorothy missed her brothers. 'I have passed one and twenty

years of my life [and regret that] the first six years only of this Time was spent in the enjoyment of the same Pleasures that were enjoyed by my Brothers and that I was then too young to be sensible of the Blessing. We have been endeared to each other by early misfortune. We in the same moment lost a father, a mother, a home, we have been equally deprived of our patrimony by the cruel Hand of lordly Tyranny. These afflictions have all contributed to unite us closer by the bonds of affection, notwithstanding we have been compelled to spend our youth far asunder . . . Neither absence nor Distance nor Time can ever break the Chain that links me to my Brothers.'[17]

William was in Switzerland in 1790, and wrote long, interesting letters to Dorothy. He asked her to pass on apologies to their brothers, as he had not had time to write to them. Dorothy eagerly followed the progress of his journey on a map, always anxious for his health and safety. William thought of her 'perpetually, and never have my eyes burst upon a scene of peculiar loveliness but I have almost instantly wished that you could be for a moment transported to the place where I stood to enjoy it.' He also regretted the absence of her precise, recording eye. 'Ten thousand times in the course of this tour have I regretted the inability of my memory to retain a more strong impression of the beautiful forms before me . . .'[18] Dorothy's powers of observation and recall were to be her greatest gift to her brother.

At Christmas 1790, William arrived to stay for six weeks. He was going through a crisis – being forced to choose between poetry and academic advancement. This was where they first talked about making a home together and where their relationship may well have deepened from fraternal affection into love. It is not unusual for siblings who have spent most of their lives apart to experience sensations of 'falling in love' when they are reunited. Byron felt this overwhelming attraction with his half-sister Augusta. Dorothy and William discovered that they could share things with each other than couldn't be communicated or understood by anyone else. Besides their emotional closeness, rooted in vague memories of childhood companionship, there was also the tremendous attraction, both physical and mental, of compatible individuals. They had played together as children. Now as adults they discovered a new mutual happiness in each other's company and a precious ability to meet each other's needs.

At Forncett Dorothy and William spent hours walking in the garden together in the unusually mild December weather, 'every morning about two hours, and every evening we went into the garden at four or half past four and used to pace backwards and forwards 'till six'. Dorothy wrote to Jane prophetically: 'I am very sure, that Love will never bind me closer to any human Being than Friendship binds me to . . . William, my earliest and my dearest Male Friend.'[19]

She was unwell throughout the summer of 1791. 'I have, during the whole of this Summer, without being absolutely ill, been less able to support any Fatigue and been more troubled with Headache than I ever remember to have been. I have of late had an extreme Weariness in my limbs after the most trifling Exertions such as going up stairs &c . . .'[20] She was increasingly tormented by her teeth, two of which had to be extracted. But part of her trouble may well have been psychosomatic, symptoms produced by the degree to which Dorothy was obliged to suppress her volatile feelings. Although by nature very highly strung, the whole of her life she immersed herself in the lives of others and concealed and suppressed her own emotions. Missing William, concerned about her own uncertain future, she began to spend time wandering alone in the gardens after dark, 'as long as I can', thinking most 'of my absent friends'.

William went to France again in November 1791. In his absence, the Rev. Cookson tried very hard to find a curacy for him. Dorothy, in particular, was very keen on the idea and does not seem to have picked up William's reluctance, even after he returned to England in December 1792. She wrote to Jane on 16 February 1793: 'I look forward with full confidence to the Happiness of receiving you in my little Parsonage. I hope you will spend at least a year with me. I have laid the particular scheme of happiness for each Season. When I think of Winter I hasten to furnish our little Parlour, I close the shutters, set out the Tea-table, brighten the Fire. When our

Refreshment is ended I produce our Work and William brings his book to our Table and contributes at once to our Instruction and amusement, and at Intervals we lay aside the Book and each hazard our observations upon what has been read without the fear of Ridicule or Censure.'[21]

Dorothy, though she may have feared 'ridicule and censure', being but an unlettered female, had a very clear critical faculty. When William's first two poems were printed (*Evening Walk* and *Descriptive Sketches*) she pounced on his coinage of 'moveless' and 'viewless', both of which he had used several times. She wrote to Jane that 'the Poems contain many Passages exquisitely beautiful, but they also contain many Faults, the chief of which are Obscurity, and a too frequent use of some particular expressions and uncommon words . . . I regret exceedingly that he did not submit the works to the Inspection of some Friend before their Publication . . . Their Faults are such as a young Poet was most likely to fall into and least likely to discover . . .' But she was particularly pleased with some of the concluding lines, verses which begin 'Thus hope first pouring from her blessed horn' referring to herself and the longed-for shared future, as she prompted Jane to infer. 'You would espy the little gilded Cottage in the Horizon, but perhaps your less gloomy imagination and your anxiety to see your Friend placed in that happy situation might make you overlook the dark and broad Gulph between.'[22]

In May Dorothy was again writing to Jane, wishing that they could meet, but she felt that she could not leave her aunt, especially after the birth of another little Cookson. She had hoped that one of her other Threlkeld cousins would come for a visit and relieve her, but this had not happened. She told Jane that she felt that she was indispensable. But, over a period of time as her attachment to William grew and the balance of her loyalties changed, this feeling evaporated and Dorothy couldn't wait to get away.

In 1792 the Rev. Cookson had been installed as Canon of Windsor and for three months during the summer, Dorothy went with them to London and Windsor and met the King and Queen. She admitted that she was not so much of a democrat that she could not 'reverence him because he is a Monarch more than I should were he a private Gentleman and not to see with Pleasure his Daughters treated with more Respect than ordinary People.' She went with a chaperon to a public ball where 'I had the most severe tremblings and palpitations during the first dance, that can be conceived by any trembling Female. My Partner was a wretched one and I had not danced for five years'.[23]

Dorothy found these public exhibitions a terrible strain and was quite glad to return to Forncett, writing to Jane that 'I have been sitting quietly though very happily at Forncett, without having been at one Ball, one Play, one Concert; indeed, I am sure I should make the worst rake in the world; I was a few days at Norwich in the course of the Summer, and returned quite jaded, and as pale as Ashes . . .'[24] She confessed to her friend Mrs Clarkson later in life that she had always been made ill by 'agitation of mind either of joy or sorrow', hot rooms or social events. 'Ever since I can remember going into company always made me have violent head-aches . . .'[25]

While in France, William had met Annette Vallon, and embarked on his first serious affair. Their daughter Anne-Caroline was born on 15 December 1792. He told Dorothy almost immediately, and she wrote affectionate letters to Annette, apparently completely unmoved by the fact of illegitimacy. Dorothy seems to have accepted William's indiscretion with complete equanimity. She referred to it in a letter to Jane, admitting that 'the subject is an unpleasant one . . . I must confess that he has been somewhat to blame, yet I think I shall prove to you that the Excuse might have been found in his natural disposition. "In truth he was a strange and wayward weight fond of each gentle &c. &c . . ." ' It was part of the accepted double standard where sexual indiscretion could be forgiven in a man, but not in a woman. Annette had been forced to hide her pregnancy, and when she eventually returned home with her child in disgrace, the baby was sent out to be fostered and she had the terrible experience of seeing the little girl carried past the door by someone else. Mary Wollstonecraft also conceived an illegitimate child in the exhilarating, liberated atmosphere of the French Revolution, and when this was eventually made public it meant social ruin for her. Annette became known in her village as 'Madame Williams' – the name Wordsworth being more than French pronunciation could cope with. It seems clear that she regarded herself as William's wife and expected him to come back to France as soon as he was able, to legalise their union and provide support for the child.

One of the usual excuses for Wordsworth's behaviour is the argument that England and France were at war, thus preventing him from going back to France to marry her. Even letters between the two countries did not reach their destinations. But there was nothing to stop him marrying her before he left, as soon as her pregnancy was discovered, and sending for her later. In fact, William lingered in France for several months before returning to England, leaving Annette to have his child, alone, with the vague promise that he would come back and marry her at some point in the future when he was able to do so. Although money was a problem, a way could have been found to support himself and a wife, just as he found a way to support himself and Dorothy. The only conclusion that can be reached is that he did not care for her enough; that he had given in to the temptations of physical passion and left her to suffer its inevitable consequences. He treated Annette very badly and it preyed on his conscience for years.

It was left to Dorothy to tell her uncle of the baby's existence – a terrible task which it should have been William's duty to undertake. The Rev. Cookson did not take the information well. A curacy was now out of the question, and William was forbidden to visit Dorothy at Forncett. 'I cannot see the Day of my Felicity, the Day in which I am once more to find a Home under the same Roof with my Brother; all is still obscure and dark and there is much Ground to fear that my Scheme may prove a Shadow, a mere vision of Happiness.'[26]

Dorothy's love for her brother was passionate and total as he became the whole focus of her need to love and to be loved. 'W . . . he is so amiable, so good, so fond of his Sister! Oh Jane the last time we were together he won my Affection to a Degree which I cannot describe; his Attentions to me were such as the most insensible of mortals must have been touched with, there was no Pleasure that he would not have given up with joy for half an Hour's Conversation with me.'[27]

Her feelings for William increased with the length of their separation. Though she had not seen him since Christmas 1790, in July 1793 she was writing to Jane about her partiality. 'I must be blind, he cannot be so pleasing as my fondness makes him. I am willing to allow that half the virtues with which I fancy him endowed are the creation of my Love, but surely I may be excused! he was never tired of comforting his sister, he never left her in anger, he always met her with joy, he preferred her society to every other pleasure, or rather when we were so happy as to be within each other's reach he had no pleasure when we were compelled to be divided. Do not then expect too much of this brother of whom I have delighted so to talk to you; do not form your expectations from my account, but from that of other people. In the first place you must be with him more than once before he will be perfectly easy in conversation; in the second place his person is not in his favour, at least I should think not; but I soon ceased to discover this, nay I almost thought that the opinion which I first formed was erroneous. He is however, certainly rather plain than otherwise, has an extremely thoughtful countenance, but when he speaks it is often lighted up with a smile which I think very pleasing – but enough, he is my Brother . . .'[28]

William's affection for Dorothy seems to have been almost as great. 'How much do I wish that each emotion of pleasure and pain that visits your heart should excite a similar pleasure or a similar pain within me, by that sympathy which will almost identify us when we have stolen to our little cottage! I am determined to see you as soon as ever I have entered into an engagement . . . Oh my dear, dear sister with what transport shall I again meet you, with what rapture shall I again wear out the day in your sight. I assure you so eager is my desire to see you that all obstacles vanish. I see you in a moment running or rather flying to my arms.'[29] There are indications that he saw in Dorothy something of his dead mother. Lines in an early poem, 'The Vale of Esthwaite', addressed to his

'Sister', pose the question, 'Why does my heart so fondly lean?' and answer it, 'Why but because I fondly view/All, all that Heav'n has claimed, in you'.

Dorothy, having decided to take William's side, began to plan in secret to leave Forncett and be with William. It took on the character of an elopement. She planned a visit to her friend Jane, at Halifax, who was forbidden to mention to anyone that she had also invited William. 'I am particularly desirous that nothing should be said of William's intention to visit Halifax when I am there, as though after the meeting had taken place, I should by no means wish to conceal it from my Uncle, yet I should be very averse to his knowing it beforehand or even afterwards, that the scheme was a premeditated one.'[30] Dorothy had to wait until a family connection, Mr Griffith, came down from the north on business to escort her to Halifax on his return journey. In the six months it took to execute the plan, William was threatened by a nervous breakdown and went off walking towards the West Country, visiting Bristol on the way. The fact that he composed the poem 'Guilt and Sorrow' on this walk is indicative of his state of mind.

Dorothy longed to go north, but Mrs Cookson was 'languid and delicate' following the birth of another child and a bout of 'milk-fever'. Dorothy, caring for her aunt and the children, had to 'literally steal the moments I employ in letter-writing'. She was also still being obliged by her aunt to sleep in her bed and Dorothy found this very irksome: '. . . she goes to bed so early as nine o'clock, which robs me of the most precious of my hours as I go to bed at the same time; and as she sleeps very indifferently at nights I am obliged to lie very long in the mornings for fear of disturbing her.'[31]

Dorothy also became ill during this enforced separation, particularly with the strain of leading a double life (difficult for one so open), and bearing the brunt of the Cooksons' disapproval of William and disappointment in him. 'If I walked upstairs quicker than usual I was obliged immediately to throw myself upon the Bed, and my heart used to palpitate, and my limbs to ache to a most distressing degree . . .' She had not seen William for three years and could hardly bear the wait. 'Oh count, count the Days

my Love till Christmas how slowly does each day move! . . . Three
months! – long, long Months I measure them with a Lover's
scale . . .'[32]

In the end she gave up waiting for Mr Griffith. Early in
February she took a coach from Norwich to London and then
from Aldersgate to Halifax. It was a complicated journey for a
young woman travelling alone, and also expensive – £1 10s.
Norwich to London. Her Aunt Cookson had given her £5 towards
the holiday, which she somehow lost when she took out her purse
to change her money; she had to appeal to her brother Richard for
an advance from her allowance. In Halifax she stayed with
Elizabeth Threlkeld, now Mrs Rawson, and was joined at last
on 7 February by William.

Dorothy, loving William deeply, saw him as a superior being,
her ideal of perfection. Her life had been compassed by domesticity; he had been well educated, had travelled widely. His ideals
and opinions now became her own. Dorothy's young, unformed,
highly impressionable mind was swayed by William's and she took
up his causes as she had taken up those of her other relatives, but
with more enthusiasm. Her mind, like her body, had been 'always
in a state of dependence'. Having bent first one way at Aunt
Threlkeld's and then another at the Cooksons', it settled firmly on
the interests of the person she felt closest to emotionally. From
having actively promoted him as a clergyman and herself lived a
deeply religious conventional life, she accepted his anti-clericism
and his then dangerous democratic views as her own. It was a
considerable volte-face.

After a prolonged six-week stay at the Rawsons', William and
Dorothy went off together in April, first by coach to Kendal and
then on foot to Keswick. There they stayed at Windy Brow, a
farmhouse owned by school friends from William's Hawkshead
days – William Calvert and his younger brother Raisley. Here she
received a stiff letter from another aunt (Mrs Christopher
Crackenthorpe) reprimanding her for tramping about the countryside unchaperoned. Dorothy sent her a carefully worded reply. 'I
am much obliged to you for the frankness with which you have

expressed your sentiments upon my conduct and am at the same time extremely sorry that you should think it so severely to be condemned. As you have not sufficiently developed the reasons of your censure I have endeavoured to discovere them, and I confess no other possible objections against my continuing here a few weeks . . . except the expence and that you may suppose me to be in an unprotected situation . . . I affirm that I consider the character and virtues of my brother as a sufficient protection, and besides I am convinced that there is no place in the world in which a good and virtuous young woman would be more likely to continue good and virtuous than under the roof of these honest, worthy, uncorrupted people . . .'[33]

William and Dorothy also found time to visit their family home in Cockermouth, now 'all in ruin, the terrace-walk buried and choked up with the old privot hedge which had formerly been most beautiful, roses and privot intermingled',[34] the rest of the garden overgrown and the roof leaking. Dorothy was very distressed, wondering if their affairs would ever be settled. Return to the Cooksons was impossible, after she had disobeyed their injunctions and become a traitor. Dorothy embarked on a series of family visits, spending some months at Appleby in Westmorland and at Newcastle, and then with her old school friends Mary and Margaret Hutchinson, now living at Sockburn-on-Tees, before returning to the Rawsons at Mill House, Halifax.

Meanwhile William had remained by the bedside of Raisley Calvert, who had promised to leave him £600 in his will. He died from consumption in January 1795 leaving £900 for William, some of which could be invested on Dorothy's behalf. Like Coleridge and Southey, Wordsworth's ability to abandon traditional occupations and be free to think and write was dependent on the charity of wealthy friends. Independence was made possible, not just by this small legacy, but also by a scheme whereby William was to care for and eventually tutor the two-year-old son of widowed Basil Montagu – who had been one of his contemporaries at Cambridge, and who had been disowned by his family after an early marriage. A property at Racedown in Dorset was to be lent by a Bristol merchant, John Pinney. They were at last to have a home and a small income.

Dorothy wrote to Jane (now married) on 2 September 1795: 'I am going now to tell you what is for your own eyes and ears alone. I need say no more than this I am sure, to insure your most careful secrecy. Know then that I am going to live in Dorsetshire . . . my dearest Jane I doubt not you will rejoice in the prospect which at last opens before me of having, at least for a time a comfortable home, in a house of my own. You know the pleasure which I have always attached to the idea of home, a blessing which I so early lost . . . it is a painful idea that one's existence is of very little use which I really have always been obliged to feel; above all it is painful when one is living upon the bounty of one's friends, a resource of which misfortune may deprive one . . . the mind is then unfitted, perhaps, for any new exertions.'[35] The arrangement was all the more satisfactory, since her Aunt Cookson had written requesting her presence in Norfolk for yet another confinement.

Dorothy – such a friend and supporter of William Wilberforce – seemed not to object to the idea of accepting a house bought and maintained by John Pinney, who made his money from sugar plantations in the West Indies run by slaves. Pragmatism was to be preferred to principle.

Two other children were talked about, but neither materialised. 'It will be a very great charge for me I am sensible, but it is of a nature well suited to my inclinations. You know I am active, not averse to household employments, and fond of children. I have laid my plans as distinctly as I can but many things must depend upon unforeseen circumstances, I am however, determined to adhere with the strictest attention to certain rules. In the first place economy and an attention to the overlooking every thing myself will be absolutely necessary for this purpose . . . I shall also have a good deal of work, (needlework) to do – and I am determined to take the whole care of the children such as washing, dressing them &c upon myself . . . I mean to keep one maidservant, she must be a strong girl and cook plain victuals tolerably well.'[36]

\* \* \*

On 20 October 1795 William wrote to a friend: 'We are now at Racedown and both as happy as people can be who live in perfect solitude. We do not see a soul.'[37]

In between sewing little Basil's and William's clothes, and supervising the house, Dorothy walked. 'We walk about two hours every morning – we have many very pleasant walks about us and what is a great advantage, the roads are of a sandy kind and are almost always dry. We can see the sea 150 or 200 yards from the door, and at a little distance have a very extensive view terminated by the sea seen through different openings of the unequal hills.'

The house too suited them. 'Our common parlour is the prettiest little room that can be; with very neat furniture, a large bookcase on each side the fire, a marble chimney piece, bath stove, and an oil cloth for the floor. The other parlour is rather larger . . . and has upon the whole a smart appearance, but we do not like it half so well as our little breakfast room.'[38] Dorothy was beginning to make good the deficiencies of her education, studying Italian, taught by her brother. Under William's tutelage she was also extending her reading.

Living together, walking, reading, discussing everything, they grew ever closer to each other. Dorothy's unquestioning faith in her brother's gifts helped to eradicate his own self-doubt, which he acknowledged in *The Prelude* – 'She, in the midst of all, preserv'd me still/A Poet . . .' They also began the collaboration that helped William to produce some of his finest work. She acted as his amanuensis, transcribing all his work, and as his critic, making suggestions which he almost always adopted. But it went further than that, operating at the most fundamental level. Dorothy's gifts of observation and evocation made it possible for him to see nature in a different way. Reading Dorothy's descriptions of their walks and comparing them to William's is very instructive. His are more prosaic and allusive, less visual; hers exact, minute, imaginative and painterly. She often lamented when she took a walk that she had never been taught to 'exercise the pencil'.

Compare 'Lyme is at least eight miles and a half from Race-down. My walk over the hills was charming. I could hear the murmuring of the sea for three miles; of course I often stopped "Listening with pleasing dread to the deep roar of the wide weltering waves". This is from the minstrel . . .'[39]

Meanwhile Dorothy observed in detail: 'The sea, spotted with white, of a bluish grey in general, and streaked with darker lines. The near shores clear; scattered farm houses, half-concealed by green mossy orchards, fresh straw lying at the doors; hay-stacks in the fields. Brown fallows, the springing wheat, like a shade of green over the brown earth, and the choice meadow plots, full of sheep and lambs, of a soft and vivid green; a few wreaths of blue smoke, spreading along the ground; the oaks and beeches in the hedges retaining their yellow leaves; the distant prospect on the land side, islanded with sunshine; the sea, like a basin full to the margin; the dark fresh-ploughed fields; the turnips of a lively rough green . . .'

And: 'Walked to the top of a high hill to see a fortification. Again sat down to feed upon the prospect; a magnificent scene, curiously spread out for even minute inspection, though so extensive that the mind is afraid to calculate its bounds. A winter prospect shows every cottage, every farm, and the forms of distant trees, such as in summer have no distinguishing mark. On our return, Jupiter and Venus before us. While the twilight still overpowered the light of the moon, we were reminded that she was shining bright above our heads, by our faint shadows going before us.'[40]

Elsewhere she talks of the view making her 'more than half a poet', but she confined her poetic gifts to her journals and letters, the former providing material not just for William but for Coleridge as well.

It was for Dorothy that William wrote 'Among all lovely things my Love had been' ('The Glow-Worm'), remembering that first year at Racedown. And hers were the imagination, eyes and critical intelligence of 'Tintern Abbey', which they visited with Coleridge. Dorothy had by then become Wordsworth's 'eye and ear', teaching him to look at nature, 'The anchor of my purest thoughts, the nurse,/The guide, the guardian of my heart, and soul/Of all my moral being . . . My dear, dear Friend; and in thy voice I catch/The language of my former heart, and read/My former pleasures in the shooting lights/Of thy wild eyes . . . My dear, dear Sister!' He goes on to wish that she will be equally blessed.

> Therefore let the moon
> Shine on thee in thy solitary walk;
> And let the misty mountain-winds be free
> To blow against thee; and, in after years,
> When these wild ecstasies shall be matured
> Into a sober pleasure; when thy mind
> Shall be a mansion for all lovely forms,
> Thy memory be as a dwelling-place
> For all sweet sounds and harmonies; oh! then,
> If solitude, or fear, or pain, or grief,
> Should be thy portion, with what healing thoughts
> Of tender joy wilt thou remember me . . .

But all this was conducted against a background of domesticity. They lived the life of a married couple, complete with child. Dorothy supervised meals, disciplined little Basil Montagu, and sewed two dozen shirts for her brothers, while William dug the garden and read. They were nourished, apparently, on 'air and vegetables'.

The Wordsworths took their role as foster parents for Basil very seriously, Dorothy calling on her experience at Forncett, and William on the theories of Rousseau. Their primary stated intention was that the child should be happy – an admirable goal as he had arrived in a state of abject misery, 'perpetually disposed to cry' somewhat understandably, since he had been parted from his father and nurse, to be cared for by strangers. Their methods were questionable. If Basil cried he was put in a room – 'the apartment of tears' – by himself 'where he cannot be heard, and [obliged to] stay until he chose to be quiet, because the noise was unpleasant to us'. If his lip so much as quivered he was reminded of the solitary confinement that would result. Soon Basil, 'when he felt the fretful disposition coming on', would say, ' "Aunt, I think I am going to cry" and retire till the fit was over'. If he was late getting up in the morning Peggy, the maid-of-all-work, was forbidden to dress him or get his breakfast and he was obliged to go back to bed until the afternoon. Dorothy noted with satisfaction that he quickly learned to do what he was told and keep his emotions under control.[41] Coleridge's daughter Sara, who was a frequent visitor to the Wordsworths' during her own childhood, confided to a friend that '*entre nous* the dear W's did not make children comfortable and delicate children felt their rough management painfully.'[42]

On the other hand he was allowed to play freely outside in the fresh air and soon became as healthy and boisterous as other children of his age. Tutoring was kept to a minimum; he learned his letters and Dorothy and William endeavoured to answer his many questions about the world around him as honestly as possible, believing that his schooling, after Rousseau, should be from nature, learned 'through the evidence of his senses'.

Mary Hutchinson's sister Margaret died in March 1796 from consumption, and in November Mary came to visit, accompanied by her brother who stayed only one night before travelling on. Mary had grown into a tall, dignified young woman, extremely self-possessed and quiet, very self-conscious about a squint in one eye. She was so self-effacing, visitors rarely heard her speak – her silence a perfect counterpoint for the more volatile Dorothy. Mary was still there in March the following year and Dorothy wrote approvingly that 'she is one of the best girls in the world and we are as happy as human beings can be . . .'[43] Mary left Racedown on 5 June, via London, carrying a parcel of shirts for Richard Wordsworth, and Dorothy sent him a letter instructing him to 'walk out with her' and show her the London bridges and St Paul's, Somerset Terrace and Temple Gardens.

Mary narrowly missed Coleridge's first visit to Racedown. He arrived the day after she left. It was the first time Dorothy had met him and she, like her brother, fell completely under the spell of one William described as 'The rapt One, of the godlike forehead,/The heaven-eyed creature . . .' He was later to recall with regret that Coleridge was the 'only wonderful man he had ever known'.

_____

## Love's First Phantasies

*Low was our pretty Cot: our tallest Rose*
*Peep'd at the chamber-window. We could hear*
*At silent noon, and eve, and early morn,*
*The Sea's faint murmur. In the open air*
*Our Myrtles blossom'd; and across the porch*
*Thick Jasmins twined . . .*

Samuel Taylor Coleridge[1]

After their marriage, Sarah and Samuel honeymooned at their cottage in Clevedon, camping out in sparsely furnished rooms that contained only a bed, an Aeolian harp and a few other necessities. Joseph Cottle in his reminiscences describes how Coleridge wrote to him urgently two days after the wedding, asking him to send slippers, candlesticks, two glasses for the wash-stand, groceries, spices, a bible, a carpet, a dustpan and a kettle. But despite the domestic deficiencies Sarah was still deeply enamoured of her 'adored . . . divine husband'.[2] Coleridge insisted that she drop the 'h' at the end of her name and from then on he always called her Sara, which he thought more elegant. He was to do the same with Sarah Hutchinson. This renaming may well have been a symptom of a hidden desire to remake the women in his life into something closer to his inmost fantasies.

Caught up in the honeymoon euphoria, Sarah even began to write poetry. A letter from Coleridge to Cottle refers to 'two of Sara's poems'. The first is referred to as a 'beautiful little poetic Epistle' which Cottle claims not to have received. The second was a letter to Cottle called 'The Silver Thimble'. Coleridge added, 'It is remarkably elegant and would do honor to *any* Volume of *any Poems*'.[3] He published it as one of a series of Epistles, 'Published anonymously at Bristol' in 1796: 'The Silver Thimble – The production of a young lady'. It is signed SARA and dated 1795. Sarah told her daughter, when she edited Coleridge's work in 1847, that she had written 'but little of these verses'.[4] Which parts of the poem were exclusively hers there is now no way of knowing, since it was rewritten and polished up by Coleridge, and other poems that she wrote have disappeared, but they are evidence of the existence of a sympathetic creative impulse which was to surface later on in her fantastic invented language, and in 'Mrs Codian'. After the breakdown of their marriage Coleridge went to great lengths to deny Sarah any creative or perceptive powers at all, and it was one of the Wordsworths' most damning criticisms of her that she had no 'creative sensibility'.

The verses, addressed to Joseph Cottle, concern the loss of Sarah's silver thimble and Cottle's production of four new thimbles for Sarah to choose from.

> You much perplex'd me by the various set:
> They were indeed an elegant quartette!
> My mind went to and fro, and waver'd long;
> At length I've chosen (Samuel thinks me wrong)
> That, around whose azure rim
> Silver figures seem to swim,
> Like fleece-white clouds, that on the skiey Blue,
> Waked by no breeze, the self-same shapes retain;
> Or ocean-Nymphs with limbs of snowy hue
> Slow-floating o'er the calm cerulean plain.
>
> Just such a one, *mon cher ami*,
> (The finger-shield of industry)
> Th' inventive Gods, I deem to Pallas gave . . .

The habit of sprinkling her conversation with French phrases, such as *mon cher ami*, was one of the Bath mannerisms Sarah had picked up in her youth and which she was cruelly teased about by the Wordsworths.

Clevedon proved to be too far from Bristol for Coleridge. He had to walk to the Bristol Library and couldn't get back in the same day, so Sarah was alone overnight and not very happy. The neighbours were also rather suspicious about the newcomers. In November they had to move back to Bristol with Sarah's mother and her younger siblings in a house on Redcliffe Hill. This was far from ideal. Cramped conditions put a great strain on the young couple's developing relationship.

The vacuum in Coleridge's life created by his estrangement from Southey was gradually being filled by a closer friendship with the radical Thomas Poole, described by De Quincey as 'a stout plain-looking farmer, leading a bachelor life, in a rustic old-fashioned house,' near Nether Stowey in Somerset. He was already, at twenty-eight, a radical democrat with an inherited fortune made out of the tanning industry and a lifelong love of literature. He encouraged Coleridge to become more involved in radical politics and offered his house to Sarah and Samuel as a refuge from the proximity of 'in-laws'. Thomas Poole saw Sarah as possessing just the elements of practicality and common sense that her husband needed to function as a poet. As he remarked, 'Happy is the genius who has a friend ever near of *good sense*.'[5]

Meanwhile, things were gradually reaching crisis point for Sarah's sister Edith. Southey's family had decided that it would be a good idea for him to go out to Portugal for six months to stay with his uncle, the Rev. Hill, who was chaplain to the British Factory at Lisbon. They hoped that it would give him a chance to think about his future, and that it would separate him from Edith. They regarded her as not only impossibly compromised, but an obstacle to the healing of the family's breach with Miss Tyler.

Southey, always motivated by a strong sense of duty and honour, was afraid that 'malicious gossiping tongues' would say that he had gone away and deserted Edith because of her damaged reputation. They were married secretly at St Mary Redcliffe church on Saturday, 13 November, the day before he left for

Lisbon. Southey was forced to borrow the money for the licence and the ring from Joseph Cottle, and after the ceremony Edith returned home as usual, wearing her wedding ring round her neck. The marriage was unconsummated and Edith kept her own name since Southey could not envisage a certain time when it might be 'convenient for us to live together'. It was not a happy occasion – 'the day was very melancholy. My Edith returned home at night, and I slept as usual at Cottles. The next day we parted.'[6] Edith, still estranged from Sarah, spent the next six months staying with Cottle's sisters, who may well have been school friends of the Fricker girls, having also been educated by Hannah More.

Coleridge felt more than ever that Southey had abandoned the cause by being in Portugal while he wrote pamphlets, addressed public meetings and set up (with Cottle's assistance and Thomas Poole's encouragement) a radical Christian-democratic periodical *The Watchman* – 'Science, Freedom, and the Truth in Christ'. The prospectus proclaimed its aims: 'That all might know the Truth, and that the Truth might make us Free.'

It was also a platform for the literary efforts of the Pantisocrats. Both Coleridge's and Lovell's poems were featured. The third issue of *The Watchman* put forward the ideal that wives should be the 'free and equal companions' of their husbands and discussed the writings of Mary Wollstonecraft. Sarah was not involved in the *Watchman* enterprise. Unlike Dorothy Wordsworth and Sarah Hutchinson, she kept herself free from Coleridge's literary projects, concentrating on the creation of a secure, domestic environment for him to live in. This was, in fact, what he needed most. But, unlike Wordsworth, Coleridge had to transcribe his own work and correct his own proofs and Sarah's failure to provide him with secretarial services became one of his criticisms of their relationship.

Early in 1796 Sarah realised she was pregnant, and she was very sick. Then she and her mother contracted some kind of viral or bacterial infection loosely called 'a fever' while Coleridge was away on a subscription-raising journey for *The Watchman* in the north of England – the heart of the dissenting community where most of the subscribers were likely to be. Coleridge cut his tour short and came home because he believed that Sarah was going to lose the child. On 19 March she was so ill that they believed that she had suffered a miscarriage. Coleridge felt the loss almost as badly as she: 'the pangs which the Woman suffers, seem inexplicable in the system of optimism – Other pains are only friendly admonitions that we are not acting as Nature requires – but here are pains most horrible in consequence of having obeyed Nature.'[7] While Sarah lay ill and fearing to lose her child, Coleridge was taking laudanum to relieve his mental distress.

As soon as Sarah recovered, the Coleridges moved into Oxford Street in the Kingsdown area of Bristol, their own lodgings except for the presence of George Burnett, Coleridge's partner in Pantisocracy (and in addiction), and assistant on *The Watchman* (he died in 1811 of opium addiction in poverty after having failed in almost everything he tried his hand at). Coleridge was quite depressed by the burden of supporting not only Burnett and Sarah, but also Mrs Fricker and her youngest child George. 'My wife, my wife's Mother, and little Brother, & George Burnet – five mouths opening & shutting as I pull the string!'[8] On Sarah's side, Coleridge's notoriously unreliable habits had begun to infuriate her, and he occasionally felt the lash of her quick tongue.

For O! I wish my Sara's frowns to flee,
And fain to her some soothing song would write,
Lest she resent my rude discourtesy,
Who vow'd to meet her ere the morning light,
But broke my plighted word – ah! false and recreant wight!'[9]

The 'glowing gorgeous poetry of courtship' was rapidly being replaced by the 'meagre prose comment' of marriage.

*The Watchman* didn't last very long as the political climate changed, collapsing with the publication of the last edition on 13 May 1796 and leaving debts for the printer's bills. There were large numbers of unsold copies which their maid used to light the fire. The Coleridges found themselves in a tricky financial position. Friends tried to arrange an annuity and gave donations to pay off the *Watchman* debts, and they received a grant of 10 guineas from the Royal Literary Fund.

After the collapse of *The Watchman*, Coleridge felt that 'domestic Sorrows and external disappointments' had weighed him down so that he was below 'writing-point in the thermometer of mind'.[10] In April Cottle published *Poems on Various Subjects* by S.T. Coleridge late of Jesus College, Cambridge. It had mixed reviews, but was generally well received and this raised Coleridge's spirits a little. But somewhere around the same time, Sarah realised with consternation that she was still pregnant. In his notebook Coleridge complained of 'Privations, anxieties and embarrassments'. Coleridge found it hard to write against a background of domestic trivia and financial anxiety. 'Formerly I could select a fine morning, chuse my road, and take an airing upon my Pegasus right leisurely – but now I am in stirrups all day . . .'[11] While Sarah tried desperately to feed them on very little money and prepare for the arrival of a new baby, Samuel resorted to laudanum as an escape from the pressures. He found it hard to settle down to ordinary life. Having tasted 'the enchanted cup of youthful rapture incident to the poetic temperament', Coleridge could not afterwards submit to the 'sobrieties of daily life'.[12]

On 3 May Robert Lovell died, from 'fever'. He had been taken ill at Salisbury but had insisted on continuing his journey home despite bad weather. His death left Mary a widow at twenty-five with a baby son and no money. Coleridge helped to nurse his friend through his illness, being with him when he died. It was one of those generous, compassionate acts that made Coleridge so much loved in spite of all his shortcomings. Robert Lovell's sufferings were so terrible Mary could not bear to stay in the same room with him. 'All Monday Night I sate up with her – she was removed to the Kitchen, the furthest room in the House from her Husband's Bed-chamber . . . It was, you know, a very windy night – but his loud, deep, unintermitted groans mingled audibly with the wind, & whenever the wind dropt, they were very horrible to hear, & drove my poor young Sister-in-law frantic . . . At one o'clock the Clock in the Kitchen went down. "Ah! (said She) it is stopt . . . (A long pause)

O God! O God! my poor Love will stop' – Here her agonies became wild – hastened out, knocked up a Chairman, & had her conveyed to my House – He died ten o'clock that morning . . .' Lovell's death affected them all deeply. Coleridge wrote soberly that 'we are all become more religious than we were'.[13] Mary Lovell initially hoped that Robert's death would cause her father-in-law to soften his attitude towards her and her young son enough to provide some support for the child, but this proved illusory. She became dependent on her sisters and their husbands for her support.

Coleridge and Sarah, both low in spirits and in health, having had the additional burden of Sarah's mother being critically ill, went on a visit to Thomas Poole in Somerset, where they spent their time relaxing in the garden, reciting poetry and drinking cider. Poole's friendship was a very important factor in their lives. He thought Coleridge a creature 'divinely endowed' and dedicated a large part of his time to his concerns. Sarah loved Thomas Poole and his mother and was loved and approved in return. After she went back to Bristol at the end of May, she kept up a regular correspondence with them and Poole eventually became one of her most intimate friends.

Coleridge was still casting around desperately looking for a means of earning a living to support himself, Sarah and the imminent baby. They travelled to Derby to see Mrs Elizabeth Evans, a wealthy widow who needed someone to tutor her two young sons. Sarah and Mrs Evans got on very well together, and Samuel as usual charmed her into agreeing to employ him. Sarah later recalled in 'Mrs Codian' that the romantically inclined Mrs Evans 'admired him greatly – even thought him personable and said he reminded her of Abelard'. Everything was so satisfactory that Coleridge went back to Somerset to visit his family with a view to affecting a reconciliation (prompted by Sarah, who had still not been introduced), leaving Sarah with Mrs Evans for several weeks. It was bliss for Sarah to be in such a comfortable environment, waited upon by servants, with no meals to cook or clothes to wash. At this stage of her pregnancy, such a holiday was extremely beneficial. There were outings to Matlock and Dove Dale and to a local stately home, Oakover, to look at the Raphaels and Titians.

In Coleridge's absence Mrs Evans' brothers – the boys' guardians – took exception to her choice of tutor and the arrangement was cancelled. Sarah was devastated, but parted from Mrs Evans on good terms with a gift of Mrs Evans' own valuable baby clothes and £95 in cash. They continued to correspond over the years and Sarah made occasional visits. Thomas Poole was furious that Mrs Evans had not stood up to her brothers, declaring that he was now convinced of women's natural inferiority. But Mrs Evans married not long after and this event, which came as no surprise to the Coleridges, may also have had something to do with the change of plan.

After their return to Bristol in September, Samuel left Sarah behind to make a trip to Birmingham to investigate another tutoring arrangement, this time with Charles Lloyd, the twenty-one-year-old son of a wealthy Quaker banking family. Charles was an epileptic, of nervous disposition, and his family were willing to pay £80 a year to have him coached by Coleridge, living as part of the Coleridge family.

Two days after he left, Sarah went into labour in the middle of the night. She was on her own, having sent the servant to fetch both midwife and doctor. She had to deliver the baby herself, medical help arriving only in time to deal with the afterbirth. Coleridge afterwards blamed the incident on Sarah, writing that she had 'strangely miscalculated' her dates. Sarah was certainly very casual and absent-minded about dates, but Richard Holmes in his biography of Coleridge suggests that his absence was 'ominous' and that he may well have been running away in characteristic fashion.

The doctor wrote to Samuel straight away, informing him that he had a son. Coleridge was 'quite annihilated by the suddenness of the information – and retired to my room to address myself to my Maker – but I could only offer up to him the silence of stupified feelings.' Coleridge was totally unprepared for the emotional demands of parenthood, overcome by 'confused thoughts and shapeless feelings'. In the carriage on the way to Bristol he alternated between joyful anticipation and fear that the child might be dead by the time he arrived. There was a tearful and rather cautious reunion with Sarah and the baby. 'When I first saw the Child, I did not feel that thrill & overflowing of affection which I expected – I looked on it with a melancholy gaze – my mind intensely contemplative & my heart only sad. – But when two hours after, I saw it at the bosom of its Mother; on her arm; and her eye tearful & watching its little features, then I was thrilled & melted, & gave it the KISS of a FATHER.'[14] The baby was named David Hartley after the philosopher.

The Coleridge marriage was still a very happy one, both declaring that each was the other's dearest friend, or 'pal' in Coleridge's borrowed cockney slang. He called Sarah his Sally-Pally and she called him Esteesi – a version of his initials, STC. The baby was a bonding factor that for a while brought them closer to each other: 'for the mother's sake the child was dear,/And dearer was the mother for the child'.[15] But there were already intimations of the rough terrain in front of them. They were temperamentally very different and had little in common. Coleridge observed ominously to a friend that 'My wife's every day self and her minor interests, alas, do not at all harmonize with my occupations, my temperament, or my weaknesses.' Coleridge – first spoilt and then abandoned as a child – was looking for unconditional love, and the kind of emotional support that might be expected to come from a mother. Sarah, on the other hand, was looking for emotional and financial security and the companionship of a husband. Tired and overworked, at her wits' end to juggle the family finances, she was rapidly discovering that she was responsible for two children, not one, as well as looking after the desperately unstable Charles Lloyd.

The birth of Hartley prompted a family reunion. Robert Southey had been back in Bristol for several months, living in lodgings with Edith, without making contact with the Coleridges. However, a few days after Hartley was born Southey, to Sarah's 'great joy', wrote a letter to Coleridge quoting Schiller: 'Fiesco! Fiesco! thou leavest a void in my bosom, which the human race, thrice told, will never fill up.'[16] Coleridge responded warmly, but wrote to another friend that the relationship had been fundamentally damaged. 'The enthusiasm of friendship is not with S and me. We quarrelled and the quarrel lasted for a twelve-month. We are now reconciled;

but the cause of the difference was solemn, and blasted oak puts not forth its buds anew! We are acquaintances and feel kindliness towards each other, but I do not esteem or love Southey . . . and vice versa Southey and me.'[17]

There was a certain temperamental incompatibility between Coleridge and Southey that had not been apparent in the first heat of friendship and political sympathy. Southey was the direct opposite of Coleridge, having 'too stoical a want of passion' to be close to him. Southey came back from Portugal much changed. Although he had loved the visual richness of the country, he had been deeply homesick for Edith and England. He returned to find his best friend Lovell recently buried and his sister-in-law destitute. His first act was to try to raise some money for her support by issuing a publication. His sense of duty had already begun to overmaster his other instincts and one of his letters expresses sentiments more usual in a middle-aged man than one of twenty-two. 'How does time mellow down our opinions! Little of that ardent enthusiasm which so lately fevered my whole character remains. I have contracted my sphere of action within the little circle of my own friends, and even my wishes seldom stray beyond it . . . I want a little room to arrange my books in, and some Lares of my own.'[18] Such a view of life was totally antipathetic to Coleridge.

But Edith and Sarah were very happily reunited with each other and when the Southeys rented a house in Clarence Place, Kingsdown, they found themselves living almost directly opposite each other. Edith and Robert were living on small sums of money advanced by Cottle, until the promised annuity, payable as soon as Southey's friend Wynn reached twenty-one, arrived. The obligations of the Coleridge and Southey families to the young bookseller were enormous – his 'true and most essential acts of friendship' underpinned their lives and could never be satisfactorily repaid. 'It is not the settling of a cash account that can cancel obligations like these.'[19]

Sarah was glad of her sister's support in the autumn of 1796, since Coleridge rapidly became ill with what was identified as a 'nervous complaint'. He was suffering from anxiety and depression, experiencing what he called 'Day-mairs' and complaining of acute pains in his joints and muscles. At times he suffered neuralgia so terrible that he ran around the house naked. He was irrational and hyperactive. The doctor prescribed laudanum, twenty-five drops every four hours, unaware that Coleridge was already imbibing massive amounts of the drug, sometimes as much as sixty or seventy drops. To make things worse, Coleridge's illness affected Charles Lloyd who had a series of epileptic fits and an attack of mania. He was sent home to Birmingham to convalesce. Sarah was terrified and shared her anxieties with Thomas Poole. The lease on their house was due to end at Christmas, and Poole began to look around for some-where more suitable – and permanent – for them to live.

Coleridge had made up his mind to move into the country. This was partly because he was convinced that it was better for children to be brought up in the country than the town, but he also had dreams of self-sufficiency in the Pantisocratic mode, and talked once more of growing his own vegetables and keeping animals. Poole found a cottage with six acres of land not far from his house at Stowey in Somerset and Samuel and Sarah began to draw up schedules and calculate accounts. They decided to live as simply and cheaply as possible without any servants except Hartley's nurse Betty. They would contract out the washing, eat no meat except on Sunday and do without 'strong liquor'. Sarah, in charge of the finances, reckoned they could manage on about 16 shillings a week.

Coleridge drew up a schedule of the division of daily chores.

Six o'clock. Light the fires. Clean out the kitchen. Put on the Tea kettle. Clean the Insides of the Boiling Pot. Shoes etc. C and B. Eight o'clock. Tea things etc put out and after clean up. Sara. One o'clock. Spit the meat. B & C. Two o'clock. Vegetables etc. Sara. Three o'clock – Dinner. Half past three – 10 minutes for cleaning Dishes.[20]

Coleridge also allotted himself the cultivation of the vegetable garden and other heavy household tasks, while Sarah took care of Hartley and the sewing.

But there was Charles Lloyd to accommodate, and then Mrs Fricker decided that she would like to join them if young George could be found an apprenticeship. Coleridge had developed a growing aversion to Sarah's mother, with her religious conformity and middle-class conventionality. She is referred to in letters as '*that* Mrs Fricker' and the malignant influence of a mother-in-law is one of the features of his poem 'The Three Graves'. The only advantage of her presence would be that she would bring her furniture with her, since they had very little of their own. But in the end no one was prepared to have George as an apprentice without a considerable premium and Mrs Fricker stayed in Bristol, to Coleridge's relief.

As with all his other grand plans, Coleridge was enthusiastic (confessing to Poole a 'violence of hope', sometimes to the point of irrationality), well intentioned, but completely unreliable when it came to putting it all into practice. De Quincey wrote of him: 'Nobody who knew him ever thought of depending on any appointment he might make; spite of his uniformly honourable intentions, nobody attached any weight to his *in re futura*: those who asked him to dinner or any other party, as a matter of course, sent a carriage for him, and went personally or by proxy to fetch him; and, as to letters, unless the address were in some female hand that commanded his affectionate esteem, he tossed them all into one general dead-letter bureau, and rarely, I believe, opened them at all.' Unlike Southey, Sarah still trusted him completely.

The cottage fell through and, now driven by necessity and the end of their lease in Bristol, they found themselves forced to take another, rather dilapidated and much smaller property, at Nether Stowey. Poole, who had initially found the cottage, had second thoughts and did his best to dissuade them from taking it. He was worried, not only about its suitability for a family, but about the effects on the Coleridges (and possibly himself) of local gossip about so notorious a radical. Coleridge's reputation had preceded him from Bristol, fuelled by his lectures and articles in *The Watchman*. Rumours even circulated that the Coleridges were not married, and Sarah was cut dead by several local women she might have looked to for friendship, including Thomas Poole's sister-in-law.

They moved in on 31 December, bringing all their belongings from Bristol in a farm-wagon. The cottage on Lime Street, at the end of the village, was absolutely tiny. There were two small living-rooms on either side of a narrow passage with a kitchen built on to the back. Upstairs there were three bedrooms, all small. Outside there was an earth closet, a long narrow vegetable garden, much overgrown, and a small orchard. Water had to be carried in from a pump. The front of the cottage opened into the street right next to the main drain.

First impressions made Sarah's spirits sink. The cottage was damp and freezing cold in winter – bearing the brunt of the fierce Channel winds that flung the Atlantic storms on to the exposed west coast. All the chimneys smoked, a fault that could never be cured, and in summer the drain filled the house with stench. In wet weather the drain overflowed creating a sea of mud and filth, creating what Coleridge called 'an impassable Hog-stye, a Slough of Despond'.[21] To make things worse they were invaded by mice, which Coleridge had to catch and kill despite his beliefs in the integrity of all animal life. To 'assassinate his credulous guests' was, he felt, a 'foul breach of the rites of hospitality!'.

Sarah, usually indomitable, found the place utterly miserable, despite Poole's attempts to alleviate the discomforts. Her Bristol nursemaid Betty left in disgust and she had only the locally employed 'poor Nanny', a very young girl, uneducated and mentally slow. On the plus side she was also loyal and hardworking and willing to endure the difficult conditions, but unknown to the Coleridges she was already suffering from consumption.

Sarah, gently reared and educated in the comfortable ambience of Bristol and Bath, found herself – as Molly Lefebure graphically describes in her biography of Sarah – living the life of an agricultural labourer's wife, with all the drudgery that a tiny cottage with primitive amenities entailed. There wasn't even an oven or kitchen range on which to cook – only an open fire with pans hung from a hook. Pies and cakes had to be carried into the village bakery to cook; washday was a nightmare, with a young baby and long skirts and trousers made filthy from the mud tramped in from the lane outside. Poole made a gate into his orchard, which bordered their garden, and offered as much help as he could.

Coleridge, faced with the realities of rural self-sufficiency, abandoned the carefully drawn up divisions of responsibility and buried himself in a tragedy, *Osorio*, that he was writing in the hope that Sheridan would produce it at Drury Lane. He escaped regularly to Poole's 'windy parlour' through the orchard gate. Sarah began to feel increasingly isolated and became depressed and weepy. She missed her friends and family in Bristol and talked nostalgically of Mrs Evans' comfortable house in Derbyshire.

However, she was never one to be beaten down by circumstances and gradually her sunny personality, and the support of Poole and his mother, won the Coleridges limited acceptance in the neighbourhood. They were invited to parties occasionally and to 'musical evenings' and the sort of entertainments Sarah particularly liked. With the coming of spring the cottage too seemed a better place, surrounded by idyllic countryside, and the fruit trees blossoming in the orchard just beyond the kitchen door.

Their relationship, chipped and frayed by family pressures and financial anxieties, also improved. Coleridge abandoned himself to doting fatherhood, even changing Hartley's nappies. Sarah accused him of spoiling the child, but Coleridge's devotion to Hartley brought them closer to each other. 'He laughs at us till he makes us weep for very fondness – You would smile to see my eye rolling up to the ceiling in a Lyric fury, and on my knee a Diaper pinned, to warm.'[22] It was here that Coleridge wrote 'Frost at Midnight', a meditative poem resonant with paternal love, as he sat by Hartley's cradle late at night.

> Dear Babe, that sleepest cradled by my side,
> Whose gentle breathings, heard in this deep calm,
> Fill up the interspersed vacancies
> And momentary pauses of the thought!
> My babe so beautiful! it thrills my heart
> With tender gladness, thus to look at thee,

[ 69 ]

And think that thou shalt learn far other lore,
And in far other scenes! For I was reared
In the great city, pent 'mid cloisters dim,
And saw nought lovely but the sky and stars.
But *thou* my babe! shalt wander like a breeze
By lakes and sandy shores, beneath the crags
Of ancient mountain and beneath the clouds . . .

In the poem he hopes that God, the 'Great Universal Teacher', will teach Hartley eternal truths from the landscape. The first version of the poem, published in 1798, ends with Hartley in Sarah's arms.

Suspend thy little soul; then make thee shout,
And stretch and flutter from thy mother's arms . . .

Later versions of the poem omit Sarah altogether.

The unhappy Charles Lloyd stayed only briefly at the cottage before becoming ill again, this time being admitted to a sanatorium. With him went the £80 a year the Coleridges had counted on as a livelihood. Lloyd's father sent £10 to cover his expenses. At the same time, Charles Lamb sent a damning criticism of an epic poem Coleridge had been working on which precipitated a bout of deep depression. Coleridge took refuge once more in laudanum.

The images of lakes and mountains in 'Frost at Midnight' may well have been generated by Coleridge's increasing contact with William Wordsworth, who talked often of his childhood in Cumberland. Coleridge had already described him as 'my very dear Friend' in early 1796, and they had corresponded all through the winter. In May 1797 Wordsworth called in on his way back to Racedown from Bristol. This visit confirmed their regard for each other. Coleridge thought Wordsworth the 'greatest man he had ever met'. Poole was also initially impressed, before he began to see William as a rival for Coleridge's affections.

After Wordsworth had left, Coleridge delivered the text of his *Poems 1797* to Cottle and set off to walk to Racedown to visit

William and Dorothy, arriving on 5 June. He saw Dorothy working in the garden at the back of the house and, instead of going round to the front door by the road, he impulsively jumped the field gate, leapt a small stream and bounded across the field towards her. The precipitate gesture made a tremendous impression on Dorothy.

She wrote straight away to Mary Hutchinson, who had left the day before. 'You had a great loss in not seeing Coleridge. He is a wonderful man. His conversation teems with soul, mind, and spirit. Then he is so benevolent, so good tempered and cheerful, and, like William, interests himself so much about every little trifle. At first I thought him very plain, that is, for about three minutes; he is pale and thin, has a wide mouth, thick lips, and not very good teeth, longish loose-growing half-curling rough black hair. But if you hear him speak for five minutes you think no more of them. His eye is large and full, not dark but grey; such an eye as would receive from a heavy soul the dullest expression; but it speaks every emotion of his animated mind; it has more of the "poet's eye in a fine frenzy rolling" than I ever witnessed. He has fine dark eye-brows, and an overhanging forehead.'[23]

Coleridge was similarly taken by Dorothy, writing that 'Wordsworth and his exquisite sister are with me. She is a woman indeed! – in mind, I mean, & heart; for her person is such that if you expected to see a pretty woman, you would think her ordinary; if you expected to see an ordinary woman you would think her pretty! But her manners are simple, ardent, impressive – In every motion her most innocent soul/Outbeams so brightly, that who saw would say,/Guilt was a thing impossible in her. – Her information various – her eye watchful in minutest observation of nature – and her taste a perfect electrometer – it bends, protrudes, and draws in, at subtlest beauties & most recondite faults.'[24]

Whereas Coleridge had been attracted by Sarah's sexuality and forceful intelligence, he was attracted principally by Dorothy's quick romantic mind – what he called her 'eager soul', her creative gifts and her quicksilver personality and 'the ascendancy of imagination over intellect'. What he did not mention was that, unlike Sarah with her notions of independence and Wollstonecraft ideals, Dorothy used her 'perfect electrometer' to bend her mood to suit the men she was with. She was a much more comfortable companion, since she took care to be companionable. De Quincey described the effect she had on him as a companion: '. . . because of the exceeding sympathy, always ready and always profound, by which she made all that one could tell her, all that one could describe . . . reverberate, as it were a plusieurs reprise, to one's own feelings, by the manifest impression it made upon hers. The pulses of light are not more quick or more inevitable in their flow and undulation, than were the answering and echoing movements of her sympathetic attention.'

The three of them read poetry, rambled about the countryside and discovered that they held mutually sympathetic views about almost everything. Within a few days Dorothy was transcribing verses for Coleridge as well as her brother. It was the beginning of a long triangular love affair.

At the end of June, Dorothy and William went back with Coleridge to visit Nether Stowey, leaving little Basil Montagu with their maid Peggy. Hazlitt describes Wordsworth cutting a strange figure, all legs, and dressed in 'brown fustian jacket and striped pantaloons'. Shortly afterwards Charles Lamb arrived, still reeling from the 'day of horrors' when he discovered that his much-loved sister Mary had murdered their mother with a knife in a fit of madness. Poor Sarah had to cope with the three extra guests, Hartley and an increasingly sickly nanny, in three tiny bedrooms, with inadequate furniture. In the fuss and confusion she accidentally knocked a pan of boiling milk over on to Coleridge's foot, confining him to a chair 'lam'd by the scathe of fire, lonely and faint' for several days. The rest of the company rambled about without him. On one rare occasion when Sarah could be persuaded to leave her domestic chores and go with them, Coleridge wrote 'This Lime Tree Bower My Prison', dedicated to 'gentle-hearted' Charles Lamb, 'My Sara' and the Wordsworths. Later on, as the Coleridges' relationship deteriorated, he dropped her name from the poem, editing her out.

This period at Stowey, happy with Sarah and his young son, stimulated by the intellectual companionship of Wordsworth, buoyed up by Dorothy's open admiration of his gifts, was Coleridge's most fertile period. Here he composed the 'Ancient Mariner', part I of 'Christabel', 'Frost at Midnight', 'Kubla Khan', 'This Lime Tree Bower' and many other major poems, before domestic discontent depressed his spirits and opium and brandy clouded his vision.

Dorothy was very impressed by the countryside which she felt resembled some of the 'less grand parts' of the Lake District. They spent a fortnight at Nether Stowey wandering around the country-side looking at houses – ultimately finding Alfoxden 3 miles away, 'without any more fixed thoughts upon it than some dreams of happiness in a little cottage'.[25]

It was a beautiful Queen Anne house with nine bedrooms, three sitting-rooms, stables and a park. The parlour window looked out over the garden with lawns and shrubs and moss roses. The front windows overlooked the hills, 'scattered irregularly and abun-dantly with trees and topped with fern . . . The deer dwell here, and sheep, so that we have a living prospect.' The side of the house gave views of the sea about 2 miles away. Assisted by Thomas Poole, William and Dorothy immediately began negotiations for the lease which were finalised by the middle of July. They moved in immediately. Their chief inducement in coming to the area, Dorothy confessed, was not the scenery but 'Coleridge's society . . . so important an object that we have it much at heart.'[26]

Though the Wordsworths had moved to Alfoxden, the cottage on Lime Street remained full of summer visitors. In July John Thelwall arrived, 'a stout man with dark crop't hair in a white hat and glasses' – a radical Jacobin who had been sent to the Tower in 1794, tried for sedition, but acquitted. Sarah liked him very much. 'Energetic Activity, of mind and of hearts, is his Master-feature . . . he is intrepid, eloquent, and – honest.'[27] Whereas the Wordsworths had made her feel excluded from their conversa-tions, Thelwall talked to Sarah while she did the washing and other chores, and made it clear that he found her an attractive and intelligent companion. The 'elegance of mind' and social accomplishments that had attracted Coleridge also attracted Thelwall. For a while he entertained romantic notions of settling in their growing community, writing the following lines to Coleridge:

> Ah! 'twould be sweet, beneath the neighbouring thatch
> In philosophic amity to dwell . . .
> To share our frugal viands, and the bowl
> Sparkling with home-brew'd beverage:- by our sides
> Thy Sara and my Susan; and perchance,
> Alfoxden's musing tenant, and the maid
> Of ardent eye, who, with fraternal love,
> Sweetens his solitude.[28]

William Hazlitt was there in July and Joseph Cottle and Charles Lloyd also came to stay – Sarah was overwhelmed by guests, feeding them as often as possible on a trestle table in the garden. The domestic economy dictated that nothing more substantial than bread and cheese and locally brewed cider was put on it, but in the collective euphoria it didn't matter.

The Wordsworths gave a dinner, partly as a housewarming party, serving a huge joint of lamb supplied by Thomas Poole's mother. They hired a manservant from the village to serve at table, and later discovered that he had also been recruited as an informer by a Home Office agent sent down from London to collect information on the 'Sett of violent Democrats' now living at Nether Stowey. It was the first time that they realised that their publicly declared democratic views had put them under suspicion of being French agents. They were all under investigation, being followed even when they went for a walk, and their servants were questioned. Many local people believed the rumours and nobody would rent a house to Thelwall who had to abandon his idea of coming to live there.

The presence of the Wordsworths and the Coleridges in the village had already caused Poole both social and business difficulties because of his known espousal of their political sympathies and his close friendship with them. Poole's business was damaged, 'hampered and distressed by vexatious calumnies'. The possibility of Thelwall joining them was considered evidence of a conspiracy. Coleridge wrote: 'You cannot conceive the tumult, calumnies & apparatus of threatened persecutions which this event has occasioned round about us.'[29]

Under all the stress of visitors and political intrigue, Sarah suffered a miscarriage. Coleridge made light of it, declaring that she had only needed a day in bed to recuperate, but the truth was that Sarah had little time to be ill. And by September she was pregnant again.

From the autumn of 1797 to the spring of 1798 Coleridge and Wordsworth were occupied with *Lyrical Ballads*. They and Dorothy spent many hours rambling through the woods and valleys of the Quantocks in an intimate triad centred around poetry. They were reading, talking, writing poetry. They called themselves 'The Concern' and were constantly in each others' company. Dorothy's journal records Coleridge's visits. A typical page of entries for April and May 1798 reads: '24th [April] . . . found Coleridge on our return and walked with him towards Stowey. . . 25th [April]. Coleridge drank tea . . . 26th[April] . . . Coleridge and W drank tea . . . 27th [April]. Coleridge breakfasted and drank tea, strolled in the wood in the morning, went with him in the evening through the wood . . . Sunday 6th May . . . Met Coleridge as we were walking out. Went with him to Stowey . . . 7th [May]. In the evening, to Stowey with Coleridge who called. 8th [May] Coleridge dined . . . 9th [May] . . . Wrote to Coleridge. Wednesday 16th [May]. Coleridge, William, and myself set forward to the Cheddar rocks; slept at Bridgwater.'

Coleridge was dazzled by Dorothy and William; William and Dorothy were 'in love' with Coleridge. Wordsworth and Coleridge were opposites – the latter animated, excitable, intellectually dominant, changeable, loquacious, religious; Wordsworth taciturn, slower to kindle, deliberate, fond of moral certainties, prosaic. Coleridge was aware of these traits in Wordsworth and apparently told Hazlitt that there was in Wordsworth 'something corporeal, a matter of factness, a clinging to the petty'.[30] Richard Holmes observes in his biography of Coleridge that while it was these contrasts that 'excited and stimulated' them, it was Dorothy whose affection 'held them together'.

Coleridge described their closeness in a letter to Godwin: '. . . tho we were three persons, it was but one soul.' There has been a lot of speculation as to who was in love with who; Gittings and Manton, in their biography of Dorothy, put it that 'They were all in a state of delighted wonder with one another, a type of joyful recognition and dazed bewilderment, for which there can be no rational account.'[31]

It was a state that completely excluded Sarah Coleridge. While Dorothy felt able to leave little Basil with Peggy while she went rambling about the countryside, Sarah did not feel that she could trust Hartley to 'poor Nanny' and was hampered by her new pregnancy. So she rarely accompanied the threesome on their walks. No longer so much in her husband's company, no longer the recipient of his closest confidences, she sensed that a distance was beginning to develop between them. She was also very conscious of Coleridge's growing admiration for Dorothy, and acutely sensitive to the comparisons she knew were being made.

She was left alone more and more often. When the chimneys smoked in the cottage at Stowey, Coleridge was apt to go over to Alfoxden to sleep, leaving Sarah and Hartley to endure. She became increasingly resentful. Coleridge openly compared Dorothy and her adoring, subservient relationship with William, not to mention her unquestioning admiration of himself, to his tetchy and critical relationship with Sarah.

De Quincey also observed this process in retrospect. 'A young lady became a neighbour, and a daily companion of Coleridge's walks . . . Intellectually she was very much superior to Mrs Coleridge. That superiority alone, when made conspicuous by its effects in winning Coleridge's regard and society, could not but be deeply mortifying to a young wife . . . it is a bitter trial to a young married woman to sustain any sort of competition with a female of her own age for any part of her husband's regard, or any share of his company.'

Coleridge would not, at the time, have agreed about the intellectual superiority. He wrote that Sarah had 'an excellent understanding . . . a woman of considerable intellect.'[32] Later he was to disparage her intelligence because it was critical of himself. But he did feel, with the Wordsworths, that she was 'deficient in organic sensibility', because she was more practical and down to earth and objective and 'worldly' than they would have liked. Her relationship with Coleridge and her circumstances were sufficient to have crushed every scrap of romance out of her system and she had little time for reading.

Coleridge also disliked and distrusted educated and intellectual women, 'bluestockings', despite his Pantisocratic sentiments and his youthful acceptance of Mary Wollstonecraft's idea. He felt that such attributes 'eroded sensibility and sympathy'. Dorothy on the other hand was a 'Women of Genius' who might 'in a different style . . . have been as great a Poet as WW himself.'[33]

Years later, Sarah's daughter observed that Dorothy had 'greater enthusiasm of temperament than my mother possessed . . . *She* [Sarah] never admires anything she doesn't understand . . . her very honesty stood in the way.'[34] Besides temperamental differences there may also have been an element of snobbery. Dorothy, by birth the daughter of a gentleman, had been brought up amongst tradespeople in Penrith and Halifax. All her life she remembered being humiliated by her grandmother's servants and for all her free and easy manners was sensitive to minute gradations of class. Even her name was unfashionable and she lamented that it was now only given to maidservants and members of the 'lower orders'. Her Cumberland accent, 'a northern *burr*, like the crust on wine', was also rather uncouth to a southern ear.

By contrast, the Fricker girls were, according to Southey, born into a class superior to any of them – himself and Coleridge included. Sarah had had one of the best educations available to women at the time, been taught fashionable manners and given a 'Bath polish'. Sarah's elegance and her Bath mannerisms and her love of dressing for dinner were the things most ridiculed by Dorothy. Sarah for her part regarded the Wordsworths as quite wild, wandering over the countryside like gypsies in torn and muddy clothes. They rarely cared what they wore.

Dorothy told De Quincey about an incident after a walk, when 'the walking party returned drenched with rain; in which case she [DW], with a laughing gaiety and evidently unconscious of any liberty she was taking . . . would run up to Mrs Coleridge's wardrobe, array herself, without leave asked, in Mrs Coleridge's dresses, and make herself merry with her own unceremoniousness and Mrs Coleridge's gravity . . . one of the natural privileges of friendship . . . but Mrs Coleridge viewed her freedoms with a far different eye . . . and it barbed the arrow to her womanly feelings, that Coleridge treated any sallies of resentment which might sometimes escape her, as narrowmindedness.'[35]

Was Dorothy's spite towards Sarah motivated by jealousy? Was she really a little in love with Coleridge at the point? She later described Sarah to Marry Hutchinson as follows: 'Her radical fault is want of sensibility and what can such a woman be to Coleridge? She is an excellent nurse to her sucking children (I mean to the best of her skill, for she employs her time often foolishly enough about them) . . . She is, to be sure, a sad fiddle-faddler. From about half past ten on Sunday morning, till two she did nothing but wash and dress her 2 children and herself, and was just ready for dinner.'[36] The letter ends with a rather bitchy reference to the frequency with which she suckled her baby 'during that time'. Sarah believed in nursing 'on demand' and breast-fed her children for anything up to sixteen months – a practice that Dorothy does not seem to have believed in. Long suckling was thought to be only suitable for the lower classes and most middle- or upper-class women weaned their children early or, if they could afford it, employed wet-nurses.

Not for Sarah Coleridge the child crying in a locked room. Sarah had a very relaxed way with her children and, as a result, they were often criticised for being too boisterous and forward. Sarah was similarly easygoing as a housekeeper, sometimes chaotic, provoking even more vituperative remarks from Dorothy, who didn't feel that she looked after her husband as carefully as she should. But she did add that although Sarah 'is indeed a bad nurse for C., . . . she has several great merits. She is much, very much, to be pitied, for when one party is ill-matched the other necessarily must be so too. She would have made a very good wife to many another man, but for *Coleridge*!!'[37]

The Wordsworths did not understand, until it was too late, the part that laudanum played in Coleridge's life and its effects on his mind and on his immediate family. Thomas Poole and Sarah did and were both very apprehensive about the Wordsworths' influence, since they encouraged him to give full rein to all his inclinations, rather than exercising the common sense and restraint that Poole judged essential to Coleridge's well-being. Poole saw Dorothy and William as selfish and egotistical and feared that their society would harm Coleridge's work. Sarah saw his emotional withdrawal and the balance of his loyalties changing under their influence and feared that they would harm her relationship with her husband.

In spring 1798, *Osorio* was rejected by Sheridan and Coleridge felt desperate. He owed Sarah's mother 5 guineas for her quarterly allowance, 2 guineas for a quarter's rent, 1 for 'poor Nanny's' wages, £1 13s. to the shoe maker and £2 6s. for coal. Other debts totalled another 5½ guineas. He began to consider a Unitarian ministry and got as far as accepting one at Shrewsbury, turning down £100 offered by the Wedgwoods – a pair of wealthy brothers from Bristol – preferring the more long-term security offered by the ministry with its benefits of a pension for Sarah if he died. He preached an inaugural sermon, but was then offered an annuity of £150 by the Wedgwoods, if he would devote himself to poetry and philosophy. He accepted, resigned the Shrewsbury ministry and returned to Stowey on 9 February 1798.

It was on 20 January 1798 that Dorothy wrote the first words in her journal at Alfoxden. The MS of the Alfoxden journal went missing sometime between William Knight's strictly edited selections in 1897 and de Selincourt's publication in 1941. All that survives is Knight's bland extraction and a copy that Wordsworth made of the first entry on 20 January 1798. Many scholars have speculated about its loss. It is known that a poem of William's written about this time was destroyed after his death by a member of the Wordsworth family worried that some of its content 'would not add' to the poet's reputation. 'A Somersetshire Tragedy' was cut out of a notebook Wordsworth had given to Thomas Poole. There were also concerted efforts to hide the Annette Vallon affair.

A whole section of Dorothy's Grasmere journal has also been lost, between December 1800 and October 1801, and two more pages have been torn out, the first for entries between 5 and 9 November 1801 and the second covering entries for 26 to 28 June 1802. There are also erasures, some in Dorothy's hand, some in another's. Knight's edition of the journals contains the only surviving part of the Alfoxden journal. This largely consists of observations from nature and the occasional mention of visitors such as Poole or Coleridge. He deliberately omitted 'trivial' details from it – unfortunately for us the more interesting personal details of health, domestic activities and relationships. A comparison of the short, edited, Alfoxden entries with the vivid, meticulous records written at Hamburg or Grasmere shows us how much we have lost, and leaves the reader wondering 'Why?' The Alfoxden journal ends six weeks before the visit to Tintern Abbey with William.

On 13 April, Dorothy stayed with Sarah while Coleridge was away visiting his brother George and the Coleridge family at Ottery. Again he went alone, but this time Sarah was expecting the baby pretty imminently and travel would not have been practicable. Dorothy and Sarah seem to have been getting on reasonably well at this point and they did have some interests in common. Mary Wollstonecraft's life, a memoir by her husband William Godwin, had just been published and Dorothy received her copy on the 14th. Its contents were something of a revelation, since the exact circumstances of her life and the irregularity of her relationships with Gilbert Imlay and William Godwin were not generally known.

Sarah's family politics were once more becoming difficult. Coleridge quarrelled again with Southey and Charles Lamb, partly because of Charles Lloyd's novel *Edmund Oliver*, published in 1797, which satirised Coleridge. It included references to his love affair with Mary Evans, opium-taking, and hilarious accounts of his life as Silas Tomkyn Comberbache. Since his release from the sanatorium, Lloyd had been staying with Southey and the novel had been written there. Coleridge believed that Lloyd had got some of the anecdotes on which it was based from Southey. The title certainly came from him, since it was on Southey's own list of 'projected works' in 1796. On the other side, there was a satirical sonnet that Coleridge had published, which Southey thought was intended to make him look ridiculous. Coleridge strenuously denied that it was directed against him.

Dorothy was also involved in the misunderstanding between Coleridge and his former friends. Coleridge wrote in his notebook that Lloyd had written a letter to Dorothy 'in which he not only called me a villain, but appealed to a conversation which passed between him & *her*, as the grounds of it – and as proving that this was her opinion no less than his – She brought over the *letter* to me from Alfoxden with tears – I laughed at it . . .' As a result, Coleridge wrote Lamb a letter which Dorothy carefully copied out which began, 'Lloyd has informed me through Miss Wordsworth that you intend no longer to correspond with me . . .'[38]

Coleridge was working on Part I of 'Christabel', which shows evidence of the growing Wordsworth influence. It contains lines which echo Dorothy's journal entries and the character of Christabel may well have been influenced by Dorothy's energetic, nomadic figure, striding over the Quantocks. It was Dorothy with whom he listened to the nightingales on an April evening near Stowey, and Dorothy who appears in the poem as 'our sister':

> A most gentle Maid,
> Who dwelleth in her hospitable home
> Hard by the castle, and at latest eve
> (Even like a Lady vowed and dedicate
> To something more than Nature in the grove)
> Glides through the pathways: she knows all their notes . . .[39]

Not only was it Dorothy rather than Sarah who featured in his poems, she was also replacing Sarah in Coleridge's letters to his friends. Dorothy wrote footnotes to his letters and copied out errata for his publisher.

On 14 May 1798 the Coleridges' second son Berkeley was born, named for George Berkeley, Bishop of Cloyne, author of works on the 'relation of man to nature'. Sarah again had a very easy labour, if anything easier than her first lightning confinement. Coleridge was once again conveniently absent, having walked into Taunton to perform Divine services for a clergyman friend whose daughter had recently committed suicide.

Berkeley Coleridge was a big, lively baby, good-natured and handsome. His sister Sara later recalled that 'Mama used to tell me mother's tales, which, however, were confirmed by my Aunt Lovell, of this infant's noble and lovely style of beauty, his large, soft eyes, of a "London-smoke" colour, exquisite complexion, regular features and goodly size. She said that my father was very proud of him, and one day, when he saw a neighbour approaching his little cottage at Stowey, snatched him away from the nurse half-dressed, and with a broad smile of pride and delight, presented him to be admired. In her lively way, she mimicked the tones of satisfaction with which he uttered, "This is my second son." Yet when the answer was, "Well, this is something like a child," he felt affronted on behalf of his little darling Hartley.'[40]

But even Hartley's 'Bercoo Baby Brodder' couldn't keep Coleridge in his domestic trap for long. Two days after Berkeley's birth Coleridge set off to visit Cheddar with Dorothy and William. After a brief return to Stowey he went off to Bristol with Hazlitt, meeting up there with the Wordsworths. They then made an impulsive visit to Wales. Between the birth of Berkeley in May and Coleridge's departure for Germany in September, Sarah saw very little of him.

_____

# The German Experiment

In March The Wordsworths had to face leaving Alfoxden, as their lease was up at midsummer. The owner would not allow them to renew it – the reputation of the group as anarchists was so bad. Coleridge said that they had been 'caballed against long and loudly'. The atmosphere at Stowey was one of suspicion and unpleasantness.

It had been a bitterly cold winter and both Basil and Dorothy had been ill – the latter with cold and toothache, an increasing problem. Dorothy began to lose her teeth early, and over the next few years they were visibly in poor condition. It told on her general health and she lost a stone and a half in weight. They also had money worries, since Basil Montagu was unable to pay for the board fees for his son, and various Wordsworth relations were making noises about the return of money advanced to William and Dorothy in the past.

On 11 March 1798 Wordsworth wrote to a friend: 'We have come to a resolution, Coleridge, Mrs Coleridge, my Sister and myself of going into Germany, where we purpose to pass the two ensuing years in order to acquire the German language, and to furnish ourselves with a tolerable stock of information in natural science. Our plan is to settle if possible in a village near a university, in a pleasant, and, if we can a mountainous, country . . .' Dorothy told one of her brothers that 'we think we can live cheaper in Germany than in England. Our design is to board in a family.'[1]

The idea of going to Germany had been discussed for a while.

Coleridge wanted to study philosophy and theology at a European university. France was out of the question, given the political climate (France invaded Switzerland in February 1798 and there were fears of an invasion of England). Germany suited the Words-worths, who planned to learn German in order to make a little money doing translations.

The initial plan included Sarah and the children, but the cost and practicalities of transporting a young family across Europe soon put paid to that. Dorothy was not so hampered. Basil was not her own child. To her aunt she wrote: 'Poor Basil! We are obliged to leave him behind as his father . . . will not be able to pay the additional expences which we should incur on his account . . . the experiment of taking a child of his age into a foreign country is at any rate hazardous, and might be prejudicial . . . we think upon the whole that it is better that he should not go . . .'[2] So Basil was abandoned, passed on like a parcel to yet another foster home.

William and Dorothy left Alfoxden on Monday, 25 June, staying with Sarah and the newborn Berkeley for a week *en route* for Shirehampton, near Bristol. They stayed in Bristol partly to supervise the printing and publication of their joint publication *Lyrical Ballads*. Cottle had given William 30 guineas for his share of the project and this was to be used to finance their German expedition. They were joined by Coleridge for a visit to Wales and then Coleridge, instead of going back to Stowey to see his wife, went up to London to stay with John Thelwall and William Godwin. From London Coleridge sent Sarah £30 in cash for household expenses while he was in Germany and deputised Thomas Poole to look after her.

Sometime in September 1798, Dorothy opened her Hamburg journal with the words 'Quitted London, Friday, 14th September 1798.' According to Coleridge she and William were desperately seasick, Dorothy 'worst of all – vomiting and groaning unspeak-ably', and spent the entire crossing below deck. But the first paragraph of her journal records only her delighted first glimpses of the German coast. 'As we advanced towards Cuxhaven the shores appeared low and flat, and thinly peopled; here and there a farm-house, cattle feeding, hay-stacks, a cottage, a windmill . . . Dismissed a part of our crew, and proceeded in the packet-boat up the river. Cast anchor between six and seven o'clock. The moon shone upon the waters. The shores were visible, with here and there a light from the houses . . . We drank tea upon deck by the light of the moon. I enjoyed solitude and quietness, and many a recollected pleasure, hearing still the unintelligible jargon of the many tongues that gabbled in the cabin. Went to bed between ten and eleven. The party playing at cards, but they were silent, and suffered us to go to sleep.'

On 18 September they arrived in Hamburg and Dorothy kept a journal of their stay for two months. It is written with a novelist's skill for narrative and description, but the style is journalistic – notes and impressions. 'There were Dutch women with immense straw bonnets, with flat crowns and rims in the shape of oyster shells, without trimming, or with only a plain riband round the crown, and literally as large as a small-sized umbrella. Hamburgher girls with white caps, with broad over-hanging borders, crimped and stiff, and long lappets of riband. Hanoverians with round borders, showing all the face, and standing upright, a profusion of riband . . . Fruit-women, with large straw hats in the shape of an inverted bowl, or white handkerchiefs tied round the head like a bishop's mitre . . .'

They were appalled by the attitude of the population to strangers. They were repeatedly cheated in the local shops. On one occasion Dorothy gave the baker a shilling for four rolls and was only given two. Dorothy mimed her disapproval and took two more rolls. 'In a savage manner he half knocked the rolls out of my hand, and when I asked him for the other shilling he refused to return it, and would neither suffer me to take bread, nor give me back my money, and on these terms I quitted the shop. I am informed that it is the boast and glory of these people to cheat strangers, that when a feat of this kind is successfully performed the man goes from the shop into his house, and triumphantly relates it to his wife and family.'

Hamburg was expensive, the streets filthy and used as a public toilet, the city gates closed at six-thirty, preventing evening expeditions. Dorothy found the theatre a 'mixture of dull declamation and unmeaning rant' and the opera incomprehensible, 'the story was carried on in singing'. The tone of her journal is one of increasing disillusion.[3]

Coleridge and his friend Chester parted company with Dorothy and William on 30 September, making their way to Ratzeburg, about 30 miles from Hamburg. The parting was said to have been amicable. Their intention was, after all, to mix with the German people and learn the language, and the Wordsworths, lacking Coleridge's Wedgwood annuity, couldn't afford the style of life he aspired to. Nevertheless there was something; Charles Lamb wrote sarcastically to Southey: 'I hear that the Two Noble Englishmen have parted no sooner than they set foot on German earth.'[4] The news that they had gone their separate ways came as a relief to Sarah, Thomas Poole and the Wedgwood brothers – who shared Sarah's distrust of the Wordsworth influence on Coleridge.

Richard Holmes ascribes their separation to 'Wordsworth's desire to be completely alone with Dorothy, who ever since the Tintern Abbey expedition had become something like her brother's Muse, magically holding open the gateway back into the Cumberland childhood. The growing intensity of this relationship seems well understood by Coleridge, who came to regard it, as his German letters show, as something sacred to Wordsworth and intimately associated with his poetry.'[5] But there may also have been some acrimony between the four after Coleridge had decided to travel separately. Wordsworth did not write to Coleridge for six weeks to his 'great Anxiety & inexpressible Astonishment. Where they are, or why they are silent, I cannot even guess.'[6]

The Wordsworths headed for Goslar in Saxony, a medieval city close to the Harz mountains that had degenerated into a small provincial town populated by 'Grocers and Linen-drapers' as William put it. After initial silence, affectionate letters passed once more from the Wordsworths to Coleridge – Dorothy copying out William's verses and adding descriptions of her own, ending the letter, '. . . farewell! God love you! God bless you! dear Coleridge, our very dear friend.'[7]

Coleridge didn't think it a good idea for William to have taken Dorothy with him. He felt that it cut William off from the benefits of German society and culture: '. . . he might as well have been in England as at Goslar, in the situation which he chose, & with his unseeking manners . . .' Coleridge was also fully aware of the gossip that their relationship generated and told Sarah: 'His taking his Sister with him was a wrong Step – it is next to impossible for any but married women . . . to be introduced to any company in Germany. Sister is considered as only a name for Mistress.'[8]

*Lyrical Ballads* was published in October 1798 and Southey wrote a critical review, reserving his worst criticisms for the 'Ancient Mariner' which he thought 'absurd or unintelligible'. William's poems were equally scorned. Coleridge also had an edition of poems – including 'Fears in Solitude' and 'Frost at Midnight' – published in London by Joseph Johnson at the same time. Sarah was much surprised when Edith wrote to her that Southey had bought a copy in London: 'I thought they were to have been sent here.' 'Fears in Solitude', she observes, as though reading it for the first time, is 'very beautiful'.[9]

Coleridge wrote numerous loving letters to Sarah and Thomas Poole from Germany. By arrangement these were to be shared between them and to be copied by Poole's seventeen-year-old apprentice Thomas Ward who was to edit out all intensely private – 'foolish' – material. In the beginning, Coleridge lamented his absence from Sarah: 'Over what place does the Moon hang to your eye, my dearest Sara? To me it hangs over the left bank of the Elbe; and a long trembling road of moonlight reaches from thence up to the stern of our Vessel, & there it ends . . . Goodnight my dear, dear Sara! – "every night when I go to bed & every morning when I rise" I will think of you with a yearning love, & of my blessed Babies! . . .'[10] He pledged himself at the end of the letter 'after the antique principles of religion' to be, 'I trust, your Husband faithful unto Death'. His letters to Sarah are intense, vivid, enlivened by drawings and by verbatim dialogue, and at the same time intimate, with the easy-going, conversational quality that comes when talking to someone who doesn't need to have anything explained.

From Stowey there was only silence, and Coleridge's letters became more and more hysterical as time passed and he heard nothing from either Sarah or Poole. '26th November. Another, and another, and yet another Post day; and still Chester greets me with "No letters from England"! A Knell, that strikes out regularly four times a week – How is this my Love? Why do you not write to me? – Do you think to shorten my absence by making it insupportable to me? Or perhaps you anticipate that if I received a letter, I should idly turn away from my German to *dream* of you – of you and my beloved babies! – Oh yes! – I should indeed dream of you for hours and hours . . . and of the Infant that sucks at your breast, and of my dear dear Hartley – You would be *present* . . . and . . . with what leaping and exhilarated faculties should I return to the objects & realities of my mission. – But now – nay, I cannot describe to you the gloominess of Thought, the burthen and Sickness of heart, which I experience every post day.'[11] In this frame of mind he wrote 'The Day-Dream', subtitled 'From an immigrant to his absent wife':

> Across my chest there liv'd a weight so warm
> As if some bird had taken shelter there,
> And lo! upon the couch a Woman's Form!
> Thine Sara! thine! O Joy, if thine it were!
> I gaz'd with anxious hope, and fear'd to stir it –
> (A deeper) Trance ne'er wrapt a yearning spirit!
>
> And now when I seem'd *sure* my Love to see,
> Her very Self in her own quiet Home,
> There came an elfish Laugh, and waken'd me!
> 'Twas Hartley, who behind my chair had clomb,
> And with his bright Eyes at my face was peeping –
> I bless'd him – try'd to laugh – and fell a weeping.

It laments his absence from his children as he imagined Sarah seeing his own image in the sleeping infant's face.

> It would have made the loving mother dream
> That she was softly bending down to kiss
> Her babe, that something more than babe did seem,
> A floating presence of its darling father,
> And yet its own dear baby self far rather![12]

The reason for Sarah's silence was that an outbreak of smallpox had occurred, due to a faulty vaccine – vaccination had only recently been discovered by Edward Jenner and the process was far from perfect, though still less risky than contracting the disease. Berkeley had gone down with smallpox and both Hartley and Sarah were ill.

Thomas Poole insisted that Coleridge should be kept in ignorance of the situation, knowing too well the effect of anxiety on his mental and physical health. He wrote to Coleridge that 'Mrs C. and the children are perfectly well. Mrs C. keeps up her spirits . . .' All this was grossly unfair on Sarah who was being forced to endure a terrible situation on her own, having either not to correspond with her husband at all or to tell lies when she did. Sarah, who was always straight and direct, couldn't do it. She must also have wondered why her husband should be spared any suffering at all, even at a distance, when she had to endure so much.

On 1 November, with Berkeley out of danger for the first time, she found herself able to write to her husband. Once she had begun, every harrowing detail of her suffering poured out on to the paper.

My dear Samuel
I received your welcome letter from Hamburgh and, since that, two containing the journal (which gave us all a great deal of pleasure) and should have answered the first but I was at that time struggling under the most severe trial that I had ever had to

undergo and when you have heard my account of it I am sure you will pity me.

About three weeks after you left Stowey, Mrs R. Poole proposed to inoculate her child and sent round to the inhabitants. I objected on account of the warm weather; she was not convinced, but very politely delayed it a week when the weather changed: on Saturday her child was inoculated and ours and several others; in a few days I perceived that Berkeley had taken the infection but Hartley had not; he was inoculated again – and again – and at last his arm rose to a great head and turned, but he never had any other sign. This was pretty well, tho' not quite satisfactory and I experienced some anxiety on his account, for he had very little if any of the eruptive fever; but my dear baby on the eighth day began to droop, on the ninth he was very ill and on the tenth the pustles began to appear in the skin by hundreds.

He lay upon my lap like a dead child, burning like fire and all over he was red as scarlet; after I had counted about two hundred I could almost see them coming out and every one that appeared after that, seemed to me a little ugly messenger come bid me prepare for his death! By the thirteenth day every part of his face and body was covered except the pit of his stomach. I was almost distracted! Lewis [the doctor] was frightened – he came six or eight times a day – the ladies of Stowey also visited me and wept over this little victim, affected by my complaints, and the miserable plight of the child! What I felt is impossible to write – I had no husband to comfort me and share my grief – perhaps the boy would die, and he far away! All the responsibility of the infant's life was upon me, and it was a weight that dragged me to the earth! He was blind – his nose was clogged that he could not suck and his dear gums and tongue were covered and he was so hoarse that he could not cry; but he made a horrid noise in his throat which when I dozed for a minute I always heard in my dreams.

The night of the turn he was very ill, and Lewis gave him a larger dose of laudanum. Two of us were obliged to sit by him one on each side the cradle to hold his hands for the itching was intolerable and he would kick and beat his head about like anything mad, and the sight of this threw me into agonies which I was obliged to suppress and which made me ill in the end.

After this critical night he grew better and was never happy but lying with the nipple in his mouth; the consequence of which was, in a few days my nipples were covered with the pustles; they became swelled as big as walnuts and I could not endure him to touch me. I have now a wet nurse to seek . . . we had recourse to a glass tube through which he sucked cow's milk, tho' very reluctantly and only when his eyes were shut. My milk, which was but little, was drawn off by various stratagems, with very great torture as you may easily believe. In the midst of all this to fill my bitter cup the fuller, I was seized with a pain in my eye; it in a few hours became quite closed – my face and neck swollen, my head swimming . . .

Part of the problem with her face she blamed on the smoking chimneys in the cottage which made it impossible to sit downstairs. She nursed Berkeley upstairs, though her room had no fire in it: '. . . he is too ill to lie in the cradle so that I am obliged to sit whole hours with him in my lap or in my arms until my whole frame is benumbed.'[13] She reassures Coleridge that they are both now on the way to recovery, her milk returned, and in a postscript includes gossip about her sister Martha and the news that she is reading Maria Edgeworth's book on the *Practical Education of Infants*.

In her distraction, Sarah failed to put sufficient postage on the letter and it was returned to her and had to be sent off again. Coleridge was almost beside himself with anxiety. He wrote to the Wordsworths: 'Dear William and dear Dorothea!/You have all in each other; but I am lonely, and want you!' His dependence on their company was growing, and, unknown to Sarah, a joint residence when they returned to England was already under discussion. Coleridge told William: 'I am sure I need not say how you are incorporated into the better part of my being . . .'[14]

Though Berkeley survived the smallpox, his nursemaid, now in 'a galloping consumption', had passed the disease on to him and in his weakened state he rapidly became worse. This time Sarah refused to obey Thomas Poole's strictures on communication with Samuel, writing a vast, miserable letter which ends: 'T.P. has been here: he *insists* on my not telling you about the child until he is quite well – I am sorry I let my feelings escape me so.' Although convinced of the rightness of her actions, she felt guilty about worrying Coleridge with her problems, knowing how attached he was to his children. 'It seems cruel to vex you after so many inquietudes, but I must either write to you my griefs, or not write at all . . . I am aware that this account of the dear child will very much wound you, my dear love, but the instant that I have a glimpse of comfort I will sit down to impart it to you, and make you a partaker of my pleasures as well as my sorrows.' She makes a pathetic attempt at jocularity:

> 'There's nae gude luck about the house
> Sen my guide Mon's awa.'

Towards the end of the letter her real feelings and her longing for Coleridge's return can no longer be contained. 'I have nursed this "wan and sickly one" with "an agony of care" for these last nine weeks until my whole person is so changed by confinement that I look at least ten years older than when you left me. Oh! that I could lay my aching forehead upon your shoulder and weep until I was relieved, for my heart is very full.' But she tries to assure Coleridge that, despite everything, he must not feel that he has to return home: '. . . tho' I long to see you, I should be much hurt if you were to return before you had attained the end of your going – and I am very proud to hear that you are so forward in the language – and that you are so gay among the Ladies: you may give my respects to them and say that I am not at all jealous, for I know my dear Samuel in her affliction will not forget entirely, his most affectionate wife . . .'[15]

Berkeley had been taken ill again on 20 November with 'a violent suffocation and fever'. Various medical tortures in the form of emetics and 'blisters' were tried, to no avail. The doctor diagnosed an inflammation of the lungs and Sarah feared that he would also get whooping cough which was in the village, unless she could get him and Hartley to Bristol in time to avoid it. Dr Lewis told her that a relapse would be fatal to the child.

Sarah went to her mother's house in Bristol on 31 December 1798 in the hope that the change of air would do Berkeley some good. 'Poor Nanny' was by now so ill with consumption she had to be sent home, but no one had yet made any connection between her illness and Berkeley's. In Bristol Sarah had the company and support of her family – both Mary Lovell and Eliza were living with their mother and they took turns to sit up with her during the night as Berkeley's fever and breathing difficulties increased.

At the end of January Thomas Poole, unmarried and without children, was still writing to Coleridge that Berkeley merely had a cough which had been going around the village, nothing to trouble himself about at all. 'Let me entreat you not to over-interest yourself about your family and friends here; not to incapacitate yourself by idle apprehensions and tender reveries of imagination concerning us . . .'[16] He warns Coleridge not to indulge in the 'folly of tenderness', but to be single-minded and rational.

Berkeley died on 10 February 1799. Sarah was shattered. After his death she stayed with Southey and Edith at their house in Westbury, the breach with Coleridge forgotten in mutual grief. Southey organised the funeral and burial. Sarah seems to have undergone a breakdown, her hair fading and falling out, so that she was forced to cut it all off and wear a wig. It never recovered its former growth and was a source of mortification to her for the rest of her life.

She relied on Poole to communicate the terrible news to Coleridge and Poole was adamant that it should be kept from him so that his studies in Germany would not be interrupted. He reluctantly agreed to write a letter but delayed doing so until 15 March. It was couched in sentiments that both Sarah and her husband must have found bewildering. 'It was long contrary to my opinion to let you know of the child's death before your arrival in

England. And I thought, and still think myself justified in that notion, by the over-anxiety you expressed in your former letters concerning the children. Doubtless the affection found to exist between parents and infant children is a wise law of nature . . . But the moment you make this affection the creature of reason, you degrade reason . . . Mrs Coleridge felt as a mother . . . She is now perfectly well and does not make herself miserable by recalling the engaging, though, remember, mere instinctive attractions of an infant a few months old. Heaven and Earth! I have myself within the last month experienced disappointments more weighty than the death of ten infants . . .'[17]

Sarah was so indignant when she read the copy he sent her that she immediately wrote another vast letter to Samuel beginning:

My dearest Love,
I hope you will not attribute my long silence to want of affection; if you have received Mr Poole's letter you will know the reason and acquit me. My darling infant left his wretched Mother on the tenth of February and tho' the leisure that followed was intolerable to me, yet I could not employ myself in reading or writing, or in any way that prevented my thoughts from resting on him – this parting was the severest trial that I have ever yet undergone and I pray to God that I may never live to behold the death of another child, for O my dear Samuel! it is a suffering beyond your conception![18]

She ended the letter with a fervent wish that he would soon be home.

Coleridge felt profoundly guilty that Sarah had had to endure so much alone, while he was enjoying himself, living a life of student irresponsibility in Germany. He wrote eventually to Thomas Poole: 'I lay the blame of my Child's Death to my absence – not intellectually; but I have a strange sort of sensation, as if while I was present, none could die whom I intensely loved.'[19] His natural instinct in difficult situations was to run away. His usual behaviour when he felt that he had upset or betrayed someone was to stay out of the way. Dorothy summed it up (on another occasion) like this: 'I know that his earnest desire to return is the cause of his silence . . .'[20] Southey wrote later: 'Never I believe did any other man for the sake of sparing immediate pain to himself inflict so much upon all who were connected with him, and lay up so heavy and unendurable, [a] burthen of self condemnation.'[21]

He wrote first to Poole before sending Sarah a tactless and rather unfeeling letter: 'It is one of the discomforts of my absence, my dearest Love! that we feel the same calamities at different times – I would fain write words of consolation to you; yet I know that I shall only fan into new activity the pang which was growing dead and dull in your heart – Dear little Being! . . . although I know of his Death, yet . . . it seems to me as if I did not understand it . . .' and he goes on to discuss in a very detached way the ideas of Priestley as to the survival of the infant soul. He recalls that one of the children had been already ill before he left England, but cannot remember whether it was Berkeley or Hartley. He ends the letter: 'Yet I trust, my Love! – I trust, my dear Sara! that this event which has forced us to think of the Death of what is most dear to us . . . will in many and various ways be good for us . . .' Shared extremes of joy or sorrow, he states, 'sink deep the foundations of a lasting love.'[22]

Far from endeavouring to share the experience with Sarah, he decided to extend his stay in Germany from three months to eight – the return that Sarah had hoped for in January was now to be May, something she bitterly resented. She was also very short of money; the small amount left by Coleridge had long since been spent on medical expenses and she was forced to borrow from Thomas Poole.

Coleridge's responses to her pleas for his return were thoroughly insensitive. 'Surely it is unnecessary for me to say, how infinitely I languish to be in my native Country & with how many struggles I have remained even so long in Germany! – I received your affecting letter, dated Easter Sunday; and had I followed my impulses, I should have packed up & gone with Wordsworth and his Sister, who passed thro', & only passed thro', this place, two or three days ago . . . But it is in the strictest sense of the word impossible that I can collect what I have to collect, in less than six weeks from this day; yet I read and transcribe from 8 to 10 hours every day . . . This day in June I hope, & trust, that I shall be in England.'[23]

On 15 May, Sarah wrote an impassioned plea for his return. 'I hope you will soon be here – for oh! I am so tired of this cruel absence. My dear dear Samuel do not lose a moment of time in finishing your work – for I feel like a poor deserted thing – interesting to no one. You must not stay a minute by the way, but fly from Yarmouth and be with me at quarter-day [24 June]! Pray write a few lines from Yarmouth . . . My dear husband God almighty bless you and see you safe home to your affectionate – Sara Coleridge.'[24]

Coleridge responded by going off on a walking tour in the Harz mountains to climb the Brocken. In later life Coleridge admitted that he always ran away from situations or hid his real feelings, in direct proportion to the urgency of the duty or the depth of the feeling. Those he most loved were likely to be the worst treated. But others also saw Coleridge's behaviour towards Sarah as blameworthy. A cartoon in *The Anti-Jacobin* portrayed him as a jackass with the caption: 'He has left his native country, commenced citizen of the world, left his poor children fatherless and his wife destitute.'[25]

In Goslar Dorothy and William had found the winter bitterly cold. 'For more than two months past we have intended quitting Goslar in the course of each week, but we have been so frightened by the cold season, the dreadful roads, and the uncovered carts; that we needed no other motives . . . to induce us to linger here. We have had a succession of excessively severe weather, once or twice interrupted with a cold thaw; and the cold of Christmas day has not been equalled even in this climate during the last century. It was so excessive that when we left the room where we sit we were obliged to wrap ourselves up in greatcoats &c in order not to suffer much pain from the transition . . . We have gone on advancing in the language . . . in tolerably regular progress, but if we had had the advantage of good society we should have done much more . . . Goslar is not a place where it is possible to see any thing of the manners of the more cultivated Germans, or of the higher classes. Its inhabitants are all petty tradespeople; in general a low and selfish race . . . Coleridge is in a very different world from what we stir in, he is all in high life, among Barons counts and countesses . . . but his expenses are much more than ours conjointly . . . It would have been impossible for us to have lived as he does; we should have been ruined.'[26]

They found it more difficult than they had thought to learn the language, since they had few people to talk to. They were in cheap lodgings, with no one to make conversation with other than their landlady and two other lodgers – one of them French. They were not invited out, something Dorothy naïvely interpreted as resulting from their inability to return invitations. Coleridge was more aware of the ambiguity of their relationship in the eyes of the suspicious burghers. The Wordsworths' stay in Goslar, marooned in each other's company, became a turning point in their relationship. They were noticeably closer to each other, noticeably more lover-like, after their German trip than they had been before. The time in Goslar also generated some of Wordsworth's best poetry – notably the Lucy poems, and some narrative poems about his childhood that eventually became part of *The Prelude*.

Dorothy and William, like everyone else, expected Coleridge to go back to England in March or April. They themselves gave up trying to learn the language in such adverse conditions and began to travel back towards Hamburg, visiting Weimar and Eisenach. They kept a joint journal which Coleridge hoped to publish as part of a travel book on Germany, but the journal was lost and the book never materialised. By 13 May they were back at Sockburn on Tees staying with Mary Hutchinson and her brother. Coleridge was still in Germany. They had called on him at Göttingen briefly on their way home, spending one day together. *Lyrical Ballads*, published in their absence, had had so unfavourable a reception that Wordsworth wrote to Cottle that 'no motives whatever, nothing but pecuniary necessity, will, I think, ever prevail upon me to commit myself to the press again . . .'[27] Sarah, in a letter to Coleridge, had commented that everyone she knew had laughed at it.

Southey had written in his review: 'No tale less deserved the labour that appears to have been bestowed on this, it ["The Idiot Boy"] resembles a Flemish picture in the worthlessness of its design and excellence of its execution . . .' Wordsworth was deeply hurt, despite the fact that he had been similarly ruthless (although admittedly not in print) in his condemnation of Southey's *Joan of Arc*. He wrote to Cottle as though his motives for publication should somehow excuse its substance and absolve Southey from being honest. 'Southey's review I have seen. He knew that I published those poems for money and money alone. He knew that money was of importance to me. If he could not conscientiously have spoken differently of the volume, he ought to have declined the task of reviewing it.'[28]

The mutual antipathy between the two men was rapidly developing into hostility. De Quincey later recalled that 'Wordsworth disliked in Southey the want of depth, as regards the power of philosophic abstraction, of comprehensive views, and of severe principles of thought. Southey disliked in Wordsworth, the air of dogmatism, and the ineffable haughtiness of his manner.' Dorothy was still reserving her opinion. She wrote to her aunt: 'You ask me if I am acquainted with Southey. I know a little of him personally, that I dined three times at his house when I was in town and called there once or twice; and I know a good deal of his character from our common friends. He is a young man of the most rigidly virtuous habits and is, I believe, exemplary in the discharge of all Domestic Duties, but though his talents are certainly very remarkable for his years (as far as I can judge) I think them much inferior to the talents of Coleridge.'[29]

In May Edith came to stay with Sarah on her own, while Southey went to London where he was now studying law. The Southeys had rented a house the previous year – nicknamed Martin Hall after the birds that nested under the eaves – at Westbury, near Bristol. Southey spent a lot of his time at Dr Beddoes' Pneumatic Institute at Hotwells, talking to Humphrey Davy and inhaling laughing gas. 'Davy has actually invented a new pleasure for which language has no name. I am going for more this evening; it makes one strong and so happy! so gloriously happy! . . . Oh, excellent air-bag!'[30]

Southey was a creature of habit. He rose early, often waking at five o'clock, and in the quiet early morning hours he wrote poetry. He breakfasted at nine. From breakfast until dinner, eaten about five o'clock, he worked on various literary projects – essays for the *Quarterly Magazine*, research for his biographies and histories. In the evening he wrote letters or corrected proofs and after supper, if there were no visitors, he wrote fiction. He went to bed about ten thirty. Southey found this the only way he could write and preserve his health. If he immersed himself in one project he found that it oppressed his mind to such an extent that he could not sleep and became prey to violent 'nervous excitement'. 'I cannot work long together at anything without hurting myself,' he wrote to Grosvenor Bedford, 'and so I do everything by heats.'[31]

Southey always had a predisposition to 'nerves', controlled only by an iron will. People who met him were always fascinated by the contrarieties of his personality. His friends found it incredible that 'such rapidity of mind' could be yoked to 'such patient labour and wearisome exactness, so mild a disposition with so much nervous excitability, and a poetical talent so elevated with such an immense mass of minute dull learning.' Southey suppressed much. He wrote to Coleridge: 'Your feelings go naked, I cover mine with a bear-skin . . .'[32] Hazlitt recalled occasions when Southey's outer mask slipped briefly – a quivering lip put under strict control, a flush of anger or excitement, promptly quelled. Southey admitted that many people 'suppose I have no nerves, because I have great self-control as far as regards the surface, if it were not for great self-management and what may be called a strict intellectual regimen, I should very soon be in a deplorable state of what is called nervous disease . . .'[33]

Southey longed for a child, but none had arrived. Edith was in poor health. Letter after letter refers to her continued invalidity. 'Edith has been very unwell . . . I wish her to diet with bark, or some tonic medicine . . . Edith is better . . . hope that frequent change of air and much exercise might strengthen her. She is greatly recovered but far from being well . . .' Her illnesses may well have been rooted in depression and associated eating disorders, the symptoms being insomnia, an unwillingness to eat, stomach pains and 'wasting away'. If this was the case, then her failure to conceive would be understandable as poor nutrition and weight loss suppress menstruation. But there are other question marks – speculation as to whether the marriage had been consummated at this point, in which case the stress-related illnesses, which prostrated both Edith and Robert at various times, would also have been quite understandable. Southey kept a record of his dreams and one curious dream he had a few years later is illuminating. In the dream, 'To my great surprise I discovered that Edith had a former husband living. He was by birth or descent a Spaniard . . . he had been dotingly fond of her, and she of him, till in some action he received a musket ball in his leg, which as long as it remained there rendered him feeble . . . Upon this he abandoned his wife . . .' The impotent Spanish husband was also a poet who wrote verses in Latin which were about 'the birds in their brooding season' and which concluded 'with a reference to the happiness he had once enjoyed at Bristol, but which he had by his own folly forfeited.' The man was now perfectly recovered but Edith refused to make contact with him again 'rather because she loved him too much than too little'.[34]

While Edith stayed with Sarah at Nether Stowey the Southey marriage seems to have been going through some kind of crisis. Edith neither wrote to her husband, nor sent personal messages. Southey became almost hysterical when he received no news of her, imagining the worst. His letters, begging for a reply, make painful reading. 'Where are you my dear Edith? with people whom I know not and in a place I know not, but wherever you are Edith you think of me, and wish for me I am sure . . . Edith, I begin to be uneasy at not hearing from you. You know I always scold when you hurt yourself, and now I am angry because I am anxious . . . If I do not get a letter tomorrow Edith – but my dear, dear Edith, write to me when you receive this . . . If I am again disappointed tomorrow, I must actually write down a great oath of anger . . . and here am I writing writing writing to Stowey without knowing whether or not my letters reach you . . . I was bitterly vexed today after a long walk to look for a letter; disappointment has left an uncomfortable impression upon me . . . Edith can I help feeling something like disappointment if no tidings of you should arrive before Saturday next?'[35] He counted the days to their reunion, swearing that he would never be parted from her for so much as a week again.

In July 1799 Sarah had another visit from Edith, this time accompanied by her husband and their youngest sister Eliza, all on their way to holiday at Minehead on the Somerset coast. Edith was by now very ill, but Southey decided not to cancel the holiday in the hope that the sea air would do her good. However, he became increasingly worried by her symptoms and by the time they reached Minehead she had collapsed completely. Sarah, when she received the news of Edith's breakdown, went and brought her back to Stowey while Southey stayed on at Minehead alone in a nervous and agitated state, walking along the coast.

At the end of July, in the middle of all this domestic trauma, Coleridge came back to face the resentment and recriminations of his abandoned wife. He had been away for ten months. Sarah was still suffering from nervous and physical exhaustion and worried about her sister's state of mind. Coleridge was feeling guilty and surly. They quarrelled openly about his breach with Southey, which Sarah insisted should be made up. Thomas Poole, suspecting that much of the mischief had been Charles Lloyd's doing, supported her, and became an intermediary. Coleridge wrote a letter to Southey, followed by another from Poole, and finally at the beginning of August, Southey arrived at Stowey to join his wife. As he walked up the village street, Coleridge went out to embrace him and the quarrel was patched up. They stayed for about a fortnight before Sarah and Samuel left for Ottery St Mary, where they were to stay with Coleridge's family; Southey, Edith and Eliza travelled on to Devon as they had originally planned.

This was Sarah's first visit to Ottery and the first time she had met her husband's family. To her great relief, she found she got on well with them. But the visit had to be cut short after the new nanny was discovered to have scabies which she had passed on to Hartley and, it was feared, others in the household. Scabies was associated with dirt and Sarah felt deeply shamed. Evil-smelling Brimstone ointment was used to cure Hartley, and Sarah had to wear a mercury girdle as a preventative. The nanny was sent home.

Back in Stowey Sarah fumigated the house, while Coleridge sat in a corner reading, doping himself with opium ostensibly for a bout of rheumatism. His general unhelpfulness fuelled all the other unresolved resentments and they quarrelled more frequently. Perhaps the move to the Lakes, already discussed with a worried Poole in letters from Germany, was also an issue. Coleridge had assured Poole that he would never settle in the Lakes, that the place was totally unsuitable for Sarah on the grounds that she would have 'no acquaintance' there. But Coleridge found it difficult, after his carefree, responsibility-free period in Germany, to come to terms with the interruptions and stresses of domestic life.

In Stowey it rained constantly, Hartley fell downstairs at the Southeys' and injured himself, Sarah accidentally shut the door on his arm, and Coleridge went down with pneumonia after getting wet through on a walk. 'Our little Hovel is afloat – poor Sara tired off her legs with servanting – the young one fretful & noisy from confinement exerts his activities on all forbidden things – the house stinks of Sulphur . . .'[36]

Sarah's worries were compounded by the fact that her brother George – who had signed on as a merchant seaman – had been shipwrecked off the coast of Spain. And Eliza was being courted by an American sea captain. Sarah didn't like him, suspecting him of trifling with her sister's affections, but part of her disapproval was generated by the long absences Eliza would have to endure if she married him. 'His being a sailor would be sufficient objection to me; but I am very sore on the subject of absent husbands just at this time.'[37]

This was understandable, since Coleridge had scarcely arrived back home than he was off again. In mid-October he went to Bristol, on the excuse that he needed to chase up his book box from Germany (it arrived in Stowey two days after he left). Then, without writing to Sarah at all, he went off with Cottle to visit Dorothy and William who were staying with the Hutchinson family at Sockburn on Tees. When Sarah wrote to her sister-in-law, Mrs George Coleridge, on 2 November, she thought him still in Bristol and was expecting him back in Stowey at any moment. But he had already been in the north a week and did not write to her until December.

Coleridge and Cottle left Bristol on 22 October, arriving four days later at Sockburn. It was here that Coleridge – irked by domestic responsibility, on edgy terms with Sarah and fed up with his whole situation – first met Sara Hutchinson, the woman he would later deem to be the one great love of his life. For ten years she was to influence almost everything he wrote.

Since their shared childhood in Penrith, the Hutchinson sisters had gone their separate ways – Mary to Sockburn, Sara to Kendal. But more recently Sara had come back to Middleham, near Durham, about 15 miles away, to keep house for her brother George and the sisters were once more close together. The death of their middle sister Margaret had strengthened their affection and the bond between them was so close that Mary described Sara as her 'second self'.

It is not clear whether Coleridge met Sara on his first visit to Sockburn before the walking tour in the Lakes with Wordsworth and Cottle, or when he called again on his way back to London. She may well have been there on both occasions, though the fateful diary entry refers only to Coleridge's second visit.

Coleridge's diary entry for the meeting was written partly in Latin, presumably to conceal it from his wife's casual glance. It describes a lively evening: 'Conundrums & Puns & Stories & Laughter – with Jack Hutchinson – Stood up round the Fire, and pressed Sara's hand behind her back a long time; and then Love first wounded me with a light arrow-point – poisoned, alas! and incurable.'[38]

Sara, born in 1775, was the most forceful of the three Hutchinson sisters, better educated, with a naturally intellectual frame of mind. She was cheerful and lively, but with a managing personality and slight asperity that did not please everyone who met her. Hartley Coleridge later described her as 'Poor dear Miss Hutchinson, without a spark of malice in her heart, [who] had, from the perfect faultlessness of her own life, a good deal of intolerance in her head . . . Not that she was so illiberal as to dislike people for differing from her own opinions (she certainly and naturally liked them better when they agreed) but hers was pre-eminently a one-sided mind.'[39] Hartley's sister Sara found her egotistical, and complained of her 'exulting *my way*'.

Coleridge himself was of a different opinion, writing to a friend that 'If Sense, Sensibility, Sweetness of Temper, perfect simplicity and unpretending Nature, joined to shrewdness and entertainingness make a valuable Woman, Sara Hutchinson is so.' She was not a pretty woman, described as about five feet tall, with a stocky figure veering towards plumpness and a strong, prominent jaw, but she had a delicate complexion and beautiful light auburn hair. In hair and figure there are distinct similarities with Sarah Fricker, and, like Sarah, she possessed a quiet sense of fun, and considerable personality. Keats thought her enchanting.

Coleridge removed the 'h' from the end of her name, as he had done with his wife. Sara carried on signing her name 'Sarah Hutchinson' and Mary Hutchinson always spelt her name in the old way. Having been thwarted in this, Coleridge experimented with various anagrams of her name in Greek and English, eventually settling on Asra. 'Dear Asra, woman beyond utterance dear!'[40] Coleridge's life now alternated between two women, Sara and Asra, the one an anagram of the other in the poet's tortured mind.

Coleridge and Wordsworth left Dorothy with the Hutchinson sisters at Sockburn to make a walking tour of the Lakes. They took the mail coach over Stainmore to Temple Sowerby, accompanied by Wordsworth's brother John. Their energy and capacity for walking exhausted Joseph Cottle, and he abandoned the party at Greta Bridge. A month later Coleridge too had to turn back, having received a letter from Daniel Stuart offering him work on the *Morning Post* in London. John and William went on alone and, on 8 November 1799, William wrote to Dorothy from Keswick: 'We shall go to Buttermere the day after tomorrow, but I think it will be full ten days before we shall see you. There is a small house at Grasmere empty which perhaps we may take, and purchase furniture but of this we will speak.'[41] This was Dove Cottage at Town End.

By the middle of December it was all arranged. Dorothy wrote to her brother Richard: 'We shall set off for Grasmere on Tuesday. Tom Hutchinson will accompany us on horseback as far as Greta Bridge, where we shall take the coach for Brough, and from thence we shall be obliged to take a post-chaise to Kendal. As soon as we are settled William will write to you at length.'[42] When the time came they walked most of the way, over terrain rendered iron-hard by frost – an epic journey which passed into family legend.

Though Coleridge didn't write to Sarah, he did write to Dorothy, communicating to her his feelings at seeing the lake scenery for the first time. 'You can feel what I cannot express for myself – how deeply I have been impressed by a world of scenery absolutely new to me . . . this evening, approaching Derwentwater in diversity of harmonious features, in the majesty of its beauties & in the Beauty of its majesty – O my God! & the Black Crags close under the snowy mountains . . . Why were you not with us Dorothy?'[43]

On 24 November, Coleridge was back in Sockburn with Sara Hutchinson, Mary and Dorothy, staying for a few days before he set off for London. There were tender scenes when Mary and Sara sat with him on the sofa in close physical proximity, later remembered in the poem 'Letter to Asra', when Mary lay with her head in his lap and Sara's eyelashes fluttered against his cheek.

From London Coleridge wrote to Sarah, telling her that he had accepted a job on the *Morning Post* and that they were going to be living in London for the next few months. He didn't even know where she was, and had to write another letter to Cottle asking him to find out her whereabouts and pass on the information if his other letter had not reached her. By 19 December, after unknown recriminations and reconciliations, Sarah and Hartley were in London with Coleridge, lodging at 21 Buckingham Street off the Strand. Coleridge also wrote to Southey, asking him and Edith to join them, but this offer was declined. The atmosphere of London suited Sarah, who always preferred the variety of town life to the country. After the Lakes, Coleridge found it barely tolerable. 'London appeared to me as a huge place of Sepulchres thro' which Hosts of Spirits were gliding.'[44]

There was considerable intimacy with the Godwin family, though a marked contrast between Hartley Coleridge and the orphaned children of Mary Wollstonecraft. Hartley was lively and talkative and given a lot of freedom of expression, described by his parents as 'rough and noisy' and even 'rampant'. On one occasion he whacked 'Mister Gobwin' over the shins with a ninepin and an indignant Sarah had to endure a lecture from Godwin on the subject of her child's upbringing. Sarah was equally shocked by the unnatural restraint and 'cadaverous silence' of Godwin's children, which the Coleridges ascribed to the recent death of their mother. Mary had died tragically the previous year from puerperal fever after the birth of her namesake, the future Mary Shelley. Coleridge remarked that Mary's influence had 'greatly improved' William Godwin.

By January the Coleridges' reunion had produced its inevitable consequences – Sarah was pregnant again, and prostrated as usual by morning sickness. Living in such cramped conditions had reactivated the problems in the Coleridge marriage, now admitted for the first time in a letter to Southey, written in Latin which neither Edith nor Sarah could read. Coleridge told Southey that although she was an extremely intelligent and well-educated woman and a good mother to his children, Sarah could never understand him, or his needs and 'infirmities', nor enter into his intellectual concerns or his poetry. He went on to state that it was not possible for him to be happy with her.

Coleridge was fretting for space. He asked Poole to look for a 'House with a Garden, & large enough for me to have a Study out [of] the noise of Women & children – this is absolutely necessary for me'. Poole, jealous of the growing pull of the Wordsworths' influence, feared to lose him. Coleridge had already reassured him from Germany that he had told Wordsworth plainly that Poole was 'the man in whom *first* and in whom alone, I had felt an *anchor*! With all my other Connections I felt a dim sense of insecurity & uncertainty . . . But my Resolve is fixed, *not to leave you till you leave me*!' Poole was his 'Friend, my best Friend, my Brother, my Beloved – the tears run down my face – God love you.'[45] But there is an element of impatience in the letter which Coleridge wrote to Poole from London to allay his fears: 'How could you take such an absurd idea in your head, that my Affections have weakened towards you? . . . my affections are what they are, & in all human probability ever will be.'[46]

Coleridge regarded Poole as one of his closest friends, and expressed his affection with all the extravagance of his nature. Poole loved Coleridge with an intensity and possessiveness that lead one to suspect a more passionate attachment. And Poole's fears of Dorothy and William's ascendancy over Coleridge were well founded, though Coleridge denied it vigorously. 'You charge me with prostration in regard to Wordsworth. Have I affirmed anything miraculous of W.? . . . Do not, my dearest Poole, deem me cold, or finical, or indifferent.'[47]

On 2 March 1800 Sarah returned to Bristol. The experiment of living together again after such a long separation (they had not lived together for more than a few weeks since September 1798) had not been a success. Coleridge went to stay with Charles Lamb, and spent the first night getting drunk.

A month later (and within two days of his letter of denial to Thomas Poole) he left London for Grasmere, calling at Sockburn on the way north. In his notebook he makes reference to a lock of

Sara Hutchinson's hair in his pocket, and a poem 'The Keepsake' refers to a handkerchief given as a token, embroidered with the giver's auburn hair. Written in 1800 it refers to the cool early morning when 'dearest Asra . . . early wak'd':

> Leaving the soft Bed to her sleeping Sister
> Lightly she rose, & lightly stole along
> Down the slope Coppice to the woodbine Bower
> Whose rich Flowers swinging in the Breeze of Dawn
> Over their dim fast-moving Shadows hung
> Making a quiet Image of Disquiet
> In the smooth, scarcely-flowing River-pool.
> There in that Bower, where first she own'd her Love,
> And let me kiss my own warm Tears of Joy
> From off her glowing cheek, she sate & stretch'd
> The Silk upon its Frame & work'd her Name,
> Between the Moss Rose & Forget-me-not,
> Her own dear Name with her own auburn Hair![48]

Coleridge's reunion with Dorothy and William was ecstatic. Wordsworth had had second thoughts about *Lyrical Ballads* and solicited Coleridge's help with a new, expanded edition. The discovery of Greta Hall near Keswick clinched the matter. Sarah, searching for property near Stowey, found herself suddenly 'transported north'.

# PART TWO

---

*The Lakers*

# A Plaited Nest

*. . . reading masses of Coleridge & Wordsworth letters of a*
*night – curiously untwisting and burrowing into that plaited*
*nest.*

Virginia Woolf

Dorothy and William arrived at Dove Cottage, or Town End as it
was called then, on 20 December 1799 just before five o'clock in
the evening. They had spent the day buying essential furniture in
Kendal and hiring a post-chaise from there to Grasmere. The
weather was bitterly cold and Rydal Water 'covered with ice, clear
as polished steel'.[1] Inside the house the fire in the kitchen range
had almost burned out and the rooms struck damp and chilly.
Dorothy stood shivering beside the dying fire in a striped gown
and straw bonnet inadequate for the ravages of a Grasmere winter.

It was Dorothy's first sight of the cottage – a much smaller and
humbler dwelling than either Racedown or Alfoxden. It had once
been a pub called the Dove and Olive Branch, and was more like
the little cottage the Coleridges had rented in Nether Stowey.
Roles were being reversed. There were three good-sized rooms on
the ground floor; the front door opened into a big living-room with
stone-flagged floor and black range, and opening off that was a
kitchen which had another open range and a deep sink. Through
the kitchen was a pantry and larder with a small beck running
through to keep it cool. Also opening off the kitchen was a small
parlour. All the downstairs rooms were panelled in wood which
made them rather dark. Upstairs there were two bedrooms, one of

which they decided to use as a sitting-room, the other occupied by William; a lumber room which did duty as an upstairs pantry and storage space; and a small 'outjutting' which, papered with news-print to insulate it, became an extra bedroom. Dorothy quickly converted the downstairs parlour into a bedroom for herself, covering the stone floor with matting. She slept in a 'camp' bed large enough for two people, which had to be shared with female guests.

William wrote to Coleridge four days after they arrived, that they had both succumbed to colds. 'D is now sitting by me racked with the toothache. This is a grievous misfortune as she has so much work for her needle among the bedcurtains &c that she is absolutely buried in it . . . D is much pleased with the house and appurtenances the orchard especially; in imagination she has already built a seat with a summer shed on the highest platform in this our little domestic slip of mountain. The spot commands a view over the roof of our house, of the lake, the church, Helm Cragg, and two thirds of the vale . . . D is so much engaged, she has scarcely been out since our arrival; one evening I tempted her forth; the planet Jupiter was on the top of the hugest of the Rydale mountains . . .'[2]

Raging toothache and domestic chores kept Dorothy indoors, despite William's attempts to get her out. The fires smoked and there were all the household arrangements to supervise, doors to be mended, rooms painted. They employed a local woman to come in for two or three hours a day to light fires, cook, wash dishes and do other heavy chores. All this for 2 shillings a week and her dinner on Saturday when she came in to do the 'scouring'. Some washing was done every week (petticoats, stockings and waistcoats), but most of the household linen, sheets, shirts, etc. was kept for the 'great washes' which took place every five weeks in an outside wash-house. There were also visitors to cater for.

Hospitality was not lavish. Harriet Martineau complained that she couldn't get enough milk in her tea, and was horrified to find that visitors were asked to pay for their board. Walter Scott was so shocked by the meagre catering that he sneaked out after dinner and went to the local inn for a decent meal. Dorothy and William never seemed to notice the privations. They used oatmeal a great deal, it being cheaper than flour. Dorothy was very fond of oatcakes with butter and they often ate porridge twice a day, sometimes as 'hasty pudding' – the oatmeal boiled in salted water without milk. They drank water most of the time, unless friends had sent a barrel of ale, and when they offered tea to visitors, the tea-leaves were dried afterwards to be reused. Home-grown vegetables formed a large part of their diet and they only ate meat when they could afford it.

Their younger brother, John Wordsworth, arrived in January and stayed with them for eight months. He was shy and sensitive and initially worried about intruding on their privacy but became a deeply loved member of the household. Mary Hutchinson also arrived at the end of February for a five-week stay. William's interest in Mary as anything other than a friend was either not apparent at this time, or had not yet developed, since John fell in love with Mary during her stay at Dove Cottage and cherished hopes of marriage. It was with John, not William, that Mary explored the local beauty spots, their wanderings later remembered with nostalgia. Coleridge arrived on 10 April and stayed until 4 May. After he left, William went over to visit the Hutchinson family at Gallow Hill near Scarborough taking John with him, but not Dorothy.

Dorothy felt the separation from William very keenly. Since Alfoxden they had rarely been apart. The opening words of her Grasmere journal on 14 May are: 'Wm and John set off into Yorkshire after dinner at half-past two o'clock, cold pork in their pockets. I left them at the turning of the Low-wood bay under the trees. My heart was so full that I could hardly speak to W when I gave him a farewell kiss. I sate a long time upon a stone at the margin of the lake, and after a flood of tears my heart was easier. The lake looked to me, I knew not why, dull and melancholy, and the weltering on the shores seemed a heavy sound.' It was the separation that had spurred her on to start a new journal 'of the time till W and J return, and I set about keeping my resolve, because I will not quarrel with myself, and because I shall give William pleasure by it when he comes home again.' The entry ends, '. . . oh that I had a letter from William.' Dorothy was lonely and intensely melancholy on her own, counting the days until they came home again.

While William was away Dorothy spent her time walking and exploring in the mild spring weather. She admitted to having some of her 'saddest thoughts' as she walked, but her journals give no details of the reflections that made her so miserable, though they may well have been retrospective. She still thought of Racedown, not Alfoxden, as 'the place dearest to my recollections upon the whole surface of the island . . .'[3] It had been her first home with William and their surrogate child Basil. In the evenings she continued the reading programme begun at Racedown, getting through *Macbeth*, *King John* and *A Midsummer Night's Dream* while William was away.

Gittings and Manton refer to Dorothy's journals as a chronicle of 'the practical business and never-ending effort of one woman's existence'. Dorothy did, however, have a maid-of-all-work to help with the housework, the heavier chores and the cooking, while Sarah Coleridge had had to make do with a young, inexperienced nursemaid in her struggles at Stowey, doing all the cooking and heavy work herself. Apart from domestic details and the descriptions of the landscape, Dorothy's journals are also social documents, recording the profound rural poverty they were surrounded by. Hardly a day goes by without someone calling at the cottage, or being passed on the road, destitute and in need of relief. If ever there was evidence of the need for a welfare state it is here. 'A little girl from Coniston came to beg. She had lain out all night. Her step-mother had turned her out of doors; her father could not stay at home "she flights so" . . .'[4] The journals are also at times embarrassingly private narratives, revealing with complete openness and naïvety the day-by-day intensification of Dorothy's relationship with William.

Dorothy's feelings of isolation when parting from William were reflected in the almost hysterical joy with which she greeted his return. 'I was walking out alone when he arrived. I had gone by the lake side towards Martindale. Jane [a neighbour's servant] met me and told me he was come. I believe I screamed, when she said so, and ran on. I then recollected myself, and told her to run on before and tell him that I was coming, in order that he might meet me; but she was stupid, and so I met him in the parlour – he looked delight-fully, but it was a sort of flushing in his face, for he was fatigued with his long ride – he got tea and very soon went to bed.'[5]

The closeness of their relationship soon gave rise to local gossip, recorded by De Quincey: '. . . there was an unnatural tale current . . . even in London, of Wordsworth having been intimate with his own sister – The reason for this story having birth seemed to be that Wordsworth was very much in the habit of taking long rambles among the mountains, & romantic scenes near his habitation – his sister, who is also a great walker used very frequently to accompany him and indeed does so still – It is Wordsworth's custom whenever he meets or parts with any of the female part of his own relations to kiss them – this he has frequently done when he has met his sister on her rambles or parted from her and that in roads or on mountains, or elsewhere, without heeding whether he was observed or not: and he has been perhaps seen by hinds and clowns or other persons who have repeated what they have seen:- and this simple fact, occurring probably under the eyes of those . . . who have not the slightest idea of pure love for any one or of that fine tie which forms the affection between a brother & a sister, has been made up into the abominable accusation bruited about, to his prejudice amongst his coarse-minded neighbours.' But it wasn't just the local people who believed that their relationship was incestuous, 'the upper and better-informed classes' were talking too. Despite local gossip, De Quincey believed in the innocence of their affection, but is hardly a reliable witness on the subject, since in the same essay he also firmly stated his belief in the platonic nature of the relationship between Lord Nelson and Lady Hamilton!

The problem for the Wordsworths' contemporaries, as it is for us, was the closeness – mental, physical and emotional – of the two and the intensity of Dorothy's feelings for her brother. When he went away she walked restlessly to Rydal every day looking for letters from him and was sadly disappointed if none came: '. . . only a letter for Coleridge – I expected a letter from Wm.'[6] If the post hadn't arrived at Rydal she would walk 7 or 8 miles down the road to meet it. 'The post was not come in. I walked as far as Windermere, and met him there. No Letters! no papers . . . I was sadly tired, ate a hasty dinner and had a bad headache.'[7] The disappointment made her ill, but when letters did come, the emotional upheaval also precipitated the prostrating sick headaches she was increasingly prone to: '. . . a letter from Wm and from Wm and from Mary Hutchinson . . . sate in the evening under the trees. I went to bed soon with a bad head-ache.'[8]

When they were together, he was the total focus of her being. Her journal records the daily intimacy of their life together. 'William went up into the Orchard and finished the Poem. Mrs Luff and Mrs Oliff called. I went with Mrs O to the top of the White Moss. Mr O met us and I went to their house – he offered me manure for the garden. I went and sat with W. and walked backwards and forwards in the orchard till dinner time. He read me his poem. I broiled Beefsteaks. After dinner we made a pillow of my shoulder – I read to him and my Beloved slept. I afterwards got him the pillows and he was lying with his head on the table when Miss Simpson came in. She stayed tea. I went with her to Rydale – no letters! A sweet Evening as it had been a sweet day, a grey evening, and I walked quietly along the side of Rydale Lake with quiet thoughts – the hills and the lake were still – the Owls had not begun to hoot and the little Birds had given over singing. I looked before me and I saw a red light upon Silver How as if coming out of the vale below,

> There was a light of most strange birth,
> A light that came out of the earth
> And spread along the dark hill-side.

Thus I was going on when I saw the shape of my Beloved in the road at a little distance. We turned back to see the light but it was fading . . . There were huge slow-travelling clouds in the sky, that threw large masses of Shade upon some of the Mountains . . . William kindled and began to write the poem. We carried cloaks into the orchard and sat a while there. I left him and he nearly finished the poem. I was tired to death and went to bed before him – he came down to me and read the Poem to me in bed.'[9]

Shelley accused Wordsworth of being a 'solemn and unsexual man', and Dorothy has also been described as 'asexual' and naïve. Coleridge wrote that she had an 'innocent soul' and that 'Guilt was a thing impossible with her'. But this appearance of innocence and physical coldness does not mean that they had no sexual passions. There was a strong element of physicality in their relationship. One of Dorothy's greatest pleasures was to sit with William in front of the fire, watching him. 'The fire flutters and the watch ticks I hear nothing else save the Breathing of my Beloved and he now and then pushes his book forward and turns over a leaf.'[10]

It is deeply significant that when William went away, and occasionally even when he was there, Dorothy sometimes slept in his bed. 'Went to bed at about 12 o'clock. I slept in Wm's bed, and I slept badly, for my thoughts were full of William.'[11] She does her best to occupy herself during the day. 'I *will* be busy, I *will* look well and be well when he comes back to me. O the Darling! Here is one of his bitten apples! I can hardly find in my heart to throw it into the fire.'[12] When he kisses her on his return, the full lover's kiss that caused so much gossip, she observes that 'his mouth and breath were very cold when he kissed me. We spent a sweet evening . . . We went to bed pretty soon and we slept better than we expected and had no bad dreams.'[13] When they sit together at the table for breakfast she is acutely aware of his physical presence: '. . . he, with his Basin of Broth before him untouched and a little plate of Bread and butter he wrote the Poem to a Butterfly! He ate not a morsel, nor put on his stockings but sate with his shirt neck unbuttoned, and his waistcoat open while he did it.' Neither of them felt easy with this state of affairs and the journals give a sense of the tiny cottage highly charged with unspoken emotional turmoil: 'We dined and then Wm went to bed. I lay upon the fur gown before the fire but I could not sleep – I lay there a long time – it is now half past 5 . . . William rose without having slept – we sate comfortably by the fire . . .'[14]

In this heightened emotional state, Dorothy was doubly aware of the beauties of the landscape around her: '. . . as I climbed Moss the moon came out from behind a mountain mass of Black clouds – O the unutterable darkness of the sky and the earth below the moon! and the glorious brightness of the moon itself! There was a vivid sparkling streak of light at this end of Rydale water but the rest was very dark and Loughrigg fell and Silver How were white and bright as if they were covered with hoar frost . . . Once there was no moonlight to be seen but upon the Island house and the promontory of the Island where it stands . . . I had many very exquisite feelings and when I saw this lowly Building in the waters among the Dark and lofty hills, with that bright soft light upon it, it made me more than half a poet. I was tired when I reached home. I could not sit down to reading and tried to write verses but alas!'[15]

That Dorothy was in love with William is indisputable. His feelings for her were also very great, but he, perhaps more than Dorothy, was aware of the nature of his involvement and the dangers of their situation. He focused his romantic and sexual feelings on other women – notably Annette Vallon and then Mary Hutchinson. So, it seems equally irrefutable that Dorothy and William were not physical lovers. Both had very strong moral principles, whatever the temptations might have been. It seems impossible that Dorothy could have written so openly and with such naïvety of their relationship in her journal if she had been fully aware of the implications of her entries. Also, at a time when birth control was rudimentary to say the least, intercourse had inevitable consequences. Byron's affair with his sister produced a daughter. But all this does not preclude the possibility that there may have been physical lovemaking between them, stopping short of actual intercourse.

In his book *Wordsworth: A Re-interpretation*, scholar F. W. Bateson posited the theory that repressed sexual passion for

Dorothy was the source of much of Wordsworth's creativity – its peak period being the years they were together at Racedown, Alfoxden and Dove Cottage. Bateson edited and softened the second edition of his book in response to an outcry from critics such as T. S. Eliot who were seriously distressed by the notion. The nature of their passion for each other is a nettle left ungrasped by most subsequent biographers.

Dorothy occupied some of the time that William was away at Sockburn by carrying on negotiations with Mr Jackson, the owner of Greta Hall, on Coleridge's behalf. Coleridge was playing a double game; while Sarah and Thomas Poole were looking for a house in Stowey, Dorothy and William were trying to rent Greta Hall for him, both acting on Coleridge's instructions. However, at the beginning of June the lease of Greta Hall finally became a firm offer and Coleridge made up his mind to come north to be near the Wordsworths. Sarah, Samuel and Hartley arrived at Grasmere on 29 June 1800. The Coleridge stayed at Dove Cottage for three weeks while Greta Hall was being made ready for them. Coleridge was continually ill and in bed for several days dosing himself with laudanum. The least agitation caused him to feel the blood in his head 'rushing in & flowing back again like the raking of the Tide on a coast of loose stones.'[16]

On the last night they all rowed out to the island in the lake, boiled a kettle hung on a fir branch over a fire of pine cones and drank tea sitting on the grass watching the sun set behind the mountains whose images trembled in the glass-smooth lake. Later in the evening they made a bonfire, dancing round it with 'ruddy laughing faces in the twilight'. This intensely happy moment, which all present hoped was the prelude to deepening friendship and creative collaboration, would later be remembered with nostalgia as the last sunny interlude before what was one of the most miserable periods of their joint lives.

Sarah wrote to her sister-in-law, Mrs George Coleridge, after her arrival in Keswick:

By the date of this you will have perceived that we are transported far North; you will remember my speaking of Samuel's predilection for this country when I was with you . . . Samuel had seen a house at Keswick that was being built and was to be let this midsummer – he urged me to take it – but three hundred miles mean mighty and numerous objections! But the time was come that made it necessary to be settled somewhere – a home must be procured; this house was accordingly secured for us by means of Mr Wordsworth. My mother and family were much against our removing to such a distance; indeed it was the only objection on my part, for we are most delightfully situated, we have a large and very convenient house furnished with every article of comfort (but without elegance) and we are to pay a very moderate rent. The circumstances of removing the furniture so far would have prevented our coming hither if we had been obliged to it, but the gentleman who built this house offered to furnish it also as he had a furnished house (beside his own) in the town of Keswick which was left him by a relation, very recently, and he had it removed for our use which suited us exactly; so our goods were sold, except the linnen which came hither by water.

Since our arrival the neighbouring families have most of them visited us: a Colonel Peachy who lives in the Summer in a very beautiful house on an island in the Lake Derwent Water – it is just opposite to our house about a mile across; a Mr Spedding and his wife and her unmarried sisters, all young persons, seem to be an agreeable family – and they live here all the year. The Revd Mr Wilkinson; Mr Losh etc – all of whose visits Samuel has returned, but my present situation precludes me from accompanying him as I look every day for an addition to the family and do not chuse to exhibit my figure before strangers.[17]

Greta Hall was described by De Quincey as a 'very plain, unadorned family dwelling'; for the adult Hartley Coleridge it was a place of suffering – 'a House of Bondage'. Its situation was dramatic. It was perched on a little rise above the River Greta, and the valley opened out in front. To the south lay Derwentwater, its islands visible from the upper windows, to the north Lake Bassenthwaite, and beyond the lakes the mountains of Newlands and the 'gorgeous confusion' of Borrowdale. Behind the house, towering above it, was the massive bulk of Skiddaw. Today Greta Hall is part of Keswick Grammar School and has been used as dormitories. Although its graceful Georgian frontage remains, its dramatic situation has been lost behind tall modern buildings, and the vistas are clogged with the sprawl of twentieth-century housing estates. But the interior is still much as it was in Coleridge's time with original fireplaces, flagged floors and, in the kitchen, a large built-in dresser and the cast-iron range.

Half the house at Greta Hall was occupied by the owner, Mr Jackson, and his housekeeper, Mrs Wilson, who became the children's beloved 'Wilsy', a mother-figure not only to them but also to Sarah who found it 'no small joy' to have a 'good affectionate motherly woman' on the other side of the wall. Hartley, in particular, spent a great deal of time there, to the delight of the childless Jackson. He was a 'modest & kind man, & a singular character'. He had been a carrier, was self-educated and had a considerable library of about five hundred books, which for Coleridge was one of the advantages of the house. The garden was large, and initially part of it was a nursery. From the garden walks, overhung with mature beech trees, there was a dramatic prospect towards Crosthwaite church with Bassenthwaite lake in the background.

Coleridge wrote that 'from the Window before me there is a great *Camp* of Mountains – Giants seem to have pitch'd their Tents there – each Mountain is a Giant's Tent – and how the light streams from them – & the Shadows that travel upon them!' Such was the view that he could not shave in front of the window without cutting himself: 'I offer up soap & blood daily,' as an offering to the 'Goddess Nature'.[18] Neither Sarah nor Coleridge was aware of the structural defects of the house, erected quickly by Jackson to take advantage of the new influx of 'Lakers'. The front elevation faced the prevailing winds and was so poorly built that cold, fierce draughts penetrated the house. Southey called it the 'Palace of the Winds'. Two years later the front showed signs of collapse and had to be rebuilt.

On 10 September Dorothy wrote to her friend Jane: 'We have spent a week at Mr Coleridge's since his arrival at Keswick. His house is most delightfully situated, and combines all possible advantages both for his wife and himself, *she* likes to be near a Town, *he* in the country – it is only half or quarter of a mile from Keswick and commands a view of the whole vale. Mrs Coleridge is going to lye in, her little boy, Hartley, who is an original sprite is to come and stay with us during that time, he is a sweet companion, always alive and of a delightful temper, I shall find it very difficult to part with him when we have once got him here.'[19] Hartley was described by his father as 'a spirit dancing on an aspen leaf'. Dorothy yearned for children. Always critical of Sarah's handling of her offspring, she was convinced that Hartley (and subsequently his siblings) was better off with her than with his mother.

After Sarah's confinement with her third child, Derwent, on 14 September 1800, the Southeys – now in Portugal – complained that neither Coleridge nor Sarah had written to them, 'which is I think somewhat uncivil.' Southey didn't approve of the name either, considering it 'heathenish'. Coleridge gave the excuse that his brothers had already taken all the available 'Christian-like' names for their children, so that he was forced to fall back upon the 'poetical & the novellish'.

Derwent – named for the river (if it had been a girl Coleridge had been going to call her Greta) – was a very big baby, but Sarah once again gave birth with ease, and was up in the parlour drinking tea only a few days later, when the custom was to 'lie in' for a month. Although he was initially very healthy, by 28 September Derwent had been taken ill and when he breathed 'made a noise exactly like the creaking of a door'. Sarah was beside herself with terror that, like Berkeley, he would not live. So firmly did everyone in the household believe that the baby was dying that he was baptised – against Coleridge's inclinations, but to Sarah's great comfort. Coleridge wrote to a friend: 'She is now sobbing & crying by the side of me . . . alas! I fear, he will not live.'[20] On 4 October, Coleridge escaped to Grasmere leaving Sarah alone with Hartley, a new, very sick baby, and the servants, only a couple of days after complaining that he was 'prevented by Mrs Coleridge's distress' from writing. Sarah did not even have a member of her own family there to support her.

At Dove Cottage Wordsworth and Coleridge worked on a new edition of *Lyrical Ballads* and Dorothy copied out the manuscript. While Derwent was ill and Coleridge at Greta Hall, Wordsworth had sent off a preface which was severely critical of Coleridge's 'Ancient Mariner', revealing 'a critical blindness and disregard for the feelings of a fellow poet'. Wordsworth objected to the inclusion of the poem, which Coleridge had revised after the first edition, and was determined to distance himself from it, regardless of the hurt and offence that he might be causing to Coleridge, who never saw the comments until they appeared in print. The essence of William's comments was that 'the Poem . . . has indeed great defects . . . the imagery is somewhat too laboriously accumulated . . . the metre is itself unfit for long poems . . .'[21] Lamb protested and this section of the preface was omitted in the next edition.

Coleridge now read 'Christabel' to Dorothy and William but, although initially enthusiastic, William refused to allow it to be included in *Lyrical Ballads*. Dorothy's journal records on 6 October: 'Determined not to print Christabel with the L.B.' Their decision was entirely selfish. 'Upon mature deliberation' Wordsworth found – and Dorothy agreed – that 'the style of this Poem was so discordant from my own that it could not be printed along with my poems with any propriety.'[22] The second volume of the *Lyrical Ballads* had none of Coleridge's poems in it at all.

The rejection of 'Christabel', coming on top of Wordsworth's public criticism of the 'Ancient Mariner', affected Coleridge deeply but Dorothy and William seem to have been oblivious of their negative effect. Southey observed that 'Wordsworth and his sister who pride themselves upon having no selfishness, are of all human beings whom I have ever known the most intensely selfish. The one thing to which W. would sacrifice all others is his own reputation . . .'[23] What Southey left unspoken, but implied in the text, was that Dorothy also cared about her brother's reputation to the exclusion of all else. Such was Coleridge's admiration for Wordsworth he too was prepared to sacrifice his own interests for those of his friend.

The effects of Dorothy and William's 'cold praise and effective discouragement' on Coleridge had been feared by Sarah and his friends. Coleridge could see this years later, after he was free of their influence, writing in 1818 that they had discouraged 'every attempt of mine to roll onward in a distinct current of my own' and that though they 'admitted that the Ancient Mariner [and] the Christabel . . . were not without merit . . . were abundantly anxious to acquit their judgements of any blindness to the very numerous defects.'[24]

This paralysed Coleridge to such an extent that he wrote to Thelwall: 'As to Poetry, I have altogether abandoned it, being convinced that I never had the essentials of poetic Genius, & that I mistook a strong desire for original power.'[25] Wordsworth he believed to be 'a great, a true Poet' and accepted William's depreciation of his own work on those terms. If Wordsworth thought his work bad, then it was. Coleridge needed the Wordsworths to validate his genius, just as William had needed Dorothy to sustain his belief in his poetic gifts. This support, neither William nor Dorothy was willing to give. A crisis of confidence, coinciding with a bout of sickness that necessitated the consumption of more laudanum which in turn produced a prolonged state of procrastination, stopped Coleridge from writing and he was in a state of despair. 'The Poet is dead in me – my imagination . . . lies, like a Cold Snuff on the circular Rim of a Brass Candle-stick . . . I was once a Volume of Gold Leaf, rising and riding on every breath of Fancy – but . . . now I sink in quicksilver.'[26]

The other circumstance that disordered his mind and body, and was rapidly eroding his wife's good will, was his growing obsession for Sara Hutchinson. Coleridge's health was poor all the autumn. Colds, inflammation of the eyes, and boils kept him in bed and in a laudanum-enhanced state. Sarah was not only looking after him and nursing Derwent, but also caring for Hartley who had become ill with a stomach complaint and jaundice. A brief visit to Dorothy at Dove Cottage in December provided some respite, but relations between the two women had begun to deteriorate, as Dorothy increasingly blamed Sarah for Coleridge's unhappiness. Sarah was also becoming aware that, like Thomas Poole, she could well lose Coleridge to the Wordsworths in the battle for his affections, and she began to fear that they were poisoning his mind against her. Her attitude to the occupants of Dove Cottage became hostile and her cool manner towards them was marked.

This hostility was reciprocated. In Dorothy's journal, inserted at 15 May 1802, is a sheet of blotting paper with all their names upon it, written out as a family tree with Coleridge at the centre. The inscription echoes the famous 'Rock of Names' on the road above Thirlmere, where they all carved their initials in the summer of 1800: WW, MH, DW, STC, JW, SH. Sarah Coleridge's name is missing from both lists. And in 'The Naming of Places', where the 'gentle tribe' named for themselves their favourite spots in the landscape – John's Grove, Sara's Gate, Mary's Seat, Dorothy's Dell, etc. – Sarah was also unrepresented.

Dorothy, meanwhile, was 'daily more delighted with Grasmere and its neighbourhood'. She had spent the summer walking and exploring the mountains or rowing out on to the lake. Fine weather had been spent in gardening, laying out a hedge around the orchard and planting roses and honeysuckle against the walls of the cottage. Dorothy had the novel idea of planting runner beans to grow up through the roses, providing a contrast of colour as well as vegetables for the table. When she went out walking, she collected wild flowers to transplant into the garden, wild thyme, foxgloves, ferns and columbine, to create a wonderful, informal display.

The only complaint she had was that the house was too small and too near the road. Inside, every noise could be heard from room to room, giving little privacy or peace and quiet for the occupants. Dorothy had even papered the walls of the upstairs pantry with newspapers to make a second spare bedroom for guests. She found their elderly servant much harder to manage than the valuable Peggy at Alfoxden; Molly was 'very ignorant, very foolish and very difficult to teach'.[27]

It is difficult to imagine the kind of snobbery that governed personal relationships. Everyone had a distinct idea of the social class that they belonged to and other classes were regarded almost as separate species. Dorothy writes: 'We are very comfortably situated with respect to neighbours of the lower classes, they are excellent people, friendly in performing all offices of kindness and humanity and attentive to us without servility – if we were sick they would wait upon us night and day. We are also upon very intimate terms with one family in the middle rank of life, a Clergyman with a very small income . . . His wife is a delightful old woman . . . chearful in her manners and much of the gentle-woman . . . The daughter, though much inferior to her mother is a pleasant kind of woman . . .'[28] On another occasion William writes to Thomas Poole for his opinion on his poem 'Michael' 'because you are so well acquainted, nay, so familiarly conversant with the language, manners, and feelings of the middle order of people who dwell in the country . . . your situation has not been altogether so favourable as mine, yet your daily and hourly intercourse with these people must have far more than counterbalanced any dis-advantage of this kind . . .'[29] William became more patrician and 'stiff-necked' as he grew older, holding his social inferiors at a distance. Dorothy found contact less difficult. She was generally on very good terms with her servants and her neighbours, yet she refused to recognise De Quincey's wife – the daughter of a local farmer – though she had known her since she was a girl.

Dorothy's primary objective at Dove Cottage was to provide the right kind of atmosphere for William to write in. This was not easy, as he suffered increasingly from what would now be regarded as psychosomatic symptoms whenever he took up the pen. Dorothy observed anxiously that his health was a subject of concern: '. . . he writes with so much feeling and agitation that it brings on a sense of pain and internal weakness about his left side and stomach, which now often makes it impossible for him to write.'[30]

Coleridge observed unsympathetically, but shrewdly, that his illness was all in his mind. William's poetry originated in 'emotion recollected in tranquillity' (Coleridge's inspired definition appropriated by Wordsworth) – but in William's case, emotions at times so powerful that they generated physical symptoms which prevented him from writing.

In December 1800 Dorothy's journal ends abruptly in midsentence and does not resume again for almost a year. There is speculation that the intervening entries were contained in a notebook which has since been lost. It seems too much of a coincidence that this year is the critical year of Coleridge's relationship with Sara Hutchinson, in which the Wordsworths were intimately involved. The missing pages from the other notebooks are also concerned with Coleridge. The first covers a period when Coleridge was staying at Dove Cottage, the second an occasion when Wordsworth had gone to Greta Hall and brought Coleridge back to Grasmere.

In November, hearing from a letter that Coleridge was 'very ill', the Wordsworths went to Greta Hall and on the 18th walked to Threlkeld to meet Sara Hutchinson, who also stayed at Greta Hall for four days. This was Sarah Coleridge's first meeting with the object of her husband's romantic imagination, and it was a chance for her to assess the nature of the threat. She found herself, like many other women in her position, utterly baffled by her rival, since there was 'nothing extraordinary' about Sara Hutchinson – quite the reverse.

Sarah was still a young attractive woman, barely thirty, with two small children, one only a few months old. She had been married for less than five years and was still in love with her husband. Her reaction to the knowledge that her husband was in love with another woman, one so intimately connected with the Wordsworth household, was as violent as can be expected. It must have been particularly galling to hear Coleridge's frequent admiration of Sara Hutchinson's auburn hair. Sarah's own hair, thick and of a similar, though darker colour, had been her own glory and Samuel's great joy. Since the death of Berkeley it was thin and straggly and she wore it cropped short, covered by a wig. It was a very deep, private humiliation.

Coleridge, as he absented himself to Dove Cottage, Yorkshire and London in order to be near Sara Hutchinson, sent Sarah a series of memoranda setting out the situation as he saw it. 'I can neither retain my Happiness nor my Faculties, unless I move, live, & love, in perfect Freedom . . .'[31] A woman did not have the right to expect a man to love only one woman, he told her. Sarah would be unreasonable if she could not accept this. Coleridge was still looking for unconditional love. 'One human being, *entirely* loving me . . . would have rendered me happy and grateful even tho' I had no friend on earth, herself excepted.' But Coleridge's needs, as both Dorothy and Sara Hutchinson would find out, were too great a burden for any woman.[32]

Coleridge – the former defender of Mary Wollstonecraft – now decided that women should be educated in the ways of pleasing men and retaining their affection: 'it is worth all the rest told ten thousand times:– how to greet a husband, how to receive him, how never to recriminate . . . the love-killing effect of cold, dry, uninterested looks and manners.'[33]

One problem in Coleridge's relationship with his wife, perhaps the greatest, was that he claimed that Sarah had no great critical faculty; that she relied on other people to tell her what was good or bad. Critics have also accused her of having no real appreciation of the worth of her husband's work, being surprised at the great regard others held him in and actually preferring Southey's poetry to Coleridge's. Much of this assessment is based on comments made by her husband or by the Wordsworths. In 1806 Coleridge wrote of Sarah's 'self-encouraged admiration for Southey, as a vindictive feeling in which she delights herself as satirizing me . . .'[34] Sarah certainly regarded Coleridge as 'unwise' to publish his fragments of 'Christabel' and 'Kubla Khan' before they were finished. But then, so did the Wordsworths. Coleridge, in the grip of opium-induced jealousies, accused her of depending upon the 'eyes and ears of others' (particularly Southey) for her opinions.

Her personality naturally inclined her towards the kind of narrative poetry written by Southey and Scott – a preference she shared with a large part of the early nineteenth-century reading public. But Sarah was more than intelligent enough to have responded to tuition. However, Coleridge did nothing to try to develop her critical faculties, deliberately excluding her by discussing his work and his theories on poetry with Dorothy and William.

Coleridge was not slow to point out Sarah's shortcomings. In a deeply offensive letter he wrote a list of them with accompanying advice: '2. Permit me, my dear Sara, without offence to you, as Heaven knows! it is without any feeling of Pride in myself, to say, that in six acquirements, and in the quantity and quality of natural endowments whether of Feeling, or of Intellect, you are the Inferior. Therefore it would be preposterous to expect that I should see with your eyes, & dismiss my Friends from my heart, only because you have not chosen to give them any Share of your Heart; but it is not preposterous, in me, on the contrary I have a right to expect & demand, that you should to a certain degree love, & act kindly to, those whom I deem worthy of my love . . . If you read this letter with half the tenderness with which it is written, it will do you and both of us good . . .'[35]

Sarah, feeling that she had been driven into a corner, sent Sara Hutchinson an anonymous letter which, like other letters from this period, has not survived. The contents of this missive, combined with a passionate outpouring from Coleridge shortly afterwards, prostrated Sara Hutchinson and confined her to bed. Coleridge was initially outraged at his wife's presumption and proposed a separation. Sarah's revulsion was so dramatic that he immediately retracted the suggestion. By March they had agreed to a reconciliation and embarked on a desperate attempt to save their marriage. A month later, to Coleridge's horror, Sarah became pregnant for the fourth time.

Towards the end of 1801 there was a turning point in the relationship between William and Mary Hutchinson. Just when friendship and affection had deepened into love is impossible to pinpoint. Mary had been part of his life for so long – the childhood friendship, the links with his mother, the early light-hearted romantic flirtation at Penrith and then over the years the warm hospitality at Gallow Hill and Sockburn and her repeated, quiet presences at Racedown, Alfoxden and Dove Cottage.

The courtship was a strange, triangular affair. Mary received joint letters from both William and Dorothy and the letters she wrote back were also shared. After they had been married some years, when William was visiting their friends the Beaumonts at Coleorton, he wrote to Mary pouring out his passionate feelings on paper, asking her 'to write to me with out reserve; never have I been able to receive such a Letter from you'. Mary wrote back: '. . . it is not in my power to tell thee how I have been affected by this dearest of all letters . . . so new a thing to see the breathing of thy inmost heart upon paper that I was quite overpowered . . . for it is the first letter of love that has been exclusively my own.'[36]

She must have known that if she wanted William she would have to have Dorothy as well. Dorothy's passionate attachment to William was completely open. When Mary chose William, she explained in a letter, Dorothy also became her 'chosen companion in life'. But there was never the depth of feeling she shared with her own sister. Whereas Sara was 'my second self', Dorothy was 'dear Dorothy', and sometimes even 'poor dear Dorothy', occasionally 'dearest Dorothy', but never the recipient of the protestations of love and affection she shared with Sara. The harmonious relationship observed by the outside world across more than forty years was only possible because of Mary's sensitivity and self-effacement. This extended also to the knowledge of William's former mistress Annette Vallon and their child.

It was when Mary returned to Grasmere in November 1801 after an absence of six months that the change in her relationship with William was finally acknowledged. That separation had made both parties realise how much they cared for each other. Both were later to recall the agonies of physical separation, Mary remembering 'that feeling which I have never wanted since [I slept with (erased)] the solitary night did not separate us' and William admitting his 'longing day and night to see you again . . . when you were at Middleham . . . those thoughts & wishes that used to keep sleep from me'.[37] Within a week of Mary's arrival Dorothy's journal records how she walked out alone with William before tea and sat with him in the slate quarry. Whatever was said, Dorothy 'sate there a long time alone' after William went back to the cottage. She slept badly for the next two nights and spent the whole of the next day in bed 'very unwell'. Their servant Molly, Dorothy wrote in her journal, 'has been very witty with Mary all day. She says "Ye may say what ye will but there's nothing like a gay auld man for behaving weel to a young wife".' Mary and William spent much of their time walking out together, 'chearful blooming and happy', before Mary had to return to her brother's farm in Yorkshire.

Mary's relatives did not approve of her wish to marry William. In a memoir written for her children she described how her Uncle Henry 'upon whom we were, as Orphans, in some measure dependent, and with whom, I had lived when I went to school at Stockton, – had no high opinion of Young Men without some Profession, or Calling; Hence knowing that he had designated your Father, as "a Vagabond", when our minds were made up to Marry, I knew it would be useless, or worse than useless to ask his *consent*.' Mary was happy to marry without it, but the disapproval of her relatives made itself apparent in the absence of wedding gifts from her side of the family. 'Whether it was in consequence of our friends thinking us an improvident Pair, I do not know – but it is a fact that we did not receive a single *Wedding Present*.'[38]

William slept badly after Mary left and was far from well. He accompanied Dorothy on nostalgic walks around the lake, and while she reminisced about their first glimpse of the cottage two and a half years ago, William enlarged 'Mary's dear name which she had cut herself upon the stone . . . to make it plainer'.[39] One of the obstacles to an early marriage with Mary was William's obligation to Annette and their daughter Caroline. There was considerable agonising discussion, and several letters backwards and forwards to France and Gallow Hill. Dorothy became more clinging and emotional towards William. 'I was stopped in my writing, and made ill by the letters. William had a bad headach; he made up a bed on the floor, but could not sleep – I went to his bed and slept not . . .'[40] Their moments together became suddenly more precious. 'After we came in we sate in deep silence at the window – I on a chair and William with his hand on my shoulder. We were deep in Silence and Love, a blessed hour.'[41]

On 22 March 1802 it was decided that William should go to see Mary and that there should be a visit to Annette in order to resolve the situation. On 7 April Wordsworth went to stay with Mary at Middleham, leaving Dorothy with her friend Mrs Clarkson at Eusemere on the shores of Ullswater. On his way back to Eusemere, he wrote the poem 'The Glow-worm', 'Among all lovely things my Love had been', which he admitted to Coleridge was written to Dorothy, remembering their time together at Racedown more than seven years earlier. After an ecstatic reunion with William, Dorothy learned the lines off by heart and repeated them to herself as she walked back to Grasmere with him.

Dorothy wrote to Mary as soon as they got back to Grasmere that she was deeply concerned to hear from William that Mary was so thin. She urges her to take more rest. 'Take no more exercise than would be proper for the regaining of your strength supposing that you were nearly as weak as you are thin – above all my dearest Mary, seek quiet or rather amusing thoughts. Study the flowers, the birds and all the common things that are about you. O Mary, my dear Sister! be quiet and happy. Take care of yourself – keep yourself employed without fatigue, and do not make loving us your business, but let your love of us make up the spirit of all the business you have.' This is an odd remark to make to someone who is in love with her brother and has just become engaged to marry him, and the tone of the letter is one of admonishment. It is as though she is warning Mary that she and William are a package deal, to love one she must love them both. From William Mary had to be content with a postscript to Dorothy's letter: 'Heaven bless you, dearest Mary.'[42]

They got very wet on the way back from Eusemere and stayed at an inn. Dorothy was soaked through. However, a visitor at the inn lent Dorothy some of her clothes and 'made a smart Lady of me at once . . .' She could not resist using the occasion to make a jibe at Sarah Coleridge: 'She did more for me than Mrs Coleridge would do for her own Sister under the like circumstances.'[43] But it was not only Sarah Coleridge's clothes that Dorothy borrowed. She had very little sense of personal property, writing on another occasion of a visit to the Hutchinsons that she was bringing very little luggage as she would depend on Sara's wardrobe to supply her needs. Not every woman was happy with this blithe exchange of intimate garments.

It was on the journey back from Eusemere, 'in the woods beyond Gowbarrow park', that they saw the daffodils and Dorothy recorded in her journal: '. . . as we went along there were more and yet more and at last under the boughs of the trees, we saw that there was a long belt of them along the shore, about the breadth of a country turnpike road. I never saw daffodils so beautiful they grew among the mossy stones about and about them, some rested their heads upon these stones as on a pillow for weariness and the rest tossed and reeled and danced and seemed as if they verily laughed with the wind that blew upon them over the lake, they looked so gay ever glancing ever changing.'[44] These lines eventually became the basis of what is arguably William's most famous poem, 'The Daffodils'. Mary also had a hand in the poem, supplying the lines:

> They flash upon that inward eye
> Which is the bliss of solitude . . .

Many of William's poems originated in incidents recorded in Dorothy's journal. 'The Leech-gatherer' was one, based on the description of an old man they had met in October 1800. 'His trade was to gather leeches, but now leeches are scarce and he had not strength for it.' Sometimes he wrote about things that only Dorothy had witnessed and William often asked her to reread entries for his poems. 'William finished Alice Fell, and then he wrote the Poem of the Beggar woman taken from a Woman whom

I had seen in May – (now nearly 2 years ago) when John and he were at Gallow Hill. I sate with him at Intervals all the morning, took down his stanzas etc . . . After tea I read to William that account of the little Boys belonging to the tall woman and an unlucky thing it was for he could not escape from those very words, and so he could not write the poem.'[45] It was eventually finished and published as 'The Beggars'. Revealingly, in William's poetry from this period, whether the events were witnessed in Dorothy's company, or were part of Dorothy's unique experience, he always used the personal pronoun 'I'.

Later in life, secure in his own eminence, Wordsworth was to deny Dorothy's contribution entirely. Mary's lines are the only ones acknowledged in 'The Daffodils' and in conversation with Aubrey de Vere he criticised the poet who 'went out with his pencil and notebook, and jotted down whatever struck him most'. The poet should have 'observed, thought, felt' and then when he got home, 'after several days had passed by, he should have interrogated his memory'. That his own memory had been constantly refreshed by Dorothy's jottings had been conveniently forgotten, and his earlier admissions that it was through Dorothy's eyes that he saw nature were now denied. 'I have hardly ever known anyone but myself,' he told de Vere, 'who had a true eye for Nature.'[46] Dorothy, after the loving tributes of 'Tintern Abbey' and 'The Glow-worm', is edited out of his later poems. The cut-off point was Wordsworth's marriage to Mary. One scholar writes that there was no longer a place for Dorothy 'in the organs of Wordsworth's poetic imagination, and she was cut out like so much decayed tissue. The uncompromising ruthlessness of it is awe-inspiring, an act of necessary cruelty, inevitable but heart-breaking . . . so Agamemnon sacrificed Iphigenia.'[47]

In June 1802 Lord Lonsdale died and his will stipulated that his just debts should be paid. At last they were to get the money due to them, and this would make a tremendous difference to their future financial security. Dorothy wrote to her brother Richard, in the light of this and of William's engagement to Mary, about her future. She assures him that William's marriage will add to his comfort and happiness. 'Mary Hutchinson is a most excellent woman – I have known her long, and I know her thoroughly; she has been a dear friend of mine, is deeply attached to William, and is disposed to feel kindly to all his family.' As to herself, she sees her future as being dependent 'upon the affection of my Brothers and their regard for my happiness'. She will continue to live with William, but asks for a settlement of £60 a year to cover her expenses and board. 'I cannot look forward to the time when, with my habits of frugality, I could not live comfortably on that sum . . . I should have something to spare to exercise my better feelings in relieving the necessities of others, I might buy a few books, take a journey now and then.'[48]

There may, possibly, have been some talk of living at Gallow Hill after William's marriage. The Hutchinsons were an extremely close family and Mary was very reluctant to leave them. There was also the problem of who would keep house for her brother once she was gone – Sara was keeping house for their other unmarried brother and their sister Joanna was still quite young. Mary must also, understandably, have had misgivings about coming to live in a household that had been run for so many years by another woman. Dove Cottage was Dorothy's home, Dorothy's creation – even the furniture had been bought with a small legacy from her Crackenthorpe relatives. Just how possessive Dorothy felt towards Dove Cottage can be seen from her reaction, years later, to the alterations made by De Quincey when he became the tenant. She refused to speak to him. Mary would not be free to organise things as she wished and as she was used to doing at her brother's houses at Middleham or Gallow Hill. Dorothy's journal entry for 24 March records that she walked with William to Rydal to collect the mail, which included a letter from Mary. The next sentence goes on to say: 'I made a vow that we would not leave this country for G. Hill' and then 'I wrote to Mary in the evening'. What William thought on the matter, she doesn't say. She did, however, have sufficient insight when describing the moment Mary arrived at Dove Cottage as William's wife to add, '. . . our dear Mary's feelings would I dare say not be easy to speak of.'[49]

John Wordsworth appears to have been deeply affected by William's betrothal to Mary. He was one of the party staying at Sockburn with William when Coleridge first met the Hutchinson sisters. Later, he had spent some weeks with Mary at Dove Cottage just after they moved in, walking with her, becoming quietly attached. He was a very shy man and had apparently said nothing of his feelings for her. But he wrote her a very sad letter after news of her engagement was broken to him: 'I have been reading your Letter over and over again, my dearest Mary, till tears have come into my eyes and I know not how to express myself – Thou art a kind and dear Creature.' He ended the letter with a quotation from William's poem 'Michael':

> But whatever fate
> Befall thee, I shall love thee to the last,
> And bear thy memory with me to the grave.

It is signed 'Thine afft. John Wordsworth.'[50] Either by accident or design, he never saw her again.

There was a turbulent emotional atmosphere after their return to Grasmere. William and Dorothy received a 'very affecting letter' from Mary on 3 June. William was ill with insomnia. Their servant Molly fell ill and Dorothy had to do all the housework herself, leaving her exhausted. She too became ill. 'I have a kind of stupefaction and headache about me, a feeling of something that has been amiss . . . William has slept well these two nights, and he looks well; this is at all times my best joy, and really it is almost a pleasure to be ill, he is so good and loving to me. I have had a bason of Broth to my dinner, which seems to settle well with me, so be under no alarm.'[51] She and William had exchanged rooms and she was now sleeping permanently in one of the single beds in William's room.

Throughout the whole of this period, the saga of Coleridge's unhappiness and emotional involvement with Sara Hutchinson continued. On 20 April 1802 Coleridge walked over to visit them carrying a huge parcel of books, much shaken after having been attacked by a cow on the road. There appears to have been talk of the Wordsworths living at Greta Hall: 'I talked with him [C] about Mrs C., told him of the letter I had written etc etc., and of our determination not to go to Greta Hall – he said something about going as lodgers for a short time; I said I could not see any good whatever to arise from this, and as I was so fully determined he pressed nothing upon me . . . Mrs Coleridge is a most extraordinary character – she is the lightest weakest silliest woman! She sent some clean clothes on Thursday to meet C (the first time she ever did such a thing in her life) from which I guess that she is determined to be attentive to him – she wrote a note, saying not a word about my letter, and all in her very lightest style . . . Is not it a hopeless case? So insensible and so irritable she never can come to good and poor C.! but I said I would not enter on this subject, and I will not.'[52]

The day after his arrival Coleridge read Dorothy and William 'the verses he wrote to Sara'. Originally a passionate account of his emotional state called 'A Letter to Asra', it was eventually published in truncated form as 'Dejection: an Ode'. The contents were deeply disturbing for Dorothy. 'I was affected with them and was on the whole, not being well, in miserable spirits. The sunshine – the green fields and the fair sky made me sadder . . .'[53] In the poem, Coleridge wrote of his unhappiness with Sarah Fricker at Greta Hall, 'those habitual Ills'

> That wear out Life, when two unequal Minds
> Meet in one House, & two discordant Wills –

Even his children, though deeply loved, have become a chain to tie him unwillingly to Sarah Fricker.

> There have been hours, when feeling how they bind
> And pluck out the wing-feathers of my Mind,
> Turning my Error to Necessity,
> I have half-wish'd they never had been born!
> *That* seldom! But sad Thoughts they always bring . . .

Visits to Sara and the happy Wordsworth household were painful because of the comparisons.

> The transientness is Poison in the Wine,
> Eats out the pith of Joy, makes all Joy hollow,
> All Pleasure a dim Dream of Pain to follow!
>     My own peculiar Lot, my house-hold Life
> It is, & will remain, Indifference or Strife –
> While ye are Well & Happy, twould but wrong you
> If I should fondly yearn to be among you –
> Wherefore, O wherefore! should I wish to be
> A wither'd branch upon a blossoming Tree?

He thinks constantly of Sara Hutchinson, prostrated by the violent emotions of his previous letter to her.

> To know that thou art weak & worn with pain,
> And not to hear thee, Sara! not to view thee –
>     Not sit beside they Bed
>     Not press thy aching Head
>     Not bring thee Health again –
>     At least to hope, to try –
> By this Voice, which thou lov'st, & by this earnest Eye –

His mind returns to 'that happy night' when he first met Sara and her sister, 'The low decaying Fire our only Light'. It is almost better never to see her than 'To see thee, hear thee, feel thee – then to part!' He wishes her 'Peace in thy Heart, & Quiet in thy Dwelling,/Health in thy Limbs, & in thine Eyes the Light/Of Love & Hope, & honorable Feeling'.

> O breathe She softly in her gentle Sleep!
> Cover her, gentle Sleep! with wings of Healing.
> And be this Tempest but a mountain Birth!
> May all the Stars hang bright about her Dwelling,
> Silent, as tho' they watch'd the sleeping Earth!
> Healthful & light, my Darling! may'st thou rise
>     With clear & chearful Eyes –

It was not a poem guaranteed to raise Sara's spirits and the fact that he chose the day of William's wedding to Mary to publish it was tactless in the extreme.

Sara was in a very difficult position. She was in love with a married man, who had two small children and claimed to be unhappily yoked, who bludgeoned her moral sense with poems and letters declaring his passion for her. His letters to her are littered with endearments: 'O dear Sara! how dearly I love you!', 'Write immediately . . . Bless you, my Darling . . . infinitely Beloved Darling . . . my darling Sara.'

On 29 April, Dorothy wrote to Mary Hutchinson that they had 'left poor Coleridge on Monday evening; we had been with him a week and a day. You know that I wrote to Sara on the Friday Evening before we went to Keswick giving her the joyful tidings that C was better, but alas! on Saturday we had a sad account of him . . . We left home at one o'clock on Sunday – and reached Keswick at about six. We both trembled, and till we entered the door I hardly durst speak. He was sitting in the parlour, and looked dreadfully pale and weak. He was very, very unwell in the way that Sara can describe to you – ill all over, back and stomach and limbs and so weak as that he changed colour whenever he exerted himself at all. Our company did him good and the next day he was much better. Since that time he has been upon the whole greatly improved in his looks and strength but he was never quite well for more than an hour together during the whole time we were there, tho' he began to form plans and schemes for working but he was unable to do anything . . . I do think he will never be quite well till he has tried a warm climate . . . He and Hartley are to come over in the first returned Chaise after tomorrow. Hartley is to stay some time with us and to go to Grasmere school. Dear little fellow! he will be as happy as a young lamb playing upon the green turf in the church-yard with our bonny little lasses. We hope that C. will grow well in a short time after he comes to us, but there is no security for his continuing so. We should have stayed longer at Keswick but our company not being so new did not do him so much good as at first, and then we are never comfortable there after the first 2 or 3 days. This of course we do not mind while we are of any essential service to him, but the same cause which makes us uncomfortable at Keswick prevents him from having all the good from us that he other wise would have.'[54] The 'cause' identified by Dorothy was, of course, Sarah Coleridge.

Dorothy's gossiping letters, full of contempt for Sarah, did a great deal to encourage Sara Hutchinson's hopes and affections towards Coleridge. Divorce, though expensive, was not unknown and the political views of the young Pantisocrats had originally embraced democratic and Wollstonecraftian notions that the marriage contract should be dissolved if the parties were in agreement. Coleridge initially, and then Dorothy, must have given Sara grounds for hope, and she apparently sent Samuel explicit letters of 'love and feeling' in the early days of their love affair. In return he sent her presents and copies of the poems that he wrote for her.

Sara kept a notebook known in the family as 'Sara's Poets'. On the flyleaf she herself inscribed 'Sarah Hutchinson's Poets', and she filled it with verses copied from both Wordsworth and Coleridge for her own pleasure. Coleridge's poems – some of them copied in his own hand – are at one end of the book and William's at the other. Coleridge's poems include 'Soliloquy to the Full Moon' and 'Tranquillity; an Ode', as well as early drafts of other poems from this period.

The Wordsworths were convinced that Coleridge's only problem was his wife, and that separated from her and in their healing company he would be restored to health and able to write. They began to discuss ways in which Coleridge could be separated from his unsuitable spouse. Their schemes also included Sarah's sons, Hartley and Derwent, who, freed from her influence, would also be 'happy as young lambs'. Hartley had become increasingly withdrawn since the move to Greta Hall, much of it due to the deteriorating temper of his father, vented not only on Sarah but on Hartley too. Under the influence of opium, Coleridge turned upon the very people he loved most, admitting to Southey that he

Must needs express his Love's Excess
In Words of Wrong and Bitterness.

Coleridge's harsh treatment of the sensitive child, and the ensuing tug of loyalty between the two families, had lasting consequences. Hartley had inherited his father's gift of talking (Harriet Martineau was one who commented on his 'wonderfully beautiful conversation'), his poetic talent, and his charisma, as well as his insecurity. Even as a child this was apparent, and Wordsworth wrote that he feared for Hartley's future.

Hartley made the projected visit to the Wordsworths' and Dorothy reported that he was 'well and happy', but reading between the lines he was missing his 'Wilsy' badly. 'He has slept very quietly at nights ever since you were here only he is long in falling asleep. He talks a great deal about Mrs Wilson. Tell her that I am sure he can never forget her . . .' Dorothy was still convinced she could be a better mother to Sarah's children than Sarah. Her appropriation of other women's children is a sad indication of the strength of her unfulfilled need for a child of her own.

Wordsworth wrote to Thomas Poole about Coleridge's condition: 'He is apparently quite well one day, and the next the fit comes on him again with as much violence as ever. These repeated shocks cannot but greatly weaken his constitution; and he is himself afraid that, as the disease (which is now manifestly the gout) keeps much about his stomach, he may be carried off by it with little or no warning. I would hope to God that there is no danger of this; but it is too manifest that the disease is a dangerous one; it is the gout in a habit not strong enough to throw it out to the extremities. At all events, as I have said, his body must be grievously weakened by the repeated attacks under which he is at present labouring. We all here feel deeply persuaded that nothing can do him any effectual good, but a change of climate . . .'[55] The object of the letter was to get Poole to advance money for Coleridge to go to the Azores.

Coleridge's symptoms of 'flying gout' were graphically described by De Quincey as the 'pains of opium': violent gastric attacks, rheumatic pains, and headaches which could only be alleviated by the consumption of more laudanum which then produced hallucinations and nightmares culminating in 'suicidal despondency'. Sometime in the spring of 1801 Coleridge discovered the notorious Kendal Black Drop, a viciously addictive concentration, retailing at several shillings a phial – a habit not likely to improve the Coleridges' tight finances. He was also consuming crude opium and wrote to friends asking them to send him supplies, promising payment 'in futura'. Samuel owed everybody money and was totally incapable of meeting his literary commitments. According to Southey he was swilling laudanum alone at the rate of a two pints a week, costing £5, and when things were bad consuming up to a pint a day, plus large quantities of brandy to 'keep it on his stomach' and raw opium as well.

Money worries, and knowledge of her husband's growing addiction, made Sarah increasingly distraught. Since the bankruptcy and death of her father, this was one of her flashpoints. In her anxiety and extreme distress she tore at Coleridge in an attempt to penetrate his drug-induced apathy. Coleridge wrote to Tom Wedgwood: 'If any woman wanted an exact and copious Recipe' in order to make her husband miserable, he could provide one: 'Ill-tempered speeches sent after me when I went out of the House, ill-tempered Speeches on my returns, my friends received with freezing looks . . .'[56] This last was a reference to her coldness towards the Wordsworths, hardly surprising in view of the fact that they were encouraging him to leave her. The Coleridges' daughter Sara later recorded that her mother's honesty was one of the greatest stumbling blocks to a harmonious relationship with her father, 'unless at the same time she had possessed that meekness and forbearance which softens everything and can be conciliating by utter silence on all unpeaceful topics and the constant recurrence to soothing cheering themes'.[57]

Unlike Dorothy or Sara Hutchinson, Sara lacked the talent for 'managing' and indulging men. She had hoped for an equal partnership with Coleridge, one in which her needs would be as important as his, believing that 'for man and woman truth . . .

must be the same'.[58] Coleridge, though he was always attracted to strong women with minds of their own, secretly hankered after one who would submit and defer, selflessly caring for him and making his needs and interests her paramount concern – as he soon saw Mary Hutchinson doing for Wordsworth, and Edith doing for Southey. 'The perfection of every woman is to be characterless', he wrote, 'Creatures who, though they may not always understand you . . . always feel you and feel with you.'[59]

Coleridge still addressed Sarah in letters as 'my dear love' and still signed himself 'your dear husband'. There were still moments when he wished, passionately, to restore what they had once had. Before illness and depression 'rendered me dead to everything', he declared, he had never 'known any woman for whom I had an equal personal fondness . . . I never saw you at the top of our Hill, when I returned from a Walk, without a sort of pleasurable Feeling of Sight . . . some little akin to the delight in a beautiful Flower joined with the consciousness – And it is in *my* garden . . .'[60] 'O Sara! dear Sara! try for all good things in the spirit of unsuspecting Love, for miseries gather upon us . . .'[61] '. . . what we have been to each other, our understanding will not permit our hearts to forget . . .'[62]

## Phantoms and Chimeras

*She was a Phantom of delight*
*When first she gleamed upon my sight;*
*A lovely Apparition, sent*
*To be a moment's ornament;*
*Her eyes as stars of Twilight fair;*
*Like Twilight's too, her dusky hair;*
*But all things else about her drawn*
*From May-time and the cheerful Dawn;*
*A dancing Shape, on Image gay,*
*To haunt, to startle, and way-lay.*

William Wordsworth

Relations between the Wordsworths and the Hutchinsons were not without their difficult moments. In 1802 Mary and Sara wrote a sharp critique of William's poem 'Resolution and Independence' – 'The Leech-gatherer' – which they found confusing. Neither Dorothy nor Coleridge could understand it either and William later agreed to amend it to make it clearer. But in a letter he upbraids Sara rather savagely for her comments: 'You speak of his speech as tedious: everything is tedious when one does not read with the feelings of the Author – The Thorn is tedious to hundreds; and so is the Idiot Boy to hundreds; it is the character of the old man to tell his story in a manner which an *impatient* reader must necessarily feel as tedious.' She is abjured to contemplate the 'moral dignity' of the old man's character. Dorothy joins the argument, admonishing Sara: 'When you happen to be displeased with what you suppose to be the tendency or moral of any poem which William writes, ask yourself whether you have hit upon the real tendency and true moral, and above all never think that he writes for no reason but merely because a thing happened – and when you feel any poem of his to be tedious, ask yourself in what spirit it was written – whether merely to tell the tale and be through with it, or to illustrate a particular character or truth etc etc.'[1] Dorothy's devotion to her brother had almost completely obscured her critical faculties with regard to his work. That Sara and Mary won the argument is reflected in the fact that when William eventually published the poem, all their corrections had been accepted and the poem edited accordingly.

By 16 July 1802 Dorothy and William were at Gallow Hill in Yorkshire where Mary was now living with her brother. On the journey Dorothy recorded one of the last moments of physical intimacy with William. 'We had a chearful ride though cold, till we got on to Stanemoor, and then a heavy shower came on, but we buttoned ourselves up, both together in the Guard's coat and we liked the hills and the Rain the better for bringing [us] so close to one another – I never rode more snugly.'[2] They went on to France via London. There Dorothy recorded in her journal the views from Westminster Bridge, which they crossed on top of the Dover coach on 31 July. It was one of the last instances of her journal providing a starting point for her brother's poetry.

They remained at Calais for four weeks in the company of Annette Vallon and her daughter Caroline, walking on the beach and talking. Dorothy's journal is silent on personal details of this meeting with Annette. What was discussed and what was decided were never revealed. William had always felt guilty about his abandonment of Annette and his inability to support their daughter. Annette's hurt at the years of silence was considerable, spilling over into letters. She had long dreamt of the moment when he would walk through the door. She wrote to Dorothy that she stood 'ready to throw myself into his arms and say to him: "Come my love, come and dry those tears which have long been flowing for you, let us fly and see Caroline, our child and your likeness." '

How she accepted the news that he was now going to marry someone else Dorothy does not allow us to know.

On 29 September Dorothy wrote to Jane Marshall just before William's marriage that she was 'exceedingly unwell' after catching cold riding in a coach from Windsor with twelve other passengers. She was too ill in London to proceed further for a few days, so that their departure was delayed, but reassures Jane that she is now 'perfectly well, except that I do not feel myself strong, and am very thin, but my kind Friends help me to take such good care of myself that I hope soon to become as strong as any body.' She also writes of her own feelings about her brother's marriage. 'I have long loved Mary Hutchinson as a Sister, and she is equally attached to me this being so, you will guess that I look forward with perfect happiness to this Connection between us, but, happy as I am, I half dread that concentration of all tender feelings, past, present, and future which will come upon me on the wedding morning. There never lived on earth a better woman than Mary H. and I have not a doubt but that she is in every respect formed to make an excellent wife to my Brother, and I seem to myself to have scarcely any thing left to wish for but that the wedding was over, and we had reached our home once again.'[3]

Once at Gallow Hill, Dorothy records that she 'was ill on Saturday and on Sunday and continued to be during most of the time of our stay' – a sentence she afterwards deleted. Also deleted was a part of the account of her emotional storm on the morning of the wedding. She was so overwrought she could not bear to be present at the ceremony and stayed in her room, leaving Sara to prepare the wedding breakfast by herself. 'At a little after 8 o'clock I saw them go down the avenue towards the Church. William had parted from me upstairs. [I gave him the wedding ring – with how deep a blessing! I took it from my forefinger where I had worn it the whole of the night before – he slipped it again onto my finger and blessed me fervently. (deleted)] When they were absent my dear little Sara prepared the breakfast. I kept myself as quiet as I could, but when I saw the two men running up the walk, coming to tell us it was over, I could stand it no longer and threw myself on the bed where I lay in stillness, neither hearing or seeing anything, till Sara came upstairs to me and said "They are coming". This forced me from the bed where I lay and I moved I knew not how straight forward, faster than my strength could carry me till I met my beloved William and fell upon his bosom.'[4] Mary was left behind as William and John Hutchinson led Dorothy to the house and tried to calm her hysteria. Even on Mary's wedding day, the focus was on Dorothy.

After an emotional departure from Gallow Hill – 'Poor Mary was much agitated, when she parted from her brothers and sisters, and her home'[5] – Mary seems to have spent much of her honeymoon looking after Dorothy who had one of her bouts of sickness. She was 'unwell' and unable to eat dinner on the second night, very sick in the coach the following day, and vomited at the inn that evening, where she was once again unable to eat. Mary put aside her own travel sickness and fatigue to go into the kitchen to make her some special broth. Dorothy even sat between Mary and William in the coach: 'Wm. fell asleep, lying upon my breast, and I upon Mary.'

The honeymoon was torment for Dorothy, travelling through places she had previously visited alone with her brother. On his wedding night at Helmsley Castle, 'I prevailed upon William to go up with me to the ruins. We left Mary sitting by the kitchen fire . . . I was pleased to see again the little path which we had walked upon . . .' and the following day, 'my heart was melted away with dear recollections – the bridge, the waterspout, the steep hill, the church. They are among the most vivid of my own inner visions, for they were the first objects that I saw after we were left to ourselves, and had turned our whole hearts to Grasmere.' Other sights were similarly emotive. Garsdale 'was a dear place to William and me.' And Staveley was 'a place I dearly love to think of – the first mountain village that I came to with Wm. when we first began our pilgrimage together.'[6]

With the arrival of Mary Wordsworth at Dove Cottage, Dorothy's detailed, illuminating journals virtually come to a halt, and apologies at the beginning of her letters for their infrequency become more common. She no longer had the privacy or the time to write, and as the family increased and the small cottage began to bulge with adults and children, she complained that she couldn't even find the time to read. Her time was taken up in childcare, household chores, transcribing her brother's poetry, gardening and walking. The change in their relationship may also have removed the will to write – her journals by her own confession had been written for her brother 'because I shall give William pleasure by it'. If they were no longer of any use to him, there was no reason to put pen to paper. She ceased to write regularly and – although she did write occasional travel journals and poems, and after 1824 began once again to keep a brief diary of daily events – she never wrote so personally or with such intensity. It was virtually the end of her life as a writer. It also marked the beginning of a deterioration in her mental and physical health. De Quincey was of the opinion that if Dorothy had developed her talents as a writer instead of devoting her life to her brother and his children at this point, she would not have suffered so much later on. Her importance to William's creative life has been noted by a number of critics, and there is consensus that 'Wordsworth's ten years with Dorothy mark an oasis of power and splendour amid endless arid tracts of middling performance'.[7]

In the November following the Wordsworths' marriage, Coleridge travelled to Wales to see his benefactor Tom Wedgwood, who was terminally ill. He managed to organise his journey so that he could spend the day in Penrith with Sara Hutchinson, who was on her way north from Yorkshire to Grasmere. This clandestine meeting seriously upset Sarah Coleridge who sent her husband a letter of rebuke which he complained had almost killed him. The violence of his reply prostrated Sarah in an uncharacteristic bout of nervous exhaustion. She wrote sadly to Mrs George Coleridge that such was the state of Coleridge's health that 'the least vexation . . . does him great injury; nothing but tranquillity keeps him tolerable, care and anxiety destroy him.'[8]

Coleridge's trip to Wales was conveniently timed, as usual, to avoid his wife's imminent confinement. From the Wedgwoods' he wrote to her that it would be 'a great comfort' if he knew that one of the Dove Cottage women was going to be with her. 'Sara rather than the other two because you will hardly have another opportunity of having her by yourself and to yourself, and of learning to know her, such as she is, really is.' He took the opportunity to remind her 'how much of our common love and happiness depends on your loving those whom I love'.[9] Nothing was more calculated to make Sarah Coleridge feel utterly, totally, isolated. For the first time before a birth, she had premonitions of disaster, confided only to her sister-in-law. 'I would to heaven those 8 or 10 days were past! for I am such a fool to get more and more a coward, and (at times) full of *fears and dread*.'[10] To make matters worse, the front of Greta Hall was still being rebuilt around her, an enormous, disruptive job that should have been completed by the end of the summer.

Perhaps, in urging Sarah to accept his lover, Coleridge had fantasies of having the kind of '*ménage à trois*' that existed at Dove Cottage. Sarah, however, was having none of it, and no invitation was issued. When Coleridge arrived back at Grasmere on Christmas Eve he received the news that Sarah had given birth to a daughter – alone as usual. She entered the birth into the family bible in her own handwriting, a circumstance some members of the family felt to be an omen.

Coleridge set off for Keswick straight away, 'bore the sex with great Fortitude', insisted that the child be called Sara and was back at Dove Cottage by 1 January. On the 4th he wrote an unforgivable letter to Sarah, still in the emotional aftermath of childbirth. 'You are a good woman with a pleasing person, and a healthy understanding – superior certainly to nine women in ten of our own rank or the rank above us – and I will be not only contented but grateful if you will let me be quite tranquil – and above all my dear, dear Sara! have confidence in my honor and virtue, and suffer me to love and to be beloved without jealousy or pain. Depend on it my dear Wife! that the more you sympathise with me in my kind manners and kind feelings to those of Grasmere the more I shall be likely to sympathise with you in your opinions respecting their faults and imperfections. I am no idolater at present, and I solemnly assure you, that if I prefer many parts of *their* characters, opinions and feelings and habits to the same parts of yours, I do likewise prefer much, very much of your character to theirs – Of course I speak *chiefly* of Dorothy and William – because Mrs Wordsworth and her sister are far less remote from you than they – and unless I am grievously deceived will in some things become less so still. God send us peace and love – My dear love! what a New Year's blessing it would be . . .' Part of the central section of the letter is missing, but he goes on to urge her to accept Sara Hutchinson, whom he intends to bring on a visit 'tomorrow night' because he has '*some few reasons* for wishing [her] to be with you immediately . . . I will tell you when I am alone with you. In one thing, my dear Love! I do prefer you to any woman I ever knew. I have the most unbounded confidence in your discretion, and know it to be well-grounded.'[11]

Whatever transpired during Sara Hutchinson's visit, Sara appears to have avoided Coleridge for most of that year. Although expected several times at Dove Cottage, she never arrived and Coleridge was intensely miserable, alternating between manic activity and paralysing depression. In his notebooks he asks '[O Sara Sara] why am I not happy! . . . why for years have I not enjoyed one pure & sincere pleasure? . . . one genuine Delight . . .' The answer lay in the medicine bottle on the desk beside him. Sarah Coleridge lamented the fact that opium had blighted their joint lives: 'I should be a very, very happy Woman if it were not for a few things – and my husband's ill health stands at the head of these evils!'[12]

In June 1803, Mary gave birth to a son, which surprised both William and Dorothy, who had been convinced the baby would be female. Mary had been unwell through most of the pregnancy, suffering from heartburn. At thirty-three she was quite old to be having her first child, but felt well enough afterwards to discharge the nurse two weeks early. Dorothy was very proud to be Mary's 'sole attendant', and doted on the little boy, christened John for their beloved brother. He was carried around in a meat basket, up mountains and on boat trips on the lake, almost from birth.

Dorothy wrote to a friend that 'he is as fine and healthy a Babe as ever was in Grasmere I verily believe . . . Would that you could see the hair growing upon his dear little head. You cannot think how bonny the bare head looks when he is sucking!' She adds in another letter: '. . . if I were not half afraid of making even you laugh at me I should say he looks as if he was not the child of ordinary parents . . .' She describes bathing and dressing him upon the floor when 'he screams lustily and is in a violent passion.' She goes on to contrast 'our' baby with the Coleridge baby with almost malicious satisfaction: 'I believe Sara Coleridge was never in a passion in her life, she is the very soul of meekness, it is quite a wonder to hear her cry when she is well . . .' The Coleridge children, even when they are ill, are 'fretful, but still in the same meek way' in contrast to John's 'angry squalls'. Pages of Dorothy's letters are taken up with details of little John's appearance and behaviour. Dorothy's love for John bordered on obsession, and according to William she was 'not quite well', her nerves wound up to fever pitch. She was physically overworked too since their old servant Molly had been ill during Mary's confinement. But much of it was due to emotional turmoil, as she admitted to a friend: '. . . when I am not in uncommon strength . . . after writing for any length of time or doing any thing that exercises my thoughts or feelings, I have a very uneasy sense of want and weakness at my stomach, a mixture of emptiness, gnawing, and a sort of preparation for sickness . . .'[13]

Coleridge, Dorothy and William had planned to go off on a Scottish tour as soon as the baby arrived. Although Dorothy had been full of enthusiasm for this trip before the birth – a rare opportunity to have William to herself for six weeks – she now had mixed feelings: 'I have no doubt I shall be as happy as they when I am fairly off, but I do not love to think of leaving home, and parting with the dear Babe who will be no more the same Babe when we return . . .'[14] Mary, understandably, did not relish staying behind on her own with the baby, especially as Sara was unable to come and stay with her. Sara had her hands full looking after her brothers during the busy time of hay and harvest. In the event her sister Joanna came, but was so ill with nerves and depression that she was of little real help.

Dorothy, William and Coleridge left Grasmere on 14 August 1803, hoping perhaps to recapture the closeness and companionship of 'The Concern'. As they passed through Carlisle on their way north, they stopped to visit Carlisle gaol, where the notorious bigamist and imposter Hatfield, who had seduced and married the 'Beauty of Buttermere', was being held prior to his execution. Dorothy 'stood at the door of the gaoler's house, where he was', while William and Coleridge went in.

Dorothy's Grasmere journal may have lapsed, but she wrote an account of her Scottish tour, edited and rewritten after her return, with a view to publication. It is the first really deliberate literary work that she embarked on. She transcribed it in full for her friend Mrs Clarkson, a job that took her two years to complete, and this is now the only surviving manuscript. William printed only fragments of the journal and many regretted that the whole was not published until 1874. Written for public consumption, it lacks the intimacy and emotional depth of her private journals, but is still a wonderful piece of travel journalism.

In a horse-drawn jaunting car they travelled through Dumfries, visiting Robert Burns' grave and calling at his home, though his wife was away. Dorothy was very struck by the contrasts of the landscape. In the lowlands 'the ground all over heaves and swells like a sea' and she was amazed to see corn growing among the gorse. Everywhere was poverty and neglect – great houses and cottages ruined and empty, and the inns and the farms where they stayed were dirty. As the land became wilder and more barren, the small villages circled by cultivation made a more striking contrast 'like a collection of patchwork, made of pieces as they might have been cut by the mantua-maker . . . so small and of irregular shapes.' There were strange and moving sights – a woman cutting corn in a field, singing in Gaelic; a partly burned-out cottage beside the road and a woman sitting motionless in the middle of the field wrapped in a grey plaid cloak. Although Dorothy lived among terrible rural poverty and need, she observes but never comments on or considers the politics behind the tragic spectacles she witnesses. Although these people attracted her ready sympathy and whatever charity she could spare, her whole emotional and intellectual focus was on William and Coleridge.

Towards Glasgow the landscape changed. The weather was bad and at times she was 'amazed by the carts and dirt, and the road was full of people . . . my head was beating with the noise of carts we have left and the wearisomeness of the disagreeable objects near the highway.' Dorothy was surprised to find Glasgow as civilised as London, with large shops and coffee houses. But further north, although the scenery became more spectacular, travelling was less easy. Many of the people they met were rude to them, some did not even speak English, the food was meagre and on one occasion William dropped their carefully hoarded supplies of coffee and sugar in the loch. Coleridge was also proving difficult company, disinclined to accompany them on walks, complaining of the cold and damp, and Dorothy often felt that she had to choose between his comfort or her brother's.

Accommodation was one of their greatest difficulties as they went further north into the Trossachs. Inns were few and far between and they had often to throw themselves upon the hospitality of crofters. William and Coleridge frequently found themselves sleeping in the barn among the hay. Dorothy's descriptions of the primitive living conditions of their hosts are rich in detail and worthy of a novelist.

When I went to bed, the mistress, desiring me to 'go ben', attended me with a candle, and assured me that the bed was dry, though not 'sic as I had been used to'. It was of chaff; there were two others in the room, a cupboard and two chests, on one of which stood the milk in wooden vessels covered over; I should have thought that milk so kept could not have been sweet, but the cheese and butter were good.

The walls of the whole house were of stone unplastered. It consisted of three apartments, – the cow house at one end, the kitchen or house in the middle, and the spence at the other end. The rooms were divided, not up to the rigging, but only to the beginning of the roof, so that there was a free passage for light and smoke from one end of the house to the other. I went to bed some time before the family. The door was shut between us, but they had a bright fire, which I could not see; but the light it sent up among the varnished rafters and beams, which crossed each other in almost as intricate and fantastic a manner as I have seen the under-boughs of a large beech tree withered by the depth of the shade above, produced the most beautiful effect that can be conceived. It was like what I should suppose an underground cave or temple to be, with a dripping or moist roof, and the moonlight entering in upon it by some means or other, and yet the colours were more like melted gems.

I lay looking up till the light of the fire faded away, and the man and his wife and child had crept into their bed at the other end of the room. I did not sleep much, but passed a comfortable night, for my bed, though hard, was warm and clean: the unusualness of my situation prevented me from sleeping. I could hear the waves beat against the shore of the lake; a little 'syke' close to the door made a much louder noise; and when I sate up in my bed I could see the lake through an open window-place at the bed's head. Add to this, it rained all night. I was less occupied by remembrance of the Trossachs, beautiful as they were, than the vision of the Highland hut, which I could not get out of my head. I thought of the Fairyland of Spenser, and what I had read in romance at other times, and then, what a feast would it be for a London pantomime-maker, could he but transplant it to Drury Lane, with all its beautiful colours![15]

It rained for days on end, so much that 'we had no hope that it would be over in less than three weeks at the least'. According to Dorothy, Coleridge declared that he had had enough and that he had determined to 'send his clothes to Edinburgh and make the best of his way thither, being afraid to face much wet weather in an open carriage.' Coleridge, in a long, chatty letter to his wife, wrote that it was William who 'proposed to me to leave them, & make my way on foot'. Years later, after Coleridge's death, his daughter Sara – who had heard both sides of the story – remembered and commented on this parting in terms that suggest it left a permanent residue of bitterness. However it happened, they shared out the remaining money and parted company by the side of the road, Coleridge to walk one way, Dorothy and William to go in the other direction 'driving heavily along' in the cart after they had lost sight of him. Dorothy's thoughts were 'full of Coleridge . . . I shivered at the thought of his being sickly and alone, travelling from place to place'.[16] Coleridge wrote to his wife, asking her to borrow money and send it to Perth otherwise he would have to beg his way home. He assured her that he kept 'the Fiend at arm's length . . . While I can walk 24 miles a day, with the excitement of new objects.'[17] The 'Horrors' only came back when he tried to sleep – phantoms so substantial he dreaded going to bed and sometimes sat by the bed and cried.

Without Coleridge, there was a chance for Dorothy to recapture some of the old intimacy with William and the delight of joint discovery. 'We talked over our day's adventures by the fireside, and often looked out of the window towards a huge pyramidal mountain at the entrance of Glen Coe. All between, the dreary waste was clear, almost, as sky, the moon shining full upon it. A rivulet ran amongst stones near the house, and sparkled with light: I could have fancied that there was nothing else, in that extensive circuit over which we looked, that had the power of motion.'[18]

Her writing conveys a poignant sense of nostalgia, as she struggled to retain the precious images in her memory. 'When we have arrived at an unknown place by moonlight, it is never a moment of indifference when I quit it again with the morning light, especially if the objects have appeared beautiful . . . I have kept back, unwilling to go to the window, that I might not lose the picture taken to my pillow at night . . . the passing away of my own fancies was a loss. The place had appeared exceedingly wild by moonlight; I had mistaken corn-fields for naked rocks, and the lake had appeared narrower and the hills more steep and lofty than they really were.'[19]

Dorothy transcribed the first two-thirds of her journal within six months of her return, spending a considerable time on its revision. But in February or March 1804, in the middle of describing a walk near the village of Kenmore on 5 September 1803, she broke off and it was a year before she took it up again. She inserted a curious memorandum in the text. 'April 11th 1805. I am setting about a task which, however free and happy the state of my mind, I could not have performed well at this distance of time; but now, I do not know that I shall be able to go on with it at all. I will strive, however, to do the best I can, setting before myself a different object from that hitherto aimed at, which was, to omit no incident, however trifling, and to describe the country so minutely that you should, where the objects were the most interesting, feel as if you had been with us. I shall now only attempt to give you an idea of those scenes which pleased us most, dropping the incidents of the ordinary days, of which many have slipped from my memory, and others which remain it would be difficult, and often painful to me, to endeavour to draw out and disentangle from other thoughts.'

The account which follows of their journey from Kenmore back to Grasmere, from 5 to 25 September, is mechanical and lacking in colour or emotion. The first entry is uncharacteristically terse: 'Sept 5th We arrived at Kenmore after Sunset.' Their return visit to the Trossachs, this time without Coleridge, is passed over: 'I can add nothing to my former description of the Trossachs, except that we departed with our old delightful remembrances endeared, and many new ones.' Among their new experiences was a visit to Sir Walter Scott and his wife which formed the basis of a lasting friendship. They heard occasional news of Coleridge, who, instead of going to Edinburgh and then home, had miraculously recovered his health and gone off on a 'wild journey' across the Highlands – walking 263 miles in eight days. He had even been 'taken up for a spy and clapped in Fort Augustus'.[20] Of the painful events, whose memories prevented Dorothy from writing up the final part of her journal for over a year, there is not a hint.

They returned to Grasmere on 25 September, having been away for six weeks. Dorothy had found the Scottish tour quite taxing. 'I was always tired when I reached the Inn at night and glad to put my Body in the state to receive all possible enjoyment of the few comforts a Scotch Inn affords. I was glad to lay my legs up and loll in indolence before the fire.'[21]

On 7 September while Coleridge was still away in Scotland and Sarah on her own at Greta Hall, the Southeys arrived. It was the first time Sarah had seen her sister Edith in two years, and the circumstances were extremely delicate – Edith's first child, Margaret, had died a few weeks earlier. Letters were despatched northwards to Coleridge somewhere in Scotland and word finally reached him at Perth. He wrote back to Southey straight away that he could not 'chit chat with Scotchmen while you are at Keswick childless' and set off south immediately.

Since their visit to the Coleridges at Stowey in 1800, Southey and Edith had both been in poor health – Edith in a deep depression 'worse than anything you can imagine', and Southey suffering from severe stress, 'disordering me now at the heart, now in the bowels, keeping me awake at night, and making me idle by day'.[22] He abandoned attempts to study law in London, a place they both hated, and took Edith off to Portugal to visit his uncle in the hope that the warmer climate would improve their health.

Edith had been much afraid of the journey and of living in a foreign country, but seems in the end to have been too depressed to care where she went. However, after a terrible voyage and near shipwreck, she found herself pleased with the small house the Rev. Hill had rented for them, and with her maid Maria Rosa – like no maid she had ever seen, 'dressed in straw-coloured gloves, fan, pink-ribands, muslin petticoat, green satin sleeves', and her hair powdered European fashion. The magic of Portugal in May, the sunshine and everything in blossom, soon began to have its effect.

In the middle of a lively group of expatriates, Edith began to regain her lost energies. There was always plenty to do in Lisbon. Edith was fascinated by the religious festivals, the riot of colour and music, but sickened by the bull fighting. A twenty-day excursion into the heart of the country with friends left her tanned and healthy-looking with a 'good squaw tint', and she happily endured nightly attacks of biting insects and rough accommodation. On one occasion Southey and his friend had to sleep on a bed of salted fish. Edith and her three female companions were, according to the men, entitled to 'an honourable place in the next martyrology. All Lisbon I believe thought us mad when we set out.'[23]

In 1801 they returned to England, after Spain declared war on

Portugal. They were reluctant to leave, despite homesickness for their families, and Southey wrote: 'I am afraid I shall pine away like a myrtle at a London window.'[24] Edith had made one good friend in Lisbon, a Miss Barker, nicknamed the Senhora, who eventually came to live beside them in Keswick.

After their return and a brief visit to the Coleridges in Keswick, Southey secured an appointment as secretary to the Chancellor of the Exchequer for Ireland, first in Dublin and then in London, and it was while in London that Edith again became ill. She was nursing Southey's dying mother and was so unwell herself that Southey felt she should not be alone. Her sister Mary Lovell was sent for to help care for Edith and old Mrs Southey, but in spite of this Edith continued in a wretched state. 'The worst part of her disease is a loathing of all remedies – her stomach rejects the diet which Carlisle recommends and half the medicines. Her spirits are beyond anything you can imagine bad.'[25] But this time it was not the 'usual affliction'. Edith had become pregnant for the first time.

They rented a house in Bristol where, unknown to Sarah Coleridge, Southey received letters from Coleridge urging him to come and live at Greta Hall, and informing him that the Coleridge marriage was, for all practical purposes, over. 'If our mutual unsuitableness continues, and (as it assuredly will do, if it continue) increases and strengthens – why then, it is better for her and my children that I should live apart.'[26] He urged the advantages of Greta Hall. 'If it suited you, you might have one kitchen, or (if Edith and Sara thought it would answer) we might have the two kitchens in common. You might have, I say, the whole ground floor, consisting of two sweet wing-rooms, commanding that loveliest view of Borrowdale . . . The highest room in the house is a very large one intended for two, but suffered to remain one by my desire. It would be a capital healthy nursery.'[27]

Coleridge's motives for inviting the Southeys to live at Greta Hall were not particularly altruistic. He was no longer close to Southey, though they were friends again, and he confessed that he could scarcely tolerate Edith's company at all. He found her boring and dreary and Mary Lovell only marginally more acceptable. Coleridge seems to have formulated the idea of inviting Southey in order to devolve responsibility for Sarah on to him so that he would be free to go and live with the Wordsworths. But one very great objection to the idea of a joint household was Sarah's aversion to the idea of living with her sister Mary who was now staying at the Southeys' lodgings with her son. The Lovell family were still refusing to contribute to their support and Southey had accepted responsibility for his sister-in-law and her child in his usual generous fashion. According to letters, her waspish disposition was the only 'canker in the bud' of the Southeys' domestic happiness. Sarah was adamant that she would not live with her. Coleridge urged Southey to be strong-minded and give Mary a small allowance in order to emancipate himself. He would then be free to come and live at Greta Hall.

Southey's one holiday in the Lakes had left him with memories of 'growling at clouds and Cumberland weather'. Edith was similarly unenthusiastic and the idea was dropped. Neither of them wished to become embroiled in the break-up of the Coleridge marriage. And in September, to the greatest possible joy, their first child, named Margaret Edith for Southey's recently deceased mother, was born. She was a healthy baby, 'grey-eyed, flat-nosed and strong as a young savage'. Edith too was well again, and managed to feed the child herself for six months before lapsing back into depression.

Eleven months later Margaret became ill, initially with teething problems and then a more serious fever with the complications of hydrocephalus – possibly meningitis. She died in the most terrible pain, leaving Edith and Robert Southey utterly devastated. It was impossible to rationalise what had happened to them. They had been given the one thing they had both longed for, had loved and doted on her for almost a year, only to have her taken away from them in such harrowing circumstances. All Southey could think of was to take Edith away from the house that had so many associations. He proposed a visit north to Greta Hall, where Sarah Coleridge had recently given birth to her own daughter.

Southey had misguided notions that seeing little Sara would somehow comfort Edith for her own loss. 'Edith will be nowhere so well as with her sister Coleridge. She has a little girl some six months old, and I shall try and graft her into the wound while it is yet fresh.' He failed to anticipate the anguish the sight of Sarah glowing with maternity would cause the newly bereaved Edith, or himself, confessing that 'I feel more pain at the sight of little Sara than I had apprehended . . . Her age, her little voice sting me to recollections that I must blunt and wear out, for they are not avoidable.'[28] There was also pain at the comparison between the blooming Sarah and her sickly sister. Sarah, despite her domestic difficulties, was, Southey reported, 'in high health. Every time I see her she seems improved.'

They arrived at Greta Hall on 7 September 1803, little realising that they had come to stay. Southey was surprised and moved by the scenery, which was not at all what he had remembered. From the library window he saw 'such shiftings of shades, such islands of light, such columns and buttresses of sunshine, as might almost make a painter burn his brushes, as the sorcerers did their books of magic.'[29]

Their social life was briefly enlivened by Hazlitt, who was staying at Greta Hall ostensibly to paint a portrait of Coleridge. His behaviour with the servants (he was apparently addicted to women 'as objects of sexual Indulgence') had already upset Sarah, and within a couple of months of Southey's arrival he was forced to leave in order to avoid 'being ducked by a mob, and probably sent to prison for some gross attacks on women,' who had 'refused to gratify his abominable and devilish propensities.'[30] Hazlitt's sexual tastes seem to have been towards the sado-masochistic, since one of the things he was rumoured to have done was to have spanked a local girl. Coleridge and Southey hid him while a local group of about two hundred vigilantes on horseback searched the countryside. He escaped under cover of darkness, making his way back to his father's house near Shrewsbury.

Mary Lovell also arrived with her young son – now about eight years old. Attempts to find her a position as a governess had come to nothing. The fact that she had been an actress was a great drawback, but her personality appears to have been the biggest obstacle. 'If she could derive from the thought, that by her own exertions she was about to make herself independent, [and exhibit] pleasure & a lightness & joyousness of Heart', Coleridge felt sure she would find a suitable position. But her pride and 'a Predetermination to be offended' stood in the way.[31] Though she was a relatively young woman, opportunities to meet eligible men were few, and it seemed unlikely that Mary would ever remarry. Coleridge and Southey were convinced that if she had only had 'Spirits & a contented mind with activity' she could have married again, so there may well have been a suitor in the offing at the time of their removal to Keswick. But as she remained widowed and dependent she was reluctantly accommodated by the family at Greta Hall, much against Sarah's will. It was a family joke that the house had become the 'Aunt Hill', because of the number of aunts living there.

It was an unusually cold autumn. The first winter ice appeared on the lake early and Southey and Coleridge, remembering simple childhood occupations, went to throw stones, making the ice hum 'like singing birds'. The magic of the landscape was beginning to enthral Southey, and when Edith, bolstered up by Sarah's practical good spirits, became pregnant again, it seemed like a miracle. So, when Coleridge talked of going abroad for his health, Southey agreed to remain at Greta Hall in his absence. Sarah was to have a share of the Wedgwood annuity to meet her portion of the household expenses, but the rent and other liabilities were to be borne by Southey. They cancelled the tenancy of their house in Bristol and Edith ordered her household goods to be crated and stored.

Shortly after the Wordsworths' return from Scotland at the end of September, Sara Hutchinson arrived at Dove Cottage, mysteriously ill and in what Dorothy described as a 'very bad hysterical way'. Her brother had been given notice to leave the farm at Gallow Hill, which upset her, and she seems to have been agitated to breaking point by Coleridge's letters, by his declarations of passion, and by the burden of her own feelings for him – feelings that are never at any time acknowledged publicly in any surviving letter. It was Coleridge who recorded her admissions of affection and caresses in his notebooks and poems, and Dorothy who observed again and again how Coleridge disturbed Sara's mind. What Sara actually felt, or what she hoped for, posterity will never know, since whatever letters there were to Coleridge, or to the Wordsworths on the subject, were consigned to an editorial holocaust after Coleridge's death.

Sara would have liked to have been married, and it is probable that if Coleridge had been free she would have married him. As a single woman and technically her 'own mistress', Sara felt often at the beck and call of other members of the family, sent for by brothers and sisters needing support and sympathy and domestic help in a crisis. 'I am often forced to submit to the bondage of prudence & circumstance.'[32] Still, she was clear-sighted enough to see the advantages of her situation: 'Old Maid as I am, don't think that, though I firmly believe that the balance of *comfort* is on our side, I am a favorer of a single life – *comfort* is but a meagre thing after all – but I have seen such misery in the marriage life as would *appal* you if you had seen it. Such millstones about the necks of worthy men! . . . Of course you will not suppose that I think all the fault belongs to the women.'[33]

Throughout the autumn of 1803, Coleridge's physical state was dreadful. His days were 'Storm . . . a dead Sleep after Dinner' and his nights were interminable: 'the horrors of my sleep and night screams (so loud and so frequent as to make me almost a nuisance in my own house) seemed to carry beyond mere body, counterfeiting as it were the tortures of guilt, and what we are told of the punishment of a spiritual world.'[34] Coleridge's tortured screaming brought Sarah running, candle in hand, woke his children and disturbed the Southeys. He confessed to Thomas Poole that one of his most frequent nightmares concerned experiences of sexual abuse at boarding school, and that, in the guilty dreams of 'shame and terror', it was impossible to tell whether he was the sufferer or the perpetrator. He decided that his only hope was to leave England for a warmer climate. Not even the prospect of Sara Hutchinson's close proximity at Park House Farm near Ullswater (which her brother had just leased) was sufficient to keep him in Cumberland. Although he gave the Wordsworths the impression that his departure was the long-urged separation from his wife, with characteristic ambivalence he allowed Sarah to believe that this was merely a temporary expediency dictated by his health. He was, typically, keeping all his options open.

On 20 December, after affectionate farewells with Sarah and the Southeys at Greta Hall, he set off for London, having insured his life for £1000, intending to sail for Malta. He broke his journey at Dove Cottage overnight where he had arranged to leave Derwent, but became so ill that he stayed on for three weeks, nursed by Dorothy, Mary and Sara. From London he sent Sara a copy of the 1658 edition of Sir Thomas Browne's *Pseudodoxia Epidemica*, writing a letter on the flyleaves of the book which ends with a poignant echo of the closing lines of the poem 'A Letter to Asra'. She responded with a letter telling him that she wanted the relationship to end.

Coleridge could not accept her decision and was unable to get her out of his mind. 'I talk loud or eager . . . or I laugh, jest, tell tales of Mirth/ & ever as it were within & behind I think, & image *you*/and while I am talking of Government or War, or chemistry, there comes ever into my bodily eye some Tree, beneath which we have rested, some rock where we have stood on the projecting road edging *high* above the Crummock Lake/where we sate beneath the rock, & those dear Lips pressed my forehead – or that Scale Force in its pride as we saw it when they laughed at us for two Lovers.'[35] At other times he fantasised that she would marry John Wordsworth.

Dorothy and Mary sat up late at night, transcribing Wordsworth's poems – more than eight thousand lines – for Coleridge to take abroad with him. For Dorothy it was a labour of love: 'Thinking of his banishment, his loneliness, the long distance he will be from all the human beings that he loves, it is one of my greatest consolations that he has those poems with him.'[36] He sailed for Malta in April 1804.

Nine months after the Southeys' arrival at Greta Hall, Edith gave birth to 'an Edithling very, very ugly, with no more beauty than a young dodo'.[37] They were both afraid that she, like Margaret, would die – 'she is too clever to live . . . I do not in my heart expect to rear her . . .'[38] Southey wrote sadly. But Edith May grew quickly into a pretty little girl with golden hair and rosy cheeks. She was very like her father, slim and elegant, and by the time she was twenty would be christened 'the Cygnet of the Derwent' by Amelia Opie. Southey was very much the proud father, thinking Edith May more good-looking and more intelligent than Coleridge's children. 'It is my belief . . . that if a child does not look quicker than other children at six months there will never be any manifest natural superiority.'[39] Hartley's poetic gifts and Sara's intellectual and literary precocity were to prove his theory wrong.

Mary Wordsworth was also expecting another child and had to wean John early because she was unwell. This was accomplished by handing him over to Dorothy who kept him out of her sight until he was completely 'reconciled to his Loss'. Friends and family were concerned that Dorothy's obsession with John had begun to grow beyond the bounds of reasonable behaviour. He was, she wrote lyrically, 'beyond measure glorious' in countenance and temper.[40] Sitting quietly minding him in the next room inspired her to write two more poems, 'Irregular Verses Addressed to a Child' and 'The Cottager to her Infant'.

> The days are cold, the nights are long,
> The north-wind sings a doleful song;
> Then hush again upon my breast;
> All merry things are now at rest,
>     Save thee, my pretty Love! . . .
>
> Nay! start not at that sparkling light;
> 'Tis but the moon that shines so bright
> On the window pane bedropped with rain
> Then little Darling! sleep again,
>     And wake when it is day.

All the love that had been focused on William was now poured out towards his son. When Mary took the little boy on a visit to Sara, now living at Park House near Ullswater, Dorothy complained that she was 'very lonely – at home without John – home without him will seem more lonely than it could possibly have been before his birth.' She was comforted by the news that while Mary had been away 'he was never happy with her and never felt himself safe but in my arms'.[41] Mary never complained at having her place in her son's affections usurped, but she must have been glad to have the opportunity to be on her own with her baby. Despite her dislike of being parted from William, she stayed away for a month.

Mary's second child arrived three weeks early, while Sarah Coleridge and her children were staying at Dove Cottage on a short visit. This time it was a daughter and William insisted that she be called Dorothy, despite protests from both his sister and Sarah Coleridge that it was an outmoded name only suitable for servants. To distinguish her from her aunt, little Dorothy was always known in the family as Doro or Dora. Initially, Dorothy was not very interested in the new baby – no one could take the place of her darling John. 'She is a nice Baby, healthy enough – stout enough – pretty enough; but in nothing *extraordinary*, as John certainly was at his birth.'[42] Later she felt guilty about her lack of feeling and did her best to 'make all up' but it was a long time before she became fond of the little girl and she was always partisan – 'it must be allowed that John is the finer creature'.[43] There may, perhaps, have been an element of jealousy, since Dora was William's favourite. He doted on her, declaring her 'the most engaging child that ever was born', and believed that she would grow up to be a beauty. Dorothy agreed grudgingly that she was 'pretty enough', but found it incredible that everybody but herself could see 'something remarkable in her'. Dora was also Coleridge's favourite after his return from Malta – his beautiful 'Cat of the Mountain', all fire and claws.

Immediately after Dora's birth, Dorothy and William went off on a walking tour, this time in the Lake District and only for a week. It was a pattern they were to repeat in the autumn of the following year. Extracts from Dorothy's 'Journal of a Mountain Ramble' were eventually published by William as part of his *Description of the Scenery of the Lakes*. They left Grasmere 'on a damp and gloomy morning . . . William on foot, and I upon the pony, with William's greatcoat slung over the saddle crutch, and a wallet containing our bundle of "needments". As we went along the mist gathered upon the valleys, and it even rained all the way to the head of Patterdale; but there was never a drop upon my habit larger than the smallest pearls upon a lady's ring.'[44] They climbed from Patterdale to Martindale and then across to Lowther and Yanwath. 'We left our horses at the mill below Brougham, and walked through the woods till we came to the quarry, where the road ends – the very place which has been the boundary of some of the happiest of the walks of my youth . . . so vividly did I call to mind those walks, that, when I was in the wood, I almost seemed to see the same rich light of evening upon the trees which I had seen in those happy hours.'[45]

Back at Dove Cottage, Dorothy and Mary lamented that they should be so 'directly in the highway of the Tourists'. During the summer they were inundated with visitors. Dorothy lamented that there was no time for walking, gardening or reading. William complained about the lack of space and the noise of the children and, like Coleridge at Nether Stowey, found himself unable to work. William, helped by Dorothy, began to build the 'Moss Hut', described by her as 'a sort of larger Bird's nest (for it is lined with moss) at the top of our Orchard, a place for my Brother to retire to for quietness on warm days in winter and for a pleasure-house, a little parlour for all of us in the summer . . .'[46]

They were already looking around for new accommodation, but postponed making any decisions until Coleridge returned. They had made up their minds that wherever Coleridge settled, they would go with him. Dorothy and William were very distressed at not hearing from him after his departure. 'We hear often from Mrs Coleridge. She is in very good health but does not know what to think of the non-arrival of letters and is very anxious.'[47] Coleridge, his where-abouts and his health, occupied Dorothy's mind continually. She wrote to Lady Beaumont, the wife of William's patron, Lord George Beaumont, of Coleridge's high opinion of herself and her literary talents and how it troubled her. She wondered 'if I am in any degree worthy of the great affection which Coleridge feels for me; but when

I think how great his regard for me is, knowing that all you know of me is from him, I really . . . am almost afraid of it, you will find me so different from what you have imagined, and (believe me) so much inferior. I have not those powers which Coleridge thinks I have . . .'[48] Lady Beaumont eventually became one of Dorothy's most intimate correspondents. In response to her request that Dorothy write more for others beyond their immediate circle, Dorothy shared thoughts on her own creativity, something she rarely discussed. 'Do not think that I was ever bold enough to hope to compose verses for the pleasure of grown persons. Descriptions, Sentiments, or little stories for children was all I could be ambitious of doing, and I did try one story, but failed so sadly that I was completely discouraged. Believe me, since I received your letter I have made several attempts . . . and have been obliged to give it up in despair . . . but I have no command of language, no power of expressing my ideas, and no one was ever more inapt at molding words into regular metre. I have often tried when I have been walking alone (muttering to myself as in my Brother's custom) to express my feelings in verse; feelings, and *ideas* such as they were, I have never wanted at those times; but prose and rhyme and blank verse were jumbled together and nothing ever came of it.'[49] Dorothy's friends often pressed her to publish her work, but she always refused.

The Wordsworths were horrified that a Liverpool merchant had bought a plot of land at a prime location in the valley and was building a large white house on it, a 'temple of abomination', which they thought 'will stare you in the face from every part of the Vale and entirely destroy its character of simplicity and seclusion'.[50] It was, Dorothy added, 'a publick sorrow'. Ironically, they were to be the first tenants of Allan Bank, as the new house was called.

Sarah Coleridge was also encountering accommodation problems at Greta Hall. Mr Jackson had decided to sell Greta Hall to a 'worthless Fellow who brought his wife with him and a *Mistress* in Boy's Clothes'. She was told that they would have to be out of the house by Whitsun. In the end the sale fell through and, after Jackson's death, Southey was able to take a lease on his half of the house and the three families had more space to expand. It wasn't easy sharing a house with so many people and although at first it was Sarah who ordered the servants and the domestic arrangements, gradually her younger sister Edith took control with quiet imperiousness and Sarah became effectively a lodger in her own house. This was very hard for someone of her temperament to endure. Even her bedroom was given up to the Southeys, and she slept in a small wing room which she eventually shared with her daughter.

Sarah took the opportunity to go away on visits to friends, staying first in Liverpool and then, surprisingly, with Sara Hutchinson at Park House. While she was away, Edith arrived at Dove Cottage in a chaise and invited Dorothy to Greta Hall. She allowed herself to be persuaded and five minutes later was bowling off down the road to Keswick. Dorothy stayed for four days and confessed with surprise that she had thoroughly enjoyed herself, something she would not have been able to do if Sarah Coleridge had been there. Dorothy's antipathy to Sarah was now such that she avoided her company wherever possible. Edith, though 'not a person of very warm feelings', could at least be tolerated for a much-needed change of scene.

Southey was away on a visit to Scotland. He was considering a return to Lisbon to write a history of Portugal, but Edith refused to go with him because of the risks to her precious baby, now a year old. Southey regretfully accepted her decision and contemplated going without her. He wrote from Scotland: 'I need not tell you, my own dear Edith, not to read my letters aloud till you have first of all seen what is written only for yourself. What I have now to say to you is, that having been eight days from home, with as little discomfort, and as little reason for discomfort, as a man can reasonably expect, I have yet felt so little comfortable, so great a sense of solitariness and so many homeward yearnings, that certainly I will not go to Lisbon without you; a resolution which, if your feelings be at all like mine, will not displease you. If, on mature consideration, you think the inconvenience of a voyage more than you ought to submit to, I must be content to stay in England, as on my part it certainly is not worth while to sacrifice a year's happiness . . . without you I am not happy. But for your sake as well as my own, and for little Edith's sake I will not consent to any separation; the growth of a year's love between her and me, if it please God that she should live, is a thing too delightful in itself, and too valuable in its consequences, both to her and me, to be given up for any light inconvenience either on your part or mine. An absence of a year would make her effectually forget me . . . of these things we will talk at leisure; only dear, dear Edith, we must not part.'[51]

His devotion to Edith did not prevent him from thinking about what might have been. Her constant depression and tendency to lapse into a 'poor and pitiable and pill-taking way' put considerable strain on their relationship and Southey was constantly faced with the difference between his sickly wife and his robust and radiantly healthy sister-in-law, Sarah Coleridge. More striking a contrast could scarcely be imagined than between Edith, whose personality Hartley Coleridge compared to 'a day never bright, even when the sun shone most serenely upon it. Never knew I a being in whom a pure and benevolent spirit was so little joyous; a morbid sensitiveness to pain and an almost apathy to pleasure . . .',[52] and her easy-going, fun-loving sister Sarah, noted for her 'dancing, frisking high spirits'.

In February 1805 Sara Hutchinson arrived at Dove Cottage unexpectedly with an urgent letter she had intercepted at Kendal. As Mary and William were out for a walk, Dorothy opened it. The letter contained news of the sinking of John Wordsworth's ship, the *Earl of Abergavenny*, off Portland Bill. It had been a cold February night and the sea very rough, and although the ship had foundered within a short distance of the land very few were saved. John had been last seen clinging to the rigging as the ship went down. It was some weeks before his body was washed ashore.

The shock made Dorothy very ill, and Mary too was deeply affected, remembering her first visit to Dove Cottage when John had walked out with her and shown her his favourite places. William insisted that *his* was the greatest loss, wrote Mary, 'because he says it is only our pleasures and our joys that are broken in upon – but [this] loss of John is deeply connected with *business*'.[53] William had given him some of their inheritance, newly recovered from Lord Lonsdale, as venture capital for the trip. Finding little solace among the women, he wrote immediately to Southey: 'If you could bear to come to this house of mourning tomorrow, I should be forever thankful . . .'[54] Southey stayed for two days and his tact and sympathy caused Dorothy to revise her original opinion of him. Initially put off by his cool exterior, she now declared that she would 'always love him'.[55] Dorothy took up her abandoned Scottish journal again and resumed copying it as a tribute to her dead brother. 'I had written it for the sake of Friends who could not be with us at the time, and my Brother John had been always in my thoughts, for we wished him to know everything that befel us.'[56] She found the mechanical business of copying 'a tranquilising employment'. She worried even more about Coleridge and had nightmares every time there was a storm. 'I am too often haunted with dreadful images of Shipwrecks and the Sea when I am in bed and hear a stormy wind . . . Heaven grant that Coleridge may be somewhere or other safe on Land!'[57]

Christmas Day 1805 was Dorothy's thirty-fourth birthday and brought its usual ambivalent feelings: 'in my inner heart it is never a day of jollity'.[58] On this occasion she wrote to her friend Mrs Clarkson in retrospective mood. 'Six Christmases have we spent at Grasmere, and though the freshness of life was passed away even when we came hither, I think these years have been the very happiest of my life, – at least, they seem as if they would bear looking back upon better than any other.'[59] When the Grasmere fiddler called on his seasonal rounds, she celebrated by dancing in the kitchen with little John until she was completely out of breath.

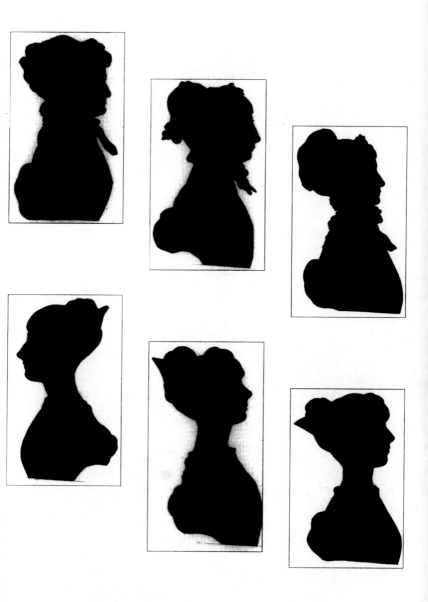

Sara Hutchinson, Dorothy Wordsworth, Mary Wordsworth, Kate Southey,
Edith May Southey, Bertha Southey. Silhouettes *circa* 1815.

The Coleridges' cottage at Nether Stowey and Alfoxden Park
where the Wordsworths lived nearby.

Sarah Coleridge in her thirties and Samuel Taylor Coleridge
as he was when she met him.

Edith Southey, aged 35,
and Robert Southey in his study at Greta Hall.

Dorothy Wordsworth as a young woman: a keepsake portrait
that she later gave to her niece Dora.

William Wordsworth at around the same time.

Dove Cottage and Rydal Mount, both from Dora Wordsworth's sketchbook.

# GRETA HALL

**SECOND FLOOR PLAN**

MAID'S ROOM
?

A SORT OF LUMBER ROOM

APPLE ROOM
INHABITED BY A BOGLE

STAIR ONCE LEADING OUT TO FLAT ROOF

NURSERY
? COTTONIAN LIBRARY

NURSERY BEDROOM
? LATER CUTHBERT'S

KATE'S AND ISOBEL'S ROOM

**FIRST FLOOR PLAN**

SPARE BEDROOM LATER EXTENDED AS BATHROOM

JACKSON'S BEDROOM LATER HARTLEY AND DERWENT

AUNT LOVELL'S BEDROOM
SHARED SOMETIMES BY ELIZA FRICKER

MR. AND MRS. SOUTHEY'S BEDROOM
HERE SOUTHEY DIED

MRS. COLERIDGE'S AND SARA'S ROOM

? GUEST ROOM LATER EDITH AND BERTHA

Duck Row

COLERIDGE'S STUDY
THE ORGAN ROOM
? USED BY JACKSON IN COLERIDGE'S ABSENCE
LATER THE SAINTS ROOM TILL 1838

SOUTHEY'S STUDY
"PETER"
? ONCE THE COLERIDGE BEDROOM

**GROUND FLOOR FLOOR PLAN**

WASH HOUSE

JACKSON'S PART OF THE HOUSE

MRS. WILSON'S BACK KITCHEN

MRS. WILSON'S KITCHEN

KITCHEN

MANGLE OR CLOG ROOM

MRS. WILSON'S BEDROOM TILL 1830
ENTRANCE HALL AFTER 1830

AUNT LOVELL'S ROOM

HARTLEY'S PARLOUR
JACKSON'S SITTING-ROOM

SOUTHEY'S PARLOUR
DINING ROOM AND GENERAL SITTING-ROOM
'PAUL' AFTER 1828 ALSO THE SAINTS PARLOUR

Greta Hall, floor plan, as described in Sarah Coleridge's memoir.

Greta Hall, as it was when the Coleridges first saw it.

The Rock of Names inscribed
(from the top) by William
Wordsworth, Mary Hutchinson,
Dorothy Wordsworth,
S.T. Coleridge, John Wordsworth
and Sara Hutchinson – but not
Sarah Coleridge.

Cousins: Sara Coleridge (left) and Edith May Southey.

Dora Wordsworth (the third of the Triad) as
bridesmaid to Sara Coleridge.

Edward Quillinan – the only known portrait.

Mary and William Wordsworth in old age.

Dorothy Wordsworth after the onset of her illness. At this time
she could no longer really write in the journal they had put on her knee.

The final entries in Dorothy Wordsworth's last
journal. Among the disconnected words can be
made out 'Torments . . . dysmal doom . . . no iron
hinges', tragic indicators of her agony of mind.

Sara Coleridge as a widow.
Her daughter used this as the frontispiece to her mother's memoir

Dora Wordsworth at the time of her engagement.
The portrait hangs in her bedroom at Rydal Mount.

# 7

## *Prejudice and Prepossession*

> *Never describe Wordsworth as equal in pride*
> *to Lucifer, no; but, if you have occasion to write*
> *a life of Lucifer, set down that by possibility,*
> *in respect to pride, he might be some type of Wordsworth.*
>
> De Quincey, Recollections

After a year's silence, a letter suddenly arrived at Greta Hall from Coleridge, declaring his intention to return to England the following month – March 1805. Characteristically he didn't arrive on English soil until 17 August 1806. It was the time of the Peninsular wars, when all ships had to travel in convoy for their protection, and the Wordsworths and Sarah Coleridge at times feared that he had been shipwrecked or captured by the French. In fact, after spending some months in Rome and a much-delayed departure, he had endured 'fifty five days of shipboard, working up against head-winds, rotting and sweating in calms or running under hard gales with the dead lights secured . . . 55 days of literal horror almost daily expecting and wishing to die.'[1] He lingered in London 'ill, penniless, and dismally irresolute' and it was another two and a half months before he came north.

The Wordsworths and Sara Hutchinson had been invited to spend the winter at the Beaumonts' country home at Coleorton in Leicestershire, rather than endure the cold and cramped conditions at Dove Cottage. Dorothy complained that 'every bed lodges two persons' and there was now another baby to be accommodated, Thomas, born in June 1806. They set off at the end of

October, having despaired of seeing Coleridge, just as he arrived in Penrith intending to see Sara Hutchinson who had been visiting her relatives there before joining the Wordsworths. Dorothy's letter records the confusion that ensued: '. . . judge of our distress at being obliged to set off without having seen him; but when we got to Kendal we heard from Sara Hutchinson that she had just received a letter from him from Penrith, written immediately on his arrival there, ie little more than half an hour after her departure from P[enrith] to meet us at K[endal]. He said he *could* not come to Kendal, just to see us, and then to part. Notwithstanding this, however, we resolved to see him and wait one day at Kendal for that purpose: accordingly we sent off a special messenger to Keswick to desire him to come over to us; but before seven o'clock that evening he himself arrived at an inn, and sent for William. We all went thither to him and never never did I feel such a shock as at first sight of him. We all felt exactly in the same way – as if he were different from what we have expected to see . . . He is utterly changed; and yet sometimes, when he was animated in conversation concerning things removed from him, I saw something of his former self.'[2] He was swollen and bloated by the amount of laudanum he had taken while in Malta, hardly caring whether he lived or died. He told the Wordsworths that he had resolved to part from Sarah Coleridge and agreed to come and stay with them at Coleorton as soon as it could be arranged. Coleridge then, somewhat reluctantly, went home to Keswick to see his wife for the first time in two and a half years.

Sarah had been overjoyed to hear of her husband's safe return, writing to Mrs George Coleridge: 'I have no doubt but we shall be enabled to live comfortably and bring up the dear children in credit.'[3] She was totally ignorant of the fact that he had told everyone in London that the prospect of 'domesticating' with his wife again was so abhorrent he would rather die. He declared that he could not even face writing to her and begged Mary Lamb to write on his behalf asking for a separation. Mary wrote to Dorothy: 'I think of the letter I received from Mrs Coleridge, telling me, as joyful news, that her husband is arrived, and I feel it very wrong in me even in the remotest degree to do anything to prevent her seeing her husband.'[4] Coleridge's duplicity is revealed by his letters to Sarah throughout September and October, promising to come to Keswick as soon as possible, full of excuses as to why he has not already arrived, addressing her in affectionate terms as his 'dear love' and signing himself 'your faithful, tho' long absent, Husband'.

When he finally arrived in Keswick Sarah was as shocked by his physical condition as the Wordsworths had been. She was also adamant that she was not going to agree to a divorce or legal separation. For a woman in the eighteenth and nineteenth centuries, divorce meant social ruin. The only legitimate grounds for putting aside a wife were adultery and promiscuous behaviour. Separations, even between members of the aristocracy, usually conferred some sort of blame on the woman. Sarah had already endured a share of notoriety for her 'liberated' conduct with Coleridge before her marriage and had then been 'talked about' in Stowey, suspected of being his mistress rather than his wife. Now, after a long absence, her husband was threatening to leave her, publicly, an action which could, and would, be misconstrued by every gossiping tongue from Keswick to London. The injustice of the situation was more than she could take. Coleridge unfairly accused her of 'a mere selfish desire to have a *rank* in life',[5] her only objection being 'that it would not look *respectable* for her',[6] because she wished the world to believe her a virtuous wife.

Eventually it was agreed that they would live apart as friends, that he would visit occasionally, that Hartley and Derwent would live mainly with him 'but . . . visit their Mother as they would do if at a publick school' and that Sara would remain with her mother. Coleridge wrote to Wordsworth that he had discussed the separation with Sarah and that they had '*determined* to part absolutely and finally . . .'[7] Sarah was under the impression that she had avoided the dreaded separation and that things would go on much as they had done for most of her married life. There is evidence that she still retained a faint hope that if he could be cured of his 'habit' their relationship could still be rescued.

It was clear that, for Sarah's sake, a public announcement of the Coleridges' separation had to be avoided. The Wordsworths, however, lamented 'the weakness which has prevented him from putting it out of her power to torment him any more'. If he did not make a public statement of the facts, people would believe that he had deserted her. Dorothy, in her loyalty to Coleridge and her firm belief in Sarah's utter unsuitability to be his wife, took upon herself the task of informing the world that their marriage was at an end. 'Mr Coleridge and his wife are separated, and I hope they will both be the happier for it . . .'[8]

Southey thought that the separation was a good thing. 'His habits are so murderous of all domestic comfort that I am only surprised Mrs C is not rejoiced at being rid of him. He besots himself with opium, or with spirits, till his eyes look like a Turks who is half reduced to idiotcy by the practise – he calls up the servants at all hours of the night to prepare food for him – he does in short all things at all times except the proper time – does nothing which he ought to do, and everything which he ought not.' Southey blamed the Wordsworths that the separation should ever have been necessary: '. . . it is from his idolatry of that family that this has begun – they have always humoured him in all his follies, listened to his complaints of his wife, and when he has complained of his itch, helped him to scratch, instead of covering him with brimstone ointment, and shutting him up by himself.'[9]

There was talk for a while of the Wordsworths coming to live at Greta Hall. Coleridge had assumed that the Southeys would now move back to Bristol and that Sarah would go with them. She had no intention of doing so, but would not have shared a house with the Wordsworths under any circumstances. Greta Hall did have the space the Wordsworths needed, although neither Dorothy nor Mary liked the house or the idea of 'taking Mrs C's place there'. When Southey heard of the proposal he immediately decided to make Greta Hall his own permanent house. He wasn't going to stand by and see Sarah turned out of her house. He wrote to a friend: 'If I had not remained here C. has so little regard to common decency of appearances that he would have brought the Wordsworths here, and his wife must have removed.'[10]

On 21 December Coleridge arrived to join the Wordsworths at Coleorton accompanied by Hartley. At first there was general joy at being together again under one roof, before the inevitable renewal of friction. All Coleridge's passion for Sara Hutchinson was revived by proximity, this time magnified by the fantasies generated during eighteen months' separation. He wrote in his notebook: 'I know, you love me! – My reason knows it; my heart feels it/yet still let your eyes, your hands tell me/still say, o often & often say, "My beloved! I love you"/indeed I love you/for why should not my ears, and all my outward Being share in the joy – the fuller my inner Being is of the sense, the more my outward Organs yearn & crave for it – O bring my whole nature into balance and harmony.'[11]

Dorothy and William were alarmed by the intensity of his passion, fearing for Sara's reputation. There was disapproval on their side, jealousy on Coleridge's and eventually there was a scene, probably sometime in January. The 'vision of that Saturday morning' haunted Coleridge for months. His notebooks are full of confused and agonising ramblings in which he imagines William beloved and adored by Mary, Dorothy and Sara, while he is only 'a Satellite'. Sara, he had begun to suspect, loved William and not himself. He pleaded repeatedly: 'I alone love you so devotedly, & therefore Sara! . . . love me! love me.'[12]

Coleridge arranged to meet Sarah and the children in Bristol, prior to a visit to his family in Ottery. Once there, he planned to break the news of his informal separation to them. Sarah would have been ostracised by the Coleridge family as a divorced woman, so she begged Coleridge not to talk in those terms, but to tell them simply that he would be working in London while Sarah remained at Greta Hall. But Coleridge, offered a schoolmaster's post by his brother George, wrote a letter without telling Sarah, in which he unfortunately revealed the current state of his relationship with his wife; they were to separate, to 'part as Friends' without a 'shadow of suspicion' on Sarah's character. While they stayed at Nether Stowey with Thomas Poole, George sent Coleridge a letter regretting that they could not be received and giving a long list of excuses. Sarah, puzzled and hurt, was given only the vaguest idea by her husband why they would not be visiting his family – a holiday she had long looked forward to. She told her sister Mary that although she longed to know the contents of the letter, she would not stoop to take it from his desk.

From Thomas Poole's they went to stay with friends at Bridgwater and there for the first time, Thomas De Quincey came into their lives. He was a young poet and an ardent admirer of Wordsworth's and Coleridge's poetry. He had given Coleridge an anonymous present of £300 on hearing that he was in need, and had also written letters to Wordsworth praising *Lyrical Ballads*. In return he had received gracious invitations to visit Dove Cottage which he had not had the courage to accept. Finding out that Coleridge was in Somerset, he gained directions from Thomas Poole and finally arrived on the doorstep and was introduced to one of the men he had idolised for so long.

He was invited to stay to dinner by Coleridge; as they sat in the drawing-room, the door opened and Sarah came in. Coleridge's reaction, in turning from animation to gloom, told De Quincey everything. 'Coleridge turned, upon her entrance: his features, however, announced no particular complacency, and did not relax into a smile. In a frigid tone he said, whilst turning to me, "Mrs Coleridge;" in some slight way he then presented me to her: I bowed; and the lady almost immediately retired.'[13] De Quincey offered to escort Sarah back to Greta Hall. This would give her the benefit of travelling comfortably in a post-chaise, and it would give De Quincey the opportunity to meet William Wordsworth. So in the autumn of 1807, De Quincey arrived at Grasmere to become another addition to what he referred to as 'the Lake colony'.

Sara Hutchinson called him 'Quince' but her younger sister Joanna thought him juvenile, rather helpless and 'dissipid'. Sara was more impressed: 'he is a good tempered amiable creature & uncommonly clever & an excellent scholar – but he is very shy and so reverences Wm & C. that he chats very little but is content to listen – he looks only like 18'.[14] Coleridge didn't share her favourable views, commenting on the 'natural tediousness' of a mind 'confused from over-accuracy and at once systematic and labyrinthine . . .' De Quincey had an amazingly retentive memory that could recall huge sections of *The Prelude* thirty years after he had read it, and he was a natural gossip with a fascination for the inconsistencies and subtleties of human relationships.

When De Quincey arrived at Dove Cottage in 1807 he found Dorothy in a very delicate nervous condition. Her eyes, he wrote, 'were wild and startling, and hurried in their motion. Her manner was warm and even ardent; her sensibility seemed constitutionally deep; and some subtle fire of impassioned intellect apparently burned within her, which, being alternately pushed forward into a conspicuous expression by the irrepressible instincts of her temperament, and then immediately checked, in obedience to the decorum of her sex and age . . . gave to her whole demeanour and to her conversation, an air of embarrassment and even of self-conflict, that was sometimes distressing to witness . . . Even her very utterance and enunciation often, or rather generally, suffered in point of clearness and steadiness, from the agitation of her excessive organic sensibility, and perhaps, from some morbid irritability of the nerves . . . caused her even to stammer . . . as distressingly as Charles Lamb himself.'[15]

It is hardly surprising that she found living with William and Mary, so profoundly happy with one another, and with Mary's fecundity, very difficult. Mary's visits to Dove Cottage for months on end as a friend were very different to her permanent presence there as William's wife. As Mary herself wrote to William, 'the blessed bond that binds husband & wife so much closer than the bond of Brotherhood' was superior to that of siblings 'however dear & affectionate a family of Brothers & Sisters may love each other'.[16] With Mary there as William's wife, the balance of power had changed. From being mistress of the house, Dorothy had gradually been sidelined into her previous position at Forncett – that of indispensable helper, nursemaid and nanny. From being the person first in her brother's affections she was now well down the list below his wife and children. Certainly Dorothy's health had deteriorated. Visiting relatives the previous summer had commented that she had 'grown so thin and old that they shou'd not have known her – lost many of her teeth and her cheeks quite sunk that it has entirely alter'd her profile'.[17] The episodes of migrainous headache and of gastric disturbance had increased – as did her intake of laudanum to cope with them. It is something rarely alluded to by the Wordsworth family. Opium is physically addictive: after a while it alters the body's chemistry so that the victim's physiology actually needs opium in order to function – addicts become ill if they try to do without it and are caught in a vicious cycle of sickness and depression.

Dorothy had begun taking laudanum to cope with her severe toothache, then to alleviate her episodes of sick headache and gastric seizure, occasionally recorded in her journal – 'ill in the afternoon, took laudanum'[18] – or her letters – 'took laudanum . . . lay in bed all day'.[19] Her symptoms of stomach cramp, lethargy and bowel disorder are so like Coleridge's opium-induced miseries it is tempting to suggest that they were caused by laudanum rather than a separate pre-condition which necessitated the intake of the drug. It was a long time before the sad facts became apparent to the family. Only once does Mary make a reference to Dorothy's 'problem' in terminology reminiscent of Dorothy's letters about Coleridge: 'She is now, thank God, perfectly well, quite strong – and if she can be prevailed upon to abide by the plan of *abstinence* from several things, which will be hard for her to do, I trust we shall keep her so.'[20]

Dorothy was not alone in becoming addicted to the drug, the only available remedy in pre-aspirin days for pain of any kind. It was even given to babies by wet-nurses to keep them quiet. Apart from Coleridge and De Quincey, Elizabeth Barrett Browning was dependent on it all her life in varying quantities, as were Elizabeth Siddall, Dante Gabriel Rossetti and many others including Dorothy's much-admired friend William Wilberforce. It wrecked their health and in some cases contributed to their early deaths.

In June 1808 the Wordsworths moved to Allan Bank, the very house they had inveighed against so bitterly. They now had the space they needed for the growing family – Mary was expecting another child in September. Dorothy was worrying about money, and wrote to William, who had gone to London to see Coleridge and was obdurately refusing to publish his poem 'The White Doe of Rylstone', fearing brutal reviews. 'We are exceedingly concerned, to hear that you, William! have given up all thoughts of publishing your Poem. As to the Outcry against you, I would defy it – what matter, if you get your 100 guineas into your pocket? . . . without money what *can* we do? New House! new furniture! such a large family! two servants and little Sally! we *cannot* go on so another half-year . . .'[21] All the worries that she had ridiculed poor Sarah Coleridge for were now hers, and her brother proved just as intransigent. 'The White Doe' went unsold, while William enjoyed himself. Wordsworth had found that he now had a certain literary celebrity in London and was not averse to its consequences. Southey wrote sarcastically that 'he powders and goes with a cocked hat under his arm to all the great routs. No man is more flattered by the attentions of the great, and no man would be more offended to be told so.'[22]

De Quincey rented Dove Cottage after the Wordsworths moved out and offended Dorothy irrevocably by altering the place to suit his needs. Sara reported: 'It is to be made very smart – the rooms new papered – kitchen under-drawn – and many other comforts – it will be almost filled with Books – and we have ordered his furniture all new (mahogany) at Kendal . . .'[23] His modifications included the demolition of the Moss Hut and the orchard hedge. 'D is so hurt and angry that she can never speak to him more: & truly it was a most unfeeling thing when he knew how much store they set by that orchard.'[24] Even though Dorothy had moved out, she regarded Dove Cottage as hers, since she had shared it for so long with William. It was her house, while Allan Bank and Rydal Mount were Mary's.

Coleridge, anxious to be reconciled with the Wordsworths and unable to keep away from Sara, came north to Greta Hall arriving on 5 September accompanied by William. They went back to Allan Bank, taking the young Sara Coleridge with them, on the 7th, the day after Mary gave birth to her fourth child, Catharine. For little Sara Coleridge the visit was a great trial. She hardly knew her father at all, for he had been absent for most of her childhood, and she was not used to being away from her mother. Sara recalled the incident in her memoirs, remembering that her mother 'did not much like to part with me, and I think my father's motive, at bottom, must have been a wish to fasten my affections on him'. Coleridge was anxious that six-year-old Sara should 'learn to love him and the Wordsworths and their children, and not cling so exclusively to my mother and all around me at home. He was therefore much annoyed when, on my mother's coming to Allan Bank, I flew to her, and wished not to be separated from her any more. I remember his showing displeasure to me, and accusing me of want of affection. I could not understand why. The young Wordsworths came in and caressed him. I sate benumbed . . . My father reproached me, and contrasted my coldness with the child-ish caresses of the little Wordsworths . . .' When asked by her father and Dorothy if she thought little Dora pretty, Sara bluntly told them that she didn't, 'for which I met a rebuff which made me feel as if I was a culprit . . . I slunk away, and hid myself in the wood behind the house . . .'[25] Coleridge's obvious preference for Dora caused Sara much pain. Nor was she happy with the fact that he liked her to sleep in his bed when she stayed at Allan Bank. He came to bed after midnight and told her 'wild tales' which fed her imagination and kept her awake. She preferred to sleep with Sara Hutchinson who went to bed early and slept soundly.

Coleridge intended settling with the Wordsworths and sent for his books and bookshelves. He had conceived the idea for a periodical called *The Friend*. His health improved with the exhilaration of being once more at work. Sara, still suffering intermittently from her mysterious debilitating illness, became his assistant. Dorothy paints a picture of their industry. 'Sara and he are sitting together in his parlour, William and Mary (alas! all involved in smoke) in William's study, where she is writing for him (he dictating).'[26] Coleridge was in bliss, having Sara so close to him. Their quiet evenings together in his study working on *The Friend* were the realisation of a dream. 'I fear to speak, I fear to hear you speak – so deeply do I now enjoy your presence, so totally possess you in myself, myself in you. The very sound would break the union, and separate you-me into you and me. We both, and this sweet Room, its books, its furniture, & the Shadows on the Wall slumbering with the low quiet Fire are all our Thought, [one dear] harmonious Imagery of Forms distinct on the still substance of one deep Feeling, Love & Joy . . .'[27]

But there is some evidence that, on Sara's part, things were not so ideal. In another notebook entry, Coleridge accuses her: 'You never sate with or near me ten minutes in your life without shewing a restlessness, and a thought of *going*, for at least five minutes out of ten.' His jealousies of William were rekindled: 'Some things incomprehensible to me in Sara's feelings concerning [me] and her [greater pleasure in] gazing on [William] . . .' He began to speculate that perhaps she only pitied, not loved, him.[28]

Sara had become aware that there was gossip about herself and Coleridge in London – possibly fuelled by Dorothy's frank letters to her friend Mrs Clarkson. There were those who believed that Sara had 'stepped over the line' where Coleridge was concerned and 'misunderstood' her character. Fully aware of the implications, Sara seems to have begun to keep Coleridge at arm's length – a kind of emotional and physical distancing that he was acutely aware of. It only served to increase his suspicions about her relationship with Wordsworth and to stimulate his irrational jealousies.

He wrote to Thomas Poole that he saw Wordsworth surrounded by his 'three wives', Sara, Dorothy and Mary, 'more and more benetted in hypochondriacal Fancies, living wholly among Devotees – having every the minutest Thing, almost his very Eating and Drinking, done for him by his Sister, or his Wife – and I trembled, lest a Film should rise, and thicken on his moral Eye.'[29]

The move across the valley to Allan Bank solved the Wordsworths' problems with space, but they found that the house had been wrongly designed and the chimneys smoked incurably. Ceilings were blackened, books, pictures and furnishings covered in soot and some rooms were uninhabitable. Sara made a joke of it in her letters. 'You can have no conception of the uncomfortableness, not to say *misery* of this House in these storms – not a chimney will draw the smoke! and one day we could not have a fire except in the Study; & then you could not see each other. In the rest of the rooms the fire was actually blown out of the Grates . . .'[30] A chimney doctor was summoned, but failed to cure the problem. The servants were continually cleaning off the filth; 'we females wish to quit the Premises immediately but the Men will not hear of it . . .'

Sara Hutchinson felt depressed by the awful weather that prevented her going out. She had also fallen into the habit of snuff-taking to keep up her spirits. 'The Waterfalls are in all their glory if one could but travel abroad to see them – I have just been stimulating my Faculties by a pinch of Fribourg out of a great Canister which came in a Box from London last night – it is in vain to attempt to give over – while Coleridge is in the House one is never out of the way of temptation.'[31] She had repeated bouts of ill-health and a permanent pain in her side which Dorothy thought was 'chiefly nervous, occasioned by her uneasiness of mind'.[32] Coleridge spent some time away, canvassing for subscribers for *The Friend*. In his absence Sara was kept hard at work transcribing a political pamphlet – *The Convention of Cintra* – for William.

*The Friend* was slow to materialise, held up by Coleridge's irregular habits. Wordsworth reproved Coleridge in terms calculated to damage friendship irreparably: '. . . it is absolutely necessary that you should always be beforehand with your work. On the general question of your health, one thing is obvious, that health of mind, that is, resolution, self-denial, and well-regulated conditions of feeling, are what you must depend upon; that Doctors can do you little or no good, and that Doctor's stuff has been one of your greatest curses; and of course, of ours through you . . .'[33]

Coleridge hated this kind of hectoring and his relationship with the Wordsworths deteriorated. *The Friend* appeared spasmodically from the beginning of June 1809. Sara was overwhelmed with work and complained to her cousin that she had been 'kept almost constantly busy in transcribing for William, and for The Friend.'[34] William often kept her at work all day until tea time, when she was 'too fagged' even to write a letter. She went on: 'I cannot have patience to write Letter[s] decently for the life of me, though I write Manuscripts for our Gentlemen most admirably, & have as much patience for it as any body.'[35]

Coleridge worked in frantic bursts which exhausted Sara and astonished Dorothy: '. . . you will hardly believe me when I tell you that there have been weeks and weeks when he has not composed a line. The fact is that he either does a great deal or nothing at all; and that he composes with a rapidity truly astonishing . . . He has written a whole Friend more than once in two days. They are never re-transcribed, and he generally has dictated to Miss Hutchinson, who takes the words down from his mouth.'[36]

Sara's health once more suffered, and in March 1809 Mary wrote to her cousin that she was 'most cruelly anxious' about her. Sara had gone on a visit to Penrith and Appleby and Mary was unsure where she was because she had failed to write. Mary was also 'uneasily uncertain' about Coleridge who had also set out for Penrith or Appleby ten days earlier in poor health.

Sarah Coleridge was a regular visitor, fetching the children to and fro on visits to their father in a borrowed carriage or a 'returned chaise'. Dorothy became more and more averse to her company. 'She [Sara junior] is to come in the spring, and Mrs C. is desirous to put off the evil day, for she dreads the contamination which her lady-like manners must receive from our rustic brood, worse than she would dread illness, I may almost say death . . . Mrs C. does not look as if any of her cares have kept her awake a single hour; but she says that she sleeps badly, and I am not disposed to doubt it: however this may be she is very fat and looks uncommonly healthy.'[37] Sarah Coleridge was adept at keeping her troubles to herself and putting a brave face on things. When she shed tears, she shed them in the privacy of her own room. And there were many tears. When Dorothy was unkind enough to remark that 'nothing hurts her', she was wrong. Sarah was too proud to advertise her distress. The famous discretion that Coleridge had so much admired in his wife actually worked to her disadvantage.

Sara Hutchinson was never much interested in small children, preferring them when they began to grow into young adults. 'You are affronted that I never mention the Babe. Why it is just like all the rest – and will be the same as Dorothy . . .'[38] Coleridge, on the other hand, always got on well with children. Sara complains in one letter that she can hear him downstairs playing with Dora and 'making enough racket for twenty'; 'he does tieze her in such a way for she cannot be too naughty for his taste; he calls her "beautiful Cat of the Mountain" & she is more like a cat with him than anything else.'[39] With Dora he was able to have the relationship he was unable to make with his own daughter.

In March 1810, as the last number of *The Friend* was printed, Sara went on an extended visit to her brother Tom, now farming in Wales. She was not particularly happy there, finding 'a great want' of intellectual stimulus 'and people must needs languish with no other thoughts from morning till night.'[40] In spite of this, she did not return until August 1811. The Wordsworths missed her terribly but were also glad that she had gone. Not only had her presence prepetuated the publication of *The Friend*, of which they disapproved, but 'he [Coleridge] harrassed and agitated her mind continually, and we saw that he was doing her health perpetual injury.'[41] The Wordsworths were totally disillusioned with Coleridge. Now that they were all living in the same house, the truth of his addiction could not be concealed. His behaviour had disrupted the entire household. His bed had to be made in the middle of the afternoon, meals provided at inconvenient times. Dorothy wrote to her friend Catherine Clarkson: 'I hope that you are sufficiently prepared for the worst. We have no hope of him . . . If he were not under our roof, he would be just as much the slave of stimulants as ever; and his whole time and thoughts . . . are employed in deceiving himself and seeking to deceive others. He will tell me that he has been writing, that he *has* written, half a Friend; when I know that he has not written a single line. This Habit pervades all his words and actions and you feel perpetually new hollowness and emptiness . . . He lies in bed, always till after 12 o'clock, sometimes much later; and never walks out . . . He never leaves his own parlour except at dinner and tea, and sometimes supper . . . Sometimes he does not speak a word.' Dorothy urged Mrs Clarkson to burn the letter, adding that although Coleridge was apt to blame his passion for Sara Hutchinson for his inability to write, this was a lie. 'Do not believe it; his love for her is no more than a fanciful dream – otherwise he would prove it by a desire to make her happy. No! He likes to have her about him as his own, as one devoted to him, but when she stood in the way of other gratifications it was all over. I speak this very unwillingly, and again I beg, *burn* this letter . . .'[42]

Coleridge's relations with the Wordsworths had begun to break down and he accused William and Dorothy of poisoning Sara's mind against him and interfering with their correspondence when they were apart. William wrote an indignant reply: '. . . you speak of Sara's Letters being written under Mary's eye and mine; these words I deem both unmanly and ungentlemanly . . . Sara's letters, either those she writes or receives do not any of them pass under my eye, and I am surprised you should so far forget yourself as to use such an expression . . .' He admits, however, that Dorothy had glanced over one of Sara's letters and seen a 'cruel sentence' which she had asked to have explained and this incident 'which you assert has occasioned you so much misery and which Dorothy tells me you have misinterpreted'[43] seems to have been the source of the trouble. Whatever happened, it was no longer possible for them to live amicably under one roof.

The Wordsworths may well have intimated to Coleridge that he was in the way, with another confinement due and the search for yet another house under way. To everyone's amazement, Coleridge went back to Greta Hall for five months in May 1810, despite having written to a friend that 'the *sight* of that Woman would destroy me'. Instead, Sarah Coleridge found herself in quiet companionship with her husband, though they no longer shared the same bed. She wrote to Thomas Poole that she was sorry to report that in that whole period 'he has not appeared to be employed in composition, although he has repeatedly assured me he was. The last No of the "Friend" lies on his Desk, the sight of which fills my heart with grief, and my Eyes with tears; but am obliged to conceal my trouble as much as possible, as the slightest expression of regret never fails to excite resentment – Poor Man!' She added that, surprisingly, 'he has been in almost uniform kind disposition towards us all during his residence here . . . his spirits too, are in general better than I have known them for years . . .'[44]

Coleridge occupied some of his time during his stay with teaching his wife and daughter Italian. Sarah was absorbed enough to continue learning on her own, teaching Sara after he had gone. Hartley was fourteen and well advanced in Greek. Derwent at ten took after his mother and was precociously good at maths, especially algebra; he nourished ambitions to go to Cambridge.

Sarah was worrying about their future and her own. She had just been told that the meagre annuity she received was liable to property tax at ten per cent, and was worried about the debts accumulated by the failure of *The Friend* and about Coleridge's lack of provision for her and their sons: '. . . heaven knows, I am so bewildered about our affairs that I know not what to wish or what to do – these Lads too, H. in particular is fast approaching towards Manhood – what can he think is to become of them if he does not exert himself . . .'[45] When their mothers, Mrs Fricker and Mrs Coleridge, died by a strange coincidence on exactly the same day, it marked the end of something indefinable, the breaking of an invisible link that seemed to be significant.

In October 1810 Basil Montagu and his wife called at Greta Hall on their way back from Scotland. They invited Coleridge to be their guest in London, offering him a place in their coach. They called in at Grasmere, where William, hearing of their plan, drew Basil aside and, understandably, warned him of Coleridge's 'infirmities and behaviour'.

Coleridge's stay at the Montagus' didn't last long. Montagu was a confirmed teetotaller who had published a book 'against the use of wine and intoxicating liquors of any sort' and would not allow drink at his table. De Quincey reported that Coleridge had violated the laws of hospitality by; firstly, asking a friend to dine (presumably without asking the Montagus) and then producing wine for them to drink. In the argument that followed Montagu repeated Wordsworth's warning to Coleridge, telling him that Wordsworth had confided that he had been a nuisance in their house. Coleridge was irreparably wounded. 'A nuisance! and then a deliberate Liar! O Christ! if I dared after this crawl to the man, must I not plead guilty to these charges and be a Liar against my own Soul?'[46] He reiterated his belief that 'No-one on earth has ever loved me.' Even Asra had betrayed him, by preferring William to himself. He even fantasised that she was William's mistress. 'O [Asra! Asra!] what have you done in deceiving him who for 10 years did so love you as never woman was beloved!'[47]

Coleridge moved in with some old friends from Bristol – the Morgans – and vowed never to see the Wordsworths again, or have anything to do with them. He could now see clearly, he declared, 'their ignorance of the deep place of my being – and O the cruel, cruel, misconception of that which is purest in me . . . my love of Asra.'[48] He even wrote a complaining letter to his wife, which Sarah (possibly with some malicious satisfaction) relayed to Grasmere. Coleridge's letter, full of his maltreatment by the Montagus and Wordsworth's infamy, neglected to tell Sarah where he was staying.

There were scenes when Sarah, supported by Edith Southey, tackled the Wordsworths about their part in the affair. Feelings ran so high that Edith was provoked into an uncharacteristic outburst. 'Never in her whole life' had Sarah Coleridge seen Edith 'so vehement, or so compleatly overcome her natural timidity as when she answered Wordsworth's excuses – She would not suffer him to wander from the true point – Never mind sir! – Coleridge does not heed what was said – whatever is true, his friends all know, & he himself never made a secret of – but that *you*, that *you*, should say all this – & to Montague – & having never at any one time during a

15 years' friendship given him even a *hint* of that state of your opinions concerning him – it is *you* Sir! *you* – not the things said, true or false!'[49]

Dorothy was extremely upset by the breach, after fifteen years of close friendship. 'It has been misery enough, God knows, to me to see the truths which I now see. Long did we hope against experience and reason; but now I have no hope, if he continues as he is . . . I am sure I have no personal feelings of pain or irritation connected with him. An injury done to my Brother, or me, or any of our Family, or dear Friends, would not now hurt me more than an injury done to an indifferent person. I only grieve at the waste and prostitution of his fine genius, at the sullying and perverting of what is lovely and tender in human sympathies and noble and generous; and I do grieve whenever I think of him.'[50] The truth was that Coleridge wore people out with his needs, alienating a succession of previously devoted friends. It was the tragedy of Coleridge's life that, however much he was loved, it was never enough to satisfy his need.

That winter, Sarah did not hear again from Coleridge. In February 1811, she wrote sadly to her 'very dear friend', the poet and painter Matilda Betham, that 'I should long since have troubled you with a few lines if I had not waited for a letter from Mr Coleridge . . . Three months & more have elapsed & he has not *once* addressed any of his northern friends, & we have heard very little of him from other persons, of course I have passed a very uneasy winter . . . I am altogether in the dark about C. & his affairs . . . I wish C. would write, both Southey & myself have often written to him, but can obtain nothing.' The letter is signed 'very affectionately yours' and a sad postscript follows the signature: 'This very day Coleridge left us 4 months ago, he had been here 5 months in better health, spirits & humour than I had seen him for any great length of time for years before – I fear he has been different since he left us.'[51] Sarah had asked Mrs Montagu to keep her informed about Coleridge, but 'I fear I made an improper request as I have not heard from her.' Sarah did not even know where Coleridge was, until someone else told her that he was staying with the Morgans. Ironically, though Coleridge could not find time to write to his wife or to Southey, he was writing elegant epistles to Matilda Betham, full of excuses as to why he had not been able to call at her London address.

In May 1811 the Wordsworths moved to Grasmere rectory to escape the smoking chimneys and the draughts of Allan Bank, but it was only a temporary respite. They found it dark, gloomy and damp. Sara Hutchinson had been left £1500 as a bequest and was now financially independent. She arrived in the autumn to make her home with them. She was much more happy and prosperous and was even on slightly better terms with Sarah Coleridge, who arrived in a party with the Southeys, as they were passing in a chaise, and held out an olive branch in the guise of an invitation to Greta Hall. 'Mrs C & S pressed me much to go to Keswick – but Southey's kind & affectionate greeting of me, & his earnest and unfeigned wishes that I should go had much more effect – and I shall certainly go – So D with whom the Ladies pretend to be affronted for her never going near them & I am to be off in a short time to K[eswick].'[52] At Greta Hall, Sara Hutchinson and Sarah Coleridge had a frank exchange of views for the first time on the subject of Coleridge. Sara reported to William that 'Mrs C and I have many a battle – but we do not quarrel – she wonders how I could ever love anyone of whom I think so ill; and thinks he ought to know what I do think of him – why, I say, everything that I say to you *have I said to himself* – and all that I believe of him now I believed formerly . . .' Sarah defended her husband against what she believed were angry and resentful reactions from Sara Hutchinson, who on her part found it difficult to believe that one who had been treated so badly and so much abused could still be so loyal. United by their love of Coleridge, they were in the end able to be friends of a kind.[53]

Coleridge came north on a visit in February 1812. He collected the boys from school at Ambleside and directed the chaise through Grasmere, past the rectory, without stopping. Sarah Coleridge found it very hard to explain to the boys satisfactorily why their father would no longer take them to the Wordsworths': 'Poor Hartley sat in speachless astonishment . . . but he dared not hazard

one remark and Derwent fixed his eyes full of tears upon his father
. . . H. turned as white, as lime, when I told him that Mr W. had a
little vexed his father by something he had said to Mr Montagu
. . . these children in the habit of going weekly to Grasmere could
not comprehend how these things were.' There were numerous,
agitated letters from Dorothy urging Coleridge to write to her and
to call before he left for London. 'But we would not go to them and
they did not come to him'[54] and the breach continued, despite
Sarah's efforts to persuade Coleridge that it was all a misunderstanding and that Wordsworth regarded it as 'a trifle'.

Coleridge returned to the Morgans' in March and in April
Wordsworth went to London. The following month, with the help
of mutual friends, there was a meeting and a reconciliation.
Dorothy directed William: 'When you see him give my Love to
him. I suppose he will now receive it, though he had indeed acted
to us all, (and Sara and I could not possibly have offended him) as
if he intended to insult us. I am sure he does not know the depth of
the affection I have had for him.'[55]

The quarrel was never properly made up. Sarah Coleridge could
not resist revealing her satisfaction: 'I may venture to say, there
will never more be *that* between them which was in days of yore
. . . it has taught C. one useful lesson; that even his dearest & most
indulgent friends, even those very persons who have been the great
means of his self-indulgence, when he comes to live wholly with
them are as clear-sighted to his failings, & much less delicate in
speaking of them than his Wife, who, being the Mother of his
children, even if she had not the slightest regard for himself, would
naturally feel a reluctance to the exposing of his faults.'[56] Sarah's
fear of exposure extended to a mass burning of family letters –
anything that might allude to their marital difficulties and
Coleridge's 'weaknesses'. It was a futile attempt to protect his
reputation and the result of Sarah's destruction was to penalise
herself, since she burned material that would have helped to give a
more balanced account of their relationship and the truth about
Coleridge's involvement with Sara Hutchinson. She made sure
that only Coleridge's side of the story could be told.

# PART THREE

---

## *The Triad*

*Come, like the Graces, hand in hand!*
*For ye, though not by birth allied,*
*Are Sisters in the bond of love . . .*
  'The Triad', William Wordsworth

# Lost Children

*Ah! how has Disappointment pour'd the tear*
*O'er infant Hope destroy'd by early frost!*
*How are ye gone, whom most my soul held dear!*
*Scarce had I lov'd you ere I mourn'd you lost . . .*

Samuel Taylor Coleridge[1]

After Coleridge's departure, given the acrimony between the women and the lack of any real sympathy between Wordsworth and Southey, it could only have been expected that contact between the two households at Keswick and Grasmere would lapse. But this didn't happen. The women put aside their disagreements and continued to visit each other for the sake of the children. Hartley and Derwent Coleridge – at school in Ambleside – joined the Wordsworth boys at Grasmere (only 5 miles away) for the weekends and Sarah Coleridge sometimes stayed there in order to see her sons more often. Without Coleridge as a source of conflict they all got on better and Sarah even goes so far as to describe Dorothy as 'my kind friend' in a letter. For Dorothy, Sarah became 'poor Mrs C.'.

There were many comings and goings between Greta Hall and what young Sara Coleridge called 'the Grasmere Hut'. She remembered childhood visits marred by 'the horrible smoke, the dirt, the irregular Scotchy ways, the mischief inflicted on the walls by the children, who were chid and cuffed freely enough, yet far from kept in good order.'[2] The Wordsworth children sometimes rose at 4 a.m., running around barefoot in the kitchen without supervision. It was all a great contrast to the gentility of Greta Hall. But in spite of the differences, close friendships began to develop among the younger girls, particularly between Dora Wordsworth, Edith May Southey and the young Sara Coleridge, who were near together in age.

In Wordsworth's poem 'The Triad', dedicated to the three girls, Edith May is the first of the Nymphs invoked.

> Who that hath seen thy beauty could content
> His soul with but a *glimpse* of heavenly day?
> Who that hath loved thee, but would lay
> His strong hand on the wind, if it were bent
> To take thee in thy majesty away?

Edith May, a tall, willowy, blonde beauty, was the link between Sara Coleridge and Dora Wordsworth, who (probably because of Coleridge's declared preference for Dora) were rather ambivalent towards each other as children. Edith May was 'first friends' with both girls. She was also a particular favourite with Sara Hutchinson and Dorothy Wordsworth. Her meek, submissive nature and sweet temper made her universally approved.

Not so the brilliant Sara Coleridge, 'Last of the Three, though eldest born'. Her physical appearance – the dramatic contrast between her dark auburn hair and white skin – was captivating and she had an ethereal, other-worldly quality which fascinated all who saw her, even Dorothy Wordsworth, who otherwise disliked the child. 'For at least five minutes I could not get over a shock which I felt at the first glance of my eye upon Sara, she seemed so very little, such a slender delicate creature, fair as a snow-drop, and was then almost as pale. But when she twirled about upon the carpet the exquisite grace of her motions, her half Lady, half Spirit Form; and her interesting countenance made her an object of pure delight. She is as quick as a Fairy – every thing about her diminutive except her eyes which may be called majestic.'[3]

Endowed with the gifts of outstanding intellect and beauty, Sara really couldn't win where Dorothy was concerned. As a quiet little girl she was too meek and insipid, but as she gained in confidence and became more boisterous Dorothy complained that 'all her meekness is gone and she is become a Snarler – a little vixen'.[4] Dorothy thought that her mother indulged her too much. Sarah Coleridge was inclined to fuss, particularly after Sara fell from a bridge into the River Greta when she was only two. She had wriggled from the grasp of the servant who was playing with her at the bottom of the field near the forge and followed her brother Derwent on to the bridge which was high above the stream. The water was extremely shallow at the time and it was a miracle that she wasn't badly hurt as she slipped through the wooden railings into the water. The blacksmith's son ran down the river bank as she was carried away by the fast current of the Greta and plucked her out. Although she was physically unhurt the accident affected the imaginative little girl severely and she was nervous and miserable for a long time afterwards. The accident also gave Sarah Coleridge a fright. She had lost one child as an infant and feared to lose another. As a result she became rather over-protective. From then on, Sara was encouraged to consider herself delicate.

Dora Wordsworth was blonde like Edith May but not as beautiful as either of the other two. Her attraction lay in her volatile personality. William idolised her and in 'The Triad' identifies her with the Muse Euphrosyne.

> Come, youngest of the lovely Three,
> Submissive to the might of verse
> And the dear voice of harmony,
> By none more deeply felt than Thee!

The contrast between Dora and Sara could not have been more striking; Dora 'with her wild eyes, impetuous movements, and fine, long floating yellow hair' and Sara with 'timid, large blue eyes, slender form, a little fair delicate face'.[5] Dora grew into a wilful, lively little girl who would not do what she was told and had to be 'imprisoned' (much like poor little Basil Montagu) in order to discipline her. 'I am sorry to tell you that we still have much trouble with Dorothy. She *can* do anything but she is extremely wayward and is desirous to master everybody. It is a woeful thing that so sweet a creature should be capable of seeking the perverse delight of making those who love her unhappy . . . sometimes we have terrible Battles – and long confinements. I hope that perseverance may conquer her . . .'[6] What Dorothy referred to as her 'waywardness' would have to be subdued. What would have been considered merely boisterousness in a boy was 'hoydenish' and unacceptable in a girl.

Dora's lively imagination and enquiring mind distinguished her among the Wordsworth children as a creative spirit – she was, like her Aunt Dorothy, 'of the dancing brood, and given to ecstasy'.[7] It was Dora who amused Dorothy by making up little songs when they went out for walks, and Dora who asked her mother, 'Do you wish you was a Butterfly, I do?' When Mary asked her why, she could only answer 'that then she could do whatever she had a mind!'[8] She had unruly hair, left unconfined during the day and put up in 'curl papers' every night, and gave the impression of being 'very pretty, very kittenish, very quick, very clever'. At the local school she became a favourite with the master and soon outstripped her brother John, who appears to have been dyslexic and was slow to learn – he was a very poor reader even at eleven. John felt humiliated by the achievements of his younger sister and Dorothy felt that it would be in the best interests of both children if Dora went to a boarding school to learn to be 'a useful girl in the family'.[9] She was 'most earnest in persuading William to let her go', which, she declared, was 'a work of pure reason' against her true feelings. Dora, she wrote, had acquired 'an abominable habit of playing tricks with her mouth, sucking her tongue when she is in a state of inaction and though she makes frequent efforts and for some days succeeds, we cannot break her of the habit with constant watchfulness when she is near us. We have some hope that her schoolfellows will shame her out of it.' The Grasmere school did not, in Dorothy's opinion, discipline her strictly enough and there was too much work to do at home with four other children to attend to – 'neither Mary nor I can sit long enough at a time with her to keep her regularly and steadily to work.'[10] Once William had been persuaded to part with his favourite child, Mary's opinion had to follow his, much against her own inclinations and her own 'motherly longings' to have Dora at home.

So, at four years old Dora was put on to the coach alone to travel to Appleby as a boarder at Miss Weir's school. Anna Weir was a friend of Sara Hutchinson and kept about twelve pupils with the help of an assistant. Two of Dora's cousins already boarded there and Miss Weir had stayed at Dove Cottage on several occasions. This, it was hoped, would make it more homely for the little girl. There was no reason, Dorothy assured her friend Mrs Clarkson, 'to dread gross vice at Miss Weir's school . . . it is more like a large family than a school . . . Much good we are sure she will get – and be saved from a great deal of pain . . .'[11] Dorothy declared that she was sure the child was 'no doubt as happy as the day is long',[12] but when William went to visit her, Dora begged him not to go, 'crying bitterly and clinging round me'.[13] Though she was allowed to come home again in 1810, she was sent back to Miss Weir a year later. Dorothy knew better than anyone how it felt to be sent away from one's family as a young child, separated from siblings and parents, and yet she actively promoted Dora's continuing exile. It was an act of deplorable cruelty and Dorothy's insensitivity seems to have sprung partly from her own blind obsession for John, and jealousy towards Dora. 'Most people think Dorothy far cleverer [than John],' Dorothy wrote, 'but that is a mistake; she is proud, and not unwilling to display what she can do . . .'[14] This was the kind of showing off the Grasmere ladies most deplored in little Sara Coleridge, and were determined to eliminate in Dora.

There was also in Dorothy Wordsworth, as there was in Coleridge, the abandoned child's compulsion to re-enact the past. Louise Kaplan, in *Lost Children*, describes how children abandoned by a parent through death or rejection may in turn reject their own children, just as parents who suffered miseries at boarding school still send their offspring to boarding school at the same young age in spite of their own experiences. Coleridge, orphaned by his father, rejected by his mother, abandoned his own children, and Dorothy, sent away from her beloved brothers at the age of six after the death of her mother, insisted that Dora was also sent away. William's own motives were also questionable, since he opposed the establishment of free infant schools for the poor on a number of grounds but partly because he opposed 'separating . . . the mother from the child and from the rest of the family, disburthening them of all care of the little one'. He talks with disgust of the streets of Preston echoing with the crying of infants being dragged to their 'school-prisons'. In any case, tuition was an insignificant part of education, he argued, life and nature being better tutors than schools or masters – 'A moment's notice of a red-breast pecking by a winter's hearth is worth it all.'[15] Sending Dora to boarding school at four was against his stated public principles.

Sarah Coleridge was scandalised, writing to Thomas Poole: 'Does it not surprize you that such clever people could not educate the daughter, at least, without paying 60, 70 pounds a year at a Boarding School?'[16]

The Fricker sisters' daily life at Greta Hall was determined by the number of children under its roof. As well as Mary Lovell's son Robert and Sarah Coleridge's three children, Edith Southey continued to add to the number. After Edith May came Southey's favourite son Herbert, another daughter, Emma, who died in infancy, grave Bertha (nicknamed Queen Henry the Eighth 'from her likeness to King Bluebeard'), Kate, garrulous and plump 'as a mushroom button', inseparable from her youngest sister Isabel, and eventually Cuthbert, a late addition to the family born when Edith was forty-five. Although Isabel and Herbert died before they reached adulthood there were still nine children in the household when they were all at home and at times it was bursting at the seams. In one letter Sarah remarks: 'There are 24 persons in the drawing room at Tea . . . and I am so tired that I can scarcely see for weariness.'[17]

When they had visitors they were, she wrote, 'like bees in a Hive – for now Eliza [Fricker] is here we are 4 women – Southey – 8 children 3 servants – & Hartley thought we were not thick enough

– so he sends for a youth of his own age to come and Scait upon Derwentwater . . . and at the same time Miss Barker had little Dorothy Wordsworth & another young lady at her house, who were half the time here'.[18] They also had to contend with visiting artists including one who painted a canvas 9 feet by 8 feet in Coleridge's study on the subject of 'A Woman on the point of a high Rock, taking her infant from an Eagle's Nest; the Eagle flying over her head' which thoroughly disrupted the housekeeping. 'This painting business creates a great deal of bustle – and running in and out, windows open to paint the scenery &c &c – which we can well dispense with.'[19]

The kitchen, a large stone-flagged room, was at the back of the house and connected to the front door by a long passageway. On the right was the parlour, doubling in use as a dining-room and general sitting-room. It looked out over the garden and Sara Coleridge remembered it 'comfortably but plainly furnished, and [containing] many pictures', watercolours, landscapes in oil and in one corner 'a frightful portrait of mama, by a young lady'. To the right of the kitchen the passageway opened into a small wing room used as a sitting-room by Mary Lovell and a 'mangling room'. 'Here were kept the lanterns and all the array of clogs and pattens for out-of-door roamings. The clog shoes were ranged in a row, from the biggest to the least.'

The staircase went up to the right of the kitchen, on to a landing filled with bookcases. Two steps down led to the bedroom occupied by Sarah Coleridge and her daughter, 'that dear bedroom where I lay down, in joy or in sorrow, nightly for so many years of comparative health and happiness, whence I used to hear the river flowing, and sometimes the forge hammer in the distance, at the end of the field'. Off this landing was also Southey's study which doubled as a drawing-room when there was company. It was a beautiful, airy room, with three windows looking out over the lake and the mountains. Here all the family portraits were hung, including those painted by Matilda Betham and Edward Nash.

Southey and Edith slept in the large back bedroom above the kitchen, and beyond that a passage led to the part of the house previously occupied by Mr Jackson. In this part was the room that Coleridge had used as a study and which Sarah insisted be kept in readiness for his return years after he left, then Mary Lovell's bedroom – 'a comfortable but gloomyish room' – a small spare bedroom and then the back stairs down to Mrs Wilson's bedroom and kitchen and a parlour used by Hartley. On the top storey of the house were six more rooms used as nurseries and maids' bedrooms. There was also a lumber room, 'supposed the abode of a bogle', which had a way out on to the roof-leads with a view out across to Blencathra.[20]

Southey once remarked that a home was not complete unless it contained a three-year-old child and a six-week-old kitten. So it isn't surprising to find that as well as the human inhabitants, there was also a whole tribe of cats with names like Pulcheria, Madame Bianchi, Lord Nelson, Bona Fidelia, Baron Chinchilla, Rumpel-stiltzchen, Hurlyburlybuss and the Arch Duchess Knurry-murry-purry-hurry-skurry. Prester John gave birth to a litter of kittens and had to be renamed Pope Joan. Their lineages, escapades and 'cat-astrophes' were recorded by Southey in 'Memoirs of Cats Eden', an essay written for Edith May, and subsequently published in *The Doctor*. 'Cats Eden' was often given as the address on his letter-headings.

Southey loved children and became a benevolent father-substitute to his niece and nephews. He regularly wrote stories and poems for them, the most famous of which is the tale of the Three Bears which has been entertaining young children ever since. He was often dragged out of his library to take the children on expeditions. 'A fine day affects children alike at all seasons as it does the barometer . . . Three or four days of dull sunless weather had been succeeded by a delicious morning . . . The glass had risen to a little above change, but their spirits had mounted to the point of settled fair . . . a holyday having been voted by acclamation, an ordinary walk would not satisfy the children:- it must be a scramble among the mountains, and I must accompany them; – it would do me good, they knew it would; – they knew I did not take sufficient exercise, for they had heard me sometimes say so.

One was for Skiddaw Dod, another for Causey Pike, a third proposed Watenlath; and I, who perhaps would more willingly have sate at home, was yet in a mood to suffer violence, and making a sort of compromise between their exuberant activity and my own inclination for the chair and the fireside, fixed upon Walla Crag . . . Oh yes! yes! Walla Crag! was the unanimous reply. Away they went to put on coats and clogs, and presently were ready each with her little basket to carry out the luncheon, and bring home such treasures of mosses and lichens as they were sure to find. Off we set; and when I beheld their happiness, and thought how many enjoyments they would have been deprived of, if their lot had fallen in a great city, I blest God who had enabled me to fulfil my heart's desire and live in a country such as Cumberland.'[21]

The children were taught by their parents. Lessons were 'short and easy, and made almost as much [a] matter of sport as of business.' Southey and Mary Lovell gave instruction in Greek, Spanish, Latin and English, Sarah in mathematics, French and Italian, and Miss Barker – the Senhora, Edith's friend from Portugal who had come to live next door at Greta Lodge – taught them music and drawing. Sarah also taught handwriting and needlework. The boys, as soon as they were old enough, were sent off to school at Ambleside, but the girls and Southey's delicate son Herbert were all educated at home, to an extremely high standard. Not one of the boys, and very few other young people in England of either sex, could boast the kind of education gained by the young Sara Coleridge, who had inherited her father's insatiable mind. By the age of twelve she was 'a good French and Italian scholar, a tolerable Latinist, and is now learning Spanish. She has begun music also, and is said by those who are competent to the subject to display most extraordinary talents for it.'[22]

She craved knowledge in a manner that worried the adults around her, for it was firmly believed that too much education could damage girls physically and mentally, making them unstable and sterile – not to mention the fact that too much knowledge made a girl virtually unmarriageable. Sara spent most of her time reading her way through Southey's extensive library. With her brother Derwent she read Tacitus, Livy, Virgil and Cicero; and when alone would turn for light relief to Ariosto, Tasso and Dante. Sarah Coleridge often had to defend her daughter: 'the *wise* Mamas, forsooth, insist upon it, that she is killed with study – but although she is fond of improvement – she is far *fonder* of play.'[23] Sara's brother Hartley took a more misogynistic view. He discouraged 'his sister's erudite propensities', telling her that '*Latin & celibacy* go together . . .'[24] Not for nothing had the eighteenth-century writer Lady Wortley Montagu advised her own daughter to hide her intellect 'with as much solicitude as she would hide crookedness or lameness'.[25]

Sara's cousin Edith May was just the opposite, being completely averse to any kind of study, particularly reading. Sarah Coleridge wished that 'each had a little more fondness for the pursuits of the other.'[26] The two girls were so dissimilar in character and interests that people were amazed that they should be so attached to each other. But the attachment was rooted in a childhood spent paddling in the river to wash their dolls' clothes together, making little gardens behind the house, climbing trees or rambling on the hills in their wooden clogs, ruining their frocks among the bracken and brambles to come home stained with bilberry juice.

There were few local families with whom the girls could mix freely. It was even a problem finding suitable servants. Keswick had several 'manufactories' which 'furnish fine clothes to the one sex & bad habits to the other: half the girls die of consumption occasioned by cotton stockings & thin clothing; – & for the other half, – there is scarcely ever a marriage which is not followed by a christening within the month . . . An inactive clergyman, negligent magistrates, cotton mills & Lakers have ruined the morals of the place.'[27] Keswick was also exposed to the same kind of political and social unrest affecting the rest of the country at the time. There were corn riots and fears of trouble from the Irish community after the Prime Minister was assassinated in the House of Commons. At Greta Hall the chickens vanished overnight, houses in the town were broken into, the mail coach was robbed and a post boy shot. Fears increased after Shelley was attacked while on a visit to

Keswick. Southey went out and bought a gun to protect the family and Mary Lovell commissioned the local carpenter to carve the statue of a man carrying a fowling-piece on his shoulder to stand at the bottom of the garden. It was lifelike enough to give several visitors a fright and was nicknamed the Apollo de Lovell.

Sarah Coleridge's friendship with Southey, begun when they were very young, was now consolidated by the difficulties in their marriages. Coleridge's drug addiction and Edith's recurring depressions drew Sarah and Southey together in a conspiracy of cheerfulness for the sake of themselves and their children. They were both by nature happy people with a great capacity for practical jokes and 'teases'. Southey nicknamed Sarah 'Bumble-cum-Tumble' because of her propensity for accidents; she called him Tomnoddycum, 'though my name, as she knows, is Robert'. Sarah's affinity with Southey had always been a source of rancour in her relationship with Coleridge who saw her 'self-encouraged admiration of Southey as a vindictive feeling in which she delights herself as satirising me'.[28]

Did Southey have regrets about his choice of wife? In January 1806, he wrote to his brother that 'a man marries his second love with sobered expectations and, as Goldsmith says, not expecting rapture, makes shift to find contentment.' But it was, he thought, 'not unfavourable to happiness to have been once disappointed.'[29] It seems to have crossed Southey's mind occasionally that he might have been happier with one sister rather than the other. He wrote to his friend Wynn on the 'abominable relic' of the law forbidding the marriage between a man and his dead wife's sister. 'Of all second marriages, I have no hesitation in saying that these are the most natural, the most suitable, and likely to be the most frequent, if the law did not prevent them . . .'[30] In reality he had the best of both worlds; for more than twenty years Southey lived in a triangular relationship with his wife and her sister, each supplying different needs. Like Wordsworth, he had two wives.

Although Sarah managed to produce a cheerful façade, all the grief that she had lived through, in such public silence, found its expression in a very unusual way. She invented her own language, a source of continual wonder and merriment at Greta Hall, and christened 'Lingo Grande' by the family. They attempted to write it down when she was 'red-raggifying in full confabulumpatus', despite her protests that they were 'persecutorums' and 'stuposities', 'threatening us sometimes that she will never say anything that ends in lumpatus again; and sometimes that she will play the very dunder; and sometimes bidding us get away with our toadymidjerings'. She called herself Snouterumpater, which she declared was 'a short way of calling Mother'.

Southey wrote an account of it to Grosvenor Bedford. 'If the children – the childeroapusses I should say – are bangrampating about the house, they are said to be rudderish and rough-cumtatherick . . . mouth is sometimes called a jabberumpeter, sometimes a towsalowset. When the word comfortabuttle is used, I suppose it may be designed to mean that there is comfort in a bottle . . . Coleridge perhaps, by the application of Kant's philosophy, might analyze and discover the principles of its construction. I, though a diligent and faithful observer, must confess that I have but little insight into it . . . If the weather is what she calls ramping and tearing, this great inventress complains of its ramposity, and says it is a toarampeter of a day . . . Has she been in dull company, she describes the conversation of such stupossums as drigdraggery. A brook she calls the running splash. When she takes a dose of physic, she says it is to give her constitution a jerk . . . I believe it gratifies her when she perceives that I cannot penetrate into the signification of an uncommonly strange and difficult neologism . . . when I hear needles called nowgurs, ladies laduls, whispering twistering, vinegar wiganar, and a mist fogogrum, or fogrogrum, I have some glimpse, though but a glimpse, of the principle upon which these mologisms are fabricated . . . On one occasion, however I was fortunate enough to see this extraordinary language in the mint, if I may so express myself, and in the very act of its coinage. Speaking of a labourer, she said, "the thumper, the why-d'ye-callder – the undoer, – I can't hit upon it, – the cutter-up." These were the very words, received and noted as they came from the die; and they meant a man who was chopping wood . . . It is much to be regretted that Mrs Coleridge's new language is not . . . investigated by some profound philologist.'[31]

Sarah's invention of her own language was deeply significant. She had denied herself a voice by refusing to speak to anyone about her problems with Coleridge, partly from loyalty to her husband, and partly from pride. By inventing a language no one else understood, she could say anything she liked. In a household of linguists and word smiths it was not only a creative, but also a subversive act. Its purpose is underlined by the fact that when she came to dictate her autobiography she called herself Mrs Codian. Southey recognised that its roots ran deep, remarking on 'the uncommon richness, and even exuberance, of her language . . . a talent or genius, – a gifted nature, which rejects the conventional terms as inadequate to its conceptions, and seeking words that burn for thoughts that breathe, brings up from the depths of its own being the natural and true vocable . . . Is it not possible that [Mrs C] . . . may actually, though unconsciously be speaking the primal language itself?'[32]

Snouterumpater 'in full confabulumpatus' was something to be reckoned with. Her epistolary style leaves the reader breathless, as when she sketches a typical Sunday at Greta Hall for Thomas Poole. 'At the hour of nine we all assembled at the breakfast table – S. his wife & two eldest daughters, myself & Sara, all well, except the good Lady of the house [Edith] who is in a very complaining way at present, (Mrs Lovell always breakfasts *alone* in the School-room & Hartley *alone* in his study). A note is brought in – Sir G. & Ly. B[eaumont]'s compliments hope to see the whole party to dinner including the young Ladies. We promise to go – Away fly the 2 cousins to Shake the Pear-tree before dressing for Church – in a minute, Edith enters, breath-less – "Aunt Coleridge, Sara has shaken something out of the Tree, into her Eye, & she is distracted with the pain". After bathing the Eye & lamenting over it, & deprecating the *folly* of the poor sufferer for near an hour, S. raps at the door with all the children ready for church, except one. Where is Kate? "She has such a bad head-ach she cant go to Church, her Mother is going to stay with her to give her James's-Powder, so I hope Sara is better & you are both ready for church." Sara was too blind to go, but I huddled on my things and got to Church as the last Psalm was reading, found our pew full, obliged to go into another, & when the communion plate was brought round, had left my purse at home, & sitting among Strangers looked very foolish . . . On our return, Kate was in a high fever; Mama [Edith] very unhappy, poor Aunt Lovell on the Couch in her *very worst way*, & on entering the bedroom, I found it quite darkened, and Sara in tears . . . We sent off for the Dr who tried with a camel's-hair pencil to clear the lid of the eye, but made it worse; prescribed for Kate who was put to bed, and Sara lay down again in despair, & I sat by her bedside reading . . . I had hardly prepared myself to be with her for the night . . . the maid comes up – Ma'am here are two Gentlemen who *must* see you, they are friends of Mr Coleridge – "pray call Hartley to them, I am nearly undressed" "Mr Hartley is just gone to the Inn" . . . Well, after sitting a full hour with these Gents; I suffered them to depart without asking them to stay supper, for which I got a trimming from S. who did not venture to ask them himself not being *sure* whether there was anything in the house to give them . . .'[33] Writing to Poole was a relief to Sarah. She could say anything to him, knowing his loyalty to Coleridge and his affection for herself. She wrote to him, she admitted, as she would to one of her sisters, 'scribbling to you these *important* adventures, which I hardly dare send off lest you should say, "Phaw. What nonsense." '[34]

In the evenings they often read aloud in the drawing-room. Sarah Coleridge had a beautiful reading voice, which might be employed in reading one of Southey's own works, or Walter Scott, and later on her particular favourite – the young Elizabeth Barrett. She was also a wonderful mimic and could entertain the others with her imitations of their friends and enemies 'to the life'. Mary Lovell, in her solitary parlour, read Virgil and Madame de Staël in an effort to keep her faculties alive.

Life at Greta Hall was not always pleasant for Sarah Coleridge and her children, particularly Sara who was at home while the boys were away at school. Both 'were doing daily services, much above the price current of reciprocal favors' and 'tho' they knew that their absence would be regretted and the house never look like itself without them, an uncomfortable sense of obligation, always lay like an incubus on their gratitude. They were afraid to move, to speak, every wrinkle of that blood-ill-temper which disorders . . . Aunt S[outhey]'s benevolence, even sometimes the young lady airs of our Lady Cousins, seem'd to their feverish apprehensions like a warning to depart.'[35] There was also an awkward daily relationship with Mary Lovell, whose temper and constant indisposition made her an uncomfortable house-mate. But there was a common bond in that both of them suffered the same humiliations and restrictions in relation to their younger sister. When Edith Southey and her friend Miss Barker ordered their new dresses from the Irish draper who called at the house, neither Mary nor Sarah could order anything without first asking their brother-in-law's permission, since he would have to pay for it. In spite of these humiliations, life for Sarah and Mary was much more fun under the protection of Robert Southey than it would have been alone. Without him they would not have been able to go out 'into society' except to visit old friends. Widows and ladies with absent husbands had their social lives circumscribed by the strict middle-class conventions of the time. With Southey in attendance the Fricker sisters could go to parties and balls and picnics, and enjoy the Southeys' reciprocal hospitality.

To celebrate the English victory at Waterloo there was a family party to light a bonfire on the summit of Skiddaw. Neighbours, such as the Wordsworths and the elderly Lord and Lady Sunderlin, were all invited to join the party from Greta Hall. The servants trudged up the mountain (3000 feet!) with roast beef, plum pudding and punch, consumed round a fire made out of tar barrels. Sarah Coleridge felt herself unable to make the long climb, in view of her increasing weight and disinclination for physical exercise. She sat up until after midnight with Lord and Lady Beaumont, who were there on a visit, waiting for the revellers to return, fretting about the descent of hill fog. But about half-past twelve a long line of torches on the mountain predicted their return and there were fireworks in the garden and a 'fire-balloon' before they all collapsed into bed.

Lord and Lady Sunderlin's home at Derwent Bank on the other side of the lake was a favourite venue. There, on summer evenings, Sarah and her young daughter would be entertained to 'illuminations, transformations and a balloon . . . with elegant refreshments and a great deal of good company.'[36] On one occasion fifty of them gathered to watch *Romeo and Juliet* performed by travelling Irish players in the drawing-room. The performance was enlivened by Romeo having drunk more than he should have done in the servants' quarters beforehand. On another occasion it was a popular opera, *No Song, No Supper*. This was more to Sarah's taste than a mountaineering expedition, especially as Lord Sunderlin thoughtfully sent his carriage for her.

More risky were excursions to Colonel Peachey's house on the island in Derwentwater which could only be reached in an open rowing boat. When the weather was bad, evening dresses were soaked, or guests were deposited on the wrong part of the lake shore in thick fog; occasionally, in order to avoid such adventures, they had to spend the night at the Colonel's house, camping out round the drawing-room fire.

In 1809 Matilda Betham came for a visit. Coleridge had first written to her in 1802, sending 'Verses to Matilda Betham from a stranger' after reading some of her poetry, *Elegies and Other Small Poems*, sent by a friend. Not only was she a published poet, but a very accomplished painter as well, and feminist in her sympathies. She compiled a dictionary of *Celebrated Women of Every Age and Country*, which was published in 1804. After some years of intermittent correspondence, she came to Greta Hall. Her visit coincided with a period of terrible weather. She and Sarah Coleridge got soaked on a walk over the Naddle Fells to St John's Chapel. Sarah, always prone to hilarious accidents, fell in a bog and had to wash her petticoat in a nearby beck. It was then captured by Southey who carried it home on his stick like a flag. Afterwards the two women had to be revived with gooseberry wine.

While Matilda was there, she painted Sarah Coleridge and both the Coleridge and the Southey children. She was a great favourite with the whole family, being witty and eccentric. Both Sarah and Southey became very much attached to her and continued to correspond after she went back to London.

Another visitor at Greta Hall was the nineteen-year-old Shelley, who stayed for several weeks on his honeymoon after his elopement with his first wife Harriet. Shelley disliked the women, observing that Edith was 'very stupid. Mrs Coleridge is worse. Mrs Lovel who was once an actress is the best of them.' Southey was also censored for having compromised his earlier, radical opinions. There were vigorous arguments in Southey's library while the women drank tea in the drawing-room. 'He has a very happy knack when truth goes against him of saying, "Ah! when you are as old as I am you will think with me" . . . I do not think so highly of Southey as I did . . . Now he is corrupted by the world, contaminated by custom; it rends my heart when I think what he might have been.'[37] The visit affected Southey too. He saw in Shelley a reflection of his younger, ardent, radical self. It was, he wrote to a friend, like meeting his own ghost.

Southey, drooping under the burden of supporting so many people 'like a hack mule', felt obliged to accept the Poet Laureateship when it was offered in 1813, although 'the laurel has certainly been tarnished by some of its wearers, and . . . its duties are inconvenient and somewhat liable to ridicule.'[38] But the money and the publicity were much needed, though the ridicule was not long in coming. 'Poor Southey! a pensioned Laureate! compelled to sing like a blind linnet by a sly pinch . . .'[39]

Wordsworth was also much changed. After the death of his brother John, and the atrophy of his relationship with Dorothy, 'a hardening of the arteries of his life and his poetry began'.[40] The young man who had thought it bliss to be alive at the dawn of the French Revolution and had been shadowed by English agents, suspected of being a dangerous revolutionary, gradually became a Tory gentleman and part of the Establishment.

Dorothy's outlook had always been narrow, caught within the

confines of her middle-class evangelical upbringing. Contact with her brother and with Coleridge had briefly introduced wider and more radical ideas, but she had few opinions of her own, reflecting theirs in general. After Coleridge's departure her contact with the outside world was much reduced and all her time was taken up with housework and childcare. Her letters to her friends Mrs Clarkson and Lady Beaumont are concerned with domestic details and gossip. She confessed to Catherine Clarkson that 'much of the knowledge which I had formerly gained from Books has slipped from me, and it is grievous to think that hardly one new idea has come in . . . the sorrows of this life weaken the memory so much that I find reading of far less use than it used to be to me, and if it were not that my feelings were as much alive as ever there would be a growing tendency for the mind to barrenness'.[41] When she went to London she was shocked to discover that some of her friends held quite radical opinions, and it took her some time to come to terms with this and learn to encompass other points of view without condemning the people who held them. Catherine Clarkson, whose political sympathies were progressively liberal, found herself 'vexed when I hear of vulgar Tory sentiments coming from those lips'.[42]

Mary's relationship with William grew ever closer. Her calm, even temperament was the perfect antidote to his highly strung disposition. She mothered him and made him feel secure. As their family increased – there were five children by 1810 – each child cemented the bond: 'those *Tendrils* that link us closer & more close to each other'.[43]

Their fourth child Catharine was partially paralysed down one side after suffering convulsions as a toddler. Mary was advised to tie up her good arm in order to encourage her to use the weak limb. Although she was able to walk, her condition continued to give concern and she required a good deal of special attention: '. . . she poor thing is obliged to follow at my skirts & this makes her fretful – it is easy to know before night by her looks & by her lameness how she has been tended thro' the day – she is however perfectly well & the arrantest Mischief that ever lived . . .'[44]

The Wordsworths were rarely parted. However, in 1810 William went to visit his patron Lord Beaumont at Coleorton, taking Dorothy and Sara south with him to spend time with the Hutchinsons' relatives in Wales. Mary was overwhelmed with work, writing to William in stolen snatches. 'I heard D[ora] leading C[atharine] upstairs in search of me – I am followed by them into every corner – I led them back & before I had put C. out of my Arms I was summoned to the door. It was the New Curate who rang . . . since which time I have *attempted* to go over the vale with the baby in my arms in search of a Man & horse to tend a part of the hay which is now ready . . . Sarah [a servant] is now preparing Supper for the hay makers & as all the children were sleeping soundly I pulled out my Stockings to mend . . . I have had to Iron & to pick & preserve Gooseberries &c . . . I have never gone to bed this week without being wearied-out from head to foot.' Yet, despite her exhaustion, she still feels guilty that she cannot give Dorothy the same attention that she gives William, knowing how demanding and jealous her sister-in-law could be. 'I have yet to write to Dorothy & now let me say while it is in my thoughts, that, as I can but write her a short letter; when you write to her you do not give her to understand that you have recd. a longer one – this would make her uneasy.' With her sister Sara she has no such qualms, William is to tell her that 'I will write to dearest Sara as soon as I have time'.[45]

While he was away William wrote Mary a series of passionate love letters. 'Every day every hour every moment makes me feel more deeply how blessed we are in each other, how purely how faithfully how ardently, and how tenderly we love each other; I put this last word last because, though I am persuaded that a deep affection is not uncommon in married life, yet I am confident that a lively, gushing, thought-employing, spirit-stirring, passion of love, is very rare even among good people . . . O Mary I love you with a passion of love which grows till I tremble to think of its strength . . . I am every moment seized with a longing wish that you might see the objects which interest me as I pass along, and not having you at my side my pleasure is so imperfect that after a short look I had rather not see the objects at all . . . my longing day and night to see you again is more powerful far, as I said before than when you were at Middleham . . .'[46] The letters reveal a very different attitude to the public stance adopted by Wordsworth with regard to the affections. The young Sara Coleridge remembered him boasting that he had never been '*in love*, properly speaking . . . in the presence of his wife' in a way that must have been hurtful to Mary.[47]

In August 1810 Mary was forty, and regretted that her hair was going grey and that she had little time or money to spend on her appearance: 'I believe the fine folks at the church style fancy as I pass with the Baby in my Arms that I am a shabby Nurse Maid at the great house – for they brush or gallop past me without ever such a thought seeming to enter their head as, that I am a Gentleman's wife . . .'[48] William responded to the hint by bringing her a new dress and a gypsy bonnet from Liverpool.

In 1812 the Wordsworths were again apart. Mary, whose health had been affected by a succession of pregnancies and a winter of influenza, was persuaded to go on a visit to her brother, now living in the Wye Valley. Wordsworth went to London to see Coleridge and try to effect a reconciliation. Dorothy and Sara stayed behind in Grasmere to look after Catharine, John and baby Willy – Dora was away at school in Appleby, and Mary took Thomas with her. Dorothy wrote letters to William keeping him informed of the children's welfare, but Mary had to rely on William's forwarding the letters to her. Letters from Dorothy often went astray, causing great anxiety to both parents. 'D said that if *I* did not hear from them I might assure myself all was well – but a small matter gives one the alarm where one has so much to love & so much to fear.'[49]

Her fears were not unjustified. At the beginning of June 1812, while Mary was on an excursion to Hereford and 'exceedingly delighted' with the 'Chestnuts in full Blossom the Thorn the Laburnum & the Lilac', her daughter Catharine suffered another bout of convulsions and died. For several days Mary wrote happy letters to William in complete ignorance of the event and later annotated the letters in black, 'Two days before Catharine died!'

and on another, '. . . our first sorrow which had overtaken our married life', recording her bewilderment and guilt that she could have been on a trip of pleasure while her child was being buried: 'Our Child had been 4 days dead!'

Dorothy wrote to William informing him of Catharine's death, but the letter arrived in London only hours after he had left. It was forwarded and finally reached him on Wednesday, 10 June – six days after her death. The tragic events are related with terrible simplicity. 'Sara and John & William and I are all in perfect health – but poor Catharine died this morning at 1/4 past 5 o'clock . . . Mr Scambler has promised us to write to you by this same post, with an account of her illness – I shall therefore say no more than that she began to be convulsed at a little before 10 last night & died this morning . . . Upon most mature deliberation we have concluded it best not to write to Mary – It would be impossible for her to be here at the Funeral; & we think that she will be better able to stand the shock when it is communicated by you, – You will be by her side to impart all the consolation which can be given. May God bless & support you both – We are as well as we can be after so sudden a shock . . . We purpose burying the beloved Girl on Monday. This we do for the best – & we hope you will both be satisfied. If we had attempted to keep her till you & her Mother could come, you would not have been able to look upon her face, she would then be so changed – & it will be a calmer sorrow to visit her Grave.'[50]

William did not reach Wales until June. Unfortunately, before he got there, a letter from Sara Hutchinson had arrived, timed by Sara to reach her brother's family after William had communicated the news to Mary. She therefore heard of the death of her daughter in the worst possible way.

In January 1812 Coleridge was talking of coming north and Southey wrote to friends that it would not surprise him if Coleridge decided to return to live with his wife again. But not only did Coleridge fail to arrive on the expected visit to Keswick, he ceased to communicate with his family at all. He wrote no letters and sent no money. Sarah declared that she 'dare not dwell upon the painful consequences of his desertion but if in the Spring he does not exert himself to pay some of my debts here – I really do not know what will be the result.'[51] Josiah Wedgwood eventually tired of Coleridge's conduct and withdrew his half of the annuity. Sarah had only the remaining portion of the Wedgwood annuity, secured by Tom's will, which, after tax, was less than £70 a year and barely covered the expenses of keeping the boys at school. Inevitably, her own expenses devolved on Southey and she felt this humiliation so keenly she began to have sleepless nights and her health, usually so robust, suffered. Southey observed her fortitude and attempts at optimism with admiration: 'Any other woman would have broken her heart ere this . . .'[52]

Sarah wept at Coleridge's neglect of his little daughter: '. . . how can her father bear to absent himself so long from her, I am sure he loves her notwithstanding?'[53] Also, far from 'having the boys with him', as Coleridge had determined, he never saw them or wrote to them either and this desertion affected them both psychologically, particularly Hartley, who had been his father's favourite. Hartley's dislike of Sara Hutchinson, which seems to date from his enforced stay at Coleorton with his father and the Wordsworths, hardened as he grew older and eventually encompassed the Wordsworths as well. Apparently at Coleorton he had overheard them gossiping around the fire about his father's relationship with Sara Hutchinson and saying unkind things about his mother. Hartley had not been happy at Coleorton, his misery manifesting itself in 'mad passions, and frantic Looks & pout-mouthing'.[54] Coleridge also seems to have tried to foster some kind of maternal relationship between Sara Hutchinson and Hartley during the visit, writing to his wife that 'your namesake takes upon her all the duties of his Mother & darling Friend, with all the Mother's love & fondness'.[55] How that must have jarred!

The Coleridge children were all very sensitive about their father and became miserable every time he was mentioned, afraid to hear unpleasant criticisms. Their memories of his spasmodic and rare appearances in their lives 'like a meteor from the clouds' were also tinged with tragedy; unkind words and thoughtless actions that left a feeling of rejection. It had often seemed impossible to please him.

Sara recalled: 'My father had particular feelings and fancies about dress . . . He could not abide the scarlet socks which Edith and I wore at one time. I remember going to him when mama had just dressed me in a new stuff frock. He took me up and set me down again without a caress. I thought he disliked the dress; perhaps he was in an uneasy mood.'[56] Sara graphically describes the effect Coleridge's moods had on his children. 'The sense that you have done very wrong, or at least given great offence, you know not how or why – that you are dunned for some payment of love or feeling which you know not how to produce or to demonstrate on a sudden, chills the heart, and fills it with perplexity and bitterness.'[57]

Hartley, perhaps the most sensitive of the three, suffered most from Coleridge's fluctuating temper. Coleridge had described him as 'a strange boy, "exquisitely wild", an utter visionary: like the moon among thin clouds, he moves in a circle of light of his own making . . . Of all human beings I never saw one so utterly naked of self . . . If God preserve his life for me, it will be interesting to know what he will become . . . all who have been with him talk of him as a thing that cannot be forgotten.'[58] Sarah Coleridge described him running around the gardens at Greta Hall at any hour of the day or night, rain or shine, 'uttering his poetic fancies aloud . . . and when we are sitting in the Parlour with the Curtains drawn, between the whistling of the wind, we hear him whizzing by'. Hartley feared most being laughed at 'and I know I shall be laughed at, for I always have been so'.[59] His father's desertion cut him to the quick and he felt rejected and humiliated when he had to rely on Wordsworth and Southey to get him into Oxford. Letters to his father on the subject were either unopened or unanswered. In the end Hartley's expenses at Oxford were met by his father's old friends, and Wordsworth and Southey solicited contributions from Lord and Lady Beaumont, Thomas Poole, George Coleridge, Joseph Cottle and Basil Montagu.

In September 1813 Coleridge's friends, the Morgans, became bankrupt. The family separated and Coleridge went into lodgings with the Morgan women. At their persuasion he gave up opium but suffered such terrible withdrawal symptoms that he wished himself dead. Inevitably he went back to the drug, this time fully recognising the hold it had over him. His only hope, he believed, was to place himself in a private madhouse under constant medical supervision. The problem was money to pay for it. Eventually, on personal recommendation, he went to live with a Dr and Mrs Gillman in Highgate. They proved very good friends, providing board and medical treatment free of charge. Within a year, his opium intake had been reduced to a manageable level, though he was never able to do without it entirely, and he was once more able to work. As Southey had predicted, he wrote to Sarah asking if she would have him back. She agreed, but Southey – remembering the terrible scenes he had witnessed and still bitter about Coleridge's treatment of his children – had changed his mind and refused to have Coleridge under his roof at Greta Hall. There seemed no possibility of Coleridge earning enough to provide for Sarah and the children anywhere else. She wrote sadly to Thomas Poole: 'It seems to me impossible we ever should live together under a roof of our own, for we have not the means.' But she added: 'Our separation has, on the whole, been for the best, you will easily see why. I grieve on the children's account, poor things.'[60] Through all that she had suffered she was still able to tell Poole, 'I blame *nobody*'.

In June 1813 George Fricker arrived at Keswick in the last stages of tuberculosis. His sisters took turns to sit with him all night and all day until he died. By a strange coincidence, shortly afterwards little Basil Montagu, now a grown man, came to stay with Miss Barker at Greta Lodge and 'the day after his arrival at Keswick he was sitting in Southey's study, [when] he began violently to vomit blood . . . *think*, what must be our astonishment & grief – when looking into the chamber, we saw this poor youth, in the same attitude, dress and much the same figure . . . just as a few months before we had seen poor George.'[61] It was feared that he too would die, but Dorothy Wordsworth came to stay for over a month and helped Miss Barker nurse her former foster child back to health.

While Dorothy stayed at Greta Lodge, she became involved in a bitter dispute between Miss Barker and the Fricker sisters who quarrelled on the very first day of Dorothy's visit, and vowed not to cross each others' doorsteps. 'I assure you the part I have had to play has not been over agreeable; for between my zeal for Miss Barker, and the hotness of their tempers, with the utter impossibility of making them look coolly either upon her supposed faults, or her virtues, I have had much ado to prevent quarrels with *me* also . . . To act as a Mediator is impossible; for Miss B would speak her opinions so plainly if any discussions were to take place between them; and *they* would be in such an outrageous passion that the Breach would only be widened.'[62] The estrangement also embraced Southey who, for the sake of his wife and her sisters, felt he could not visit Miss Barker either. Indeed, Southey may well have been one of the sources of contention. According to Dorothy, it was 'solely on Southey's account' that Miss Barker had come to England, and it was to her that he dedicated his book *The Doctor* (though it was largely transcribed by Sara Hutchinson) in which she featured as the Bhow Bhegum. But the major factor seems to have been the 'petty irritations' of living in such close proximity – Greta Lodge being only yards from Southey's back door. Miss Barker moved to Borrowdale, where she had a house built at such expense that she became deeply in debt and had to live in France.

A few months after all this upheaval, before the family had time to recover, Sara Coleridge, who was now eleven, suffered her first serious illness, experiencing 'frequent febrile attacks and . . . nervous sleeplessness' that necessitated treatment with laudanum. It had begun with a swelling in her foot, which her mother had attributed to a sprain. Other parts of her body then began to swell with fluid and she was passing blood in her urine. Southey wrote to a friend for medical advice. Sarah, he observed, was 'unhappy enough without these fresh afflictions'.[63] Medical science was helpless in the face of even the most commonplace childhood ailments. Parents lived in constant fear of losing one of their children.

Sara recovered, but she would always be subject to poor health,

and a nervous 'uneasy' tendency she believed she had inherited
from her father. After her visit to Grasmere, when she had lain
awake at Allan Bank terrified of the dark waiting for her father to
come to bed, she had had increasingly severe 'night-fears'. In the
beginning they took the form of 'lions, the only form of terror
which my dark-engendered agitation would take. My next bugbear
was the ghost in *Hamlet*. Then the picture of Death at Hell Gate in
an old edition of *Paradise Lost*, the delight of my girlhood . . . Oh
the agonies I have endured between nine and twelve at night,
before mama joined me in bed, in presence of that hideous
assemblage of horrors, the horse with eyes of flame! I dare not,
even now, rehearse these particulars, for fear of calling up some of
the old feeling, which, indeed, I have never in my life been quite
free from.'[64] When she crept down to the parlour after 'an hour's
torture', she was laughed at by Southey and scolded by her mother,
neither of whom understood the reality of her imaginary chimeras.
At her father's insistence, on his last visit to Greta Hall, she was
always able to have a lighted candle in her room.

At Grasmere Mary was still grieving for the death of Catharine,
and stricken with guilt that she had not been there for her and that
she had had no opportunity to say goodbye to her little daughter. It
was the first major tragedy of her life. Dorothy tried to comfort her
by telling her that the child's death was 'a sorrow in which comfort
is found', since Catharine would have been terribly disabled had
she lived. But although Mary recognised the common sense of this
argument, her maternal feelings and her grief were often too strong
to be controlled and on one occasion, as they walked through the
churchyard on the way home, she threw herself full length on the
grave and wept.

Great offence was caused by De Quincey's reaction to Catharine's death. She had been his favourite among the Wordsworth
children, to the extent that scandal-mongers reported that the
child was his. He referred to her as 'the darling of my heart' and
became quite hysterical after her death, writing passionate letters
to Dorothy and sleeping on Catharine's grave at night 'in mere

intensity of sick frantic yearning'. Such an extreme, and unhealthy, obsession could only cause more hurt to Mary's feelings. Sara Hutchinson, who had previously liked De Quincey, was now disgusted with him: '. . . he doses himself with Opium & drinks like a fish . . .'[65] He compounded their bad opinion of him by having an illegitimate child by Peggy Simpson, the daughter of a neighbouring farmer, and, although he subsequently married her, it was an unequal alliance they could not approve. Dorothy's tolerance towards her brother's 'weaknesses' did not extend to De Quincey. 'Mr De Quincey is married,' she wrote, 'and I fear I may add he is ruined.'

Dorothy's health was giving concern under the stress of a compulsive self-sacrifice that seemed to grow stronger as she grew older. She was gently persuaded by Mary that she was not entirely indispensable ('I *cannot* leave home . . . I *cannot* do it'), and sent on a much-needed holiday with her Aunt Rawson in July and then in November to stay with her friend Jane. It was rare for Dorothy to leave home on her own – on previous occasions she had always gone with William; her fear of leaving home alone was almost a form of agoraphobia. While she was away the children were taken ill with measles and, before she could return, little Thomas died. William met Dorothy on the road with the news and she arrived in Grasmere in a state of collapse. Once again Mary had to put aside her own feelings to minister to her sister-in-law 'with the calmness of an Angel . . . I was ashamed of my own weakness; and bitterly reproached myself that I could not bear the sorrow as she did . . .'[66]

Mary's 'striking fortitude' was dearly purchased by suppression. She had to care for William, who was once more convinced that his grief was the most intense, a prostrate Dorothy and the children – all three of whom still had measles. Sara Hutchinson did what she could to support her sister, but she herself was ill. Three weeks later, in a state of complete physical and mental exhaustion, Mary herself collapsed, overwhelmed with grief and unable to stop weeping. Dorothy roused herself to take charge and lapsed into conventional piety, writing that 'what God wills is best for all of us.'[67] It was poor comfort to a woman who had lost two much-loved children within six months.

At Greta Hall there were also a series of tragic anniversaries to be relived every year. Even the irrepressible Sarah Coleridge was depressed and sad whenever the date of Berkeley's death arrived. She talked of him all her life, telling her children that he had been the most beautiful baby, cheerful and easy to nurse. When she destroyed Coleridge's letters and her own after his death in an attempt to protect his reputation, she saved the letter she had written to Coleridge in Germany, writing a note in one corner that she would not destroy it 'for the sake of my sweet Berkeley'.

Edith Southey lost her fourth child Emma just as she started to walk and talk, but was prevented from sinking into uncontrollable grief by the fact that she had another child at the breast, Bertha, who required all her attention. Edith and Herbert also continued to thrive, but the bereavements tipped the balance of her, already fragile, mental health. Fears of further losses affected her ability to bond with her living children – she was almost afraid to love them, convinced that they too would die. The deaths of fourteen-year-old Isabel and nine-year-old Herbert, a few years later, were devastating. Altogether she lost four of her eight children and with each death sank into a more permanent state of depression.

Infant mortality at the time was about fifty per cent, though it was higher among poorer families. Sarah Coleridge, who lost one out of four, and Mary Wordsworth – two out of five – fared better than the average. Despite the fact that they had large families, and that such deaths were usual, their grief was just as great as it would be for a parent today, and anyone doubting this should read their letters and journals. When Herbert died in 1815, from 'affliction of the heart', part of Southey died too. He had feared to let Matilda Betham paint Herbert's portrait six years earlier 'lest it should ever become an object of pain' and now his worst fears were realised. He found it impossible to write and had to borrow money from a friend. It is a myth that, because such deaths were more common, the deaths of children were more easily accepted. All their lives the families remembered their lost children, and kept the anniversaries of their births and deaths. 'I have eight children,' Southey was wont to say when asked, 'but four of them are in heaven.' In Crosthwaite churchyard were Southey's 'tenderest affections, the very deepest by many degrees which he had ever known'.[68] The general effect was to make Southey more religious. He gave his eldest daughter a bible and hoped that she would read the set psalm and lesson for the day every morning. The Wordsworths also found solace in religion and even Dorothy became, once again, a regular church-goer. She found it difficult to look forward: 'I never talk of *next* year's plans, but I think of Death . . .'[69] For the Wordsworths, the view of the graveyard from the rectory windows was a constant, tragic reminder.

In 1813 the Wordsworths moved from Grasmere rectory 3 or 4 miles down the road to Rydal Mount, which was to prove the answer in their search for a permanent home. It was a beautiful old house looking out over Rydal Water, and it had a long terrace on the side of the hill. It was let to them by Lady Diana Fleming who owned the Rydal Hall estate, of which it was a part. Wordsworth had obtained, through the influence of the current Lord Lonsdale, the office of Distributor of Stamps for Westmorland, with a salary of £500 per annum, and so the family were now financially secure. Sara Hutchinson wrote her first letter from the new house on 23 June 1813. 'We are all very well and comfortable in our new residence . . . and we have so much pleasure from the beauty which is around us without doors that we care little for the want of ornament within . . . It is the admiration of everybody – the *crack* spot, and the envy, of the whole neighbourhood.'[70] The ladies of Rydal Hall were in the habit of popping in for a 'friendly cup', and the Wordsworths were given the freedom of the grounds. Being nearer to the social centre of Ambleside, within 'visiting distance', made a great deal of difference to the women's lives. They had begun to feel a certain amount of social isolation at Grasmere, once their summer visitors had left. Dorothy had had a close friendship initially with Catherine Clarkson, but when the Clarksons left

Eusemere to move south for reasons of health, she had had no one she felt close to outside the four walls of the house. Her friends felt that this was a great evil and made her too inward-looking. In Catherine Clarkson's opinion the whole family needed 'acquaintances . . . neighbours . . . the sight of *equals* . . . in whose company they must put some restraint upon themselves'.[71]

Rydal Mount was at first very sparsely furnished, but this was soon remedied after a few visits to local auctions, returning by moonlight clutching mirrors and decanters, having purchased 'the drawing room curtains with a grand cornice the length of the Room' (which Dorothy thought William had bid too much for), a meat safe and a writing desk and 'far more chairs than we know what to do with'.[72] A '*Turkey!!!!* carpet' was ordered from London for the dining-room at the unthinkable price of 22 guineas. Dorothy feared their friends would think they were 'setting up for fine Folks'.[73] Sarah Coleridge remarked sarcastically that Wordsworth's new position had more profit than honour, though 'he keeps a sort of secretary to do the drudgery'.[74] She commented drily to Thomas Poole that the Wordsworths were now 'quite in request, you have no notion how much respectability attaches to them; their society is much courted.'[75]

The women were now in their forties. Mary went through the menopause shortly after Willy's birth and resigned herself to the idea that she would have no more children. Dorothy in particular was ageing fast: 'she looks nearer 60 than 50 in her profile, owing to her extreme leanness, and the loss of teeth'. But she was still agile and still loved to dance, which some of the young girls thought was incongruous. Wordsworth on the other hand would remark with delight on her 'lively movements' and 'deep enjoyment'. Sarah Coleridge, sitting beside him, knew that William was seeing once again the 'Ardent girl', his 'Beloved Sister'. Sarah felt herself to be 'an object of commissiration; for I am so *encreased* in size, that I could no more go down a dance, or climb a mountain, than I could fly over the Derwent.' She laughed at the contrast between Dorothy's 'nut-cracker nose & chin' and her own 'full-moon phiz'.[76] When Sara Hutchinson congratulated herself on never having been a beauty and so having nothing to lose, Sarah Coleridge sighed for the loss of hers and admitted that she could not bear to look at herself in the mirror for 'it is not a bit of a matter what one puts on when one is grown such a [fright].'[77] Mary unkindly likened Sarah to 'a stuffed turkey'.

Edith Southey, now forty-five, was expecting another child after a gap of seven years and 'for many months this has occasioned so much bodily ailment and so much depression of spirits'[78] that the mood of the whole house was affected. This proved to be Cuthbert, a much longed-for son, the baby of the house and thoroughly spoilt. Edith's deepening mental disturbance began to have a very bad effect on Mary Lovell, whose health had never been good 'while there exist in the world such Things as Tea, and Lavender & Hartshorn Slops, & the absence of religious & the presence of depressing, Passions.'[79] The lively, talented girl had become a disappointed, embittered woman and she began to suffer from mysterious illnesses of a 'nervous', and possibly also gynaecological, origin as she entered her forties. Her situation was unenviable after her son went away to boarding school. During the vacations he stayed with family or friends to save the expense of travel and she didn't see him for seven years. When he finally did come home on a visit, Sarah Coleridge thought he had become a very sensible boy, 'without any of those overweening sensibilities which, I am sorry to say, distinguish his 2 cousins H[artley] & D[erwent]'. Mary was horrified to see how shabby Robert was when, in 1817, he walked all the way from London to see her. But they were all much impressed by his character: 'I think he is much more likely to be happy & perhaps to confer happiness, or, I should rather say more likely to escape giving pain to others than those whose minds and manners are so intirely different from his.'[80] The fact that Sarah mentions Coleridge in the next sentence is a good indication of her train of thought.

Southey paid for Robert to be apprenticed as a printer in London and Mary Lovell saw her son even more rarely thereafter. Without her child she was a superfluous, dependent female on the fringes of a warm and lively family circle that continually reminded her of what she had lost. Loneliness, of the kind that cannot be assuaged by being in the company of other people, a lack of personal fulfilment, and the waste of a considerable intellect, all affected her spirits and she developed the particularly female disorder that nineteenth-century doctors were all too familiar with in middle-aged, middle- or upper-class women. Sara Hutchinson commented, with her usual shrewd asperity, that what Mary needed was to get away from the 'Aunt Hill' and have some kind of occupation.

In 1818 Sara Coleridge was almost seventeen and still diminutive: '. . . she seems to have done growing and has stopt just above her mothers stature. Edith [a year younger] is still a great girl and bids fair to equal or outstrip hers . . . They have got on well with their music, I scarcely know how, except that the poor piano seems never to be at rest. And they have got on so far with their drawing that they would do very well with it, if they applied to it more.'

Dora, despite, or perhaps because of, her removal to boarding school, was not progressing as well as her early precocity had suggested. The Wordsworths thought of employing a governess – Miss Fletcher, a friend of Miss Barker's – to run a small school for Dora and some other local girls at Ambleside: '. . . the advantages to us will be incalculable – for Dorothy is the most unteachable creature alive; though as quick as thought – but there is no nailing her to her books . . .'[81]

The gifted Hartley had just gained a second class degree at Oxford, doing less well than he might have, but better than expected given the circumstances: '. . . as honourable for him, as a first class for one who has been regularly bred.'[82] Derwent was working as a tutor for a family near Ulverston and hoping to go to Cambridge to read mathematics. Southey now regarded Coleridge with contempt: '. . . when I think of the manner in which he has left these boys to sink or swim, I cannot speak of him with patience.'[83] His abandonment of his children was something that Southey could never understand or forgive.

Hartley was granted a fellowship at Oriel College, but he had begun to drink under the stress of his position – sometimes immoderately – and in the spring of 1820 he was told that because of lapses of sobriety and conduct unbecoming a fellow it would not be renewed. The situation was made more shameful for him after he went to live with the Montagus who, after several incidents of 'intemperence', asked him to leave. Hartley became very depressed and tried to keep the situation from his mother, but the Gillman family (where Coleridge was now lodging) wrote her a letter. Sarah was distraught. It seemed a repetition of Coleridge's conduct; the addiction, the lack of self-control and failure to persevere at anything. Sara Hutchinson felt 'truly sorry' for her. Sara was very fond of Hartley and felt that it was not entirely his fault, 'for what can the helpless creature do for himself!'[84] Sara and Dorothy eventually took on the care of Hartley's affairs, partly perhaps for the sake of his father. Coleridge was persuaded to write to the headmaster at Ambleside School and Hartley was offered a post there as assistant master. Southey refused to have him at Greta Hall as he had refused his father: 'I certainly will not suffer any such disturbance of my peace and comfort as such an arrangement would inevitably bring with it. Mrs C. perfectly understands this.'[85] Sarah may have understood it but she suffered bitterly from having 'no establishment in which H. can be received'. She was a guest in her sister's house and could not even have her children with her unless they gave her permission. She told Thomas Poole that she had 'bitter feelings attached to the word HOME'. Hartley referred to Greta Hall as the 'House of Bondage'. He was effectively homeless.

# *Dobrizhoffered*

*I should have been happier, with my taste, temper and habits,*
*had I been of your sex instead of the helpless, dependent being*
*I am.*

Sara Coleridge to her brother Derwent

In 1818 Southey suggested to Derwent that he could earn enough money to go to Cambridge by working on a translation of Dobrizhoffer's *Historia de Abiponibus*, a history of the Amerindian people of Paraguay published in Latin in 1784 – a text Southey had come across while writing his own *Tale of Paraguay*. Derwent felt no enthusiasm for the project, his interest being in mathematics rather than linguistics, and so his seventeen-year-old sister Sara offered to help him, beginning the third volume while he tackled the first. While it was under way a family friend offered to pay Derwent's fees and maintenance at Cambridge and Derwent abandoned the project with considerable relief.

Sara on the other hand 'felt disappointed, and said, she liked the employment "of all things", and her uncle approving of her specimen, said, if she chose to finish it, at her leisure, she might, but she must not be disappointed if nothing was gained by it, and she must *not work too hard*.'[1] Southey, while approving of female education in principle, had long since parted company with the theories of Mary Wollstonecraft that had seemed so attractive to the young Pantisocrats. He paid lip-service to the ideas of female education, but was still a misogynist at heart. His opinions matched those of his fictional character The Doctor: '. . . this question concerning the sexes was a subject which he was fond of introducing before his female acquaintance; it was like hitting the right note for a dog when you play the flute.'[2] Although he educated his own daughters and Sara Coleridge to a very high standard, like Wordsworth, he felt that literary accomplishment in a woman was acceptable only as a hobby. It was Southey who 'sent a dose of cooling admonition'[3] to Charlotte Brontë informing her that 'literature cannot be the business of a woman's life, and it ought not to be.'[4]

Fortunately Sara's mother had very different ideas and gave her daughter all possible encouragement. Sara had a naturally academic disposition and inherited from her father a love of words and ideas. Like him she was 'a library cormorant', with a precocious understanding. The completed book, *An Account of the Abipones, an Equestrian People of Paraguay*, was published anonymously early in 1822 and many people thought that it was written by Southey. It was a work of considerable scholarship and much acclaimed among those who knew the secret of its authorship. 'How she Dobrizhoffered it all out, it puzzles my slender Latinity to conjecture,' wrote Charles Lamb. Coleridge later declared: 'My dear daughter's translation of this book is, in my judgement, unsurpassed for pure mother-English, by anything I have read for a long time.'[5] Sara, only just nineteen, was paid £113, much of which she insisted on contributing to her brother's educational fund. It was ironic, since Sara, of all the children at Greta Hall, was the one who would most have benefited from a university education and was denied it because of her sex. Like many clever eighteenth- and nineteenth-century women, she helped to pay for the education of her brothers.

There was never any question of Sara making a career as a writer. Wordsworth remarked that her education and accomplishment would fit her to become a governess 'should it be necessary'. Women were domestic beings, unsuited to public life, who might turn a pretty verse or write romances, or even translate the work of great men like Dobrizhoffer, so long as it did not interfere with the real business of their lives. The plight of the female author was graphically described by Elizabeth Gaskell in her biography of Charlotte Brontë. 'When a man becomes an author, it is probably merely a change of employment to him. He takes a portion of that time which has hitherto been devoted to some other study or pursuit . . . and another merchant or lawyer, or doctor, steps into his vacant place . . . But no other can take up the quiet, regular duties of the daughter, the wife, or the mother, as well as she whom God has appointed to fill that particular place: a woman's principal work in life is hardly left to her own choice; nor can she drop the domestic charges devolving on her as an individual, for the exercise of the most splendid talents that were ever bestowed.'[6]

Fortunately, Sara's education and her situation at Greta Hall had brought her into contact with a number of female authors who either corresponded with Southey and her aunts, or visited from time to time. She was familiar with the work of the foremost writers of the day and admired the eloquence and 'the profundity of Madame de Staël, the brilliancy of Mrs Hemans (though I think *her* over-rated), the pleasant broad comedy of Miss Burney and Miss Ferrier, the melancholy tenderness of Miss Bowles, the pathos of [Elizabeth] Inchbald and [Amelia] Opie, the masterly sketching of Miss Edgeworth (who, like Hogarth, paints manners as they grow out of morals, and not merely as they are modified and tinctured by fashion); the strong and touching, but sometimes coarse pictures of Miss Martineau . . . and last not least, the delicate mirth, the gently-hinted satire, the feminine decorous humour of Jane Austen'.[7] These were her role models.

Sara's health improved dramatically while she worked on the book, but her mother noted that once she had finished and was feeling 'at a loss' it deteriorated again. This was interpreted as being the result of her concentrated labour, rather than being caused by a lack of employment for her faculties. Her inclinations were much disapproved of by the ladies of Grasmere. Sara Hutchinson, on a three-week visit to Greta Hall, wrote that 'Sara is somewhat spoilt by so much learning – she has no enjoyment of any thing else & never seems interested but when she has a classical author in her hands – takes no part in any conversation but what relates to books, & *personal beauty* – and she is perfectly useless & helpless as far as regards the ordinary occupations of life – Yet it is a wonder that she is not more spoilt for her Mother & Brothers think there is not such another Being upon earth – & be she absent or present their discourse always tends to her'. She much preferred the fun-loving, book-hating Edith May whom she referred to as a 'delight. She is just what a girl of that age ought to be . . .'[8] With Edith she discussed the latest fashions in hairstyles and morning gowns and the gossip from London, where Edith longed to go. 'The fashion for the hair is to be *stroaked up* very high behind & fastened in plaits & bows at the crown of the head . . . Green is the prevailing colour – & shoes of all colours, boots legs of one col. & feet of another the *flashyer* the better – & in spencers and Gowns the gayest most prevailing.'[9]

Sara Hutchinson had begun to spend a considerable amount of time at Greta Hall, much of it acting as Southey's amanuensis or reading her way through his library. She liked to be occupied and wrote breezily that she had 'not a moment to call my own, for there are 50 books here which I want to read, and quires to be written – which I would gladly do, if the time would serve. Southey is going to write a History of the [Peninsular] War; & he has got all Lord Wellesley's papers respecting Spanish & Portuguese affairs (including his private papers & letters) and I have been assisting to transcribe them, which has been a most delightful employment . . . I have become every day more & more attached to my occupation & this has made me prolong my stay here . . . for Southey has so much work and is so industrious that it is a good work to assist him.'[10]

She began to quote Southey in her letters: 'Southey says . . . Southey always says something *must* come out of that circumstance'; 'Southey says *this* winter began when the *last* ended'; 'S is as kind and delightful as could be. He is as lively as a Lark – always busy, & yet always at leisure . . .' Southey began to develop a very great affection for her. 'There is no woman out of my own house,' he admitted, 'with whom I am so intimate as Miss Hutchinson, or who I love altogether so well' – a sentiment which seems to have been reciprocated.[11] Sara's lively, intelligent and slightly caustic personality was like a breath of air in a household dominated by Edith's depressions, Mary Lovell's confirmed hypochondria and her disagreements with her hot-tempered sister Sarah. Even Dorothy Wordsworth felt sympathy for Southey – 'How can he be lively when his Wife is always dull and frown[s] at all his little gaieties?'[12] As an unmarried woman without children, Sara Hutchinson was completely free to devote herself entirely to Southey and his interests.

She had become slightly disillusioned with Wordsworth, and the occasional barbed comment creeps into her letters. On his inclination to fuss: 'William is doing nothing – except when he is obliged to bother himself with the affairs of his Trust which are twice as much *work* for him as anyone else.' And on his need for female attentiveness: 'He wishes Mary very much to accompany him to London – and I should suppose either she or Dorothy will; as he does not like to stir without one of [his] Females.'[13]

In the end it was Sara who went to London with William and Mary, despite her horror of coach travel – 'about a mile off [we] were favoured with the Company of a drunken young man, something like a horse dealer, who smelt of liquor & slept all the way, tossing about his legs & arms to our great disgust'.[14] From London she wrote flip and racy letters to Dora. 'I have very often wished for you my dear D. and then I have thought you were far better at home; for I am sure you would be half-killed with the delight of seeing so many gay sights – the Shops, and the Bazaars would soon steal all your money from you – and want of rest & sleep you health . . .'[15] She was introduced to Keats who referred to her as 'Wordsworth's enchanting sister', and met Coleridge for the first time since his breach with the Wordsworths. With the help of the Gillmans, he had regained control of his addiction and was writing and publishing again. He seemed eager to renew contact with Sara, who was very reluctant to reopen old wounds. 'He asked me the address, but I hope he has forgotten it – if he should ask you try to evade the question – for we [Sara and Catherine Clarkson] are neither of us ambitious of the favor, especially as an answer *would be required*.'[16] But she still cared enough to ask her cousin Tom for news of him: 'Pray have you any conversation with him? & did he inquire after "my dear" . . . Tell us what sort of figure he cuts & in what spirits he appears to be . . .'[17]

By 1820 Dora was 'a great *strapping* lass' and was applying herself to her education well enough to have risen to the top of the class at her boarding school. A Miss Dowling had taken over the school at Ambleside previously taught by the older, deaf Miss Fletcher. Anna Dowling had won the lively girl's affection and confidence and given her the stimulus needed to realise at least some of her potential. She treated Dora 'as a Friend' and under this kind and understanding management there was a marked change in Dora's manners and behaviour. Dorothy noted with approval that Dora had become 'thoughtful, steady and womanly . . . all her turbulence is gone'.[18]

Dora suffered from being Wordsworth's daughter and Dorothy's niece. She had inherited both intellect and creativity, but was discouraged from exercising either by the two dominant personalities in the household. And although manifestly the cleverest child in the family she was sent away to small governess schools with up to a dozen pupils across a wide age range where, although she was kept occupied, her mind was never stretched to the point where she was interested enough to learn much. The periods in between, when she was educated at home, were a disaster. No one in the household seemed to have the time or patience to teach her – all their time and energy were lavished on the boys.

The comparison with her older brother John was damaging to both of them. John was – even Dorothy was eventually forced to admit – 'inconceivably slow', 'the backwardest Boy I ever knew', needing special tuition to get him through the necessary exams. Even as an adult he found reading difficult, confusing similar words – 'stores' with 'stories' and 'requite' with 'require'. Sara Coleridge observed that he seemed to have inherited the temperament of his dead uncle, Captain John Wordsworth, and to be happier in physical rather than mental exercise. The older John Wordsworth had apparently also been labelled as a dunce when at school because he loved fishing and 'social boyish sports' better than learning. Dorothy was full of admiration for her favourite nephew's physical prowess. John was 'never tired in Body – a proof that he is very strong. This thought of his strength strikes now suddenly upon me many and many a time – and my heart is humbled . . .'[19] John suffered from being Wordsworth's son, forced into a career of scholarship for which he was totally unsuited.

Willy also failed to achieve academic success, having been very spoilt by his father after the death of Thomas and over-protected by his mother who kept him at home because she feared for his health. When they were eventually persuaded that it would be better for his education to go to school he was sent home ailing and the experiment was never repeated. John managed to struggle through Oxford and became a clergyman; Willy, after trying unsuccessfully to get a commission in the army without his parents' knowledge or approval, eventually became his father's deputy and inherited his position as Distributor of Stamps. His parents fussed over his health almost as much as Dora's.

Dorothy later admitted that their handling of the children had been at fault. The boys should have been sent to school earlier and treated more firmly. But with Dora they had been too harsh. She had been sent to boarding school because she required, Dorothy had written in 1812, the 'utmost strictness', but a few years later she was forced to admit that 'if we had been less anxious about her and taken less pains she would have done much more for herself'.[20]

Dora was terribly homesick at boarding school, her eyes filling with tears at each mention of home. She visited Rydal Mount sometimes on Sundays when it could be arranged, but despite the fact that Ambleside was only a short distance away, the family did not go to see her, Dorothy explained, because Dora became so upset when they left and there were emotional scenes. She was still rather immature; at fifteen she had as yet 'no womanly breadth', but Dorothy was glad, for reasons of her own, 'that she continues a child so long'.[21] Dora suffered badly from acne and tried various remedies including soap and fine sand – even the spa waters at Harrogate – without much effect.

Though the school at Ambleside seems to have been much better than the establishment attended by Charlotte Brontë in Yorkshire, being smaller and more homely, communal living conditions encouraged the spread of infectious diseases and, like the Brontë sisters, Dora contracted tuberculosis. As a small child she had always been prone to coughs and colds, which were slow to clear, and in adolescence she suffered from chronic chest problems which improved with the warm, dry summer weather, but returned each winter with the cold and damp. She also began to develop a curvature of the spine; '. . . she fancies that her ill-made clothes are the, or rather, *cause* the appearance of a "*hump*" as she calls it – However I do believe it is her stays that have pushed out her shoulder blades for they do stick out terribly. I was quite shocked with them yesterday & it really is no fault in her holding herself now but stick out they will . . .'[22] Dora's ill health caused continual anxiety, but it was several years before the serious and insidious nature of the illness was finally realised.

Dora left school at eighteen and Miss Dowling gave a ball to celebrate her graduation. There were more than forty-three adults present, 'all the Beauty and Fashion of the neighbourhood', including her friends Edith May Southey and Sara Coleridge. The last guest left at almost four o'clock. 'You may be sure we are happy to have her at home,' Dorothy wrote. 'She is not yet in *confirmed* good health, though not so subject to take cold as formerly, and, as she has no apparent weakness we trust that fresh air and exercise (she cannot now bear long walks) will in the course of a few months restore her.'[23] Dora stayed at Greta Hall as often as she could, though it was more often Edith May and Sara who came to stay at Rydal Mount, for Wordsworth had become possessive since Dora's return from school and Sara Coleridge complained that he could not 'bear her absence for many days together' and would not let Dora stay for long at Greta Hall.[24]

Dora got on well with Southey, who wrote lilting letters to her in broken English calling her his 'pretty', his 'dear young wife', signing them 'your dutiful old husband, Robert Sootée'.

In 1820 Dorothy, William and Mary went for an extended visit to France and Italy, partly to retrace William's 1790 journey and partly to accompany Mary's cousin Tom Monkhouse on his honeymoon. Dorothy, as usual, kept a journal to record their travels across Europe. Her letters record a catalogue of illness as her old complaints of exhaustion, headache and diarrhoea recurred under the stress of the journey: '. . . so very unwell that I could hardly speak at all . . . My Bowels were much affected . . . At Brussels again I fatigued myself – I did not go out as much as others . . . I was . . . overpowered and exhausted . . . It is my way now not to be able to sleep in the mornings – but my legs ached so from the state of my Bowels that I was forced upon the bed again.'[25]

The journal was written up after her return from notes taken at the time, but lacks spontaneity and the fresh colour of intense personal feeling. Much of it is backward-looking, remembering other excursions, other experiences, of which she was constantly reminded. She found copying it out afterwards a tedious chore and admitted that she was no longer able to 'sit steadily to writing by the hour together'.[26] The result, she admitted, was 'utterly unsatisfactory' even to herself. Her friends agreed that it was 'a hurried composition', well below the standard of her 1803 Scottish journal. Dorothy wrote two more journals (apart from the daily journal which she still kept intermittently), covering a tour of Scotland made in the company of Joanna Hutchinson in 1822 and one of the Isle of Man in 1828. Though they never reach the high literary standard of her earlier work, she was still capable of writing arresting phrases such as: 'The moon rose large and dull, like an ill-cleaned brass plate . . .'[27] She continued to keep journals until the end of her life in a spasmodic fashion. She hoped that they would be of interest to posterity, 'when we are dead and gone, any memorial of us will be satisfactory to the children'.[28] William tried to arrange for publication of Dorothy's 1803 Scottish journal, but the idea made her very uneasy. She had so many 'scruples and apprehensions' it took her a long time and much persuasion to assent. Even then she was unwilling to 'sacrifice my privacy for a certainty *less* than two hundred pounds',[29] and in the end the project came to nothing.

Dorothy was, Mary acknowledged, 'a most industrious journalist', and Mary feared to 'injure her report' by her own efforts. However, Mary's 'Memorials of a Tour on the Continent' is a very readable and talented account, well worth publication, but though she was urged to publish she always refused. Mary's journal is much more personal than Dorothy's and written with a dry wit. On one occasion she observed that, although she was up and about, William was still in bed 'hurting himself with a sonnet'.

In 1821, the year Dora left school, a new name began to feature in her letters. Edward Quillinan was an army officer retired on half-pay, son of a Portuguese wine merchant, a published poet and admirer of Wordsworth, who had come to live in Ivy Cottage at the bottom of the lane leading up to Rydal Mount. He was married to the daughter of Sir Egerton Brydges and had two children, Jemima (named for her mother and always shortened to Mima) and Rotha (named for the river that runs into Grasmere). Quillinan was a very shy man, who found his first introduction to Wordsworth something of an ordeal. When he finally plucked up courage to respond to Wordsworth's invitation and presented himself at Rydal Mount, he found the poet much offended by the delay. 'He seemed quite angry, twirled a chair about, and made short and stiff remarks. I was getting indignant and thought him disagreeable.' The entrance of Dora Wordsworth into the room temporarily lightened the atmosphere, but 'Soon, however, the fine patriarchal expression vanished, the poet resumed his frigidity and his twirl of the chair.' It took Sara Hutchinson's particular blend of tact in the management of difficult men to set things right. 'I was about to retire, much disappointed, when in came Miss Hutchinson, who saw at once that there was some awkwardness between us: she relieved me in a moment with that fine talk and benign politeness th[o]roughly understood only by women. She civilly accosted me, rallied the poet for twirling the chair, took it from him and appropriated it to her own use, made herself mistress of the cause of our restraint, laughed him into a good humour, and sent him out to show me the garden and the terrace.'

It was Quillinan's first meeting with Dora, a brief but vivid glimpse, recorded in his diary. 'Suddenly the door opened, and a young lady, rather tall of good features perhaps, not handsome – but of most engaging innocence and ingenuousness of aspect, stood at the door, seemed impressed at seeing a stranger, and half drew back . . . It was a most timely interruption. I have loved that sweet girl ever since.'[30] Quillinan was one of the party who attended Dora's ball at Ambleside and was soon a regular visitor to Rydal Mount. Sara Hutchinson observed with approval that he was 'agreeable & *suitable* to Doro & Willy – he flirts with Doro & plays with Willy . . . Doro & he have had a *poetical* correspondence since he went to Lancaster – And Sara Coleridge who is here is quite as fond of him as Doro – So you may guess what a nice good-humoured creature he is . . .'[31] The 'poetical correspondence' took the form of letters in rhymed forms. One of the few to survive (though Quillinan apparently kept and treasured them all), written on 31 December 1821, begins:

> You man of the Moon!
> Who were once a Dragoon . . .
> I hope you'll come soon
> From the banks of the Lune . . .

The monorhyme is sustained for several pages of nonsense before ending with a threat.

> . . . Ere I fly to Lake Shun
> For a bright Honey-moon
> With my own sweet Baboon.

It is signed 'Little simple/Dora Dimple'.

Quillinan's wife was in poor health, having been suffering from severe post-natal depression since the birth of her second daughter, Rotha – Dora's god-daughter. In the spring of 1822 Mrs Quillinan was found beside the kitchen range with her clothes on fire and, although the flames were beaten out, she was badly burned and died several days later, devotedly nursed by Dorothy. Dora looked after the two girls, nicknamed 'the Trotts', and grew rapidly fond of them. It may well have been at this point that she began to fall in love with their father. Dora had a very passionate nature and was prone to violent affections for both men and women. After Quillinan left, taking his children to live at Lee Priory in Kent, Dorothy observed that Dora was 'neither well nor ill . . . but looks wretchedly and . . . is dull in spirits and sluggish in motion'.[32] She was also extremely bored, having nothing to do at Rydal Mount except a few desultory domestic duties in a house already amply served by women. In May 1823 she was still thinking constantly of Quillinan and his daughters, desiring Dorothy to send 'a thousand Loves' with her letters. 'She never lets half a day go by without talking of you all.'[33] Dora was still very young for her age – as late as 1825 her letters are ingenuous and even childish – but this was hardly surprising as her parents kept her so 'close' at home and allowed her hardly any opportunities to mature and develop an independent personality. She suffered from the ill that Mary Wollstonecraft had identified for young women, that 'dependence of body naturally produces dependence of mind'. Dora remained a 'child-woman' all her life, a quality that could be quite attractive to men. Hartley Coleridge called it 'the childishness that has always hung upon her womanhood'.

In 1822 Sara Coleridge accompanied her mother on a visit to London. She had rarely been away from home in her life – visits to Rydal Mount and a single excursion with her mother to stay with family friends in Liverpool were the sum of her social round. Her innocence and naïvety were as obvious as her beauty and accomplishment – Sir Walter Scott, on a visit to Keswick, noted that in spite of her precocious intellect, she had an 'extreme ignorance of the World'.[34] Lord and Lady Beaumont had made plans to launch

Sara into London society in style. There were many people who were eager to meet her. William Collins, on a visit to the Lakes, had painted her portrait as 'The Highland Girl' which had caused something of a sensation when it was exhibited at the Royal Academy. This, as well as her authorship, gave Sara some celebrity. Southey thoroughly disapproved of the plan. 'If Lady Beaumont has formed any indiscreet scheme of showing off Sara, I am afraid Mrs C. would enter into it too readily, & set down any caution which might come from me, to a wrong motive . . . But I believe the Wordsworths are going to Coleorton, & they will prevent this kind of mischief . . .'[35] The planned event came to nothing.

It was a tremendous ordeal for Sara to go to London, since her reputation as a beauty and a bluestocking had already preceded her and its effects were very apparent. 'My bluestockingism is gone abroad,' she wrote to Derwent. 'I hope my dear brother don't countenance these scandalous reports. I'm really become a perfect bugbear. One gentleman expatiated most pathetically on the *fright* he was in when he first approached our house, the den of the monster.'[36] Her unusual looks also caused consternation in a city where beauties were numerous. The 'Highland Girl' was rapturously described as 'a form of compacted light, not of flesh and blood, so radiant was her hair, so slender her form, so buoyant her step, and heaven-like her eyes', and designated the 'Flower of the Lakes' and 'Sylph of Ullswater'.[37] On one occasion when she attended a public gathering everyone stood up spontaneously when she made her entrance. Sara's astonishing beauty was a burden to her (when Hartley ingenuously told her she was 'a visible soul', she retorted that he was 'a visible fool' for saying so) and one of her first essays was 'On the Disadvantages resulting from the possession of Beauty'.

It was hoped that the visit to London would separate her from an unsuitable attachment. Among the many dazzled young men who haunted Greta Hall was a Mr May who laid siege to her affections in a very determined way. Sara became romantically involved with him and fancied herself in love. She was persuaded to assent to an engagement, but when John May's father forbade the match and Southey expressed his disapproval, Sara quickly realised that she had mistaken her own feelings and the engagement was broken. The young man, however, was quite persistent in his attentions and it was hoped that Sara's absence and her introduction into a wider social circle would put an end to the affair.

One of the major events of Sara's stay in London was a visit to Coleridge at Highgate. It was the first time she had seen her father in ten years but the awkward meeting passed off reasonably well despite Sara tactlessly disagreeing with her father by saying, 'Uncle Southey doesn't think so.' Having Southey thrown in his face had always irritated Coleridge. But he was so enchanted with his beautiful, erudite daughter that the remark was passed over. Sara visited Coleridge at the Gillmans' for about three weeks, discovering with delight that she and her father were 'likeminds'. With her shrewd gift for appraising people, a watchfulness developed in childhood, she observed that Mrs Gillman had become one of Coleridge's idealised women, though he was not quite as obsessed as he had been by Sara Hutchinson. The renewal of the relationship with Sara was not without problems. One of Sara's cousins observed: 'My uncle does not seem very affectionate towards her.' There was a distance between them, a crevasse filled with guilt and sadness, resentment and all the other impossible emotions, that could not be crossed in a matter of weeks. On Coleridge's side there was the memory of the awkward little girl who refused to caress him; on Sara's side was the knowledge that Dora Wordsworth and even her brother Derwent's fiancée Mary Pridham had come before herself in her father's affections. It was all too much for Coleridge. After the initial visits he became too ill to leave his room, as he often did under stress, and did not see his daughter again during all the months she was in London.

It was in the Gillmans' drawing-room that Sara met her cousins John Taylor and Henry Nelson Coleridge, the sons of Coleridge's brother James. They were great admirers of Coleridge's work, finding the man himself – whatever the family said of him –

'delightful and astonishing'. Both were lawyers. Henry, the younger of the two, had just begun to practise as a Chancery barrister after a brilliant academic career at King's College, Cambridge. Both Henry and his brother were sophisticated men-about-town with 'Eton Bronze' and not likely to be susceptible to the charms of a 'country cousin'. Henry wrote to his favourite sister Fanny that he wagered five to one that Sara would 'commit waste' among the young regimentals in London. With all the confidence of immunity he admitted that she was 'a lovely creature; small, but not in the least diminutive or dwarfish . . . her hair like Mary's and her eyes like a dove's; fair with a nice carmine; little features. Mrs C. is not prepossessing; she was wonderfully kind and attentive and watchful; I even read *design* in her eye. She dressed most unbecomingly. Sara neat and elegant . . . She does not seem at all formidable; you need not alarm yourself. She uses no hard words and seems very ordinary in her wishes and thoughts . . . You would split to hear the way I *romanced* to Sara!'[38]

They had a great deal in common, though very different personalities. Henry was extrovert and sociable; Sara introverted and rather shy in company. But both shared a delight in intellectual pursuits and a taste for the discussion of 'philosophy and abstract ideas' that terrified many of the other young men who were attracted to Sara. She had an intensity and seriousness that were considered inappropriate in a woman, but this was no deterrent to a man as brilliant as Henry Coleridge. These qualities were also apparent in the strength of Sara's feelings for Henry. 'When she loved,' Hartley wrote, 'the fate/Of her affections was a stern religion . . .'

Three months later they entered into a secret engagement, known only to Sara's mother and Henry's sister Fanny. Henry had two rings made from Sara's hair, one set with pearls to give to her and the other for himself. They were both afraid that, as they were penniless, their families would forbid the engagement and they resolved to keep it secret until they had the means to marry. They were also aware that the Coleridge family's main objection to the match was not their financial circumstances but Sara's '*Mad*

Father'. During Henry's childhood Samuel Taylor Coleridge had been held up to the cousins as a tragic example *not* to be followed. After a visit to the Coleridge family at Ottery St Mary, where she was universally approved despite her parentage, Sara returned to Greta Hall in a highly emotional state, not knowing when she would be able to see Henry again. Dorothy Wordsworth was relieved that Sara had 'returned to her native mountains unspoiled by the admiration that has been showered upon her'[39] and thought her much improved by her town polish.

In 1823 it was Edith May's turn to be taken to London by her father. She enjoyed it so much that she stayed for two years. Southey wrote letters to her addressed to his 'very magnificent and most dissipated Daughter'.[40] She was out such a great deal that Southey complained that the only time one could be certain of seeing her was at breakfast. Edith May was now a 'very striking person' and thought to be much like her mother at the same age. Hartley thought it likely that she would marry into the nobility which, for the elegant, though penniless, daughter of the Poet Laureate, was a possibility.

Back at Greta Hall Sara Coleridge and the younger Southey girls began the task of cataloguing Southey's library of over 6000 books. It was, Sara remarked, a dreary task, but it filled otherwise empty days. Time hung on their hands as they followed the normal pursuits of upper-class girls – they paid calls, embroidered silk covers for albums, went for walks and waited for husbands. Sara was depressed and miserable and her mother often found her in tears. It was very hard 'to be separated from one for whom one feels so much . . . and that is nothing compared to the dread of losing his affection from long absence, which it is impossible entirely to remove from one's mind.'[41] Dorothy's keen eye observed that she had become extremely thin: 'I could not but think of a lily Flower to be snapped by the first blast . . .'[42]

At Grasmere, in her new offices of amanuensis and 'regular tea maker' – an 'important part of feminine duty' – Dora Wordsworth became idle and moped. She went to Stockton on Tees with Sara Hutchinson and Sara reported that she found it dull: 'She does not

like *this sort of Town* life at all & is very industrious – but London
where there is so much novelty would make her quite wild . . . for
this is the most stupid place in the world . . . there is no *society* – &
for the Country it is detestable. Yet we have exceedingly enjoyed
ourselves . . .'[43] Dora began to read Horace and teach herself
German, having no trouble at all learning things when she was
interested and motivated enough.

Sara Hutchinson and Dorothy Wordsworth were away visiting
family and friends for increasing amounts of time, now that there
were no children to look after and little to do for William who
wrote less and less. Dorothy had a great desire to be needed and
willingly went wherever she felt useful: '. . . there being now so
little occupation at home . . . I feel as if I could have done more
good elsewhere . . . I should shrink neither from pain nor fatigue
could I lend a helping hand or alleviate distress.'[44] In Dorothy's
absence, Dora began to fill her place in William's life. He had
trouble with inflamed eyes and Dora read to him and transcribed
his poetry and letters for him while he lay on the sofa with his eyes
closed. She was also a source of inspiration for him at a time when
his creativity had reached a low ebb. He came to regard her as
indispensable.

Sara Coleridge quickly found herself a new task to alleviate her
boredom. She began a translation of an early French text whose
title ran to two and a half lines, *The Right Joyous and Pleasant
History of the Facts, Tests, and Prowesses of the Chevalier Bayard,
the Good Knight without Fear and without Reproach: by the Loyall
Servant*. It was in some respects more difficult than Dobrizhoffer
but Sara was fortunate in having Southey's library to draw on. Old
French and Italian dictionaries proved invaluable to translate
obscure chivalric terms, though the amount of reading required
to research the book properly strained her eyes. 'It is all about
battles and sieges,' Sara explained to Henry, 'things which puzzle
my little feminine brain. However, I am quite enamoured of my
hero, the more so as he reminds me of my first love, Amadis de
Gaul, over whose dreadful adventures I used to cry . . .'[45]

It was published anonymously in 1825. Southey wrote to a

friend that it was, 'as you have guessed, translated by Sara Coleridge, who gives herself wholly up to such employment – not a little (in my judgement) to the disqualifying herself for those duties which she will have to perform whenever she changes from the single to the married state.'[46] Although her engagement was secret, her attachment to Henry was already much talked about in the family.

In 1824, Henry had planned to visit Sara and her mother at Greta Hall as part of a tour of the Lakes and Scotland. But, like Sara, he had been a delicate child and was far from robust as an adult. A renewed bout of rheumatism caused him to postpone the journey and he went to stay with his father at Ottery instead. Whether this was the real reason for the alteration in his plans isn't clear and several biographers have speculated that there may well have been problems between the two young people. One difficulty was the rejected John May who had assiduously renewed his attentions and would not accept Sara's repeated refusals. Sara, bound by secrecy not to reveal her engagement, was forced to ask Henry's brother to write to him on her behalf.

While at Ottery, Henry took the opportunity to broach the subject of a possible engagement with his father. The result was more devastating than the young couple had expected. Colonel James Coleridge demanded that any 'understanding' already entered into should be terminated and Henry was rapidly packed off to the West Indies with another Coleridge cousin, ostensibly for his health. John Coleridge wrote to Sara telling her that she was to regard herself as 'entirely disengaged'. Sara wrote him a spirited letter in return.

I may be disengaged, but my own feelings will never permit me to think myself so – in the eye of the world I might be justified in bestowing my affections elsewhere, since Henry cannot assure me of his hand as well as his heart; but after what has passed between us, after the vows that we have interchanged, I must ever think that for either of us to make such a transfer . . . would be a faithless and falsehearted thing . . .

For my own part, I knew from the beginning that there was but little chance of our being ever united – I knew also that if I entered into the sort of negative engagement which Henry wished, for an indefinite term till he should think it advisable to ask his father's consent, such a plan would very probably prevent my settling in life . . . for a man may marry almost when he chooses, but with a woman, especially one in my situation, the season is soon past and after dedicating my affections to him for so long a time how could I calculate upon stifling them all of a sudden and marrying another? – No! when I gave my heart to him I gave it for good and all and never will I take it back till I perceive that he is weary of the gift – then I certainly will never trust any of his sex with it again.[47]

Sara had also to counter disapproval nearer home. Hartley considered Henry too lightweight for her. When Henry published an account of his travels in the West Indies on his return in 1826, Hartley found it 'flippant and vulgar' and felt that it reflected badly on Henry's quality of mind and suitability as a husband for Sara. Support came from an unexpected source. A reference in Henry's book to the author's love for a beautiful cousin alerted Coleridge to his daughter's attachment and he wrote to his wife that he did not want to see his only daughter '– and *such* a Daughter – condemned to a miserable Heart-wasting'. He was hurt that Sara had not felt able to confide in him and promised to do all that he could to promote the match.

In 1823 Dora Wordsworth spent some months teaching at Miss Dowling's school, filling in for the absence of one of the Dowling sisters. Dora enjoyed the occupation and was 'well and happy', her health improving with her spirits. She was responsible for instructing 'the whole school (thirty 8 or 9) in penmanship – the younger classes reading and French – walking as Governante of the tribe, superintending drawing and music lessons – and having the charge of 5 or 6 little ones in her Bedroom'.[48]

On her return home, Dora was presented at a public ball in

Penrith for the first time and was wildly excited, though her father grumbled a great deal at having to accompany her. Afterwards she was much disillusioned with what she called '*quadrilling* it away at Penrith . . . Daddy & Mammy looking on I will never go again – to me it is perfectly detestable'. She had no time at all for friends who 'talk to me of nothing but balls & routs concerts and Officers of the 7th Hussars &c &c'. Dora managed to persuade her father to allow her to travel to London with Miss Dowling's sister Jane. Edith May was still in town. So, too, was Quillinan, accompanied by his elder daughter Mima. Dora was apparently corresponding with him at this point and he sometimes sent poems for her to transcribe. How aware he was of her romantic hopes and fantasies, no one can know, but it is not surprising that she found him attractive – a handsome poet, thirteen years her senior, with a tragic history, Edward Quillinan was the very stuff of romantic novels.

The London visit was a great success. Dora went to the theatre and the opera and, in spite of her protestations, led a life of lively dissipation. When her parents and Dorothy came south, Dorothy took Dora to Lee Priory to stay with Quillinan and 'the Trotts'. There – chaperoned by her aunt – Dora walked with him and listened to the nightingales in the garden and could hardly tear herself away: 'I am sure I could have stood all night listening and not have been wearied.'[49] After they had left, Dorothy wrote a letter of thanks on behalf of herself and her niece. 'I will not say a word of Lee and the nightingales – I was too sorry to leave them – and poor Doro could think of little but what she had left behind, for some miles of the journey.'[50]

In such low spirits Dora was no longer in a condition to enjoy the diversions of London, and a journey to Wales with her mother had little appeal. So when Wordsworth declared that he had had enough of the city and pressured Dora to accompany him back to Grasmere, she gave in, cutting short her visit by several months, and in doing so sacrificed the opportunity to see more of Quillinan. Dorothy did not approve at all. 'I assure you this arrangement does not please me . . . Doro will write to you herself a day or two after her arrival at home – and she will tell you how she sickened at the thought of her Father's going without her – how he yielded – and also how desirous he was to take her with him. The point he most dwelt upon was, that her absence from home and from her Mother and himself would be too long – more than could be afforded – "nine or ten months being a long portion of human life after 53 years of age", but I am insensibly getting into details that I wished to avoid.'[51]

The relationship between Dora and Edward Quillinan was very one-sided at this point. Though Quillinan conducted a sporadic and lively correspondence with her, he does not seem to have considered the possibility of a love affair, and Dora's letters to Quillinan give no clue as to her real feelings for him at all. In the beginning they are playful and flirtatious, then – after a long gap – friendly but formal. During this period Quillinan was writing to Sara Hutchinson in a much more intimate vein, taking liberties only a much younger man could get away with. She was his 'dearest Hutton' and, in a Valentine, 'Larah my dear, my love; my life'. Sara was the recipient of his confidences. Describing his problems appointing a suitable governess for Mima and Rotha, he confessed that he could not trust himself 'with a governess under 35'. Quillinan got on well with women and there was more than one romantic possibility in his life. When one of these attractions married someone else he told Sara that though he 'could not have afforded her for myself . . . yet I had a sort of dog-in-the-manger feeling about her . . . you are shrewd enough to comprehend obscure phrases and develop darky meanings . . .' In the next letter he urged Sara to find him a wife. 'I wish I was married. I am sick of this stupid life of selfish dissatisfied freedom.'[52] The thought of Dora as a lover seems not to have crossed his mind and Dora, during Quillinan's long absences in Portugal and France, seemed able to put him firmly out of hers. A phrase in a letter written two or three years later suggests that Quillinan had done something to put an end to any romantic hope she might have cherished.

Back at Rydal Mount (or 'Idle Mount' as she quipped in letters)

Dora once more had nothing else to occupy her mind but the state of her health, which began to deteriorate almost immediately. Sara Coleridge witnessed her decline. She noticed that Dora had 'lost bloom' and become 'liny and in some respects old-looking'. Sara's friendship with Dora strengthened as they grew older. She was, Sara wrote, 'one of the most interesting women I have ever known'. Her major fault was that she was 'all tenderness and attention to others and self-postponement.'[53]

By 1826 Edith Southey was already beginning to show symptoms of mental disturbance, graver than the bouts of depression she had always been prone to. Southey exhorted her to look after herself: '. . . if you will but take due means for keeping yourself in a healthy state by regular exercise, generous food and occasional medicines, chearful thoughts and wiser ones will put an end to all unhappiness of mind.'[54] But in July their fourteen-year-old daughter Isabel became ill with a sore throat and fever and on Sunday the 16th she died, plunging Edith into an abyss from which she never emerged. In a lucid moment, she told Southey that she feared that she was going mad.

Isabel's death caused considerable trauma among her sisters and friends. Though they had been saddened and bewildered by Herbert's death ten years earlier, this was the first family death they were old enough to fully comprehend. Southey wrote the girls an awesome letter, urging them to confront their own mortality: 'Who may be summoned next is known only to the All-wise Disposer of all things . . .' They must, he urged, prepare themselves by correcting faults and cultivating 'a meek, submissive, obliging disposition', in order to inherit the Kingdom of Heaven. Both Dora Wordsworth and Sara Coleridge were devastated. The 'fair knot of Girls' was snapped.[55]

Isabel's death occurred on the eve of Sara's departure for London. It was a visit that had been planned for some weeks in order that Sara could spend the winter with her father. She had also been invited to stay with Lady Beaumont, whose husband had recently died. But the major objective of the visit was to meet

Henry, who had now returned from the West Indies. Complicated arrangements had been made for her travel, since a young, single lady could not travel alone. Mr Gee, a friend and neighbour, had offered to take her in his barouche, travelling in easy stages, since she suffered from motion sickness. When the day came, Sara was so emotionally overwrought by her own fears, endless sleepless nights and grief over Isabel's death, that she was able to go no further than Kendal. Her mother had gone with her, intending to visit friends there, and so was able to bring her back. At Greta Hall she was gradually nursed back to health 'but her disappointment is so keen that all here are of opinion, that if she is suffered to remain here all the winter brooding over the impossibility of her being able to take the journey, that it will have a bad effect upon her health as she grows daily thinner – and looks almost as white as this paper'.[56]

Sarah Coleridge was also worried that Henry would believe Sara reluctant to see him and bestow his affections elsewhere unless the attachment was quickly renewed, and she was afraid that Coleridge, bitterly disappointed at not seeing Sara and now in very precarious health, would not live to see his daughter again. She arranged to take Sara to her friend Mrs Evans in Derby for a short holiday and send her on to London from there.

At Rydal Mount there was a very different account of the affair. Sara Hutchinson wrote a sharp letter to Quillinan that 'Celestial Blue' (as he called Sara Coleridge) had 'set off for Town with Mr Gee about a month ago – but unluckily her mother accompanied her to Kendal & there persuaded her she was not fit for the journey, dosed her with Laudanum to make her sleep at a time when she could not have been expected to sleep if she had had the feeling of a stone . . . and brought her back – leaving poor Gee to go alone – after having waited 17 days for her convenience & procured a Carriage in which she could travel at ease – & have the advantage of staying on the road at Night. Now S[ara] is in despair – Her Father disappointed – Her Lover too (but why does he not fetch her?) . . . So if you want to succor a distressed Damsel you may go thither & escort her up by *slow stages* which is the only mode by which she can travel. – O how I do pity her! & hope that if she gets rid of her Mother that she may turn out something useful before she ceases to be ornamental.'[57]

In London Sara was relieved to discover that not only had her relationship with Henry survived their separation, but the time that they were now able to spend together strengthened the bond between them. Sara felt 'the chain grow tighter and tighter every day'. She was ecstatically happy when Colonel James Coleridge wrote from Ottery finally giving his grudging consent to their engagement. All that was needed now was sufficient money to live on. 'To judge from my present feelings,' she wrote to Henry, 'from the moments of deep delight I have felt in your society and from hearing the sound of your beloved voice, I know and feel sure that if to this were added a sense of security and permanence, if the sad perspective of parting, of possible disasters and various dreaded contingencies were not before me, my condition would be one of real happiness.'[58]

There were many who considered Sara totally unsuited to marriage and motherhood, since she did not have the expected aptitude for domestic pursuits. Even Henry himself seems to have had misgivings. Sara assured him that the 'tendency in my nature to speculation and dreaminess' would not 'render me an unfit wife to you. Does not Wordsworth point out to you how the most excursive bird can brood as long and fondly on the nest as any of the feathered race?'[59]

One incompatibility that was rapidly becoming apparent was Sara's reticence in sexual matters and Henry's open acknowledgement of his desire for her. Sara gave Henry her most intimate commonplace book to read, a collection of quotations from texts that had moved her most deeply. Henry kept the album for almost a year, annotating her entries with marginal notes. Beside a love sonnet he wrote: 'If my passion for you, Sara, is not pure, then human love can never be so. There is appetite in it; it is the tongue of lambent flames which speaks to *Sex*; but appetite is subordinate to reason with me, and scarcely any thing else but an effect to an intense desire to actualize my affection. I am sick for complete Union.' Sara's view of love as a high-minded, spiritual affection,

Henry argued, was 'not human' and 'falsely denies the body and its needs'. Sara's romantic notions of love, fed by her readings of Dante and Petrarch, were about to founder on the realities of physical desire. Part of an essay on love written in her album by Henry has been crossed through and several pages torn out. Henry's last entry reads: 'I shall return this book to you this evening. When I see it again, let it have been enriched a thousand-fold: Make it your friend, your confessional, your notebook. Write everything in it that has any reference to the heart.' Sara never wrote in it again.

Quillinan's father died in 1826 and he was often in Portugal in connection with the family wine business. He returned in the spring of 1827, to settle briefly in London. He chided Dora for not writing to him while he was away and received a cool response. 'I more than once thought of writing . . . but your ingenious excuse for getting rid of so *heavy* a correspondent two or three years back occurred to me, and I was content to remain in ignorance . . .'[60] In his absence Dora had not been without her share of suitors. William Crackenthorpe of Newbiggin Hall wanted to marry her and so did her cousin Thomas Robinson who wrote to Wordsworth in January 1826 asking for permission to 'pay his respects'. He was refused because he had no money. Wordsworth recommended him to 'look out for some lady with a sufficient fortune for both of you.'[61] The wording of the letter indicates that Dora's feelings were never consulted.

Ivy Cottage had a new tenant, the Rev. William Ayling, who soon became a regular visitor at Rydal Mount. His sister Fanny got on well with Dora and they were soon 'first friends' – Dora developing a passionate attachment for Fanny. But when William fell in love with Dora and was refused, the relationship soured. The Wordsworths insisted that Dora should no longer call on her friend Fanny, who felt understandably aggrieved and began to entertain 'all *her* friends & *ours* with her own version of the story . . . it is impossible for me to hear all this without being hurt'. Dora was wounded even further by the discovery that her love for

Fanny – 'too enthusiastic to be wise I grant' – had never been reciprocated. Dora had been 'in love with *her for her own sake – &* *liked her brother for her sake* – whilst she thought I *loved her for her* brother's sake as she in fact only liked me – but now I am convinced that I am the only one of this bright triad that ever was in love or they *could* not have behaved as they have done . . . & they only wanted me among them because I was Wordsworth's Daughter . . .'[62]

Dora had several intense female friendships. One of them was the young authoress Maria Jane Jewsbury who had written to Wordsworth in 1825 'with the most genuine sentiments of respectful admiration' and ventured to present him with 'the accompanying little volume; and to hope that my having dedicated it to you without your permission will not be deemed an unpardonable liberty'. The work enclosed was *Phantasmagoria*, a collection of prose and verse. Dora wrote back on her father's behalf and was soon adding postscripts to his letters that developed into an independent correspondence. Jane visited the Wordsworths at a rented summer house – Kent's Bank – where the two girls began what seems to have been a passionate relationship. One of the fruits of their summer collaboration was the *Kent's Bank Mercury*, a mock-newspaper they published during the holiday. After Kent's Bank, Jane's letters to Dora become increasingly intimate – Dora becomes 'the Fairy Dorabelle', and Jane is Dora's own 'Jug-Jug'.

Throughout 1826, the entire household was engaged in transcribing and correcting for a new edition of William's poetry in five volumes. It was wearisome work and his temper became frayed. He later apologised to Mary for his 'ungovernable impatience' and harsh treatment of her: 'I often pray to God that He would grant us both life, that I may make some amends to you for that, and all my unworthiness . . .' He admitted that Dora also had cause for complaint.[63] The edition didn't come out until 1827, held over due to the failure of the printer's business.

Dora had not been in particularly good health since her trip to London; Isabel's death and the unpleasant emotional upheaval of the Ayling affair all seem to have affected her. In the autumn she became critically ill with what was described as a 'bilious fever'. She had diarrhoea so badly that Mary Wordsworth and Sara Hutchinson had to take turns to sit up with her for eleven nights. A 'physician of great practice' was called in, but agreed with the local apothecary that there were no consumptive symptoms. The propensity of tuberculosis to invade other parts of the body, including the stomach, skeleton and brain, was not generally known at that date. Dora was still ailing and confined to her room in March and the family talked of taking her to Italy in the hope that the warmer climate would help. Dora's enforced confinement was brightened by the presence of Edith May, who came to stay for two months.

In June the Wordsworths and the Southeys took the two girls to Harrogate to take the waters. The change of scene and amusement effected the hoped-for improvement in Dora's constitution, though her mother remarked that 'this happy state is only to be depended upon so long as the beautiful weather lasts; she is a complete *air* gage; as soon as damp is felt the trouble in her throat returns.'[64] Mary wisely decided that, as Italy was unaffordable, she would take Dora south to winter among friends.

Quillinan visited Rydal Mount in August, his presence once more coinciding with Dora's improved health. Dora wrote to Jane Jewsbury: 'I am glad you have seen & *like* Mr Quillinan he is certainly the *most agreeable man I ever* met with & my prime favorite . . .'[65] They spent some time with the Southeys at Greta Hall and had a 'gypsy bonfire' and picnic at Raven Crag overlooking Derwentwater. Dora's memories of her visits to Keswick were of 'balls, plays, tea drinkings on the Islands &c &c', and the girls being 'worn off their feet pleasuring'. In November Quillinan joined Dora and Mary Wordsworth in Herefordshire where they, and Edith May, were staying with Mary's Hutchinson relatives. By 11 May they were all in London staying at Quillinan's house in Bryanston Street. There Dora wrote to Jane that 'the whirl has been so great that I am astonished I have any head left – what with calling, and receiving calls, writing, and replying to notes – Dinners, breakfasts, Luncheons, routs – Operas, Theatre, Dioramas, exhibitions and last though not least *shopping* – we are overpowered not to speak of the *weight of talent & learning*, this is magazinish is it not?'

Visits to the theatre, galleries and the opera were very much to Dora's taste and she allowed herself to be fashionably dressed. 'I have got such a hat! and had a Frenchman last night to dress my hair for the opera, who cut off all my dangling curls, and made my head precisely like the ladies you see in their windows.' Dorothy feared that she might have her head turned and lose her 'simplicity of character', but Dora, though entertained, was not seduced by London life. 'The more I see of the world the more satisfied and convinced am I, that my lot is one of the happiest in the world oh I would not exchange my mountain dwelling for all the [wealth & grandeur this] city has to offer.'[66]

While they were in London Wordsworth had the idea of going on a tour of Belgium, Germany and Holland in the company of Coleridge. Dora was to accompany them, while Mary went to stay with her son John, who had just accepted a living as curate of Whitwick in Leicestershire. The ill-assorted party of 'two Poets and their amiable Daughter' left on 22 June 1828: Coleridge short, plump, vague, fussy and now quite white-haired; Wordsworth thin, tall and kitted out like 'a mountain farmer' in long brown overcoat, 'striped duck trousers, fustian gaiters, and thick shoes'. It was Dora's task to look after her 'two fathers' and she found this more arduous than expected, with Wordsworth's confirmed hypochondria (his letters are a catalogue of minor ailments, from indigestion to piles), and Coleridge's 'fiddle-faddling' and bouts of exhaustion.

The renewed acquaintance with Quillinan in London, after a gap of three or four years, brought a renewal of their correspondence. By March 1829 they were once more writing regularly to each other – though Quillinan was the more frequent correspondent. This time the tone is altogether different. On 16 April he wrote: 'My dear Dora, If I were to tell you that I am in love with you for your last letters you would answer, "Why you wretch, you have told me that a thousand times before!" Well, then. I am more in love with you than ever . . .' He asks, playfully, 'What sort of a

Housekeeper do you make in the absence of all the elder (not elderly mind) store-room Guardians? but indifferent I suppose – Are you Butler, too?' Her reply, addressed to 'My dear Mr Quillinan', is another light-hearted verse epistle.

> Know that of my keys the jingle
> Yet with father's verse doth mingle;
> Know, that I preside in state
> O'er each Pie's and Pudding's fate . . .

She threatens him with a rival lover – someone she actually disliked.

> Fie upon you Mr Quilly!
> Rogers shall be friend of mine –
> You shall be but Porcupine!

His slightly joking, but probably genuine, protestations of love are not alluded to – which he may have interpreted as a rebuff. By July 1829 it is Dora who is complaining that he is 'very sparing' of his letters.

In late May, Jane Jewsbury came for a month's visit to Rydal Mount. Her relationship to Dora had by this time become very intimate. A typical letter would begin 'My very, very dear Dora' or 'My dearest love', and emotions are explicitly described. 'I think away enthusiasm & work away feeling . . . I could not bear those brimming eyes of yours, brimming with lustrous tears – but you may *tell me when you write* that you love me, for that will be a comfort.' She sent Dora a copy of Surrey's poem 'To His Mistress' and hoped that Dora would be alone when she read her letters. Dora assured Jane that she read out only the *suitable* portions to the rest of the family. Dora had a great capacity for love and the intelligent and fascinating Maria Jane became the focus for her affections. 'Your restrictions as to the extent of my love amuse me not a little – Much like Canute's commands to the Sea "thus far shalt thou come & no farther" – You do not expect this (wise I grant) advice to be followed I know; nor am I *quite sure* you would wish it; that I should not is pretty certain.'

After leaving Rydal, Jane wrote a mournful letter to 'my own dearest Dora': 'I have been a dead thing all day . . .' Departure had made her 'heart sick'. But 'Whilst I can send a packet for 1d I felt as if I were not, could not be, far from you . . . oh do write to me at Lancaster – my own, my own – do not love me if it makes you sad, love me just as much as loving affects your happiness – no more – and love in hope, in the expectation of reunion – you will travel south – then I shall see you – I shall travel north . . . we *know* that the human heart must, & does strangely get above the dominion of grief – the past will soon give pleasure only . . . my own dear love . . .'

An undated letter from Dora among the Jewsbury MS almost certainly belongs to this period, since it refers to Jane's. 'My very dear Friend. You well know with what feelings your letter was seized & read; a thousand thousand thanks – for the first time in my life I have had to struggle against the feeling that distance & death only differ in name – when I had you by [m]y side I *could* not think so – now alas at times it weighs me to the ground – when I pass your door – when I throw myself on the sofa – when I stroll into the garden. I feel mournful *stillness* – sad mournful as the stillness of death – This I know will wear away, but the love & affection which *now* call out the feeling will *never* fade . . . When you left me I turned to the only fountain, whence pure hope, comfort & consolation can be drawn – then I read your letter & then what do you think I had strength & courage to do – In compliance with your wish I burnt *all* your letters except those written to me during your illness these treasures I will never part with – by the time I had done this – Father & Mother were returned from their drive to Grasmere & found me *bright* as usual & ready to read to them which – I did – But when I retired to my own room oh it was more than I had strength for – then I did give way & wept myself to sleep long before you had gone to rest . . . I wish I might just be alone for a few days – my heart sickens at the thought of *appearing* joyous, my thoughts *will* turn to you I feel what I have parted from, I know not if ever I shall again have those eyes overflowing with love cast upon me – & that thought causes mine to overflow with tears – "Dora" "Dora" – calls my "austere" Papa – I must go . . .'

The letter has a passionate postscript. 'Friday morning will bring me pleasure: – letters are something – are they not? and distance is not death – I will not think so it is wicked . . . I have seen you – & I know you love me – & I trust I shall always deserve your love & I am happy & thankful & God bless you adieu my dearest Friend . . . how I long for you last Evening such a sunset! the mountains were of burnished gold – the Lake – I know not what it was like – something out of faery Land and *now* the Green – with its living carpet – but I am longing for you every hour every moment – A bird cannot sing – A shadow fall – a cloud float past my window no nor Neptune look nor the Doves coo but I miss you . . . where is the friend who at all times was ready to listen to my nonsense, my hopes, my fears, – my joys, & my sorrows she is gone – but her love remains – & I do prize it . . .'

Jane's reply was written at 5 a.m. on 29 June. 'I cannot sleep here . . . Pray let me have an immediate reply & say you will not unlove your testy friend, who yet would never be testy to you – & never tired of you – & never weary of looking at you – My own sweet Dora, you know not the "sweet influences" cast on me by Rydal – & mornings & evenings rise upon me – now I am among "Phantoms of Delight" dreams coloured with beauty . . . & I hear your voice – a haunting sound, that makes me "long to steal away to weep".'

By the end of July Jane was back in Manchester, but no less unhappy. 'My own dearest Dora, Have I been separated from you only three weeks! My heart feels it three months – what would I not give for one glance of you tonight . . . my own heart is pregnant with remembrances, & of each *you* are near to me as ever – I dare not say how near – or you will think it needful to be wise and rebuke me!'[67]

In 1831 Jane married Mr Fletcher – much against her father's wishes. She was, she confessed to Dora, not in love with him 'but in a very morally prudential state of mind'. 'The affections of a woman of thirty', Jane explained, 'are not so easily got hold of as those of unsuspecting and romantic seventeen.' The motive may well have been escape from her father's domination and, as she admitted, 'being maintained instead of having to maintain' herself. She told Dora that she had been worn down by Mr Fletcher's persistent devotion. 'I doubt my own power of resisting the wear & tear of miserable looks. *I am a coward.*' Although the intensity of their relationship had cooled since Jane's visit to Rydal, Jane assured Dora of her constancy: '. . . can I ever cease to love to my best ability – yourself – now lapsing into the chosen circle of "old friends" – but remembered by me, as having called forth an enthusiasm that no living creature will awake more . . .' Jane was in the process of writing the first part of a trilogy, the *History of an Enthusiast*, which is the story of two women – one who becomes a writer and one who elects to fulfil her domestic role. It is tempting to draw parallels between the story, published in 1830, and Jane's relationship with Dora Wordsworth.

Jane asked Dora to burn all her letters, and although Dora agreed to comply with the request the passionate love letters from 1827 onwards are preserved at the Wordsworth Trust. In 1832 Mr Fletcher was offered a chaplaincy in India where, to Dora's great grief, Jane contracted cholera and died shortly after her arrival.

The young John Wordsworth, newly installed as curate at Whitwick, confided in his aunt that he was finding the long dark autumn evenings very dull. 'Poor Fellow!' Dorothy wrote, 'he wanted me sadly to go with him . . .' Dorothy needed little encouragement to travel south and keep house for him during the winter: 'I intend to stay at Whitwick, six months without stirring from the spot . . .'[68] The village was only 3 miles' walk from her friend Lady Beaumont at Coleorton and she went there whenever she could spare the time. She was kept busy with housework and parish visiting among the dilapidated cottages of what was a poor and industrial area – a landscape scarred by coal mining, brick kilns and stocking mills.

At the end of March 1829, Dorothy, now fifty-six, contracted influenza. Complications quickly set in similar to her usual gastric attacks but this time more acute, identified as 'internal inflammation' accompanied by excruciating pain. She became so dangerously ill the servants at her bed-side, believing her to be unconscious, talked amongst themselves about their belief that she would die. The doctor was convinced that there was an obstruction in her bowel and after the application of strong emetics, she began to improve.

Two weeks of illness left her unable to get out of bed and scarcely able to speak. Mary Wordsworth left for Whitwick as soon as she heard of the gravity of Dorothy's condition, in order to nurse her. William was very shaken by the news: 'Were She to depart the Phasis of my Moon would be robbed of light to a degree that I have not courage to think of . . .' Dora Wordsworth, Sara Coleridge and her mother stayed at Rydal Mount to keep him company and administer regular doses of 'pity and compassion'.[69]

Dorothy spend some months at her Aunt Rawson's in Halifax as soon as she was well enough to travel. There she had a relapse in the form of what she called 'Cholera Morbus'. She came back to Rydal in September, thankful and happy but 'not to be depended upon'. She still suffered from fatigue, an 'uneasiness' in her bowels and recurrent rheumatism. Her symptoms were remarkably similar to Coleridge's 'flying gout' but, as Gittings and Manton have pointed out in their biography, may well have been further attacks of the colitis which she seems to have suffered from all her life. It is also possible that she was suffering from gallstones, since foods such as butter were certain to precipitate the pain. Dorothy was treated, as usual, with laudanum and brandy, the dosage increasing with the severity of the spasms. By November Dorothy had become a confirmed invalid, convinced that 'acting the invalid, however strong and well I feel myself to be' was the best course for her since 'exercise amounting to the slightest degree of fatigue invariably disorders me.'[70] A short stroll along the terrace, or being driven by Dora in the pony chaise, were her only excursions. During the winter she kept more and more to her room; 'I find the best remedy against uncomfortable feelings has been the shutting out of cold. Hence I have a fire in my Bedroom – morning and night.'[71] After a lifetime of self-sacrifice and devotion to others, Dorothy was overcome with lassitude and enjoyed the sensation of being waited on by her niece and her sister-in-law. It proved to the orphaned child that she was indeed *loved*, and satisfied the deep-rooted, only partially suppressed craving she had always had to be the centre of attention – in fact to be mothered. A year later she wrote: 'I still enact the Invalid; but am in truth perhaps in better health than any one in the house . . .'[72] When Dora was not there to help her, Mary was at times exhausted by the demands of nursing Dorothy, managing the house and looking after William. '*She* is sometimes overdone with her exertions – and looks wearied – but spirits never fail her – she lies on the sofa for ½ an hour's rest and rising restored, never shrinks from any fresh call of duty.'[73]

At some time during this period Dora's relationship with Quillinan appears to have deepened. His letters are addressed to 'La mia Dorabella'. A letter interrupted by William, requesting Quillinan's company on a walk, has the scribbled postscript, 'the truth being that he is afraid I am making love to you all this time', which was an accurate description of the contents of the letter. Dora's letters to Quillinan are serious, rather formal – very unlike the earlier ones – and there is no expression of feeling as there is in her letters to Jane Jewsbury. Her mood was sober – 'years rob one of one's joyous spirits, & I have gloomy forebodings of what may happen before we meet again prey upon me'. Quillinan's own emotions appear to have blown hot and cold in response to the lack of encouragement. In letters to Dora he apologises for 'playing with her affections' and acting the 'social butterfly', behaviour that she was unable to deal with except by withdrawing behind a defensive shell.

One of the reasons for Quillinan's caution was his awareness of Wordsworth's disapproval. It is difficult to judge the exact moment when the family first became aware of the developing relationship, or when Quillinan first broached the possibility of marriage to Wordsworth. Whether it was mentioned to Dora is unclear. Some critics have opted for 1828 and some for 1832 as the critical dates when her father's approval of a match was sought. But the letters reveal that it was not until 1836 that Dora and Quillinan admitted the extent of their mutual affection to each other. It seems also from the letters that it was not until after Jane Jewsbury's marriage and her death, with all their emotional repercussions, that Dora began to turn once more to her long-standing friend. Whatever the disputes about the date of the first marriage proposal, scholars are unanimous in their agreement as to Wordsworth's reaction, which was discouraging to say the least. He did not want Dora to marry. He felt that she should wait, though no definite period of time was ever mentioned. Dora felt that it was her duty to remain with her parents. Dorothy – who seems to have been Dora's only ally in the affair – declared very firmly that she did not approve of making people wait to get married until 'all the life of life is gone'.[74] Wordsworth's justifications for his decision were Dora's uncertain health and the poor state of Quillinan's finances, but as one scholar puts it, his deepest objection was 'his selfish paternal desire to keep Dora beside him'.[75]

But it was not just Dora's father who was the problem. Mary Wordsworth had very strong views on the kind of life she wanted for her daughter; had she been in favour of the marriage, William might have been persuadable. A close friend of the family wrote in his diary that 'Mrs Wordsworth has all her life wished her daughter to be above both marriage and authorship'. When Dora's ambitions on both counts became apparent Mary found it 'hard to submit to those vulgarities on her behalf'.[76]

Part of the Wordsworths' objection was to Quillinan's Catholicism. Much as Wordsworth liked him as a man, Quillinan was irredeemably tainted by his religious beliefs. Whereas Sara Coleridge could write that 'there was nothing that insulted or endangered our Church in a Romanist's sitting in Parliament directly – and the principles of toleration and equal dealing with all religions, *as such*, seemed to demand the concession', William was fervently against Catholic 'emancipation'. He explained that his two or three years on the Continent had left him with a disgust of 'Popery' and the admission of Roman Catholics into Parliament could only be 'a dangerous experiment'. The Roman Church was at its root 'Idolatrous' and persecuting, the shade of its branches 'deadly and the fruit poisonous'. It could never be 'a temple of the true God'.[77] The influence of his judgment seems also to have affected Dora, who was, he wrote, 'a staunch Anti-Papist – in a woman's way', and there were times when she was unsure of her own feelings and doubted whether she should marry Quillinan.[78]

Dora was in very good health as she always was when fully occupied, 'all life and activity', looking after her aunt, acting as housekeeper for her mother, and as 'sole amanuensis' for William. Nevertheless the Wordsworths watched her anxiously, observing that she was 'as yellow as a gipsy and as thin as a Lath' – this comment in a letter being dictated to Dora herself who added a protest in parentheses '(is it not too bad to *insist* upon *my* writing this?)'.[78] On another occasion she crossed out her father's comments on her looks and health and added a postscript to the letter, which was to Quillinan. It was all 'Nonsense . . . which I have taken the liberty of putting out.' They tried to convince her that she should take the Blue Pill for her liver, but neither they nor the doctor could prevail. 'She says – "if I were *ill* I would take *that* or any thing; but being well I *will not*.' She changed her bedroom, having taken a dislike to the room in which she had been incarcerated for a whole winter,[80] and went for a holiday with a school friend. A further fortnight of gaiety with Edith May at Keswick effected a transformation better than any Blue Pills and for a while she was perfectly well. It was a relief to get away from the family who watched her with misguided affection for every minute variation in her health. Even at Keswick she was pursued by letters containing 'requests and exhortations'. 'Never *walk* to church but always go on your Poney – and avoid fatiguing yourself by walks in any direction. – Eat some animal food however small a quantity at luncheon, and ride every day if possible . . . I now begin to fear that the *heat* will be too much for you . . . move about according to your strength . . . and if you can, let us hear that your appetite is improved. Do not hang over any sort of Books – above all beware of novels – and do not take too much of German!'[81] Southey felt strongly that Dora was better anywhere than at home, where Wordsworth's 'extreme anxiety for Dora worries her'.[82] Over-watched, over-protected, Dora was a victim of the tyranny of familial love.

# The Legacy of Genius

*Was not that Woman blest above her peers,*
*Upon whose head worth, genius, beauty set*
*Their triple crown, – whose infant glances met*
*The starlike eyes of poets and of seers . . .*[1]

In 1829 Southey wrote: '. . . last week we had a marriage from this house – next to a funeral methinks the most melancholy of domestic events, where it compleatly takes away the member of a family.'[2] Southey's sadness at losing Sara Coleridge inclined him to feel less than optimistic about the marriage: given that both Sara and Henry had such poor constitutions, he feared it boded ill for the health of the children to have two such sickly parents.

Sara Coleridge was married in Crosthwaite church on 3 September in glorious weather, surrounded by her family and friends. Southey gave her away, her childhood playfellow John Wordsworth was the clergyman and Dora Wordsworth, Edith May, Bertha and Kate Southey were among the seven bridesmaids dressed in pale green satin, carrying armloads of late roses. Sara wore a dress of white silk brocade, flossed with tulle and trimmed with white satin, and, throughout the ceremony, gave her responses in a firm, clear voice.

A few days before the marriage she had written a last letter to Henry looking back on seven years of continuous correspondence. 'My beloved, my head is at this moment full of tender, affecting thoughts of all that is past and of all that is to come. What an interesting, agitating yet consoling interchange of letters are we now about to terminate! I could almost weep to bid farewell to such a correspondence, would that other imperious, though blessed thought, of all we are about to commence, suffer me to dwell long enough upon that . . . O may our union be still more blest, more unmixed, than our correspondence has been. I am sure it will be so, for all the trying subjects of dissension are now at rest, and hereafter it will be my pride as well as my duty to comply with your wishes, and you, beloved, will, I trust, be happier and more satisfied than you have hitherto had cause to be . . . I trust I shall never encroach upon your privileges, or abuse your gentle nature, asserting the reign of feminine too pertinaciously . . .'[3]

Hartley didn't come to the wedding, though Sara had hoped he would give her away. He had tried unsuccessfully to run a small school at Ambleside and since its failure he had been without regular work, trying to maintain himself by writing poetry and essays for *Blackwood's Magazine* or 'the Annuals'. According to the Wordsworths he spent much of his time 'getting drunk in low company, and running away from every engagement to skulk in pot houses'. Shortly afterwards he lost his lodgings and Dorothy reported sadly that he was 'wandering about like a vagabond, sleeping in barns . . . and picking up a meal where he can.'[4] Much of Hartley's misery was due to a split with his father which had occurred in 1822 and been concealed from his mother and sister. All the resentments and rejections of his childhood had grown in him until they could no longer be contained and erupted in an awful interview, when Coleridge was confronted with his failure as a parent. The resulting outburst led to an estrangement and great grief on both sides.

Before the wedding Hartley had written a bitter letter to his mother, articulating his feelings of isolation and a sense of his own worthlessness. 'I remain alone, bare and barren and blasted, ill-omen'd and unsightly as Wordsworth's melancholy thorn on the bleak hill-top. So it hath been ordain'd, and it is well.'[5] Hartley did manage to see his sister on her honeymoon, observing that although she looked 'so pensive and so meek', underlying her submissive demeanour 'there was an angel with her/That cried Beware!'[6]

Sarah Coleridge had made up her mind to leave Greta Hall after her daughter's wedding. Edith Southey's attitude to Sarah's presence there had become increasingly hostile and unpredictable since Isabel's death. Sarah underwent considerable heart-wrenching at the thought of leaving the house that had been her home for so many years, but she felt that her position there would be untenable without her daughter's company. Henry and Sara's new house in London was too small to accommodate a parent, so Sarah went on a farewell visit to Rydal Mount after the wedding and on 28 September travelled to Cornwall to stay with Derwent and his wife at Helston. Southey too felt a considerable degree of pain at the parting, though he admitted reluctantly that the change was 'for several reasons to be desired'. Sarah wrote to Thomas Poole that 'it ought not to be matter of *very great moment* where the time is past between the present and the Last home – but old age is full of doubts, fears, and cares, unknown to earlier years'.[7] Sarah did not know her daughter-in-law and had no idea how they would get on under the same roof.

Sarah Coleridge was devastated that Hartley did not come to see her before she left. Careful arrangements were made for his welfare out of a small legacy left to Sarah by Sir George Beaumont. She would at least, Dorothy wrote by way of comfort, have 'the satisfaction of knowing that you . . . have done all you can to guard him from perishing of cold and hunger.'[8] The Wordsworths undertook responsibility for finding him board and lodgings and promised to remit strict accounts to Sarah for the money laid out on his behalf. Given Hartley's reputation for unsteadiness, finding good lodgings was not going to be easy. Sarah could not resist sending her son reproachful letters, urging him to better himself by his own efforts. Hartley, laden with guilt about what he saw as his failures and inadequacies, stayed away from his mother at the final parting. For Sarah, who loved her children intensely, this was a severe blow. She accused Hartley of having ceased to love her. He replied in an anguished letter: 'You cannot, do not seriously suspect this, for if you did, no profession, scarce any performance of mine, could exorcise the evil spirit from your soul, for dead affections have no earthly resurrection . . . I never ceased to love you, tho' times have been, when that love was more remorse and agony, proclaiming aloud the duties which it gave no strength to perform.' It was not indifference that had prevented him calling to see her at Rydal Mount. He was afraid, he confessed, fearing reproaches and 'the eye of offended love'.[9]

Southey was now alone with a rapidly deteriorating Edith and only his daughters and the morbidly depressed Mary Lovell to keep him company. 'It is as well for me that I have now acquired a habit of concentrating my thoughts either on their present occupation or busying them in retrospective and excursive speculations . . .' He refused to look into the future, since it seemed full of evils − 'possible, likely or calculable and certain'.[10] As Edith's condition worsened, Southey tried to be stoic: '. . . my life has had its share of good and evil; no man has enjoyed greater blessings, and few have had keener griefs, but these have been medicinal, and so I trust will be the bitters on which I am now dieted.'[11]

Even more bitter for Southey was the knowledge that he had met a woman with whom he felt he could have been happy, had he been free to marry her. She was the authoress Caroline Bowles, a much-indulged only child, left by the death of her parents to support herself at the age of twenty-nine. She did what many other women did in similar circumstances − she took up her pen and wrote a romance. Since she was already an admirer of Scott and Southey, her tale was written in 'metrical verse'. In 1818 she had ventured to send it to the Poet Laureate with a letter admitting that she was 'startled at her own temerity' since she 'shrank like the sensitive plant from the touch of a cold answer'. But her letter was articulate and confident and full of wit, drawing a sympathetic response from Southey. He offered to find a publisher for *Ellen Fitzarthur* but warned her that 'The success of a poem . . . does not depend on its merit . . . Booksellers . . . are necessarily tradesmen; and a constant attention to profit and loss is neither wholesome for the heart nor the understanding'. Then as now, only six or seven out of five hundred were published and of that only half made a profit. Caroline was one of the lucky few.

They continued to correspond and their letters to each other gradually became more intimate, particularly after Southey met Caroline on a visit to London. In 1823 she stayed for two months at Greta Hall and subsequently Southey visited her house at Lymington almost every year. They discussed literature and the problems of composition, as well as their private lives. By 1824 Caroline was writing: 'What would I give for only one poor half-hour of your society now and then!', and Southey replied: 'You are lonely, God knows; yet, if you could know how often I was with you in thought, you would feel that there is one person in the world who regards you as you ought to be regarded – as you would wish him to regard you. How difficult is it when we mean a great deal, not to say either too little or too much . . .'[12]

Caroline suffered from periods of severe depression – 'a dark-ness of spirit' which brought 'absence of memory, a confusion of ideas' and rendered her 'hardly able to see, hear, or understand'. When it passed away she was overwhelmed with the exquisite delight of sensory perception, as if everything was being viewed for the first time. Southey was her anchor. 'You met and took me by the hand on the brink of that dreary, unknown country; I found in you what I had never met with, even in my lost Eden, and while you hold me fast, I shall not want courage to go on . . .'[13]

A parallel tragedy was taking place at Grasmere, as Dorothy Wordsworth's health began to deteriorate again. In December 1831 she suffered a recurrence of the severe 'internal inflamma-tion' she had had at Whitwick and spent the entire winter and early summer of 1832 in bed or confined to her room. Though she rallied during the summer, with the onset of winter she worsened alarmingly. Her legs were swollen and began to develop black spots which the doctor feared were symptoms of 'mortification'. He increased her dosage of brandy and opium, though she was already completely in the grip of the drug. Soon, though she was 'in a quiet state of mind', there was evidence of mental deterioration and she became incontinent.

Dora wrote to a friend on 23 February 1833 that, on the previous

Monday, 'neither we nor our medical attendant had the slightest hopes that another Sun w'd rise upon my dear Aunt. The Cross was in mercy allowed to pass from us and since that trying night she has rallied slowly but regularly . . . Father was mercifully supported that sad sad night when he thought he had taken leave of his sister for the last time – indeed all through this trying winter – but surely such love as he bears to her is of no common nature . . .'[14] Knowledge of Dorothy's illness was kept from Coleridge, who was himself in a fragile state in London. 'Were she to die he would not be told,' wrote Sarah Coleridge. His health was too frail to withstand bad news.

Dorothy's condition was, Southey thought, a case of 'premature old age' and some contemporary analysts have concluded that she was suffering from Alzheimer's disease. But although there are similar symptoms many of the manifestations of her illness do not fit the pattern of Alzheimer's development, which is usually progressive. The geriatric consultant whose report is included in Gittings and Manton's fine biography noted that he 'had always been troubled' by the length of time she lived after developing the disease and 'by the letters she wrote during her demented period' – and not only letters, but poems. Her length of life and periods of self-awareness and articulacy are virtually unknown to sufferers from Alzheimer's, though they are occasionally able to have flashbacks and short periods of lucidity. But the one vitally important fact which the eminent physician does not seem to have taken into account in his consideration of Dorothy's mental degeneration, and which is not even mentioned in the report, was her opium addiction. Opium does not just attack the body, it affects the mind, and in someone as highly strung as Dorothy could well have been the determining factor in her final disintegration. In the opinion of her brother William, it was indeed the cause.

By 1835 Mary wrote that Dorothy was totally 'confused as to passing events', but 'remembers and recollects all but recent things perfectly, and her understanding is, as far as her strength will allow her to think, clear as ever it was'. Her literary judgement, reasoning and ability to converse 'upon any point of Literature' remained unimpaired. William reported that she was subject to severe cravings: 'I feel my hand shaking, I have had so much agitation today, in attempting to quiet my poor Sister, and from being under the necessity of refusing her things that would be improper for her . . .' She was, he wrote, 'in a sad state when the action of the opium is not upon her'.[15] William added tellingly, in a letter to his brother, that 'I have always thought that this weakening of the mind has been caused by the opium which was thought necessary on account of her great bodily sufferings'. But attempts to reduce her intake of the drug by half failed to bring about the hoped-for 'restoration of the mental powers of recollection'.[16]

In a clear moment Dorothy wrote in a letter: 'A Madman might as well attempt to relate the history of his doings and those of his fellows in confinement as I to tell you one hundredth part of what I have felt, suffered and done.' And to Dora she confessed: 'My own thoughts are a wilderness – "not pierceable by power of any star" . . .' In her periods of dementia she composed doggerel verses for her attendants which Mary described as 'not very elevated'. When she was lucid she produced poetry of an altogether higher order.

> No prisoner am I on this couch,
> My mind is free to roam,
> And leisure, peace and loving friends
> Are the best treasures of an earthly home.
>
> Such gifts are mine, then why deplore
> The feeble body's slow decay,
> A warning mercifully sent
> To fix my hope upon a surer stay?
>
> And may I learn those precious gifts
> Rightly to prize, and by their soothing power
> All fickle murmuring thoughts repress
> And fit my fluttering heart for the last hour.

It seemed incomprehensible to Dorothy that so many of her friends could find release in death while she struggled on. 'Poor Peggy Benson lies in Grasmere Church-yard beside her once beautiful Mother. Fanny Haigh is gone to a better world. My Friend Mrs Rawson has ended her ninety and two years pilgrimage – and I have fought and fretted and striven – and am here beside the fire.'[17]

Her journals, which she had begun to write again in 1824 as purely private jottings, reveal her decline. At times the writing tails off in an unintelligible scrawl; there are gaps and pages cut out. She charts her own decline – tiredness, lack of concentration, a weakening of the eyes – and talks sometimes of herself as a prisoner. 'How I long to be free of the open-air! The Birds are all singing, Rooks very busy. The earth & air & all that I behold seem a preparation for worship.' But her fascination with people continues as she relates the story of a poor woman refused lodgings by a neighbour who slept rough in bad weather and gave birth the next day, alone, to a dead child. One of Dorothy's last coherent entries is in November 1835: 'I take up the pen once again after a trying illness I have risen to dinner – without pain at present Wm is at Workington – John has been in Radnorshire – Dora most unwell . . .' It ends with a poem:

> My tremulous fingers, feeble hands
> Refuse to labour with the mind
> And *that* too oft is misty dark & blind.

The last pages are scrawled with disconnected words. Among them 'Torments . . . dysmal doom . . . no iron hinges' are clearly discernible as tragic indicators of her agony of mind.

Sara Coleridge began married life in rented rooms in Gower Street, but an early pregnancy meant that a search for larger premises had to be made shortly afterwards. A few months after the marriage they were able to rent a 'cottage' in Hampstead. This was close enough for Sara to walk across the fields to visit her father, but too far out of London for Henry to travel backwards and forwards to his chambers every night. He came home only at the weekends and in between he and Sara wrote each other letters. Their relationship became, by this accident, a boon for the biographer.

The new house was big enough to accommodate Sara's mother and Sara was anxious that Mrs Coleridge should be there for her confinement. Mother and daughter had so rarely been parted that Sara found their separation a 'material drawback' to her happiness. For Sarah Coleridge it was the 'safe ground' she had longed for. She had written to Derwent when it became apparent that she would be forced to leave Greta Hall that 'I have not been on safe ground for a very, very long time – I trusted long to frail reeds which broke, one by one, from my grasp, and never helped me to good land!'[18] Sarah was much changed by the events of her life, more inclined to worry over trifles than she had been in her youth, and even more inclined to fuss over her children and their lives in an attempt to prevent them making the same kind of mistakes as their parents.

Although Sara loved her mother, she was not sentimental about her. 'She has no power over her mind to keep the thought of petty cares and passing interests (the importance of which is often mere matter of fancy) in abeyance. She never compares on a wide scale the real importance of the thing with the degree of energy and time and vital spirit that she spends upon it; and though her talents are above mediocrity and her understanding clear and good – on its own range – she has no taste whatever for abstractions and formerly had less toleration for what she did not relish than now.' Sara called her mother 'Frettikins', but bore it all with loving fortitude.

On 7 October 1830, Sara gave birth to a healthy son weighing over eight pounds. She called him Herbert after her beloved Southey cousin who had died at the age of nine. Coleridge's doctor, Mr Gillman, attended her during the labour and was very impressed by her determination and courage. Most people were amazed that one so small and delicate could have given birth to such a large baby with so little trouble. Dora visited her soon afterwards and described Herbert as 'a baby beautiful as she'. Mrs C. was 'happy, proud and anxious', but for once, the 'happy and proud outweighed the anxious thoughts and feelings'. Bertha Southey thought that Herbert, being such a big, handsome baby, looked 'unnatural' in the arms of his diminutive mother.

Sara didn't enjoy breast-feeding her children. She found it enervating and, despite drinking brandy and raw egg in the morning, pints of milk and stout and occasional glasses of port to stimulate her constitution, she felt 'pulled down' by the process. Unlike her mother, who had fed each of her children until they were sixteen or seventeen months old, Sara weaned hers early. Perhaps Hartley's jokes about 'tugging Piggy-wiggies' had something to do with it. Sara was extremely fastidious and reticent in 'matters of the body'. By weaning her babies early Sara lost out on the contraceptive effects of lactation and a year after Herbert's birth she was pregnant again.

On 2 July 1832 Sara had a daughter, named Edith for her favourite cousin. Edith was a plump, contented baby, less attractive than Herbert, but easier to manage. Herbert had grown into a 'dear villain of a boy' according to his father, quick and precociously intelligent.

Despite having been in a 'sad, weak, depressed state' for much of the year Coleridge was well enough to attend Edith's christening, declaring that he was determined to stand beside 'Mrs C.' to prove 'that the lack of Oil or Anti-friction Powder in our Conjugal Carriage-wheels' did not prevent them from fulfilling their duties as parents and grandparents.[19] Coleridge talked with his old eloquence and intensity. 'The life & vigour of his mind so illuminated his house of clay that few people, especially strangers . . . perceived its decaying condition.'[20] Although Sara was able to carry Edith to the church for baptism, she was very unwell and shortly afterwards was diagnosed as having puerperal fever, though this was her father's interpretation of her illness, to which Dr Gillman seems to have assented. Her symptoms were, however, those of severe post-natal depression.

By the end of September her 'nervous debility' was so bad she 'was obliged to think seriously of [not] feeding my darling'. Her symptoms were treated, as usual, by laudanum which Sara had been taking regularly since 1825 for insomnia. She had confessed to a friend: 'I am unable to sleep at all without laudanum, which I regret much, though I do not think I shall find any difficulty in leaving it off . . .' When mentioned in connection with De Quincey or her father it was a '*horrid* drug', but not for herself – 'in me this is rather ungrateful as it has done me much good and no harm – and I might exclaim with Mrs O'Neil "Hail lovely blossom that can'st ease the wretched victims of disease".'[21]

The effects of the drug enhanced her depression, sharpened her mood swings and made her brittle. In the autumn of 1832 she had a complete collapse. 'I cannot shed a tear – I seem sealed up – a creature doomed to despair . . .'[22] Her mother wrote to Thomas Poole that Sara would 'sit in a Carriage (wh: we hired by the hour to drive on the Heath with the children and nurses) and never speak one word to the poor babes the whole time'. Sara was terrified by the idea of another pregnancy and begged Henry to allow her two or three years' respite from child-bearing. This assurance Henry felt himself unable to give. They were newly married – he had an ardent nature; abstention was unthinkable. He was convinced that all she needed was firmness of will and the determination to get well.

Sara Hutchinson wrote Sara bracing letters, urging her to pull herself together. 'Only let me say dearest little Sara try to rouze yourself – believe me "quiet" & the presence of the same objects will not so speedily work your cure as change of scene & occupation . . .'[23] Sara became unable to eat or sleep and 'all things [were] wrong in the interior'. On the advice of doctors Henry took her to Brighton, in the hope that the sea air might effect a cure. The journey was a nightmare. Henry rode outside the coach in the pouring rain, ostensibly to leave more 'air' for Sara and her mother. For Sarah Coleridge it was 'one of the most weary journeys I ever experienced'. Sara became hysterical: '. . . she said, oh, I shall go into convulsions if I cannot get out! the rain pouring the whole way, yet, at any change of horses she darted out and walked rapidly up and down the road like one distracted . . . I shall never forget that night . . .'[24]

At Brighton Sara improved only marginally, being less prone to 'nervous terrors' and with more appetite for food, but her mind, her nerves and her hormones, disarranged by childbirth and the effects of opium addiction, were beyond the soothing influence of changed scenery. Part of the problem was the alteration in her circumstances. Her husband was away most of the week and her friends at a distance. Sarah Coleridge observed shrewdly that Sara had been 'transported from a *too* bustling family, to one of utter loneliness'. Where once her days at Greta Hall had been occupied by 'Reading, writing, walking, teaching, messing, mountaineering . . . with occasional visiting', now in London as mistress of a household and mother of two young children she had 'house orders, suckling, dress and undress, walking, serving', formal visits and 'at homes' with 'very little study of Greek, Latin and English' to fill her days.[25] Sara needed intellectual stimulation for her mental health. Caught in a spiral of pregnancy and child-rearing she simply did not have the time for the 'life of the mind' that was as vitally important to her as it had been for her father. This was something that Henry did not completely understand.

In desperation, unable to sleep or work, Sara resorted to even larger doses of opium. By the summer of 1833 she was feeling better and was once again helping Henry by copying out his Chancery papers – a work of terrible drudgery, which she found strangely calming. Academic employment had always had a steadying effect on Sara's nerves. Freed from domestic duties by her poor health, she began to read again. She read Cunningham's *British Painters*, all the contemporary biographies, reread Shakespeare and Ben Jonson and then, with Henry's encouragement, embarked on a study of Dryden.

Her own creative work was initially neglected after her marriage. She gave herself up to her children, feeling that it was essential for them to have a happy childhood free from 'shock and irritation'. Looking back at her own turbulent past, she declared: 'I should be

[ 274 ]

a different creature now, perhaps, but for the mental agitations and disproportionate bodily exertions of my childhood and youth . . .' She tried very hard to shield her own children from 'the troubles and constraints which so often came . . . like frosts and wintry blasts'. She made resolutions, based on her own experiences. 'I would never say "Alas – why don't you love me?" . . . Love is an emotion and cannot be compelled . . .' Sara hoped to educate her children by patient and understanding love.[26]

There were occasional conflicts with her mother. As a grand-mother, Sarah Coleridge was much more indulgent than she had been with her own children. Sara reprimanded her for spoiling Herbert. 'I have a very *decided opinion*, and one that runs counter to all my present comforts and inclinations and therefore can only proceed from the verdict of my deliberate judgement, that what-ever pain it may cost at the time it is our duty to bring Herbert, as far as we can, into more independent and manly habits . . .' When her mother argued that he was only a child and could be allowed a little licence Sara retorted that 'I was far more restricted than he and the *restraint was good for me*.'[27]

Sara worried a great deal that Edith was considered by everyone to be a plain child, particularly in comparison to Herbert. 'Poor little dear! How gladly would I transfer to her any remnants there are of my former faulty sort of prettiness . . .' And if her plainness should continue into adulthood, Sara resolved that 'Our peskin girly shall have more money left her than Herby . . . She must be very accomplished and we must let her learn the piano.' Sara was cynically aware that in society, beauty, money and accomplishment were the only things for which women were valued.

In the summer of 1833, before she had fully recovered from her depressive illness, she became pregnant again – this time with twins. She had a bad pregnancy, made worse by the amount of opium she was now consuming for her 'nerves'. Florence and Berkeley, born in January 1834 after a difficult delivery, died a few days later. They became the first family entry in what came to be known as Sara's 'Death Book'. Sara Hutchinson wrote to Edward Quillinan: 'Of poor Sara Coleridge the account, I grieve to say, is most deplorable . . . she had Twins, which both died – & for a short time after they had hoped the Mother was recovering her spirits – if not her strength of body – but she has relapsed into her former state & they seem perfectly hopeless – (as she is herself poor Dear) as to her ultimate restoration . . .'[28]

In January 1834, Edith May married John Warter, a scholarly clergyman who had been chaplain to the British Embassy at Copenhagen. He was the son of a well-connected country gentleman and had been granted a living in Sussex by the Archbishop of Canterbury. The marriage and loss of a favourite daughter finally tipped the delicate balance of her mother's sanity over into mania. Southey wrote to Edith May on 3 April 1834, regretting that her mother could not. 'She is at present very unwell in spirits, but better disposed than usual to use all proper means for getting better – that is, to take John Edmondsons tonics, and to go out of doors. And if she will but venture upon the tepid shower-bath, or upon a system of spunging that may in some degree answer the same end, I trust she will soon be set up.'[29] Edith May's way of dealing with the tragedy was to ignore it. Communications with her father and her sisters virtually ceased. Southey was very distressed. In a letter to Bertha, he expressed the wish that she would never be 'so far lost to me' as her sister Edith May had become.[30]

Edith was taken to the Retreat near York, accompanied by a trusted family servant and her own personal maid. The York Retreat had been established by Quaker philanthropists and pioneered the humane treatment of psychiatric illness. Its ideas of 'moral management' seemed to offer the best hope for Edith's recovery. At York she had to be removed from the carriage by force and although she quickly improved, sleeping better, accepting food, being aware of her surroundings, she remained depressed and seemed reluctant to go home. Southey wrote to Grosvenor Bedford that 'the worst symptoms seem to have been subdued, or mitigated. But an alternative treatment by which a great change is to be produced must necessarily be slow in its operation. Indeed the rules of the Institution require that a quarters board be paid in advance; which is proof enough that speedy recovery is never to be expected . . . I am, as you may suppose, much shaken.'[31]

Edith passed the last eighteen months of her life in another world. 'Time passes with her as in a dream, or a succession of incoherent dreams, no fancy keeps possession of her mind long, but none are of a cheerful kind.'[32] Edith Southey's mental state seems to have been due, in part, to the operation of circumstance on an already melancholy disposition. The deaths of four of her children, Margaret, Emma, Herbert and Isabel, played an incalculable role in her final disintegration, and the departure of her daughter Edith May must have seemed like another death. She had also fretted all her life over money – a legacy of her father's bankruptcy – and Southey's letters to her are full of reassurances that their position is secure.

But questions also have to be asked about the nature of her marriage to Southey. Southey declared that he had been happy, despite Edith's repeated breakdowns. But his unquestionable, dutiful, devotion to Edith did not prevent him forming attachments with Sarah Coleridge, Sara Hutchinson and then Caroline Bowles – each of whom provided elements missing in his relationship with Edith, i.e. intellectual stimulation and a sense of fun. He lamented that the only thing he lacked was 'the presence of someone who could fairly enter into my views and feelings, and partake the interest which I take in such researches'.[33] On Edith's side, the breakdown in her health that occurred after her marriage is a good indicator of her state of mind and happiness. It is a recognised fact in psychiatry that unhappiness within a relationship is a major cause of mental and physical ill health. Edith's psychosomatic symptoms and periods of depression would seem to indicate that all was not well in the Southey relationship as far as she was concerned.

With both her friends married, Dora felt very isolated. Edith May had been the last of her unmarried friends of the same age and her going was a great loss. 'What is to become of me', she asked, 'when all that are dear to me are gone . . . & everybody married that [I] care about – but if they are made happy I must be made happy too – but I find it very difficult to live on the happiness of others.'[34] It seemed to Dora that she might never be allowed to marry. Her position was made even harder by the fact that in 1830 Dora's brother John, now with a living at Moresby on the Cumbrian coast, had married her friend Isabella Curwen, heiress to the Curwen family of Belle Isle on Windermere, after only a few months' engagement. John Wordsworth had only a very small living, though his prospects of advancement were quite good, and Isabella's health was as uncertain as Dora's. The Curwens' generosity towards their delicate daughter was a stark contrast to the Wordsworths' reluctance to allow Dora independent happiness.

Visitors to Rydal Mount in August 1834 noticed that 'Dora looks cheerful before other people, but is in a sad, melancholy way and eats nothing, says nothing, and goes nowhere.'[35] She wrote to Quillinan in Portugal, quiet, restrained letters written in what seems to have been a hopeless frame of mind. Not surprisingly, her health once more suffered. The Wordsworths talked repeatedly of sending her to warmer climates, but the expense was always a bar. 'We are so poor,' was William's repeated plea. Something must be done for John, and then there was the 'heavy' expense of Willy's tour of the Continent, where he had been sent after the family despaired of finding him any kind of employment. So the idea of taking Dora abroad again 'must be given up'.[36]

Before he left for Portugal Quillinan had stayed at Rydal Mount for several weeks, lingering 'longer than he intended'. He may well have mentioned the subject of marriage to Dora. Afterwards he wrote to Wordsworth, and to Dora, asking permission for Dora and Sara Hutchinson to be joint guardians of his daughters in the event of his death. Dora wrote back: '. . . allow me to assure you (which I think I need not scruple to do after the very flattering mark which you have given of the unbounded confidence you place in me) of what I have so long and so often thought and felt – that long as life is given to me your Darlings will have one friend who must always think of them with a Mother's anxiety and love them with a Mother's love and whose only regret will be or rather is that her power of serving them falls so far short of her desire to serve . . .' These words are the strongest possible hint that Dora, although she did not admit that she loved Quillinan and would not agree to marry him until 1836, was aware of the significance of what she had been asked to do. She appears to have known that Quillinan wanted to marry her. Denied the right to be their stepmother by her father's intransigence, Dora was willing to take on the office of guardian to Quillinan's children.

Quillinan's reply brought a stiff letter from William overruling Dora's wishes. 'I am sorry to learn that you have been led to entertain so confident an expectation that Dora would undertake the charge of Jemima and Rotha . . . I infer that her feelings must have betrayed her into the expression of sentiments on this point very different from what would find sanction from her own understanding, uninfluenced by such feelings or rather unblinded by them. It is incumbent on me, as her Father, and as the Friend of the Children and yours, to assure you that she is utterly unfit both from her health, strength, temper, and circumstances to stand pledged for such an anxious responsibility.'[37]

Dora's amusements at this time were few. She drove her father round Scotland in a little four-wheeled phaeton, taking Dorothy's place on a visit of reminiscence, and spent time at her brother's house with her sister-in-law Isabella and a growing brood of nieces and nephews. At Rydal Mount she accompanied Dorothy as her aunt was pushed round the garden in a bath chair, or acted as her father's amanuensis, since his eyes were now in too poor a state to allow him to read and write for himself. In the absence of Sara Hutchinson, who spent most of her time at Keswick or with her relatives in Wales, Dora, now thirty years old, was sole attendant on three elderly people, two of whom declared themselves unable to do without her. Only Dorothy, in her more lucid periods, could wish that Dora would go away more on pleasure trips and by discreet emphasis in her letters indicate her disapproval of William's need to have his daughter beside him.

Mary, too, clung to her daughter, particularly after the death of her sister Sara in 1835. While Dora was away Mary felt her absence like a physical pain. She wrote to her of the pleasure she had taken from wearing one of Dora's aprons and, putting her hand thoughtlessly into the pocket, finding a piece of paper with Dora's handwriting on it 'and thinking you had put it there – It was just like the shock of pleasure . . . I used to feel upon hearing, at some distance, your baby voices when you were *new* to me. I do not know if even *you* can understand this.'[38] She worried about Dora travelling: 'I was awe-stricken last night to read of the disaster to the steam P.[Packet] between London and Thurness, to think how near the time of your travelling by such conveyance that same course, and when awaked by the dreadful thunder storm at 4 this morning, I had a multitude of sad feelings, and wished we were altogether . . .'[39] Loving her parents as she did, Dora was racked by guilt at the thought of leaving them, when they so clearly needed her.

Coleridge died on 25 July 1834 in Highgate and the Wordsworths were shocked and sad at the news of their 'ever-to-be-lamented Friend's decease'. Within a fortnight of his death an advert appeared in the press stating 'that the afflicted widow of a lately deceased poet earnestly requested all persons having letters or papers of his to place them in her hands &c'. Sarah Coleridge's holocaust to try to protect her husband's reputation, even at the expense of her own, was about to begin.

Sara Hutchinson, who had visited him just before he died, thought that his death had had a beneficial effect in rousing his daughter '& she now seems determined to be well – & God grant that she may – for it is a deplorable thing to see a young creature who seems to have every wish of her heart gratified given up to fanciful despondency.'[40]

Sara Coleridge was still bedridden with depression when Coleridge died, only six months after the death of the twins, eating little and dosing herself with opium in order to sleep. She had lost so much weight she stopped menstruating for a time;

but at least this temporarily freed her from the risk of another pregnancy. A series of articles in the press, including De Quincey's 'Recollections', so enraged her with their inaccuracies and misconceptions that she decided she must do something about it. Sara set herself the task of helping her husband to edit her father's work and defend his reputation in print. The Wordsworths did not entirely approve of her enterprise. Mary Wordsworth wrote: '*I* say, "the least said is soonest mended" – and I do wish poor dear indefatigable Sara would let her Father's character rest. Surely that great spirit has left sufficient to gratify the craving for literary fame in any one, without that dear Creature worrying her brain in her endeavours to increase, or justify it – which with all her pains she will never accomplish.'[41]

Sara's post-natal depression had freed her from many of the responsibilities of housekeeping and motherhood. She had fallen into the childhood habit of letting her mother look after things, including herself, while she lay on the sofa 'reading from morning to night'. As Elizabeth Barrett also discovered, freedom from domestic duties provided the time and space in which to work. As well as sorting her father's papers and rereading his entire works, Sara began the task of educating her brilliant young son. At three he could read and she found herself 'obliged to get up my geography and sacred history even to instruct a child of this age – four years old on Tuesday'.

Doctors warned her of the dangers of stretching his mind too early, but Sara knew that her own mother had endured similar strictures with regard to herself and she had the confidence of experience. Herbert was never pressured to learn anything, she insisted, but taught purely as amusement. What he enjoyed he would learn. Her aim was to 'put works of simple natural history and geography into his head instead of sentimental trash. Give him classical Fairy Tales instead of modern poverty-stricken fiction – shew him the great outlines of the globe instead of Chinese puzzles and spillikins'.[42]

In order to make the boring aspects of education such as Latin grammar and the minutiae of history more palatable, she wrote a series of verses designed as mnemonics for her children.

> *Lupus* means a wolf,
> *Ursa* is a bear,
> *Vulpes* means a fox,
> *Lepus* means a hare;
>
> Tea is brought from China;
> Rice from Carolina,
> India and Italy –
> Countries far beyond the sea.

Not all were so didactic.

> Fast, fast asleep my Edith lies,
>    With her snowy night-dress on;
> Closed are now her sparkling eyes;
>    All her merry thoughts are gone.
> Gone! ah me! perhaps she dreams;
> Perhaps she views the crystal streams,
> Wanders in the grove and field –
> What hath sleep to her revealed?

The occupation was beneficial to her health and Henry encouraged her to compile her verses into a small volume which was published in the summer of 1834. Although Dora Wordsworth thought them 'wretched doggerel', *Pretty Lessons in Verse* fitted well with the Victorian fashion for didactic literature and became a modest best-seller. It was still in print in 1927.

One of the poems in the volume is the revealing 'Poppies', in which for the first time Sara publicly acknowledged her dependence on opiates. Her brother Derwent and his wife felt that it was a mistake for Sara to include the poem. The posthumous publication of Coleridge's *Collected Poems* had brought a flood of revelations in the press about his private life including his drug addiction. Derwent felt that Sara's poem would not add anything to the family's reputation. Sara conceded the point: '. . . the Poppy poem in *Pretty Lessons* should have been left out . . .' But in subsequent editions it remained.

> The Poppies Blooming all around
> My Herbert loves to see,
> Some pearly white, some dark as night,
> Some red as cramasie;
>
> He loves their colours fresh and fine
> As fair as fair may be,
> But little does my darling know
> How good they are to me.
>
> He views their clustering petals gay
> And shakes their nut-brown seeds.
> But they to him are nothing more
> Than other brilliant weeds;
>
> O how should'st thou with beaming brow
> With eye and cheek so bright
> Know aught of that blossom's pow'r,
> Or sorrows of the night!
>
> When poor mama long restless lies
> She drinks the poppy's juice;
> That liquor soon can close her eyes
> And slumber soft produce.
>
> O' then my sweet my happy boy
> Will thank the poppy flow'r
> Which brings the sleep to dear mama
> At midnight's darksome hour.

Despite her father's awful example, Sara too had become an addict and, like Coleridge in the early stages of his addiction, she still believed that she could control the drug.

During 1834 Dora's health took a new and more ominous turn. She had been suffering from loss of appetite and indigestion and then began to have pains in her neck and shoulder which the doctor diagnosed as 'inflammation on the spine' – almost certainly tuberculosis. She was confined to bed or sofa and subjected to 'blistering and bleeding' – both painful and weakening, but the universal medical treatment for almost everything. Dora's recovery was once again hampered by her refusal to eat. Quillinan wrote from Portugal to chide her. It was wilful and pernicious of her to adhere to her 'system of starvation'. She must know how harmful it was, 'as sure though not as speedy a suicidal process as any other', yet 'you still persist in your *determination to be unable to eat.*' For anorexics, control over their own bodies is the only power they feel they have.

Quillinan confessed to suffering from '*saudade*' – a Portuguese word meaning 'tenderness, sorrow, solicitude, longing, and every kind and melancholy thought and wish, all blended into one feeling . . . How I wish you could be here.'[43]

While Dora lay on her sofa, too weak to do anything more taxing than read novels, and Dorothy's mind began to wander more and more often, less able to be recalled, Sara Hutchinson – the 'sheet anchor' of the household, always to be depended on – became ill with rheumatic fever. It began suddenly while she was at home in Rydal. She was interrupted writing a letter and, after bending down to fasten her clog, had a sudden spasm of what she believed to be rheumatism, 'without the least previous warning of Lumbago as I suppose it is – tho' I never had a hint of the disease before – & now my back is as stiff as a tree & I could scarcely get in & out of the Carriage'.[44] Five weeks later, on 23 June 1835, she died.

Mary was devastated. She and her sister had been so close she had described Sara as her 'second self'. Wordsworth wrote to Southey describing Sara's last moments: 'She had no acute suffering whatever, and within a very short time of her departure – when Dora asked Mr Carr if something could not be done to make her easier – she opened her eyes in strength, and with a strong and sweet voice, said, "I am quite, I am perfectly comfortable". Mr Carr supposed that her debility produced a suffusion on the brain, which was the immediate cause of her death. O, my dear Southey, we have lost a precious friend; of the strength of her attachment to you and yours, you can but imperfectly judge. It was deep in her heart.'[45]

Sara's death shattered the remaining vestiges of Dorothy Wordsworth's fragile hold on reality. She was noticeably worse. As a last resort, the Wordsworths decided to try a new experiment. They began the painful process of withdrawing opium from Dorothy and wrote to friends asking them not to visit. 'I think it right to let you know, that it would add to our distress if you should be a witness of the anxiety we are undergoing on account of the experiment now in progress, and drawing towards a conclusion . . . You know I believe how much Opium has been thought necessary for her – We expect in the course of a fortnight to get rid of it altogether . . . but her present sufferings appear to be, from withdrawing this medicine so severe, that we would rather you were not conscious of them to the extent that would be unavoidable if you were with us . . .'[46]

A month later Mary reported that, although Dorothy had been without opium for four days, the effects were disappointing. The experiment had 'brought no comfort with respect to the *mind* – The recollection of passing objects is indeed greatly restored – but is more than counterbalanced by increasing irritability, which when her wishes are necessarily opposed amounts to rage and fury.'[47]

With Sara Hutchinson dead and Dorothy confined to her room with dementia, there was now no one to plead Dora's cause with her parents. Quillinan was at Rydal Mount during August and early September 1836 and it seems to have been during this period that Dora admitted to Quillinan that she loved him. In 1839, Quillinan talks of a period 'three years before' when he first

realised that his feelings for Dora were reciprocated. But Wordsworth was implacable on the subject of marriage. Sara Coleridge
was very critical of the Wordsworths' selfish attitude to Dora. 'It is
strange that Mr and Mrs Wordsworth do not see how much the
least of two evils their consenting to Dora's marriage with Mr
Quillinan would be than letting her pass her life in regret and
uneasiness . . . Their dreams are now over that she prefers single
blessedness – and they must see that she is not likely to make any
other match . . .'[48]

Quillinan returned to Portugal in November with his emotions
in turmoil. On the way out he and Jemima narrowly escaped
shipwreck when the engines of the steamship they were on failed in
a storm off Cape Finisterre. His brush with death seemed only to
intensify his feelings for Dora. 'You do not know what yearnings of
the heart you have awakened in me by your remarks about Willy
and his love; how differently might many of my past years have
gone by, if I had been wiser in money-guarding, and wiser in
woman's heart . . .' Quillinan was now forty-five and lonely. He
suggested that Dora come out to Portugal with one of her
Hutchinson cousins and once more broached the subject of
marriage. 'How happy we might be in my Brother's house on
the seaside all the spring & all the summer!' Dora rejected both
proposals. Her health was too uncertain, her parents' need for her
too great; Quillinan should consider himself free to find someone
more suitable. His reply was a masterpiece of resignation. 'So you
are not only *not* coming, but you would not if you could! . . . Then
you add that I shall like you better for such a resolution: now there
you are mistaken: I *could* not have liked you better than I did, but I
do like you a little less for this confession of yours. – Never mind
. . . It is best that you should be there, and I should be here; it is
best that you should be a Nun at large and your own Lady Abbess;
and it is best that I a widower of 45, not inexperienced in troubles,
should at last look out for a rich widow or a maiden heiress . . . I
shall be a philosopher in time.'[49]

The following spring Wordsworth went on a trip to France and
Italy, leaving Dora behind though she had longed to go with him.

Her health, he told her, would never stand the travelling, though she was well enough to visit Edith May in Sussex and Sara Coleridge in London, and to see the Hutchinson family in Wales, while he was away. Apart from toothache she was in excellent health and spirits. Quillinan returned to England in September, but Dora missed seeing him as she had promised to escort her father home to Rydal. It is possible to wonder whether Wordsworth's insistence on her company and the timing of his return to Grasmere were designed to prevent her reunion with Quillinan. However, Isabella Fenwick, an old and respected family friend, decided to take an interest in the affair. She invited Dora to return southwards to spend the winter with her at Dover and the family were persuaded to agree in the best interests of Dora's health.

Dora's troubled relationship with Quillinan continued by letter, as she struggled to understand the fluctuation of her own feelings during their long separation. Sometimes she felt that it would have been fairer to release Quillinan from the attachment and leave him free to find someone else. At other times she longed to be with him. Quillinan complained that her letters and her public demeanour were cold and that it was only with difficulty that he could discern the 'least manifestation of preference' towards himself. In November, while he was staying at Rydal and she was at Dover, Dora wrote telling him that 'My love for you is a spiritual Platonism such as man might feel for man or woman for woman . . . I wish for your own sake you were fairly married to someone else . . .' Dora's mother chanced upon the letter while Quillinan had it on the writing table and asked to read it. Mary was very uneasy when he responded with evasions, alerted to the fact that the relationship of which she and William so disapproved was still alive. The reply that Quillinan was writing as Mary came into the room accused Dora of heartlessness: 'I am not spiritualised enough for you – you – frigid disagreeable thing! . . . it is a wood-pecker's tap on a hollow tree in my ears: it is a squirt of lemon-juice in my eyes, and it is gall and wormwood on my tongue.'[50] The letter contains a poem which betrays the extent of his feelings.

Yes Dora, on *his* hearth and *thine*
With vagrant hopelessness I pine
  And so would fain depart,
And wander forth – in search of what? –
My *home*:- t'is not where Thou art not –
My home is in thy heart.

It concludes with instructions 'to be burnt when read on honor'.

A further, passionate letter was despatched to Dora at Dover after Quillinan left Rydal. He apologised for past fickleness and for having played with her feelings at times: 'My love for you has certainly in one sense not been a happy one: but without it, I should have been dead long since; nothing else could have sustained me through what I have endured of evil; lighter affections might have buoyed my spirit up under common troubles; but I have had some troubles so severe as nothing but a rational and thoughtful and downright and resolute, though *passionate* love for a good and virtuous girl could have given me fortitude to bear . . .'[51]

He was a frequent visitor to Dover, where Isabella Fenwick became a benevolent matchmaker. One of Dora's problems was that although her early romantic attraction for Quillinan had matured into a deeply loving platonic relationship, she does not seem to have experienced the passionate sexual attraction felt by him for her. Nor do her own letters express the same level of passion that is evident in her correspondence to Jane Jewsbury. Although she loved Quillinan and she loved his daughters as if they were her own, she found it difficult to know whether this was enough for marriage, particularly in the face of implacable parental opposition.

Dora wrote to her father in April 1838 telling him that she had definitely decided to marry Quillinan. Wordsworth's reply to Dora was adamant. His opinion had not changed since the matter was first mentioned. 'I take no notice of the conclusion of your Letter; indeed part of it I could not make out. It turns upon a subject which I shall never touch more either by pen or voice. Whether I look back or forward it is depressing and distressing to me, and will for the remainder of my life, continue to be so.'[52]

To Quillinan he wrote that his financial position, his religion and Dora's health made the prospect of marriage impossible. Although Dora was now thirty-four and of an age when she should have been free to make her own choice, she was completely under the domination of her father, bound by both affection and duty. Her will was not strong enough to do something that would incur his displeasure and cause him immense pain. Dora stayed away from home for fifteen months, and after her return it was made plain that Quillinan was no longer welcome at Rydal Mount.

In May 1835 Southey brought Edith home from the Retreat 'in a state which was pronounced to be all but absolutely hopeless'. But Edith was rather calmer at home, though possessed by a 'settled melancholy'. 'This certain good has been obtained by it, that she herself is relieved from the distress of being separated from her family which she felt deeply; and it is much better for my daughters to have the object of their solicitude always with them, and find relief in the performance of their duty, than to be anxiously expecting reports from a distance.'[53] 'For fifteen months', he wrote to a friend, 'my wife has been a maniac . . . This used to be a hospitable house; we see no company now and . . . can have no abiding guests . . .'[54] Edith could not tolerate the presence of strangers in the house.

The situation was hardest for her daughters, Bertha and Kate, who rarely went out except to visit a neighbour or to a family dinner. They took turns to sit with their mother, who became restless and irritable if left alone. The house had come to resemble a private asylum, shuttered and silent, with a pervasive atmosphere of dread. Southey lived in 'an uneasy dream', thankful when Edith passed a quiet day: 'generally she is manageable, tho . . . she always seems unwillingly to do what she is requested . . .'[55] Sometimes there would be a brief interval when she looked or spoke like her former self; at other times there were 'violent paroxysms' of anger when Edith would have to be held down by force. After these episodes she would sink into a deep sleep.

Southey was increasingly unable to bear the enforced confinement with his wife and left her with Bertha, Kate and Mary Lovell to go on a four and a half month trip to show Cuthbert the scenes of his childhood: 'a land flowing with cyder and clouted cream and wherein apples, better than which never grew in Paradise, are not forbidden fruit'.[56] He visited Sarah Coleridge, who was staying with Derwent in Cornwall, Joseph Cottle in Bristol, Southey's elderly aunt in Taunton and Edith May in Sussex, where he made the acquaintance of his first grandchild. He also paid a visit to Caroline Bowles near Lymington. His relationship with Caroline was gradually and imperceptibly changing with the anticipation of Edith's imminent demise. Although 'it was impossible that either of us could look upon such an event as among the contingencies of fortune' there appears, at this point, to have been an 'understanding' between them.[57] He came back to Greta Hall refreshed by Caroline's support and better able to cope. For his younger daughters there was no respite.

In August 1837 Mary Wordsworth stayed for a few days at Greta Hall on her way back from her son's house and Bertha Southey took her in to see Edith, hoping that it might help her mother to see an old friend, "but she would not look up, but kept *muttering* to B. 'I said I would not see her. I'll speak to nobody – dirty slut to bring her – dirty – dirty slut". Seeing her thus disturbed, I did not sit down as B. wished me to do, but said a few words of greeting and left the room. She is an affecting object – but what a contrast in regard to beautiful neatness and cleanliness to our poor sufferer.'[58]

On 16 November 1837 Edith died, to the great relief of everyone around her. But it was relief mixed with grief and guilt. Bertha was now free to marry her cousin Herbert Hill, a fellow of New College, Oxford, as soon as he was in a position to support her. Kate had no such happy event to look forward to, and took months to recover. She was sent away to stay with her sister Edith May and then taken to London by Isabella Fenwick, where it was hoped that 'novelty and chearful circumstances may bring her spirits into a healthier state'.[59]

Southey was also ill during the winter and planned an expedition to France with Cuthbert. Although only sixty-four he had aged considerably in the space of the previous year. He was very lonely. 'Whether Hope and I shall ever become intimate again in this world, except on the pilgrimage to the next, is very doubtful . . . I am haunted in dreams more distressingly than can be described. At times the burden of loneliness seems to weigh me down.'[60] After his visit to France he went to stay with Caroline Bowles and wrote to Bertha and Kate announcing his intention to marry her. 'I have known Miss Bowles more than twenty years; and since Miss Hutchinsons death there has been no woman with whom I have been so intimate, or for whom I have entertained so high a regard. For many years I have never travelled to the South without making Buckland one of my resting places, and it was always the place at which I wished to rest longest. No persons could be more prepared for the relation in which we now stand to each other . . . You and Kate both know enough of my long friendship for her and the grounds upon which it has rested, to understand how suited to each other we are in all respects.' The marriage was planned for the following June and Southey hoped that it would add to Bertha and Kate's comfort: 'I am perfectly satisfied Caroline will be to you as an elder sister . . . You will love her the more for having made me myself again which under any other circumstances I never should have been.'[61]

Unfortunately, Southey was being naïve. His announcement of remarriage came less than twelve months after the death of the girls' mother and they found the thought of it utterly repugnant. Caroline was fifty-two and Southey sixty-five when they married. Southey's physical state was already deteriorating and he was unable to consummate the marriage. On holiday in France he had lost his way in hotels, had lapses of memory and became physically unsteady. More recognisable symptoms of stroke appeared in August 1839 when he 'lost himself for a moment; he was conscious of it, and an expression passed over his countenance which was very touching – an expression of pain and also of resignation.'[62] He gradually became more confused and bewildered and incapable of any kind of literary activity. When Wordsworth visited him in July

1840 Southey failed to recognise him. A year later he could not even recognise his wife.

Caroline's entrance into the household was the source of considerable conflict. Neither Kate nor Bertha could stand seeing their mother's place at Greta Hall usurped, and they had no wish to have their home altered by a stranger. Caroline was hot-tempered and apt to 'stand upon the letter of the marriage contract', which was an additional source of grievance since Southey was – in Wordsworth's words – 'incapable from failure of mind to fulfill the Contract in the sense which the Law requires'.[63] Caroline sacked the Southeys' elderly servant and refused to allow the girls to nurse their own father as they wished to do. After considerable argument Kate was told she could see him only once a week. Kate quarrelled irrevocably with Caroline over these and many other things, and gradually the entire family became involved. When Edith May took Caroline's part against Kate and Bertha, arguing her rights as a wife, the breach between the sisters was too wide to be bridged. Eventually Kate, Cuthbert and Mary Lovell were forced to leave Greta Hall, to the indignation of other members of the family and close friends. Mary Lovell made a home with Cuthbert Southey, though she does not seem to have been very popular with his wife. Kate remained unmarried and rented a cottage on Vicarage Hill in Keswick.

One of Sara Coleridge's first tasks after the death of her father was to assist Henry in the production of *Table Talk*, a collection of Coleridge's conversations compiled from careful notes kept by Henry over a series of years. Sara contributed little, lamenting the fact that she had never recorded her talks with her father. Her input was editorial – helping Henry to untangle her father's complex lines of reasoning. Though she was still 'morbidly depressed', her mental equilibrium remained in fragile balance so long as she was occupied.

She professed herself to be very much in love with her husband. He was the 'colour of life' for her, she declared: without him she would shiver 'in the gloomy vestibule of winter'. Her letters are full of feeling. 'My beloved I think of you with the deepest love, and am drawn nearer to you by all the events of life; if others disappoint my hopes I seem the tighter bound to you; if kindness and friendship abound, I rejoice in it as a common good with you; yet think what a nothing it is compared to your love – the great source of heartfelt happiness.'[64]

Yet Sara was deeply unhappy in her role as wife and mother. She had inherited too much of her father's disposition. She was highly strung, imaginative, fearful and lacking a tough outer skin to shield her from the wear and tear of ordinary life. The 'visible soul' Hartley had observed, was without protection. She was flayed by self-doubt and driven by an inner creative force she was helpless to control. This double-headed monster returned again and again like Prometheus' eagle to tear at her. Whereas Virginia Woolf personified her own demon as a black fin on an ocean of water, Sara saw hers as 'a black vulture', revealingly masculine, which came to cast 'his grim shadow over me, and give me a sight of his beak and claws. Now he holds me down upon the ground in his horrid gripe . . .'[65] And, as with Woolf, Sara's dark visitant was inextricably bound up with her creativity – 'my nervous trials have been the source of some of my most valuable mental acquisitions'. They were also a projection of her guilt. She was constantly torn between her own desires and needs and her duty towards her husband and children. Always a perfectionist, she felt a failure because she could not be entirely selfless in the role of wife and mother.

It was a double bind felt by most women writers of the time. Anne Finch, Countess of Winchelsea had articulated the same feelings a hundred years earlier, in the grip of the same depression.

> O'er me alas! thou dost too much prevail;
> I feel thy force, whilst I against thee rail;
> I feel my verse decay, and my cramped numbers fail.
> Thro' thy black jaundice I all objects see,
>     As dark and terrible as thee,
> My lines decried, and my employment thought
> An useless folly, or presumptuous fault . . .[66]

During her severe depression in 1834, following the death of the twins, Sara had begun an essay on 'Nervousness'. It was an attempt to analyse her mental and physical condition from an intellectual standpoint as a means of understanding her own psyche. Composed more than twenty years before the birth of Freud, it is a fascinating example of self-analysis, written in the form of a dialogue between the Invalid and her alter-ego 'Good Genius'. Its message is the Victorian credo of Self-Help. For sufferers of 'nervous derangement' there was no 'all competent tribunal' outside the Self to appeal to. 'Self-Management' was the only answer, since each individual was unique and needed a unique solution, but the first step was self-knowledge. 'We shall be our own counsellors, if we will but be true to ourselves, and if we have full *information* on the subject in question . . .'

Her observations are acute, informed by years of living with her aunts, and by personal suffering. 'Nervous derangement manifests itself by so many different symptoms that the sufferers themselves are puzzled what to make of it, and others, looking at it from different points of view make wrong judgments on the case. Those who perceive only how it affects the mind are apt to forget that it also weakens the body . . .'

Sara, more at home with the workings of her mind than those of her body, found it hardest to make sense of the eating disorder that accompanied her depression. 'During one part of my illness I suffered from a total loss of appetite – with despair I heard that a generous diet was absolutely necessary for me, & saw my friends exerting their calming imaginations to devise concentrated essences of meats, by which the largest possible quantity of nourishment might be conveyed in the narrowest space with the least opposition from the shrinking stomach. Then came a craving fit: whatever I took seemed as if it were cast into a yawning gulf and did nothing perceptible toward contracting the gulf, while I felt conscience stricken at every morsel – because how could one with such digestive powers, and without the aids to digestion of air & exercise, profitably or safely dispose of such a load of food?'

A more complex moral problem was her reliance on laudanum

to alleviate her symptoms. 'Another case of conscience with me is in regard to the use of stimulants and narcotics, particularly laudanum. Every medical man speaks ill of the drug, prohibits it, & after trying in vain to give me sleep without it, ends with prescribing it himself.' Close observation of her father had still not brought the realisation that addiction to the drug was physical and not the result of a weakness of will – 'it is the liability to become a habit that is the chief evil of laudanum taking, rather than the bodily effects. But we must never suffer it to become a habit – but every time we have recourse to it must ask ourselves if it really be as necessary as it was at first . . .' What was done cautiously and rationally 'can never become a bad mental habit'. Good Genius commands her: 'If you have reason to think you shall become a slave to it, give it up whatever it costs you . . .' The same applied to the wine and spirits thought necessary as a tonic, or to 'keep the drug on the stomach'. She had first been given regular glasses of port wine as a nine-year-old child on the advice of doctors.

Sara's inability to give up either the drug or the stimulants had been seen as another humiliating personal failure. In the persona of Good Genius, Sara castigated those who, like Sara Hutchinson, told depressives to pull themselves together and that 'by reasoning and perseverance alone we can triumph over that which is a bodily weakness'. One might just as well try 'to curb the wind with a bit & bridle!' Believing such a doctrine was fatal. 'We fail and the failure causes disappointment and irritation; such a notion entertained by others must lead to wrong and harsh judgments expressed or understood, whereby the sufferer's heavy burden is rendered more galling than before . . .' Sara adds regretfully, 'Had I but known as well as I do now what it is possible to achieve & what must be submitted to as inevitable how much regret and bitterness of spirit I should have been spared.'

She was violently opposed to the new electric shock treatment for nervous disorders. What did the most good was understanding: 'Sympathy is like rain on the brown grass. Mingle admonition with sympathy according to the Lucretian prescription – let them feel that they are fully understood.'

Henry's father died in 1836 and Sara accompanied her husband on a long-overdue visit to the Coleridge relatives at Ottery. Sara hated travelling – the swinging and bumping of the coach always made her ill – and the thought of a five-day journey into Devonshire was a nightmare. But with the death of Colonel James, the family visit could not be put off any longer.

During her stay at Ottery, Sara was very withdrawn and remained in her room for much of the time, reading and making notes for a new edition of her father's work. She became increasingly paranoid about the journey back to London. She eventually left with the children and their nurse, leaving Henry and her mother to follow later, but by the end of the first day she was in a state of total breakdown and at Ilchester declared that she could go no further. It seemed a repeat of her ill-fated trip to London in 1826 when she had collapsed at Kendal. Henry, Mrs Coleridge and the children travelled to London without her.

Sara stayed in a quiet inn, totally alone, without mother or children or husband. Her room was cleaned and her meals prepared without any effort on her part and, for the first time in her life, she found herself free to write, read or simply sit and think without anyone requiring anything from her.

Henry wrote long letters pleading, cajoling, even commanding her to come home. Her replies were almost hysterical. 'If I reach Hampstead paralyzed or dead what will it signify that husband, mother, and children are there – what good will my return do then?' She professed to feel great grief at being separated from Henry and her children, yet in the same letters she begs to be allowed to stay for several months. 'Your feelings will be sad when you hear that I cannot proceed with my journey. God in heaven, to whom I fervently pray, knows that I cannot. I . . . had no sleep last night, and in attempting to set out today found I could not do it . . . I know not what will happen. I *cannot* bear the misery. I never suffered as I have done for 24 hours. Judge kindly of me my beloved, & write to comfort me at Ilchester. *Indeed* I would go if I could. I would suffer pain – but their terrors are too dreadful & my prostration too great. If I am now quiet I shall gradually recover but if I proceed I never shall . . . My notion is that I may after a time return to Ottery and be in Aunt Luke's house or some lodging for the winter. This is dreadful – the separation from you but it cannot be helped.'[67]

A few weeks later she was arguing desperately for the right to remain where she was, at least until Christmas. 'Say that I may rest here till my shattered nerves have recovered some degree of tone, and I shall be happy: but assuredly that will not be in ten days, nor perhaps in ten weeks. For the rest of my life I would keep my expenses within the closest bounds possible.' By the middle of November the letters have become more barbed. 'Your *expressions* my love are fond & gentle, but you virtually deny all my requests, which nothing but absolute necessity induced me to prefer.' Sara was, in part, running away from an impossible situation, as her father had done so often. She genuinely loved her husband, but he also represented all the things that made her miserable. She had discovered that it was virtually impossible, as Southey had predicted, to combine the roles of writer and scholar with that of the 'Angel in the House'. It was simply not possible for a married woman to opt out of her domestic responsibilities. Chronic ill health, as Elizabeth Barrett and Florence Nightingale discovered, offered virtually the only retreat.

Continually grieving at the separation from her children, driven by the desire to have the time and privacy to work, Sara calmed her night terrors with large doses of laudanum and during the day she wrote. The fears and phantoms of her mind were spilled on to paper in a fantastic tale, 'a string of waking dreams', that became her fairy-tale *Phantasmion*, supposedly written for children but very much an adult book. In doing so, she encountered that other demon of women's writing, the rock against which so many productions were shattered. She found that it was not possible for her to 'write the body'. 'I reject all those burning expressions which suggest themselves to my mind in crowds & will endeavour to write only at the dictation of that highest mind which has nothing in common with the body. O who will deliver me from this body of death!'[68]

She remained at Ilchester for six weeks, initially fearing that she might be pregnant. Throughout her life she recorded not only the day but the time her menstrual periods arrived, and any variation in the cycle: '33 hours after the time . . . 4 days late. Alas! Alas!' On more than one occasion she took drugs to 'bring on' her 'monthly courses'. Towards the end of November Henry's patience ran out. He arrived at the inn with a 'bed carriage' and insisted that she accompany him back to London. By 23 November she was 'once more lying on the longed for little bed in Mama's little room' in a state of convalescence.

*Phantasmion* was published anonymously in 1837 and is an escapist fantasy, depicting a world where the sick are miraculously healed, lovers live happily ever after and dreams come true. It ends with Iarine standing before Phantasmion, 'her face beaming bright as ever in full sunshine, the earnest that all he remembered and all he hoped for was not to fade like a dream.' The *Quarterly Review* thought that, though not a poem, *Phantasmion* 'is poetry from beginning to end'. It was, the reviewer observed, probably the last fairy-tale for adults 'ever to be written in England'. An American critic compared it to Fouqué's *Undine*. But unfortunately fairy-tales were out of fashion, and *Phantasmion* did not sell well. It remained the 'beautiful conception of a rarely-gifted mind'.

## From Poetry to Prose

> *It is politic to tell our own story, for if we do not, it will*
> *surely be told for us, and always a degree more*
> *disadvantageously than the truth warrants.*
>
> Sara Coleridge[1]

In February 1839 Quillinan wrote to Wordsworth hoping that he had not completely forfeited his friendship. Quillinan had been invited to Ambleside as Isabella Fenwick's guest, and so renewed contact would be inevitable. Isabella had been trying to effect a reconciliation for some time and the visit seemed to do some good, although, despite Isabella Fenwick's persuasive talents, Wordsworth was still implacable on the subject of marriage. Quillinan wrote to Dora that he wished he could say 'what would be quite satisfactory to Miss Fenwick, for then you and I would be happier than we are as yet, though my visit has, I trust, removed the ill-omened gloom that darkened your house to me.'[2]

In April 1839, Mary and William went to Bath with their son Willy so that he could take the waters for a stomach and bowel complaint. While they were there Quillinan wrote to Dora asking her if she would 'dare to run the rough chance' and marry him despite his relative poverty, even without her parents' approval. Dora sent her father an extract from the letter and told him of her own desire to marry Quillinan. Wordsworth was outraged. He felt that to ask Dora such a thing 'during the absence of her parents' was scarcely the action of a gentleman. Isabella Fenwick was upset that Quillinan had been so tactless as to undo all her diplomacy.

'Cannot you prompt a more conciliatory letter?' she asked Dora. 'Why cannot this attachment be put on the footing it seemed to be when Mr Q left Ambleside? – a patient waiting for happier circumstances, your father reconciling himself to all objections and willing to consent when there could be any reasonable security of your being provided for . . .'[3]

Unfortunately, Quillinan had waited a long time and felt that to be asked to wait even longer was unreasonable for him and unfair to Dora. 'I have been mortified enough already, and you have suffered the torments of suspense too long; you have had too painful a conflict between your love for your father and your kindness for me . . .'[4] His reasoning was not irresponsible. He was not a wealthy man, but he was not a pauper and Dora had £40 a year of her own left to her by Sara Hutchinson. Between them they had a great deal more than Mary and William had had when they decided to embark on married life. The Wordsworths were also in a position to settle money on their daughter if they had felt inclined. But Wordsworth pleaded poverty and the prior claims of Dora's brothers. 'Mr Q is, I trust, aware how slender my means are; the state of W[illy]'s health will undoubtedly entail upon us considerable expense, and how John is to get on without our aid I cannot foresee.'[5] Dora reproached her father with his parsimony. After all, she argued, the Southey girls had been allowed to marry poor men, so why couldn't she? Dora was accused by her mother of lack of proper respect. 'All the feelings for your sake, that he has extinguished – should not indeed my Dearest have been met in this spirit . . .'[6] But Dora's long separation from her parents, first with Isabella Fenwick and then during the Wordsworths' absence in Bath, had given her confidence in her own judgment and strengthened her resolution.

The root of the matter was Wordsworth's tenacious patriarchal desire to keep Dora at home, perhaps hoping 'to recapture, in her companionship, the eyes and ears which Dorothy had given to him many years before . . . Not only did he love her as a daughter, but as a virgin who might tend the flame upon his altar.'[7] This manifested itself in a deep-rooted possessiveness. 'I cannot think of parting with you with that complacency, that satisfaction, that hopefulness which I could wish to feel,' he wrote. So it could not be thought of. In the end another reconciliation was brought about by Isabella Fenwick and Quillinan had a 'weary interview' in which he pleaded his case. Faced with Quillinan's genuine distress and the risk of losing his daughter's affections, Wordsworth gave in, half-heartedly. 'As the event is inevitable, I told him I felt it my duty to try to make the best of it; but how I should succeed I could not tell. But said I blame no-one.'[8]

Mary wrote to Dora: 'To spare you as much anxiety as I can I send you *direct* a copy of the letter your Father has written this morning to Q . . . Heaven forbid that the reply may not be a satisfactory one – and if it *be* satisfactory, I shall ever deeply regret that you suffered us to quit home, as you are to be taken so soon from it. We have been too long separated of late . . . But I must not look at the matter in "this point of view"; rather let me hope and trust in the Almighty that all may go well with you . . .'[9]

But in reality very little had changed and the prospects of their being able to marry in the near future were as remote as ever. Quillinan's finances had been entangled since the death of his wife and his father's estate had proved to be in a similar muddle. There was also a trial hanging over him, the result of a fraudulent transaction by his wife's family to which he had been an innocent signatory. Quillinan was a long way from being able to support Dora in the way her father required. 'Something must turn up in our favor,' he wrote to Dora, 'the cards have been against us so long . . .'[10] The following year Dora accompanied Isabella Fenwick south and stayed for ten weeks, accompanying Quillinan in public for the first time. Friends interpreted this as sign that the engagement was to be openly acknowledged. Dora brought Jemima north to Rydal when she returned and Quillinan came a few weeks later for the summer. Thus they were able to spend most of the year together. Dora's health was good enough at the end of August to ascend Helvellyn on a pony, accompanied by her father and Quillinan. When he left there was a grudging agreement that a marriage might be contemplated the following summer.

But at the beginning of March 1841 Dora again accompanied Miss Fenwick south to be with Quillinan and on 25 April Dora wrote to her cousin that she was to be married in three weeks' time. It was all due to Miss Fenwick's kindness, she explained, that 'minor difficulties have been removed . . . and I am thankful, very thankful, not to have so many weeks as I expected to look forward to a point in one's life w'h when quite resolved upon the sooner it is got over the better for body and mind . . .'[11] She still had mixed feelings and many fears about 'the awful event'. Many of their money worries were to be banished by a trust set up by her uncle Christopher Wordsworth, who settled £1000 on Dora, his kind action a rebuff to his less generous brother.

Dora was married to Edward Quillinan on 11 May 1841 from Miss Fenwick's house in Bath. She was elegantly clad in a white poplin dress trimmed with lace at the collar and cuffs and wore a white silk bonnet with a short veil held in place by a sprig of orange blossom. Her brother John officiated and Willy gave her away. William had fully intended to come, but he had 'a sudden outburst of feeling' at the last moment and stayed behind in the house while the others went to church. The emotional stress was almost too much for Dora. Quillinan observed anxiously that she was 'in much agitation till it was over, her face was as white as her dress & she tottered so that I thought she would fall.'[12]

Mary felt the loss of her daughter keenly: 'My spirits are too much bewildered . . .' Quillinan took Dora to Wells for their wedding night and the following morning they all met at an inn for breakfast before setting off for Bridgwater, Stowey and Alfoxden. It was the first time either Mary or Dora had seen the house they had heard so much about. Mary described it as a '*pilgrimage*' which for Wordsworth brought painful memories of Dorothy – 'the thought of what his sister . . . was then and now is'. It was, Wordsworth wrote, 'a farewell visit for life'.[13] The next day brought a 'sorrowful parting' as Dora went back to Bath with Quillinan and William and Mary travelled on to London.

In London Mary went to visit the Coleridges and had 'a long sit' while the ladies dressed themselves to receive company. She was detained longer than she had intended to stay by 'so many family questions', mainly about what was happening at Greta Hall, Mrs Coleridge's concern for Hartley, and the tragic disappearance of Mary Lovell's son Robert. He had gone on a tour of the Continent and been last heard of at Marseilles. Enquiries by the Foreign Office and the efforts of friends failed to reveal any trace of him.

Sara invited the Wordsworths to dinner the following evening. Mary's dislike of the young Sara and her mother was unabated. She wrote to Dora that Sara had become 'a silly prating forward thing – I was so sorry to hear her put in, not her word only, but advance opinions, so glaringly, that even Father felt and mentioned it to me'.[14] Though Coleridge and Wordsworth could hold the stage for hours at a time until the listener felt 'bethumped with words', women – even very learned women – were supposed to remain silent. Sara, however, 'prosed away in learned matters all dinner time and after, to the Pastor of the Parish on her right hand, and now and then a word to the Poet on her left – I sat between H. and a brother Lawyer . . . Poor dear Mrs C. like a *stuffed Turkey* opposite me – and that was our party.'[15]

Four weeks to the day after her marriage, Dora wrote to Isabella Fenwick of her gratitude. 'I *cannot* let this last happy day of four happy weeks pass away without one word of deep & heartfelt thanks to *you* to whom I owe it all . . . a happier or more thankful spirit than mine cannot walk this bright earth.' Dora was glad that Isabella had continued her course of diplomacy with her parents. 'The fear that my Father might be yet more discontented with the path I had chosen when we were irrevocably started upon it haunted my waking & sleeping hours . . .'[16]

But happiness had come almost too late. Early in 1842 Dora had a relapse at Quillinan's house in Spring Street. The tuberculosis had invaded her stomach and she found it almost impossible to eat. The Wordsworths were in London at the time and were dissatisfied with Quillinan's handling of Dora's illness. They immediately took over her care, Mary Wordsworth being convinced that she knew what was best for her daughter. Dora was continually urged by her mother to eat more since she ate 'about as much bacon as a sparrow might pick, no liquid, for she is afraid of wine, with a little rice. She took tea – and poor thing, she has retired to hide, or to keep off greater suffering . . . really the food she takes is insufficient one would imagine to support life. I am sadly out of heart about her . . .'[17] Wordsworth tried to get her to promise to eat a small spoonful of minced 'animal food' at least once a day. Dora found it difficult to eat, and attempts to make her 'bolt' in order to build up her constitution made her nauseous. Food became repulsive and she was, under pressure, gradually starving herself.

Dora had been treated by Dr Davy, formerly very high in Wordsworth's estimation. Now, yet another physician was called in for an opinion, this time Dr Ferguson, who discounted Dr Davy's diagnosis and prescription and ordered wine. Mary reported: 'He assures us there is no vital disease, but an obstinate derangement of the nerves of the stomach which extend over the whole frame – and that there is no doubt of this being brought on by anxiety; and that rest, mental and bodily, is what she needs, – and advised her 'to Bolt', as he expressed it. This she would not listen to, saying that she could nowhere be so quiet as by remaining here . . . And it annoyed me to find her scheme is not to go with us to Hampstead . . . She fight[s] with me against going . . .'[18] But Dora was not allowed to have her own way and be comfortable in her own home amusing herself playing chess with her step-daughters. Her husband backed up the Wordsworths' opinion that the air of Hampstead would be better for her and so she had to go. 'Doro, tho' we had a struggle to get her away, was cheerful during her drive but sadly exhausted afterwards; she appeared however for a couple of hours again after dinner, from which she retired, and this morning, as is usual, she is bright again – tho' I fear sleep and she had little to do with each other . . . I trust if Dora can but reconcile herself to being absent from the girls – and her own diseased clinging to home – this lovely spot and this fine air and kind friends, could not but benefit her health.'[19] But Dora couldn't wait to get back to her own home, away from parental pressure, and moved back to Spring Street as soon as she could.

\*     \*     \*

In the year following Sara's breakdown at Ilchester, she suffered a series of miscarriages. As many women discovered, laudanum is lethal to the unborn child. Dante Gabriel Rossetti's wife Elizabeth had a still-born baby and Sara's friend Elizabeth Barrett Browning, also addicted, managed to have only one living child from a number of pregnancies. Sara was dimly aware that there might be a risk, but was unable to do without the drug. She wrote to Dora during her pregnancy: 'I know that to abstain would be the safer side . . . the longer I am ill the more puzzling my complaint is to me & the less I know how to act for the best.'[20]

The Coleridges' financial position was improving rapidly. Henry had inherited money from his father and was now earning a good living at the Bar. He showered Sara with gifts – silk dresses and jewelry and ermine muffs. She was still beautiful and he declared that he liked to see her 'to advantage'. There was also enough money to enable them to move to a larger house. As soon as Sara felt strong enough, they moved to Chester Place in Regent's Park. Sara regretted the loss of the countryside, confessing that she always felt 'insecure in a street', but was determined to concentrate on the advantages of the move. 'We have some pleasant neighbours in the adjoining terraces, and the Park with its miles of greensward, clumps of trees, and bleating sheep, is more rural and pleasanter to roam in than we expected to find it . . . But there is no water near us, running or at rest; and this to me, who have in my early days, luxuriated so in water, is a great want.'[21] The house was close enough to London for Henry to be able to live at home during the week. It also brought them within calling distance of London society, which for Sara was another disadvantage.

In 1840 she again carried a child to full term and in July gave birth to a girl – Bertha Fanny. Sara had a very difficult time and was completely prostrated afterwards, requiring rest and absolute quiet and the administration of drugs. As she lay in a semi-conscious state in the darkened room, she was aware of Henry sobbing as he leant over the crib in the nursery next door and realised that their daughter had died. Sara tried very hard to distance herself from the death of this baby, having been aware from the beginning 'that the little darling was not for this world'. Henry was extremely upset, he 'suffered more than I could have imagined'. Sara talked consistently of the baby as a stranger, resisting the bonding process – what she referred to as the ability of 'these little speechless creatures, with their wandering, unspeaking eyes,' to 'twine themselves around a parent's heart from the hour of their birth.'[22] Yet she kept a five-page journal of Bertha's pitiful eleven days of life.

Six months later Henry himself became ill and throughout 1841 was only able to work intermittently. In a period of respite, he travelled to Belgium with Sara. Despite her hatred of travelling, Sara had a wonderful time visiting churches and looking at art – particularly Rubens; 'the fire, life, movement and *abandon* of his pictures quite unfit one, for a time, for the sedater excellencies of Hemling and Van Eyck!'[23]

By May 1842 it was clear that Henry's illness was of a serious and probably fatal nature. He began to lose the use of his legs and by the end of the year was completely bedridden and in great pain. The relationship with his wife was now reversed. Sara looked after him and took on his role as head of the household, managing all their affairs. Henry deteriorated rapidly, becoming emaciated and almost unrecognisable. The children were kept away, both parents feeling that it was better for them not to see him in that condition.

In her letters to friends, Sara wrote in an attitude of resignation, accepting the inevitable: 'when I once know that it *is* God's will, I can feel that it is right . . .'[24] But in her diary she could be more truthful: 'He looks worn – but his countenance is quiet – though with more ghastliness about it. He talks a little – slowly and at intervals. He embraced and kissed me this morning . . . O my beloved – how thou sleepest – Alas is this the prelude to the sleep of the grave? . . . Even thus I would fain keep thee ever by me.' Henry was not so composed. When his brother asked him, 'Are you resigned?' he replied bitterly, 'What can a man be else!' Henry was delirious towards the end – 'heartrending' for Sara to witness. He died on 26 January 1843 and Sara kissed 'his beloved face –

over and over again' before writing to her son Herbert, at Eton, to tell him of his father's death.

On the next day she suffered an emotional reaction. 'After two o'clock a heavy black cloud came over me. It seemed as if the prop of my spirits had fallen away and all was crushed into flatness. I am better now – but very low. I am resigned to the blackness and desolation of feeling that I must go through.'[25] Henry was buried in a vault in Highgate cemetery and Sara arranged for her father's coffin to be placed beside him, rather than in the damp mausoleum where the Gillmans had interred him.

In the months following Henry's death Sara had to come to terms with her ambivalent feelings about her widowhood. 'Not only had I lost *Henry*, but I was without a husband and lover – one to whom I was everything and who was everything to me. Nobody was now left who loved me more than all the world beside, took an interest in whatever concerned me, and saw my whole mind and person through glorifying golden mist. I seemed to be laid bare – reduced from poetry to prose . . .' But, though she dreamt at night of Henry's return, 'having sad disappointments in waking', she was forced to admit that 'it was ever the lover more than the protecting husband that I missed . . . I feel content with singleness and begin even in some respects to prefer it, which I once thought impossible.'[26] It was Henry as lover that she grieved for, Henry the lover who had given her moments of happiness; Henry as husband stood for everything that had made her life intolerable. With his death she embarked on a new freedom.

On 4 October 1842, Mary wrote to her friend Isabella Fenwick of her forty years of happiness with William: '. . . from this day we look back upon 40 years of wedded life with grateful thanks to our heavenly Father for leading us thro' such a long course of uninterrupted harmony. We, like all mortals, have our sorrows, but these have been endeared to us by perfect sympathy, and only drawn us more closely to each other. Then this beautiful region in which we have been permitted to live – and in such home-society!' The letter is interrupted by William calling her to the end of the terrace to look at the view, 'a more visionary scene of loveliness was never witnessed.'[27]

William too, in a moment of introspection, made a tribute to Mary's patience and self-control. 'I have to thank God for his goodness towards me . . . that for more than forty years I have had a companion who can bear with my offences, who forgets them, and enters upon a new course of love with me when I have done wrong, leaving me to the remorse of my own consciousness.'[28] Mary was not always able to bear things with saintly fortitude. She gave in occasionally to exhaustion and depression under the strain of caring for her sister-in-law, and constant worry about Dora's health and the state of her son John's marriage. His wife, Isabella Curwen, had long been ill with consumption. Continental spas, residence in Italy and other measures had all been tried without result. During these long absences, Isabella's relationship with John Wordsworth had deteriorated and their marriage had become 'a wearisome wasting thing'.[29] Isabella eventually died at Pisa in 1848, leaving John free to remarry.

There had been a great change in the Wordsworths' circumstances. Sara Coleridge observed: 'The latter years of that family have not been like the earlier ones . . . Then there were April showers, and vernal gusts of pettish weather. But now there is settled dullness – no Lyrical Ballads – no Excursions . . . No gladsome Miss Wordsworth and cheerful Miss Hutchinson to say alternately sharp and kind things; no naughty but mirthful Willy at the door – the careless children turned to anxious men and women – the bard shorn of his vigour by age, and of his gentleman-like courtesy of manner.'[30]

Both the Wordsworths were now in their seventies. Mary's eyesight, always bad in one eye, was fading. William's health, actually quite robust under the obscuring screen of minor ailments he continually complained of, was also imperceptibly declining. Mary reported that 'a *change* in spirits and habits I am sorry to say has taken place . . . he sits more over the fire in silence etc etc and is sooner tired on his walks'.[31] But they were both still fit enough to go south on extended visits to friends and relatives. Sara Coleridge reported that William could still walk 7 or 8 miles a day 'but is always losing his way, and making out *he* is obliged to look sharp after his wife, whose eyesight is grown so bad that she is not to be trusted.'[32] Wordsworth was still much fitter than most of his contemporaries. Sarah Coleridge, whose health had been excellent throughout her life, was now suffering great discomfort from rheumatism and angina. Southey was wasting away at Greta Hall.

Southey died on 21 March 1843, having been a complete invalid in body and mind for some years. When Wordsworth and Quillinan attended the funeral at Crosthwaite church, to which they had not been invited, they found that Caroline Southey and her friends were not speaking to them. The quarrel also affected the relationship between Sara Coleridge and Edith May. By taking Kate and Bertha's part against Caroline – after seeing letters written by Edith May – Sara alienated her favourite cousin.

There were mixed opinions in the general assessment of Southey's life and work after his death. Many agreed with Byron's satirical poem, written some years earlier:

> He had sung against all battles, and again
>   In their high praise and glory; he had call'd
> Reviewing 'the ungentle craft', and then
>   Become as base a critic as e'er crawled –
> Fed, paid, and pamper'd by the very men
>   By whom his muse and morals had been maul'd:
> He had written much blank verse, and blanker prose,
> And more of both than anybody knows.[33]

Southey himself provided the best response. He had once written to Walter Savage Landor that 'I might have done more in this way, and better. But I have done enough to be remembered among poets, though my proper place will be among the historians . . .'[34] Wordsworth was very concerned that there should be a proper memorial to him, but the task of collecting his letters and constructing a memoir seemed inevitably to be devolving on to Cuthbert Southey who Wordsworth, and others, felt was unequal 'to the arduous office of determining what part of his Father's papers is fit for publication, and what ought to be held back – or destroyed.' The family quarrel, which divided even Southey's executors, made Cuthbert's job even more impossible. Decisions about what to leave for posterity, 'a matter of no small difficulty and delicacy', were taken only after many arguments – Kate, Bertha and Cuthbert on one side and Caroline, Edith May and Southey's brother Henry on the other.[35]

Henry Coleridge's death wrought a substantial change in Sara. During her marriage, much to Henry's regret, Sara had declined to accompany her husband into society, pleading ill health and a dislike of social intercourse. As a widow she began to go out a great deal. 'I seem to crave a brightly-lighted room, and lively faces and animated conversation . . . I cannot now bear to live a quiet life – I want either society or brisk intellectual occupation to keep me from brooding . . .'[36]

She met the poet Aubrey de Vere, ten years younger than herself, who appears to have been fascinated by her – the admiration of a young man for a beautiful and quite extraordinary older woman. Sara was probably a little in love with him. She had always needed the company of clever men. Few women were able to converse with her on the same intellectual level. She was frequently in de Vere's company when he was in London and corresponded at length with him when he was not. His conversion to the Church of Rome in 1850 caused her some pain, but their friendship lasted until she died. She wrote poems for him, enclosed in her letters, which show that she may well have fantasised about him as a possible lover. One of them, titled 'Dream Love', begins:

> The union of thy heart and mine,
> Ah yes! I know 'tis all a dream:
> For I am dark, in life's decline –
> Round thee the noon-day splendours beam:
> But let this fair tho' flickering gleam
> Of fancied love one moment shine;
> Thou mayst afford at least to seem
> For one brief moment to be mine.

There were other friendships too. In 1845 Elizabeth Barrett sent Sara a copy of her new volume of poems with a letter showing how fully she understood Sara's inheritance as Coleridge's daughter, referring to her as '*you*, who have sate all your life under a living laurel'. Sara was harshly critical of Elizabeth's poetry, as she was towards most other female authors. Elizabeth Barrett's poems were 'all ambition and effort, but full of undisciplined power', and on another occasion, 'a more than *quantum sufficit* – in my opinion – of affectation and bombast'. Were her writings from the hand of a man, Sara went on, 'they would be set down as unsuccessful productions exhibiting some portion of poetic power and merit and never have made the tenth part of the *noise* which as the *poems* of Miss Barrett they have created. Epics and Lyrics and Dramatics of female authors at most are but *splendid failures . . .*'

Sara never seems to have analysed very deeply why this should be so. It was true that mediocre productions by women were often praised beyond their merits simply because their author was a woman – the 'performing dog' syndrome. But it was also true that it was harder to get published as a woman and much, much harder to be taken seriously on a literary level with men. Sara, educated at the hands of Wordsworth and Southey, judged the work of her literary sisters by masculine criteria and found them wanting. So she could reject the 'falsetto muscularity' of Harriet Martineau and Elizabeth Barrett and approve Jane Austen's 'peculiarly feminine genius' which gave 'an especial charm and value to her writings',[37] totally oblivious that it was this essential 'charm and femininity' that kept women's writing in the margins of literature. When *Jane Eyre* was first published, Sara was convinced that it was written by a man. Charlotte Brontë's novels had 'a spirit, a glow and fire about them, a masculine energy of satire and of picturesque description, which have delighted me'. But, when their female authorship had to be taken into account, 'they also abound in proofs of a certain hardness of feeling and plebeian coarseness of taste'.[38]

Though she herself struggled to conform to ideas of female modesty in her own writing she occasionally yearned to be 'very tall, strong and striking' in the literary 'crowd'. In another revealing letter she shows how much her ideas of what was appropriate for a woman gender her writing: '. . . politics and history are subjects which I have less of my desultory, feminine sort of information than some others which seem rather more within my compass. Divinity may be as wide a field as politics; but it is not so far out of a woman's way, and you derive more benefit from partial and short excursions into it . . .'[39] It wasn't just style and tone (ideally feminine and modest) but subject matter that constrained women's writing.

Sara exchanged letters with Elizabeth Barrett before she married Robert Browning and went to live in Italy. They finally met on one of the Brownings' rare visits to England and Sara found that she was not as drawn to her as she had expected. Elizabeth struck her as 'cold and self-involved at first and very plain, with a small ungraceful figure and a wide mouth . . . Her eyes are fine, and there is something about their deep, subdued expression, the pallid cheek and plaintive voice which made me think of Goethe's Mignon . . .'[40] When they spoke, it was to discuss their use of opiates.

Sara had begun to use morphine, taking a massive dose every other night. On these occasions she did not sleep at all, but lay all night in a comfortable state of waking dream. The following night she was able to sleep deeply and wake refreshed and in a happy mood. Regulated in this way, she was able to control her addiction in a manner that enabled her to live and work as normally as possible. Elizabeth Barrett, with Robert Browning's help, had achieved a similar discipline.

Henry's death had left Sara very short of money. He had previously lent Derwent and one of his own brothers–in–law substantial sums of money and after his death they did not seem to see any urgent need for the repayment of the debt. They often failed to pay even the interest. This left Sara severely straitened. Another inheritance which could have eased her way was also paid to her in 'dribs and drabs' without any consideration for her circumstances. As with the majority of women at that time, Sara had only limited control over her own finances. The actual legal status of women from birth to death was that of dependent child.

Sara's capital was 'held in trust' by her male relatives and she was at the mercy of their economic management. The passing of the Married Women's Property Act in 1870 was the beginning of a much-needed change.

Sara had been collaborating with Henry on a number of editorial projects just before his death. She was now faced with the task of editing her father's work by herself – something she was uniquely fitted to do, and she applied herself with great energy and a clear sense of direction. Coleridge's *Aids to Reflection* appeared in 1843, accompanied by an essay of her own 'On Rationalism', written just before Henry died, and arising from reflections on her father's religious ideas. It is a long, discursive document, but full of brilliance. Hartley remarked that, of the three Coleridge children, it was Sara who was 'the inheritrix of his mind and genius'.

After the publication of *Aids to Reflection*, Sara meticulously prepared a second edition of *Biographia Literaria* to appear in 1847. The latter was dedicated to Wordsworth and Sara acknowledged herself on the title page his 'Child in heart and faithful Friend'. *Notes and Lectures upon Shakespeare* and *Essays on his Own Times* followed in 1849. Almost inevitably she was accused of writing 'immodestly', but as she wrote to her brother-in-law, it would have been of little use to 'intersperse modest phrases' when the 'arrogance – if such there be – counts in doing the thing at all'.

Sara's notes for these editions were exhaustive – a boon for modern scholars – but occasionally bewildering. In some places there are footnotes to the footnotes! But it was utter drudgery. 'No work', Sara wrote wearily, 'is so inadequately rewarded either by money or credit than that of editing miscellaneous, fragmentary, unmethodical literary remains like those of S.T.C.'[41] When she wasn't busy with research, she was copying out the text, correcting proofs, writing essays and reviews or dealing with tardy or incompetent publishers.

Editing her father's work, reading his most intimate letters and journals, brought Sara closer to her father than she had been at any time when he was alive. 'Indeed he seems ever at my ear . . . speaking not personally to me, and yet in a way so natural to my feelings, that *finds* me so fully, and awakens such a strong echo in my mind and heart, that I seem more intimate with him now than I ever was in life.'[42] This knowledge of her father brought her also to a profounder understanding of herself. 'It was not self-sacrifice, but self-realisation', as Virginia Woolf put it. 'She found her father, in those blurred pages, as she had not found him in the flesh; and she found he was herself. She did not copy him, she insisted; she was him.'[43]

Much of Sara's editorial effort was aimed as a defence of her father against critics who accused him of a multitude of offences, including plagiarism. She did not attempt to deny Coleridge's use of other people's work, but she argued strenuously that, though he was careless in his attributions, he was innocent of any intent to mislead. Similarly she was quite frank about Coleridge's use of opium, maintaining that he took it from necessity 'that the power of the medicine might keep down the agitations of his nervous system, like a strong band grasping the jangled strings of some shattered lyre'.[44] Her candour was effective, and even De Quincey – one of Coleridge's fiercest critics – acknowledged that her 'mode of argument' was 'unassailable'.

Sara felt it a justification for her efforts. The 'many mornings, evenings, afternoons . . . hunting for some piece of information in order to rectify a statement – to decide whether to retain or withdraw a sentence, or how to turn it . . . the silent avoidance of error. The ascertainment of dates, too, and fifty other troubles of that kind.'[45] But it was 'something to myself to feel that I am putting in order a literary house that otherwise would be open to censure here or there.' Behind all her efforts was the spurned child on a visit to Grasmere, longing for her father's approval and affection but treated coldly because she did not approve of Dora, put down from his knee because he did not like her dress. She sought to please, to win his approval after his death as she had not been able to do as a child.

Her preoccupation with her father's work and reputation, together with her responsibilities as a single parent, once more curtailed her own creative work. Sara wrote to Henry Reed that her leisure time was 'short and liable to interruption . . . The various calls of a London life to a widow with children, and a Father's multifarious literary productions to take care of, are such that they render it generally out of my power to transfer from the tablet of the brain to the sheet of paper the many epistles mentally written in sleepless nights . . .'[46] This situation frustrated and distressed her. 'I do sometimes feel as if I had been wasting myself a good deal . . .'[47] Yet she felt unable to do anything else until it was too late. Suddenly aware of her own mortality, suspecting that her lifespan might be cut short, she wrote a poem, addressed to her father, found among her manuscripts after her death.

> Father, no amaranths e'er shall wreathe my brow. –
> Enough that round thy grave they flourish now: –
> But Love mid' my young locks his roses braided,
> And what car'd I for flowr's of deeper bloom?
> Those too seem deathless – here they never faded,
> But, drench'd and shatter'd dropp'd into the tomb.
>
> Ne'er was it mine t'unlock rich founts of song,
> As thine it was ere Time had done thee wrong: –
> But ah! how blest I wander'd nigh the stream,
> Whilst Love, fond guardian, hover'd o'er me still!
> His downy pinions shed the tender gleam
> That shone from river wide or scantiest rill.
>
> Now, whether Winter 'slumbering dreams of Spring,'
> Or, heard far off, his resonant footsteps fling
> O'er Autumn's sunburnt cheek a wanner hue,
> While droops her heavy garland, here and there,
> Nought can for me those golden gleams renew,
> The roses of my shattered wreath repair.
> Yet Hope still lives and oft, to objects fair
> In prospect pointing, bids me still pursue
> My humble tasks: – I list – but backward cast
> Fain would mine eye discern the Future in the Past.

The Wordsworths were still unhappy with Dora's chosen way of life and felt that the climate of London did not suit her health. Wordsworth's interference led him to write to Dr Ferguson urging him to persuade Quillinan that sea air was what Dora needed and that she was well enough to withstand a 36-hour rail journey to the Lakes so that she could take the sea on the Cumbrian coast at Allonby! Their motives were not so much the bracing effects of sea air and a warmer climate, all of which could have been provided within 70 miles of London, but her presence near them. In March 1843 they succeeded in their object. Dora and Quillinan came north to rented lodgings in Ambleside which cost them £5 a month.

In June 1844, Dora and Quillinan went to stay at Flimby, near Maryport on the Cumbrian coast. Dora was not in good health and a letter from a visiting cousin to the Wordsworths alarmed them so much 'that Father after advising with Mr Carr (Dr Davy to whom he first went, being out), he determined not to wait till Monday, but go off next morning (Saturday) to Flimby to bring her home in the Mail. However thank God he found her so much better, from the effect of a blister – that I trust their previous plans need not be changed . . .'[48] At Flimby, Wordsworth's disapproval of his son-in-law and fears for his daughter's well-being led to words being exchanged. William wrote to Dora as soon as he returned to Rydal: 'I hope that nothing that passed between us dearest D will at all disturb you or retard your recovery. If I thought so, I should be quite miserable . . .' Her parents, he wrote, had both spoken from their 'sense of right'. Dora, understandably, was very angry.

The problem was Edward Quillinan. 'The worst of it is', Wordsworth explained to a friend, 'that Mr Q. seems incapable of regulating his own temper according to the demands which his Wife's indispositions too frequently make upon it. And it is not to be doubted that his way of spending his time is little suited to make the day pass pleasantly for others. He never scarcely *converses* with his wife or children; his papers, his books, or a newspaper engross his whole time. This is surely deplorable, and yet, poor creature, she is very fond of him . . .'[49] Wordsworth accused Quillinan of laziness – he could earn a decent living if he chose. 'He has now taken again to hard labour on his translation of Camoen, a work which cannot possibly turn to profit of any kind either pecuniary or intellectual . . .' Literary activity was something he should have been doing in his '*leisure* hours'.[50] Quillinan's published poetry, his novels and translations counted for nothing to Wordsworth the Victorian Father. In his strictures and complaints he seems to have forgotten the attitude of his own relatives towards his 'indolence' and reluctance to enter remunerative employment before Raisley Calvert's generosity freed him to dedicate his life to poetry. He was censoring Quillinan for merely trying to do what he had done himself.

Although the breach at Flimby was smoothed over, relations with Quillinan deteriorated. Wordsworth initially refused to give Dora an allowance, which would have been the customary action of a middle-class parent in his position. Isabella Fenwick taxed him with his neglect in a letter, but he wrote back assuring her that he would never allow Dora to suffer from lack of money. However he deemed it 'fit and right' that she should be 'straightened, acting as she has chosen to do with my strongest disapprobation.' Dora was being financially punished for marrying Quillinan. The Wordsworths gave her money for servants and for the hire of a carriage, at one point up to £70 a year. But she could never count on this money and it had to be asked for and was given with strings attached, keeping Dora in the position of a dependant.

There was also trouble over Dora's marriage settlement. She owned a field, always referred to as 'Dora's field'. This was part of her settlement and – as was usual with women's property – held in trust for her by her father. However, Wordsworth proposed building a house on it, not for Dora, but for Isabella Fenwick to live in on her visits to Cumbria. Only after the Wordsworths' deaths and Isabella's death would it pass to Dora. Isabella wrote back that she could not possibly contemplate living there under those circumstances – she refused to allow Wordsworth to build a house for her while Dora was without one. But Wordsworth would not move on the subject. If Isabella did not want a house then he would not build one for Dora 'situated as she is'. Dora remained in lodgings and Isabella Fenwick was so angered by Wordsworth's attitude towards his daughter that she refused to come north for her usual summer visit. Wordsworth's behaviour was a repeat of his failure, first to maintain, and then to provide an adequate marriage settlement for his French daughter Caroline – a continuing source of bitterness for Annette Vallon.

In 1845 Quillinan proposed taking Dora to Portugal in the hope that the warm climate might improve her health. Dora was ecstatic at the prospect, but the reaction of 'Old Daddy and Mammy' – especially the latter – to the idea caused her to abandon her plans temporarily. 'We talked of Oporto, & all agreed that it was a most desirable experiment for D. – One person only said nothing – & it was too evident that she was very low on the subject – Mrs Wordsworth. – Dora when we came home intimated to me that she was thrown into an uncertainty about going by her Mother's fears & dislike of the scheme.'[51]

But Quillinan's persuasions and the allure of Oporto won in the end. Although in April Wordsworth was writing confidently that 'Dora has given up the thought of going to Portugal, in consequence of her Mother (who knows her constitution perfectly,) being averse to her doing so when the summer heats are so near', Dora sailed for Oporto on 7 May 1845 with Quillinan and her stepdaughter.

Quillinan's brother had lent them a pretty villa overlooking the sea at the mouth of the River Douro, for as many months as they cared to stay. Though initially troubled by homesickness, Dora was enchanted with its beauty and the views out over the water. 'It was at night; the signal gun of our English steamer roused me from a deep sleep. I got up; opened the shutters. A full moon was shining brilliantly; the white breakers of the bar were as visible as they were audible; beyond the bar, southwards, the sea was a plain of burnished – not gold, nor yet silver, but something between – which now glistened, now glittered as the waves rolled gently along. To the north all seemed wrapped in gloom; but in that direction my heart lay. I again looked anxiously into the deep gloom, and a heave of some friendly wave brought into view a galaxy of bright stars floating upon the waters: it was as if a constellation had come down from the heavens . . .' Dora was confined to bed shortly after their arrival with an attack of what was described as 'rheumatic fever', but she was soon riding 'a beautiful Andalusian poney' (in full English riding costume to the astonishment of the Portuguese) and reported herself 'in the 7th Heaven'.[52] Quillinan was still quietly at work on the translation of Camoen's *Lusiad*, to Wordsworth's annoyance.

Dora loved the Portuguese *festas*; '. . . a certain fashionable and wealthy tailor of Oporto was not content with illuminating his house brilliantly and sending his rockets up into the air, but he must send them down into the street too, to see, for the fun of the thing, the consternation they would cause among the passers-by; and a rocket actually set fire to a lady's petticoat as she was walking home from the opera.' Dora hated being importuned by beggars, but was fascinated by pet pigs. 'Ours was a pretty, round, plump, short-legged little fellow . . . he would mount two or three of the steps, and there squeal and squeak until we went to him, and he would not quit the place until something was given to him. He knew our voices perfectly . . .'

Below their house the *lavendeiras* scrubbed washing on the river bank, singing as they beat the clothes on the stones. 'Picturesque figures are forever passing to and from the city; fish girls, fruit girls (their pretty baskets always on their heads) tripping along with a gay, light step . . . Groups of fishermen are spreading their nets to dry, or sitting on the ground before their cottage doors, in the full sunshine . . . little children darting in and out of these same doors like rabbits . . .'[53]

Dora remained in Portugal for a year. She wrote to Sara Coleridge that the sunshine and exercise had so improved her health she 'slept like a top and ate like a plough-boy'. Dora was in no hurry to come back and they returned on a leisurely trip through Spain and France. She wanted to see 'Seville, Gibralter, Grenada, the Alhambra!' and the Pyrenees. Dora was keeping a journal of her tour which she hoped to present to her parents when she came back, and she also did a series of drawings which came to the attention of the Duke of Saxe-Coburg (elder brother of Prince Albert) who – much to Dora's embarrassment – asked to see them and was much 'gratified by her performance'. Sketching was not always easy. In parts of Spain she was 'literally mobbed by men, women and children', and in some areas the mere appearance of a pencil and pad caused great offence.

Dora loved travelling, particularly the strange assortment of people she met in the hotels and lodging houses. 'Our table-d'hote dinner is very amusing; fresh faces every day; and one or two old ones we are always pleased to see. An elderly gentleman with a most benignant countenance, is so quietly attentive, that I long to talk to him . . . There is another regular guest whom I should like to talk with too – a young man with a very large black moustache; and to him I should say "it is not gentlemanly to sit with your hat on and *smoke* all the time you are not eating, when ladies are dining at the same table as you".'

The Alhambra was everything Dora had hoped for. 'The reality far, far surpassed aught my fancy had pictured . . . palm-like columns . . . marvellous pendent ornaments like perfect stalactites, and walls covered with the finest lace-work, marble floors, fountains at play in the centre of almost every room.' The surroundings too surprised Dora. 'All this sublime beauty in the distance . . . air perfumed with flowers; groves of orange and lemon; the shade-loving fig tree, the gadding vine, the sky-seeking cypress, and the aloes and prickly pears . . . And then the nightingales!'

The long stay in Portugal, the warm climate and freedom from parental control had wrought a great change in Dora. She 'looks like a rose', Sara Coleridge commented when they met – 'The improvement in her is marvellous.'[54] The Quillinans stayed with Isabella Fenwick for a while and then lingered in London before returning to Rydal in July, fourteen months after they had left. They settled at Loughrigg Holme near Rydal. Wordsworth, always over-anxious, was disappointed that Dora had not put on more 'Beef!' while she was away and thought her 'sadly pulled down'.

But by October he was reporting her 'wonderfully strong and well'.

On her return she published the journal of her travels, in two volumes, dedicated 'in all reverence and love to my Father and Mother, for whom they were written'. There was much of interest in it, William wrote, since 'women observe many particulars of manners and opinions which are apt to escape the notice of the Lords of the Creation'.[55] Quillinan thought Dora's book 'clever' but was afraid that Portugal was too obscure a country to arouse much interest among the reading public. It appeared anonymously in the spring of 1847. The Wordsworths affected to disapprove of Dora publishing her book, 'authorship and marriage' being the two things that they had abhorred in connection with their daughter, but they excused her conduct by saying that she needed the money. It was, Sara Coleridge remarked, hypocrisy: 'Mr & Mrs W's way on this and kindred subjects was a sort of semi-pretense . . .' They had published everything, even Sara Hutchinson's 'insipid verses', so why did they pretend? Sara declared that she would never allow her own daughter to publish anything for money that she would not have published for its own sake.

In 1845, while her daughter Sara was on a visit to Oxford, Sarah Fricker Coleridge died suddenly from a heart attack in London, in the act of washing her face before dressing for the day. 'How strange', Sara wrote, 'that I should be absent from her at the last – after living all my life with her . . . The death-silence is awful.' Aubrey de Vere called on a visit of condolence and found Sara grieving 'almost in the dark except for two faint candles'. The death of her mother was of greater moment than that of her father, permanently affecting her happiness. Not only did it cut her off from her family history and the 'common remembrances' that were so important to her sense of identity, it left her feeling very isolated. 'I did not apprehend during her life to what a degree she prevented me from feeling heart-solitude . . .'[56] Sarah Coleridge left behind the uncompleted 'Mrs Codian's Remembrances', dictated to her daughter to record the Fricker family history and the circumstances of the Fricker sisters' courtship and marriage.

This attempt to 'tell her own story', in the face of gross mis-representation after Coleridge's death, had been abandoned.

Though the Wordsworths had not had much contact with 'Mrs C.' for several years, her death brought several days of sorrowful recollection to Rydal Mount. William wrote a letter of consolation to Derwent reminiscing about his first meetings with Sarah and Coleridge in Bristol, memories which brought back feelings it was impossible to expect anyone else to be able to understand. 'Link after link is broken,' he wrote.[57] Dorothy, too, was lucid enough to take in the news and remember how Coleridge had leapt the fence and run across the field all those years ago at Racedown.

Sarah was buried beside her husband and her son-in-law in the family vault at Highgate. She had been greatly loved and greatly misunderstood. Sara wrote savagely in her journal that though Mary Wordsworth had the reputation of being a saint, it was all appearances: 'who except her spouse – will weep for her as a few wept for my poor mother when she died'.

In December 1846 Dora went to Carlisle to help her brother Willy prepare a house for his forthcoming marriage to childhood friend Fanny Graham. While there she caught a severe chill which seems to have reactivated the tuberculosis which had lain dormant since her visit to Portugal. She was in poor health all winter, causing her husband and her parents considerable anxiety, though they all hoped that this was only her 'usual winter cold'. But the warm spring weather failed to bring the expected improvement and the dreaded word 'consumption' was finally uttered. A devastated Quillinan insisted that Dora be told the truth about her condition. 'She asked me several particulars, to every one of which I answered faithfully; so she was put in full possession of the truth. The spirit with which she received the awful intimation, and with which she continues to bear to look it in the face, is in every respect admirable; so humble, so self-censuring for faults of temper which the delicacy of her conscience magnifies, yet so cheerful, so hopeful of the mercy of God, so willing to live yet so resigned to die, and so loving withal, and so considerate.'[58] Quillinan was distraught.

May, he had once written to Sara Hutchinson, was a month of horror for him. His mother had died in May when he was a child, then his first wife in the spring of 1822, and now he had been told that Dora also faced death.

By 24 May 1847 she was ill enough to be brought to Rydal Mount to be nursed by her mother, who chronicled her decline in letters to her brother's wife Mary Hutchinson. 'A *tendency* to Diarrhea last evening exhausted our Darling so much that when I left her at ½ past 1 oc this morning I scarcely expected to see her revive, so far as to meet her again as I did at ½ past 7 oc. sitting up in bed looking and speaking cheerfully – she having written the enclosed – which she gave me, saying, "tell her I have more than 7 lives".' The Wordsworths were still clutching at straws and, on a recommendation, persuaded Dora to try cod liver oil, having been assured by the doctor that it would do no harm. 'Poor Mr Q. clings to the hope, and dear John: it will be a satisfaction to him that the trial is made – You will say with me and with us all God's will be done.'[59]

Mary feared that Friday 29 June was Dora's last day, but three hours later at half-past nine she had revived a little. Mary was very angry with her sister-in-law for destroying the last letter Dora had ever written to her. 'I particularly remember begging you to save this and the former letter I sent you . . . I feared at the time they might be her last, so wished to preserve this memorial – *this is no mistake of mine*. I did not wish to "brood over them".'[60] Dora was now too weak to read, or even to listen to anything being read, but took comfort from the recitation of the hymn 'Just as I am – without one plea,/But that thy blood was shed for me/ And that thou bidst me come to Thee./ O Lamb of God, I come!'

Dora's last sufferings were terrible. 'Since 3 oc yesterday Morning she has a *respite* from an almost continuous *Diarrhea* of 36 hours previous, and the racking pains and helplessness of every-part of the body – being consequently disturbed by the necessity of constant changing (to free the sad sores that sink *deeper*, and become more numerous where the parts are subject to pressure and where the bones wear thro!) cause suffering beyond what aught but the most patient heroism could sustain. Yet the noble Wreck is full of thankfulness . . . she has snatches of sleep and ease when in a quiescent state – and *so chearful* – joking even, about her *fat* – dropsical swellings which have appeared, and move from one part to another for some days past. Hence, even in her face the extreme *emaciated* look is changed.'

Her brother John gave her the Sacrament three times. Only her willpower was keeping her alive. 'It is marvellous how she rallies – Yet she has *at times every day* those sinkings that seem to be the forerunner of immediate dissolution. And dearest Mary, that will be a thankful moment – for nothing but increased suffering can be expected from the sores and weakness. There is no cure for a body exhausted and worn as hers is – and she cannot be moved from one painful part without being thrown upon another.'[61]

Towards the end she began to have a delusion – 'one peculiar symptom of this insidious fatal disease' – that she was recovering. Mary Hutchinson offered to come to support her sister-in-law, but Mary wrote back: 'By no means think of coming to me, I shall find my support in the quiet example she has set me. No change will she admit that she knows of, in the house on her account – We are to sit as usuall in the room below – the breakfast and dinner bell is to be rung as usual – "No fuss" – is her watchword.'[62]

She did not die until 4.45 a.m. on 9 July and she was buried beside Thomas and Catharine and her aunt Sara Hutchinson in Grasmere churchyard. Sara Coleridge found that Dora had left her a strange inheritance. When Sara Hutchinson died she had given to Dora a sonnet that Coleridge had written for her at the height of his passion – 'Dear Asra, woman beyond utterance dear!' Dora left it for Sara Coleridge with a letter. 'Dearest Sara . . . I give it to you knowing how precious it must be to you for all their sakes, and being sure it will be prized for mine also as a memorial of a lifelong friendship, and of my undying love . . .'

Dora also left behind her album, originally a gift from Felicia Hemans, always known as 'Dora's Book' – a record of the literary visitors to Rydal Mount, with entries by Tennyson, Southey, Jane Jewsbury, Matthew Arnold, Walter Scott, Mary Lamb, Walter

Savage Landor, Leigh Hunt, and many others. Coleridge, towards the end of his life, had written for the woman he regarded as a second daughter:

> Now! It is gone. – Our moments travel post,
> Each with its deed or thought, its *What?* and how?
> But, know! each parting Hour gives up a Ghost,
> May live within thee, an eternal NOW.

William was utterly crushed by Dora's death – 'the blank is terrible'. He shut himself in his room and suffered paroxysms of weeping. Mary feared for his health and sanity. Mary herself shrank from painful recollections of Dora's suffering. For Quillinan it was 'a *horrible desolation*, and I cannot yet call it anything else . . . All my usual occupations were so blended with her presence and encouragement, that I *cannot* yet fix myself to any of them.'[63] Isabella Fenwick came north for the first time in years to comfort her friends, but after her departure, almost inevitably, the old gulf opened up between Wordsworth and Quillinan. In reply to her anxious enquiries William wrote: 'You kindly express a hope that Mr Quillinan and I walk together – this has not been so, I cannot bear to cross the Bridge and Field that leads to his Abode; and he does not come hither . . .'[64] Excursions of any kind became a problem, since almost every prospect reminded Wordsworth of Dora. Mary wrote: '. . . where can we find a place or an object on earth to look upon that is not beset with like hauntings!' By February 1848 Wordsworth was 'bowed to the dust . . . His mind and spirits . . . in the lowest state of *humiliation* and deep sorrow.'[65]

The Wordsworths went to stay with their son John at his living in West Cumbria, and then to Carlisle to see Willy – a visit which brought awful recollections, since William believed Dora had caught the fatal chill there, going to furnish the house for Willy's wedding. Their youngest son's marriage to Fanny Graham had not turned out quite as expected either. Fanny had very definite opinions about where she wanted to live, which did not coincide with those of her in-laws, and was very firm that 'the air of Rydal' did not suit her health. As a result, Mary lamented, they rarely saw her.

Throughout it all, Dorothy 'continued in her usual way . . . She is more restless than ever, and it is a perpetual move from her own chair to that of her Brother the whole time she is downstairs.'[66] She insisted on having an enormous fire roaring in the grate even on a hot summer's day to keep 'uncomfortable feelings' at bay, and the Wordsworths complained that it was a great drain on their finances. The continual washing was also a problem, especially when the weather was bad.

Like the first Mrs Rochester in *Jane Eyre*, Dorothy haunted the upper rooms of Rydal Mount. When the Wordsworths had visitors to stay they had to sleep in a distant part of the house: 'We can give her no neighbours but ourselves, or she would terrify strangers to death. She is however in many things much improved – tho' not in her *manners*. But her memory is wonderfully mended – and at times if you heard her talk, without seeing her, you would think nothing ailed her. It is a strange case.'[67] Almost to the end she could be perfectly lucid, write letters and have a conversation in a way that astounded those around her, but the rest of the time she lived in the world of the child, incontinent, irrational and self-willed.

She liked to play with soap and a bowl of hot water, making suds, and was quite happy to be taken out in the garden '2 or 3 hours at a time'. This helped her to sleep and was a mercy for her attendants. She no longer walked and had begun to put on weight. 'Her countenance is often the image of child-like innocence and simplicity, and her *pleasures* in perfect accordance with that expression, except when she is angry . . . she asks the same questions a dozen times a day.' She was also highly entertained by the gift of a cuckoo clock: 'I thought she would have dropped from her chair, she laughed so heartily at the sudden exit of the little Mimic.'[68] She was often violent, knocking her nurses about the head and tearing their clothes. Mary was lucky that there were women who had been fond of Dorothy and who were willing to serve her devotedly until the end.

One of John Wordsworth's little boys became very attached to his great aunt, despite fears that she would frighten him. He insisted on saying his prayers in her room and rode around the garden with her, 'sitting at her feet, with a cord fastened round *Dolothy's* waist, which he whips along, calling her his *horse*, and he the *diver* – he is crazy about horses, poor little fellow.'[69] The garden gates were locked when Dorothy was being wheeled round the terrace, to prevent tourists coming in.

The Wordsworths were fed up with tourists. By 1848, people were coming from far afield, even from America, to see 'the Poet'. William greeted them all cordially, but Mary was inclined to hide, pretend she was not at home and allow a servant to show them the public parts of the house. Lakeland tourism was growing, especially since the development of the railways: 'The Country is strangely changed – think of an Hotel – Omnibus and Carriages running at different hours in the day between Grasmere and the Train! And of numbers pouring in by Monster trains . . . to the tune of nearly 4 score . . . upon this front and the Terraces. We have however *seen* nothing like this.'[70] William had been much opposed to the building of the railway, fearing just such an incursion, and Hartley Coleridge had written a letter to the papers accusing Wordsworth of wanting to keep the Lakes for himself and his rich friends.

Besides the tourists, there was also an influx of writers, those who came on extended visits like Felicia Hemans, and others who came to live in the Lakes. Mary was annoyed by Harriet Marti-neau, who had come to live in Ambleside. Mary went out for a walk every day in the afternoon specifically to avoid her calls. 'She is a pest . . .'[71] Miss Martineau smoked a pipe and tramped the narrow lanes in leather leggings and men's shoes with a knapsack on her back, causing considerable amusement in the district.

In later years, Mary acted as William's secretary, though her eyes were at least as bad as his, and the double portrait of Mary and William by Margaret Gilles shows her sitting at a table beside him with her pen in hand waiting for his dictation. With Dorothy an invalid, Sara Hutchinson and Dora dead, the full burden of

William's work fell on Mary. She wrote to a friend that he required 'almost all the time I have to spare from household concerns', leaving her no time for her own personal correspondence. Though the stamp office duties had been passed to her son Willy, Wordsworth had been appointed Poet Laureate on the death of Southey and there was still a voluminous amount of paperwork.

Dorothy made it difficult for Mary to leave home for a rest and was particularly demanding towards William. 'Dorothy, who tho' I think *mentally* better (bodily she is well and *strong*) in *some* respects, is become so much the Master of her Brother, who humours all her waywardnesses as quite to enervate him – so that whether he will have the heart to deprive her of his indulgences (which she is much happier without) by our leaving home – is doubtful.'[72]

In December 1848, Mary was sending bulletins to Sara Coleridge on the failing health of Hartley. Sara feared the worst: 'His illness has brought up strongly before my mind all my past early life in connection with my dear brother. I feel now more than I had done before how strong the tie is that binds me to him. Scarce any death would make me anticipate my own with such vividness as would his.'[73] Derwent was staying with the Wordsworths and was there when Hartley died on 6 January 1849. Even though she had expected it, his death was a terrible shock for Sara Coleridge. In the space of seven years, Sara had entered the names of her husband, her mother, her brother and one of her closest friends in the Death Book. She admitted: 'Nothing has ever so shaken my hold upon earth . . . I feel as if life were passing away from me in some sort; so many friends of my childhood and youth removed, so few of that generation left. It seems as if a barrier betwixt me and the grave were cast down.' She had hoped to see Hartley again, and remembered how he had been 'in my girlhood so deep a source of pride and pleasure, and at the same time the cause of such keen anguish and searching anxiety'. She felt it some comfort that he was to be buried in Grasmere churchyard beside 'dear bright-minded kind-hearted Dora who never mentioned his name but to say something of praise or affection.'[74]

Mrs Gillman had voiced what was to be the prevalent sentiment with regard to Hartley's life, in an earlier letter to Sara. 'I never could endure human judgement to be passed on him, having myself always believed, that there was some hidden cause for his conduct, some defect in the powers of his moral Will, which however did not extend to his Intellect – and which leaves him, as it were blameless, an innocent Being, without vice, yet fulfilling none of his duties, giving only pain to those he loves and by whom he knows himself beloved.'[75] The 'hidden cause', as Sara knew very well, lay in Hartley's childhood and in the genes he had inherited from his father. It was a legacy that was also very damaging to herself. William Wordsworth wrote of Sara and Hartley that 'but for being their father's children both would be larger figures in English literature.'

Sara was determined that there should be a new edition of Hartley's poems and essays, prefaced by a memoir. She was too busy herself to undertake the task, so it was entrusted to Derwent. Both were very clear that the account of Hartley's life should be as truthful as possible. 'It is not to be expected in these days, that what is to be lamented in Hartley's life and character can be "veiled in silence;" . . . if his prose and verse live, his personal history will live also . . .' It was better, Sara wrote, that it should be told 'by one deeply interested than by any one else'.[76]

Over the following year tentative steps towards a reconciliation between Wordsworth and Quillinan began. There were short visits, and the girls, Jemima and Rotha, occasionally came to stay. In January 1850 Wordsworth, now eighty, was invited to Lough-rigg to dine with Quillinan and Matthew Arnold – 'a trial which I feel I am unable to bear as with due submission to God's Will I ought to do.'[77] But he did accept the invitation. Quillinan himself never fully recovered from the blow of Dora's death and died in 1851.

During the year following Dora's death, Mary observed that William's memory gradually became 'clouded', and in the early spring of 1850 William had what Mary described as an 'ugly attack'. By 6 April 1850 he was confined to bed, though conscious. Despite great exhaustion he kept asking to have his back and his stiff leg scratched. 'Since Tea he has awaked and so sweetly! asking me "if I thought he would ever get well?" and upon my expressing my thoughts and explaining why he was so weak and what was to be done to regain lost strength, he jocosely observed – "You preach very nicely – Now read to me". This office I turned over to Eliz, to whom he said "You must excuse me if I fall asleep" – And truly it is even so – Yet at this instant Sister is come to see him, rather innopportunely – as he is too sleepy to be kept awake, and this is not desireable just now.'

William's illness had a strange effect on Dorothy, rousing her from her torpor. Quillinan was astonished to find that 'Miss W. is as much herself as she ever was in her life, & has an almost absolute command of her own will! does not make noises; is not all self; thinks of the feelings of others (Mrs W's for example), is tenderly anxious for her brother; and in short but for age and bodily infirmity, is almost the Miss Wordsworth we knew in past days.'[78]

On the Tuesday morning Mary wrote in increasingly tremulous handwriting that the hopes which had lingered in her heart 'have after a quiet night, passed away, and I feel I must – and I feel I must no longer . . . rest them *here*.'[79] William died at twelve o'clock midday on 23 April.

Mary was immediately plunged into problems as literary executrix. She was made very unhappy by some of the arrangements for publication of memoirs and a collected edition of William's poems which Dora and Isabella Fenwick had been working on before the former's death. This, with all notes, had been transferred to William's nephew Christopher. There was also the mass of unpublished material, including *The Prelude*, and it was Mary who arranged for the poem's publication and gave it the title.

Henry Crabb Robinson, in his memoir of Wordsworth, wrote succinctly on the debt William owed to the women he and Lamb had jokingly called his 'three wives'. 'If Providence had not blessed him with a wife, a sister, a wife's sister, and a daughter, whose lives were bound up in his life, as his was in theirs, and who felt that his poems were destined for immortality, and that it was no small privilege to be instrumental in conveying them to posterity, it is probable that many of his verses, muttered by him on the roads or on the hills, or on the terrace-walks of his own garden, would have been scattered to the winds . . .'

Sara Coleridge, while admitting that 'never was a Poet so blest before in the ladies of his household', commented caustically that he might have acquired more dexterity in the use of a pen if he had had to exercise it himself. But she acknowledged her own in-tellectual debt to Wordsworth when she had roamed the hills with him on her visits to Rydal Mount. 'My mind & turns of thought were gradually moulded by his conversation . . .' On a personal level she admitted that she was 'indebted to the character and daily conduct' of Southey. In the absence of her father she had been influenced by both as a growing girl 'yet I never adopted the opinions of either *en masse*'. In maturity she had discarded many of the opinions she acquired from them, achieving intellectual and spiritual independence.[80]

Sara guarded her children jealously from the stresses and incon-veniences of her own position. She didn't want them to suffer as she had suffered. Herbert was happily making a name for himself as a brilliant scholar at Oxford and eventually obtained a double first. Sara was very proud that she had helped by giving him extra tuition in Greek and Latin. Herbert's many prizes were as much a tribute to his mother's scholarship as to his own.

Edith was less scholarly and like Herbert had very little interest in poetry. Sara lamented that 'If Edith takes up a poem . . . it is for the sake of the story it contains, not for its imagery and poetic tone.' She wanted Edith to have as much fun as possible and took her, clothed in her own cut-down dresses, to balls and breakfasts. This lively social round meant that Edith was much more com-fortable in company than Sara had ever been. 'No child', she wrote, 'can have grown up more at ease, with less pressure from *anxiety* of any kind. A keen sense of the infelicity which certain anxieties and constraints caused me in my childhood and girlhood, has made me careful to guard her from the like . . .' Sara had no time for people who asserted that suffering was beneficial and instructive. 'Though these fretting trials *may* be turned to good account, may strengthen the mind, and do certainly purchase considerateness and reflective habits, their direct tendency is to injure: all pain is injurious unless made otherwise by an effort of the will.'[81]

At some point in 1849 Sara became aware of a lump in her right breast. Her physician, when she mentioned it, assured her that it was probably benign. But in the summer of 1850 it began to increase in size and another lump appeared in the lymph glands under her arm. The doctors she consulted told her that the tumour could be benign or cancerous – there was no way of knowing, and they were reluctant to operate. Sara was devastated, and her first thoughts were for Herbert and Edith. 'Alas! I live in constant fear . . . My dear, dear children.'

In the knowledge that she might well be terminally ill, Sara made what became the last entry in 'Dora's Book' – a sonnet entitled 'Prayer for Tranquillity'.

> Dear Lord, who, at thy blessed will,
> Didst make the raging wind be still,
> And smooth the tossing of the Sea,
> Oh! cause our stormy griefs to flee,
> Our wild tempestuous thoughts allay,
> And fires of passion send away.
> Conduct us here to perfect peace,
> When all our earthly transports cease,
> And lastly, while to Thee we cling,
> Our souls to that blest haven bring,
> Above the sphere of Care and Woe
> Where earthly blasts can never blow,
> With Thee to dwell, supremely blest,
> Anchored on everlasting rest.

Sara herself was far from tranquil. She fought with herself and the disease, raging against the injustice of it all in violent hysterical outbursts. She was homesick for Keswick: '. . . shall I really die, and never, never see thee again? . . . all the loveliness transfused, the hope, the joy of youth! . . . Oh! this life is very dear to me!'[82] She had so much work still to do and her children were not fully fledged. Herbert, in his second year at Oxford, had become engaged to a solicitor's daughter – much against Sara's will. But she became reconciled to the early match, feeling that at least Herbert's future would be assured. Edith, still in her teens, decided that she would live with her brother and his wife after her mother's death.

Sara continued to work on an edition of her father's poems, assisted by Derwent – so minimally that when the volume was published Derwent disclaimed any real part in it, saying that his contribution had been 'little more than mechanical'. Sara also began – secretly – to write her autobiography for the benefit of her children, particularly her daughter. It is addressed to 'My dearest Edith', and begins: 'I have long wished to give you a little sketch of my life. I once intended to have given it with much particularity, but now *time presses*: my horizon has contracted of late. I must content myself with a brief compendium.' She planned it in four parts, childhood, youth, married life and widowhood, intending to conclude each part with 'some maxim which it specially illustrated, or truth which it exemplified, or warning which it suggested'. Her life story was intended as a moral example for her daughter – an extension of Sara's hopes that her children would avoid the pitfalls of her own life. For a private document it is highly edited – skating over the Coleridges' marital difficulties – but fairly frank about Sara's ambivalent feelings towards her father. Sara's great attachment to her mother illuminates the pages from the first statement that 'the entry of my birth is in my dear Mother's hand-writing, and this seems like an omen'. She admits to having been a nervous and insomnolent child, unable to sleep unless cradled in her mother's arms. 'This weakness has accompanied me through life.' The memoir perfectly illustrates the division in Sara's psyche –

torn permanently between the safe, domestic haven symbolised by her mother, and the 'star-paved road' her father walked; a dichotomy aggravated by early nineteenth-century assumptions about women's capabilities and their role in society.

Sara's account ends in mid-sentence. 'On reviewing my earlier childhood I find the predominant reflection . . .' It is as if she put down the book to reflect, and found the conflicts and oppositions of her own life too difficult to reduce to an exemplary platitude. 'And like so many of her father's works,' Virginia Woolf remarked, 'Sara Coleridge remains unfinished . . .' The task of explaining herself for posterity was too difficult.

The disease advanced inexorably. 'When I see the sad state of the tumour I feel heart broken. But I sustain my poor heart and bind it up again by saying – It is only the body – *not the mind – not the mind* . . .'[83] By December 1851 she was confined to her bedroom and the adjacent sitting-room. 'I endeavour not to speculate – to make the most of each day as it comes . . .' She was still in very little pain, due to the large doses of morphine, but felt oppressed by 'sinking' sensations and an overwhelming fatigue. She wrote to her brother, 'Dear Derwent, I am dying. I feel it.' Isabella Fenwick sent £100 to ensure that her final months were spent in comfort. Sara longed to be buried, not beside her husband at Highgate, but in Crosthwaite churchyard: '. . . now I long to take away Mama's remains from the place where they are now deposited, and when my own time comes, to repose beside her, as to what now *seems* myself, in that grassy burial-ground, with the Southeys reposing close by. My husband I hope to meet in heaven; but there is a different feeling in regard to earlier ties . . .'[84]

In the spring of 1852 an announcement appeared in the columns of the London journals: 'May 3 at 10 Chester Place, Regent's Park, Sara Coleridge aged forty-nine years, only daughter of Samuel Taylor Coleridge, and widow of Henry Nelson Coleridge esq.' It was her fate, as with other remarkable women of her generation, to be defined in death, as in life, by the men to whom she was either married or related. Not 'Sara Coleridge poet and author', but 'Sara Coleridge daughter and wife'.

Aubrey de Vere wrote a moving tribute in a letter to Edith. 'Few', he told her, 'have possessed such learning,' yet 'with all her high literary powers she was utterly unlike the mass of those who are called literary persons . . . To those who knew her she remains an image of grace and intellectual beauty that time can never tarnish . . . She moved with the lightest step when she moved upon the loftiest ground. Her feet were "beautiful on the mountain-tops" of ideal thought. They were her native land, for her they were not barren; honey came up from the stoney rock.'[85]

Mary Wordsworth's right eye – her good one – had been gradually darkened by the formation of a cataract. But she found that her other eye, which had always had a squint and 'lurked in the corner', gradually improved as she struggled to use it and that after practice she could just see to read and thread a needle, though she found letter writing difficult. She was also lame with arthritis in her hips. But there was to be no rest for her, despite her age and infirmity. Her sister-in-law Dorothy, now eighty-two, was still alive and required constant attention, though the unpleasant work of washing, feeding and cleaning was done by servants. Whenever Mary's conscience and her own health allowed, she managed to get away for short visits to friends and relatives.

In 1853 Dorothy had one of her surprising periods of lucidity and wrote a letter to Mary, who was in London visiting Isabella Fenwick and other friends. Although written as simply as a young child might write, the letter is quite clear.

My dearest Sister, I have had a good night so I think I will write. The weather was rough. I was in bed all day. I am well today. My love to Miss Fenwick and Miss Jane – love to Hanna.
                                        Dorothy Wordsworth.
Mrs Pearson is very poorly and the Doctors say she cannot live. We have got a cow and very good milk she gives. I only wish you were here to have some of it.[86]

Dorothy celebrated her eighty-third birthday in bed, 'the best place for her, poor thing', on Christmas Day 1854. On 22 January she appeared to be in a state – 'had any other Invalid been in question' – of dying. But on 25 January at 5.20 p.m., Mary wrote, 'our dear Sister was released after her gradual but *fitful* sinking and some few hours of peaceful and anx[ious] waiting.'[87] The letter is blurred with tears. Both Mary's sons were with Dorothy at the end. Mary wrote to her niece: 'Last Wednesday the Remains were laid under the Thorn in the South East corner of the Church Yard by the side of the Grave of her loved companion my Sister [Sara Hutchinson].'[88] She was relieved that Dorothy had died before her: 'I shall forever feel thankful for the Almighty's goodness for having spared me to be the solitary lingerer . . .'[89] Mary herself only survived another year. She was, in the words of one obituary writer, the last 'of that constellation of bright particular stars'.

There were few left to mourn her – she had outlived them all. Only Derwent Coleridge, Cuthbert, the Southey girls and her sons John and Willy had survived. Mary had been a strong, self-sufficient woman who kept her thoughts and feelings to herself and was therefore difficult to know. Her whole life had been bound up in her family and a few close friends. A tribute to Mary appeared in the newspapers on 26 January 1856: 'We have seen her in her joy and in her sorrow – in the full enjoyment of her husband's honourable fame, in the thankful possession of his boundless love, respect, and gratitude; we have heard her with fearless truthfulness, combat his prejudices and maintain her opinions when he was flattered by the great and the noble, and but for her saving influence, might have been injured by it.'[90] For those who knew the Wordsworths, her greatest achievement had been the clear and measured gaze through which she looked at the world – albeit through a narrow aperture – and the pragmatism that acted as a counterpoise to her husband's susceptibilities.

# References

KEY

AJ Wordsworth, Dorothy, *Alfoxden Journal*
CCL Southey, C. C., *The Life and Correspondence of Robert Southey*
CNB Coburn, Kathleen, *The Notebooks of S. T. Coleridge*
DC Dove Cottage manuscripts
DQ De Quincey, Thomas, *Recollections of the Lakes and the Lake Poets*
GJ Wordsworth, Dorothy, *Grasmere Journal*
G&M Gittings and Manton, *Dorothy Wordsworth*
HRHRC UTA MS Harry Ransom Humanities Research Center, University of
  Texas at Austin
JTH PW Thelwall, John, *Poetical Works*
LLW&MW Darlington, Beth, *The Love Letters of William and Mary Wordsworth*
*Minnow* Potter, Stephen, *A Minnow among Tritons*
MWL Burton, Mary E., *The Letters of Mary Wordsworth*
NSLC Curry, Kenneth, *New Letters of Robert Southey*
PW Coleridge, S. T., *The Complete Poetical Works*
SCML Coleridge, Edith, *Memoir and Letters of Sara Coleridge*
SHL Coburn, Kathleen, *The Letters of Sara Hutchinson*
STCL Griggs, E. L., *Collected Letters of Samuel Taylor Coleridge*
UL STC Griggs, E. L., *The Unpublished Letters of Samuel Taylor Coleridge*
WW&DWL De Selincourt, Ernest, *The Letters of William and Dorothy
  Wordsworth*
  EY The Early Years
  MY The Middle Years
  LY The Later Years

## *Preface*

1. Angela Locke (after a haiku by Claire Harman)
2. DC
3. SHL
4. Adrienne Rich, *On Lies, Secrets and Silence*, Virago, 1980
5. 'The Other Side of the Mirror', *Poems of Mary Elizabeth Coleridge*, 1908
6. Sara Coleridge, *Phantasmion*, London, 1836

## *Chapter 1*

1. DQ
2. NSLC vol. i p. 150–1 September 1797
3. CCL
4. 'Mrs Codian'
5. Dowden, *Correspondence of Robert Southey with Caroline Bowles* L 52
6. Dowden, *Southey*
7. NSLC vol. i p. 27 14 July 1793
8. NSLC vol. i p. 37 December 1793
9. NSLC vol. i p. 48
10. NSLC vol. i no. 36
11. Haller, *Early Life of Robert Southey*
12. NSLC vol. i no. 83/84 October 1794
13. NSLC vol. i p. 84 October 1794
14. 'Mrs Codian'
15. STCL vol. i pp. 347–8
16. Letter to Asra, 1800 MS, DC
17. STCL vol. i p. 63
18. STCL no. 65
19. NSLC vol. i p. 58
20. STCL no. 50
21. STCL no. 51
22. NSLC vol. i p. 72 August 1794
23. STCL no. 65
24. Joseph Cottle, *Early Recollections*, 2 vols, 1837
25. STCL no. 77
26. STCL no. 59
27. STCL no. 522
28. STCL no. 1169
29. STCL no. 73
30. STCL no. 77
31. NSLC vol. i no. 76 August 1794
32. NSLC vol. i

33. 'Mrs Codian'
34. STCL no. 65
35. STCL no. 76
36. STCL no. 58
37. STCL no. 93
38. DQ
39. PW vol. i p. 64
40. STCL no. 238
41. WW&DWL EY, WW to Matthews 1795
42. ibid.
43. STCL no. 81
44. NSLC vol. i p. 93
45. Mrs Henry Sandford, *Thomas Poole and his Friends*, London, 1888
46. DQ
47. STCL no. 93
48. Sandford, *Thomas Poole and his Friends*

### *Chapter 2*

1. *Prelude* V, II
2. WW&DWL EY no. 293
3. WW&DWL EY no. 3
4. WW&DWL EY no. 5
5. WW&DWL EY no. 1
6. WW&DWL EY p. 421
7. WW&DWL EY no. 2
8. WW&DWL EY no. 28, 16 February 1793
9. WW&DWL EY no. 6
10. ibid.
11. WW&DWL EY no. 7
12. ibid.
13. WW&DWL EY no. 14
14. WW&DWL EY no. 9
15. WW&DWL EY nos. 9 and 11
16. ibid.
17. WW&DWL EY no. 28
18. WW&DWL EY no. 10
19. WW&DWL EY no. 30
20. WW&DWL EY no. 19
21. WW&DWL EY no. 28
22. ibid.
23. WW&DWL EY no. 26
24. WW&DWL EY no. 19
25. WW&DWL EY February 1804

26. WW&DWL EY no. 30
27. ibid.
28. WW&DWL EY no. 31
29. WW&DWL EY no. 32
30. WW&DWL EY no. 31
31. ibid.
32. WW&DWL EY no. 35
33. WW&DWL EY 21 April 1794
34. WW&DWL EY no. 277
35. WW&DWL EY no. 50
36. ibid.
37. WW&DWL EY no. 52
38. WW&DWL EY no. 55
39. WW&DWL EY no. 52
40. AJ 26 February 1798
41. WW&DWL EY no. 65
42. Broughton, *Sara Coleridge and Henry Reed*
43. WW&DWL EY no. 65

## Chapter 3

1. PW 'Reflections on having left a place of Retirement'
2. STCL no. 91
3. STCL no. 92
4. PW vol. i p. 104
5. Poole MS BL ADD 35, 343
6. NSLC vol. i p. 102
7. STCL no. 112
8. ibid.
9. PW vol. i p. 94
10. STCL no. 126
11. ibid.
12. DQ
13. STCL no. 124
14. STCL no. 142
15. PW vol. i p. 154
16. HRHRC UTA SC to ML 1843
17. STCL no. 136
18. Dowden, *Southey* p. 60
19. NSLC vol. i to Cottle
20. CNB 283 G 280
21. STCL no. 262
22. STCL no. 176
23. WW&DWL EY no. 70

24. STCL no. 195
25. WW&DWL EY no. 72
26. WW&DWL EY no. 83
27. STCL no. 200
28. JTH PW 1805 pp. 129–31
29. STCL no. 204
30. William Hazlitt, *Selected Writings*, ed. Ronald Blythe, Penguin Classics, 1987
31. G&M p. 66
32. STCL no. 317
33. STCL no. 178
34. Griggs, *Coleridge Fille*
35. DQ
36. *Letters of Dorothy Wordsworth*, ed. A. G. Hill
37. ibid.
38. STCL no. 243
39. PW vol. i p. 264 'The Nightingale'
40. SCML

## Chapter 4

1. WW&DWL EY nos. 85/6
2. WW&DWL EY no. 93
3. *Hamburg Journal*, ed. William Knight
4. *Letters of Charles and Mary Lamb*, 3 vols, ed. E. V. Lucas, London, 1935, vol. i no. 141
5. Holmes, *Coleridge*, vol. i pp. 209–10
6. STCL no. 259
7. WW&DWL EY no. 105
8. STCL no. 270
9. HRHRC UTA
10. STCL no. 254
11. STCL no. 262
12. DC
13. HRHRC UTA
14. STCL nos. 266 and 268
15. HRHRC UTA
16. Sandford, *Thomas Poole and his Friends*
17. ibid.
18. HRHRC UTA
19. STCL no. 277
20. WW&DWL EY no. 235
21. NSLC vol. ii nos. 3–4
22. STCL no. 275

23. STCL no. 276
24. HRHRC UTA
25. STCL no. 305f
26. WW&DWL EY no. 106
27. WW&DWL EY no. 119
28. WW&DWL EY no. 120
29. WW&DWL EY no. 93
30. Dowden, *Southey* p. 69
31. NSLC vol. i
32. Dowden, *Southey* p. 133
33. ibid. pp. 111–12
34. Dowden, *Correspondence of RS with CB* p. 369
35. NSLC vol. i pp. 183–95
36. STCL no. 294
37. HRHRC UTA
38. Raysor, 'Coleridge and Asra'
39. Griggs ed., *Letters of Hartley Coleridge*, p. 136
40. PW, 'To Asra', a sonnet, 1801
41. WW&DWL EY no. 124
42. WW&DWL EY no. 125
43. STCL no. 299
44. CNB I 1592
45. STCL no. 255
46. STCL nos. 318, 277, 255 and 318
47. STCL no. 330
48. DC

## *Chapter 5*

1. WW&DWL EY no. 126
2. ibid.
3. WW&DWL EY no. 127
4. GJ 18 May 1800
5. WW&DWL EY no. 169
6. GJ 27 May 1800
7. GJ 20 May 1800
8. GJ 24 May 1800
9. GJ 17 March 1802
10. GJ 23 March 1802
11. GJ 14 February 1802
12. GJ 4 March 1802
13. GJ 16 February 1802
14. GJ 14 March 1802
15. GJ 18 March 1802

16. STCL no. 341
17. HRHRC UTA
18. STCL no. 342
19. WW&DWL EY no. 140
20. STCL no. 353
21. STCL vol. i p. 602
22. STCL vol. i p. 643f, NY Public Library MS
23. NSLC vol. i p. 449
24. STCL vol. i p. 631f, NY Public Library MS
25. STCL no. 369
26. STCL no. 390
27. WW&DWL EY no. 140
28. ibid.
29. WW&DWL EY no. 157
30. WW&DWL EY no. 140
31. STCL no. 470
32. Raysor, 'Coleridge and Asra'
33. *Anima Poetae* p. 195
34. UL STC
35. STCL no. 470
36. LLW&MW 1 and 2
37. LLW&MW
38. MW Memoir, DC
39. GJ 31 January 1802
40. GJ 6 February 1802
41. GJ 2 June 1802
42. WW&DWL EY no. 169
43. ibid.
44. GJ 15 April 1802
45. GJ 13 March 1802
46. Aubrey de Vere, *Essays Chiefly on Poetry*, 1887 vol. ii pp. 276–7
47. Bateson, *Wordsworth: A Re-interpretation*, pp. 202–3
48. WW&DWL EY no. 171
49. GJ 6 October 1802
50. WW&DWL EY
51. WW&DWL EY no. 172
52. ibid.
53. GJ 21 April 1802
54. WW&DWL EY no. 160
55. WW&DWL EY
56. UL STC, vol. i p. 215
57. Griggs, *Coleridge Fille*
58. Mary Wollstonecraft, *Vindication* ch. 3, London, 1792
59. CNB
60. STCL no. 683

61. STCL no. 517
62. STCL no. 591

## Chapter 6

1. WW&DWL EY no. 172
2. GJ 13 July 1802
3. WW&DWL EY no. 178
4. GJ 24 September 1802
5. ibid.
6. ibid.
7. Professor Garrod in F. V. Morley, *Dora Wordsworth: Her Book*
8. HRHRC UTA
9. STCL no. 474
10. HRHRC UTA
11. STCL no. 481
12. MS NY Public Library
13. WW&DWL EY no. 205
14. WW&DWL EY no. 189
15. Knight, *Recollections of a Tour made in Scotland*, Saturday 27 August
16. ibid. Monday 29 August
17. STCL no. 514
18. Knight, *Recollections of a Tour made in Scotland*, Saturday 3 September
19. ibid.
20. STCL no. 516
21. WW&DWL EY no. 192
22. NSLC vol. i p. 211
23. NSLC vol. i p. 243
24. NSLC vol. i p. 145
25. NSLC vol. i p. 271
26. STCL no. 417
27. STCL no. 449
28. NSLC vol. i p. 324
29. Dowden, *Southey* p. 88
30. WW&DWL EY no. 206
31. STCL no. 489
32. SHL no. 46
33. SHL no. 52
34. CNB
35. CNB ff10–10v; Raysor, 'Coleridge and Asra'
36. WW&DWL EY no. 211
37. Dowden, *Southey*
38. NSLC vol. i pp. 372, 369
39. NSLC vol. i p. 326

40. WW&DWL MY no. 209
41. WW&DWL EY May/June 1804
42. WW&DWL EY no. 226
43. WW&DWL MY no. 135
44. Knight, *Journal of a Mountain Ramble*, 7 November 1805
45. ibid. 12 November 1805
46. WW&DWL EY no. 237
47. WW&DWL EY no. 237
48. WW&DWL EY no. 239
49. WW&DWL MY no. 14
50. WW&DWL EY no. 242
51. Dowden, *Southey* p. 95
52. Simmons, *Southey* p. 105
53. MWL no. 2
54. WW&DWL EY no. 246
55. WW&DWL EY no. 263
56. WW&DWL EY no. 272
57. WW&DWL EY no. 293
58. WW&DWL MY no. 60
59. WW&DWL EY no. 292

*Chapter 7*

 1. WW&DWL MY no. 58
 2. WW&DWL MY no. 48
 3. HRHRC UTA
 4. WW&DWL MY nos. 19–22
 5. WW&DWL MY no. 55
 6. STCL no. 642
 7. WW&DWL MY no. 55
 8. WW&DWL MY no. 134
 9. NSLC vol. i p. 451
10. ibid.
11. CNB 15, f115
12. CNB ff. 45–7
13. DQ
14. SHL no. 6
15. DQ
16. LLW&MW no. 5
17. WW&DWL EY no. 278f
18. GJ 23 May 1802
19. WW&DWL EY no. 164
20. MWL
21. WW&DWL MY no. 102

22. NSLC vol. ii
23. SHL no. 7
24. SHL no. 12
25. SCML
26. WW&DWL MY no. 255
27. *Anima Poetae*
28. ibid.
29. STCL no. 525
30. SHL no. 5
31. ibid.
32. WW&DWL MY no. 101
33. WW&DWL MY no. 157
34. WW&DWL MY no. 342
35. SHL no. 23
36. WW&DWL MY no. 184
37. WW&DWL MY no. 176
38. SHL no. 5
39. SHL no. 6
40. WW&DWL MY no. 188
41. ibid.
42. ibid.
43. WW&DWL MY no. 115
44. *Minnow* L 6
45. ibid.
46. UL STC
47. CNB, *Anima Poetae* p. 254
48. Raysor, 'Coleridge and Asra'
49. STCL no. 859
50. WW&DWL MY no. 225
51. Betham, *A House of Letters*
52. SHL no. 11
53. DC
54. *Minnow*
55. WW&DWL MY no. 243
56. *Minnow* L 7

## Chapter 8

1. PW 'On Receiving an account that his only Sister's Death was Inevitable'
2. SCML
3. WW&DWL EY no. 395
4. WW&DWL EY no. 272
5. SCML p. 17
6. WW&DWL MY no. 255

7. WW&DWL MY no. 81
8. LLW&MW no. 2
9. WW&DWL MY no. 234
10. WW&DWL MY no. 225
11. WW&DWL MY no. 226
12. WW&DWL MY no. 158
13. WW&DWL MY no. 150
14. WW&DWL MY no. 87
15. WW&DWL LY no. 408
16. *Minnow* no. 20
17. *Minnow* no. 15
18. *Minnow* no. 8
19. ibid.
20. SCML
21. *Colloquies* no. 6 vol. i pp. 116–9
22. NSLC vol. ii p. 119
23. *Minnow* no. 8
24. *Minnow* no. 19
25. Jones, *A Glorious Fame*, p. 180
26. *Minnow* no. 19
27. Betham, *House of Letters*
28. WW&DWL MY no. 55
29. NSLC vol. i pp. 413, 418
30. CCL vol. v
31. Warter, *Selections from the Letters of Robert Southey*, 14 September 1821
32. ibid. 24 December 1822
33. *Minnow* no. 16
34. ibid.
35. Griggs, ed., *Letters of Hartley Coleridge*
36. NSLC vol. ii
37. Shelley, Letters to E. Hitchener, 2 and 7 January 1812 (in Dowden, *Southey*)
38. NSLC vol. ii pp. 65–6
39. Reformists Register, 22 February 1817
40. DQ
41. WW&DWL MY no. 307
42. *Correspondence of Henry Crabb Robinson*, ed. Morley, vol. i no. 159
43. LLW&MW no. 2
44. ibid.
45. ibid.
46. LLW&MW no. 3
47. Sara Coleridge, 'Reasons for not placing Laodamia in the First Rank of Wordsworthian Poetry', HRHRC UTA
48. LLW&MW no. 4
49. LLW&MW no. 18
50. LLW&MW

51. *Minnow* no. 9
52. NSLC vol. ii p. 98
53. *Minnow*
54. STCL no. 643
55. STCL no. 638
56. SCML p. 16
57. SCML p. 15
58. SCML p. 3
59. *Minnow* no. 10
60. *Minnow* no. 18
61. *Minnow* no. 11
62. WW&DWL MY no. 318
63. NSLC vol. ii p. 99
64. SCML p. 20
65. SHL no. 25
66. WW&DWL MY no. 273
67. WW&DWL MY no. 272
68. DQ
69. WW&DWL MY no. 305
70. SHL no. 17
71. Morely, ed., *Correspondence of Henry Crabb Robinson*
72. WW&DWL MY no. 304
73. WW&DWL MY no. 305
74. *Minnow* no. 8
75. *Minnow* no. 19
76. *Minnow* no. 18
77. SHL no. 67
78. NSLC vol. ii p. 192
79. STCL no. 525
80. *Minnow* no. 15
81. SHL no. 18
82. NSLC vol. ii p. 194
83. NSLC vol. ii p. 196
84. SHL no. 66
85. NSLC vol. ii p. 235

## Chapter 9

1. *Minnow* no. 21
2. Southey, *The Doctor*, ch. LXXXV
3. Dowden, *Correspondence of RS and CB*
4. E. Gaskell, *Life of Charlotte Brontë*, ch. VIII, London, 1857; CCL, vol. VI
5. SCML pp. 27–8
6. E. Gaskell, *Life of Charlotte Brontë*, ch. XVI

7. SCML pp. 52–3
8. SHL no. 61
9. SHL no. 23
10. SHL no. 30
11. Dowden, *Correspondence of RS and CB*, no. LXXVI
12. WW&DWL MY no. 460
13. SHL no. 29
14. SHL no. 48
15. SHL no. 36
16. SHL no. 40
17. SHL nos. 40 and 41
18. WW&DWL LY nos. 18 and 25
19. WW&DWL MY no. 253
20. WW&DWL MY no. 395
21. WW&DWL MY no. 552
22. SHL no. 69
23. WW&DWL LY no. 52
24. *Minnow* no. 28
25. WW&DWL MY no. 600
26. WW&DWL LY no. 1
27. Knight, ed. DW Tour in the Isle of Man 26 June 1828
28. WW&DWL LY no. 30
29. WW&DWL LY no. 88
30. DC Notebooks of Edward Quillinan
31. SHL no. 78
32. WW&DWL LY no. 74
33. WW&DWL LY no. 99
34. *Familiar Letters of Sir Walter Scott*, 1894, vol. ii no. 342
35. STCL vol. v p. 268n
36. MS Fitzwilliam Museum, Cambridge
37. Towle, *A Poet's Children*
38. Griggs, *Coleridge Fille* p. 43
39. WW&DWL LY no. 102
40. NSLC vol. ii p. 261
41. HRHRC UTA to Derwent Coleridge
42. WW&DWL LY no. 140
43. SHL no. 84
44. WW&DWL LY nos. 18 and 159
45. HRHRC UTA
46. NSLC vol. ii
47. HRHRC UTA
48. WW&DWL LY no. 108
49. DC DW to EQ 1824
50. WW&DWL LY no. 135
51. WW&DWL LY no. 137

52. DC EQ to SH 17 September 1826
53. Broughton, *Sara Coleridge and Henry Reed*
54. NSLC vol. ii p. 305
55. CCL vol. v
56. *Minnow* no. 30
57. SHL no. 117
58. HRHRC UTA
59. ibid.
60. DC DW to EQ 22 December 1827
61. WW&DWL LY no. 214
62. *Dora Wordsworth: The Letters*, ed. Vincent, no. 33
63. WW&DWL LY no. 1145
64. WW&DWL LY no. 295
65. *Dora Wordsworth: The Letters* no. 5
66. *Dora Wordsworth: The Letters* no. 13
67. Letters of Maria Jane Jewsbury, DC
68. WW&DWL LY no. 379
69. WW&DWL LY no. 428
70. WW&DWL LY no. 483
71. WW&DWL LY no. 496
72. WW&DWL LY no. 511
73. WW&DWL LY no. 523
74. WW&DWL LY no. 270
75. *Dora Wordsworth: The Letters*
76. Henry Crabb Robinson, *On Books and their Writers*, ed. E. J. Morley, 1938, p. 262
77. WW&DWL LY Appendix
78. WW&DWL LY no. 428
79. WW&DWL LY no. 502
80. WW&DWL LY no. 496
81. WW&DWL LY no. 514
82. Dowden, *Correspondence of RS and CB*

## Chapter 10

1. Anon MS signed 'W.' Library of Pennsylvania
2. NSLC vol. ii p. 344
3. HRHRC UTA; Griggs, *Coleridge Fille* pp. 62–3
4. WW&DWL LY nos. 241 and 505
5. Griggs, ed., *Letters of Hartley Coleridge*
6. 'On the Death of Henry Nelson Coleridge, January 1843'
7. *Minnow* no. 34
8. WW&DWL LY no. 454
9. Griggs, ed., *Letters of Hartley Coleridge*

10. NSLC vol. ii p. 346
11. NSLC vol. ii p. 434
12. Dowden, *Correspondence of RS and CB* nos. XXI and XLIV
13. ibid. no. XLVI
14. DC; WW&DWL LY no. 750n
15. WW&DWL LY nos. 912, 917 and 921
16. WW&DWL LY no. 928
17. WW&DWL LY nos. 1176 and 1207
18. HRHRC UTA
19. STCL no. 1752
20. SCML, Sara Coleridge to Hartley Coleridge 5 August 1834
21. DC
22. Griggs, *Coleridge Fille*
23. SHL no. 153
24. *Minnow* no. 40
25. *Minnow* no. 34
26. SCML
27. Griggs, *Coleridge Fille*
28. SHL 17 March 1834
29. NSLC vol. ii p. 405
30. NSLC vol. ii p. 478
31. NSLC vol. ii p. 416
32. NSLC vol. ii to Lightfoot
33. Dowden, *Correspondence of RS and CB*, no. L
34. Vincent, ed., *Dora Wordsworth: The Letters* no. 34
35. Morley, ed., *Dora Wordsworth: Her Book* (Samuel Rogers to his sister)
36. WW&DWL LY no. 450a
37. WW&DWL LY nos. 705 and 706
38. MWL no. 83
39. MWL no. 82
40. SHL no. 158
41. WW&DWL LY no. 2096
42. Griggs, *Coleridge Fille*
43. DC EQ to DW 1835
44. SHL no. 169
45. WW&DWL LY no. 899
46. WW&DWL LY no. 944
47. WW&DWL LY no. 959
48. Griggs, *Coleridge Fille*
49. DC EQ to DW 26 November 1837; WW&DWL LY no. 1172n
50. DC; WW&DWL LY no. 1189n
51. DC; WW&DWL LY no. 1225n
52. WW&DWL LY no. 1225
53. NSLC vol. ii p. 422
54. NSLC vol. ii p. 434

55. NSLC vol. ii p. 441
56. NSLC vol. ii p. 462
57. NSLC vol. ii p. 479
58. MWL no. 81
59. NSLC vol. ii p. 470
60. Southey, Letters to Henry Taylor and Caroline Bowles
61. NSLC vol. ii p. 480
62. Dowden, *Southey*
63. WW&DWL LY no. 1465
64. Griggs, *Coleridge Fille*
65. ibid.
66. Anne Finch, Countess of Winchelsea, 'The Spleen', *Poems*, 1713
67. SCML 16 October 1836
68. SCML 10 October 1836

## *Chapter 11*

1. SCML SC to Hon. Mr Justice Coleridge February 1849
2. WW&DWL LY no. 1292
3. WW&DWL LY no. 1308n
4. DC EQ 17 April 1839; WW&DWL LY no. 1312n
5. WW&DWL LY no. 1312
6. MWL no. 102
7. Morley, *Dora Wordsworth: Her Book*
8. WW&DWL LY no. 1327
9. MWL no. 100
10. DC EQ 5 December 1839; WW&DWL LY no. 1389n
11. WW&DWL LY no. 1502n; BL MS
12. Letters of Edward Quillinan, DC
13. WW&DWL LY no. 1544
14. MWL no. 88
15. MWL no. 104
16. DC DW to IF June 1841
17. MWL no. 113
18. MWL no. 114
19. MWL no. 115
20. DC
21. Griggs, *Coleridge Fille*
22. SCML SC to Mrs Joshua Stanger, 10 August 1840
23. SCML 27 October 1841
24. SCML January 1843
25. Sara Coleridge diary, HRHRE UTA
26. SCML
27. MWL no. 118

28. WW&DWL LY no. 1814
29. WW&DWL LY no. 1964n; Sara Coleridge
30. Griggs, *Coleridge Fille*
31. WW&DWL LY no. 1985
32. SCML
33. Byron, 'Vision of Judgement'
34. CCL vol. v
35. WW&DWL LY no. 1683
36. Griggs, *Coleridge Fille*
37. SCML SC to ET 24 January 1830
38. SCML SC to Ellis Yarnall, 28 August 1851
39. SCML
40. ibid.
41. ibid.
42. DC
43. V. Woolf, *The Death of the Moth*, Hogarth Press, 1942
44. *Biographia Literaria*
45. Griggs, *Coleridge Fille*
46. Broughton, 3 July 1850
47. Sara Coleridge diary, 28 October 1848
48. MWL no. 121
49. WW&DWL LY no. 1814
50. WW&DWL LY no. 1828
51. DC Crabb Robinson Correspondence, 8 April 1845
52. WW&DWL LY no. 1911
53. Dora Quillinan, *Journal of a Few Months Residence in Portugal*
54. Morley, ed., *Dora Wordsworth: Her Book*
55. WW&DWL LY no. 2010
56. SCML SC to the Hon. Mrs Henry Taylor, 8 December 1845
57. WW&DWL LY no. 1920
58. WW&DWL LY no. 2054n; EQ Poems p. 38
59. MWL no. 127
60. MWL no. 129
61. MWL no. 130
62. MWL no. 132
63. WW&DWL LY no. 2066n
64. WW&DWL LY no. 2066
65. MWL no. 137
66. MWL no. 136
67. MWL no. 98
68. MWL nos. 97 and 107
69. MWL no. 83
70. MWL no. 142
71. MWL no. 163
72. MWL no. 143

73. SCML
74. SCML January 1849 and April 1850
75. Griggs, *Coleridge Fille* p. 70
76. ibid.
77. WW&DWL LY no. 2126
78. Morley, ed., *Correspondence of Henry Crabb Robinson*
79. MWL no. 151
80. SCML
81. Griggs, *Coleridge Fille*
82. Towle, *A Poet's Children*, SC to Aubrey de Vere
83. Diary 9 September 1851
84. SCML SC to Aubrey de Vere 1 October 1851
85. SCML Aubrey de Vere to Edith Coleridge
86. WW&DWL LY no. 2132
87. MWL no. 177
88. MWL no. 178
89. ibid.
90. *Witness*, Edinburgh 26 January 1856

# Select Bibliography

BATESON, F. W., *Wordsworth: A Re-interpretation*, Longman, 1954.

BETHAM, ERNEST, *A House of Letters*, Jarrold and Sons, 1905.

BROUGHTON, L. N., *Sara Coleridge and Henry Reed*, Cornell University Press, 1937.

BURTON, MARY E., *The Letters of Mary Wordsworth 1800–1855*, Clarendon Press, 1958.

COBURN, KATHLEEN, *The Letters of Sara Hutchinson 1800–35*, Routledge and Kegan Paul, 1954.

—— *The Notebooks of S. T. Coleridge* (3 vols), Routledge 1957.

COLERIDGE, EDITH, *Memoir and Letters of Sara Coleridge*, Henry S. King and Co., 1875.

COLERIDGE, S. T. C., *Anima Poetae: From the Unpublished Notebooks*, ed. E. H. Coleridge, London, 1895.

—— *Biographia Literaria* 1817 (2 vols), 1847 (3 vols), ed. Sara Coleridge.

—— *Collected Letters* (6 vols), ed. E. L. Griggs, Oxford, 1956–72.

—— *The Complete Poetical Works* (2 vols), ed. E. H. Coleridge, Clarendon Press, 1912.

—— *Unpublished Letters* (2 vols), ed. E. L. Griggs, Constable, 1932.

CURRY, KENNETH, *New Letters of Robert Southey* (2 vols), Columbia University Press, New York and London, 1965.

DARLINGTON, BETH, *The Love Letters of William and Mary Wordsworth*, Chatto and Windus, 1982.

DAVIES, HUNTER, *William Wordsworth*, Weidenfeld and Nicolson, 1980.

DE QUINCEY, THOMAS, *Recollections of the Lakes and the Lake Poets*, 1862, 1970 (Penguin, ed. David Wright).

DE SELINCOURT, ERNEST, *The Letters of William and Dorothy Wordsworth*, Clarendon Press.

—— Vol. i *The Early Years* (1935) Revised Chester L. Shaver 1967

—— Vol. ii *The Middle Years* (1970) Revised M. Moorman (2 vols)

—— Vol. iii *The Later Years* (1979) Revised A. G. Hill (4 vols)

DOWDEN, EDWARD, *Southey*, Macmillan and Co., 1884.

DOWDEN, EDWARD, *The Correspondence of Robert Southey and Caroline Bowles*, Dublin University Press, 1881.

DUNN, JUDY, *Sisters and Brothers*, Fontana, 1984.

GILL, STEPHEN, *William Wordsworth: A Life*, Clarendon Press, 1989.

GITTINGS, ROBERT and MANTON, JO, *Dorothy Wordsworth*, Clarendon Press, 1985.

GRIGGS, E. L., *Coleridge Fille*, Oxford University Press, 1940.

GRIGGS, E. L., *Wordsworth and Coleridge*, Princeton University Press, 1939.

GRIGGS, E. L., ed., *Letters of Hartley Coleridge*, Oxford University Press, 1941.

HALLER, W., *The Early Life of Robert Southey*, New York, 1917.

HILL, ALAN G., ed., *Letters of Dorothy Wordsworth: A Selection*, Clarendon Press, 1985.

HOLMES, RICHARD, *Coleridge*, Vol. I, Hodder and Stoughton, London, 1989.

HYMAN, EIGERMAN, *The Poetry of Dorothy Wordsworth*, Columbia University Press, NY, 1940.

JONES, KATHLEEN, *A Glorious Fame*, Bloomsbury, 1988.

KAPLAN, LOUISE J., *Lost Children: Separation and Loss between Children and Parents*, HarperCollins, 1995.

KNIGHT, WILLIAM, ed., *The Journals of Dorothy Wordsworth*, London, 1897.

LAMB, M. E., *Sibling Relationships*, Lawrence Erlbaum Associates, 1982.

LEFEBURE, MOLLY, *The Bondage of Love*, Victor Gollancz, 1986.

MADDEN, LIONEL, *Robert Southey: The Critical Heritage*, Routledge and Kegan Paul, 1972.

MOORMAN, MARY, *William Wordsworth: A Biography* (2 vols), Clarendon Press, 1957.

—— *Journals of Dorothy Wordsworth*, Oxford University Press, 1971.

MORLEY, E. J., ed., *Correspondence of Henry Crabb Robinson with the Wordsworth Circle*, 1935.

MORLEY, F. V., ed., *Dora Wordsworth: Her Book*, Selwyn and Blount, 1924.

MUDGE, BRADFORD KEYES, *Sara Coleridge: A Victorian Daughter*, Yale University Press, 1989.

POTTER, STEPHEN, *Minnow among Tritons: Mrs S. T. Coleridge's Letters to Thomas Poole* (1799–1834), Nonesuch Press, 1934.

QUILLINAN, DOROTHY (Dora Wordsworth), *Journal of a Few Months Residence in Portugal*, Longman, Green and Co., 1895

RAYSOR, Professor, 'Coleridge and Asra', *Studies in Philology* XXVI, July 1929.

SHOWALTER, ELAINE, *The Female Malady: Women, Madness and English Culture*, Virago, 1987.

SIMMONS, JACK, *Southey*, Collins, 1945.

SOUTHEY, C. C., *The Life and Correspondence of Robert Southey*, London, 1850.

SOUTHEY, ROBERT, *The Doctor*, ed. M. H. Fitzgerald, London, 1930.

TOWLE, ELEANOR A., *A Poet's Children*, 1912.

VINCENT, H. P., *Dora Wordsworth: The Letters*, Chicago, 1944.

WARTER, JOHN WOOD, *Selections from the Letters of Robert Southey* (4 vols), Longman, Brown and Green, 1856.

WHALLEY, GEORGE, *Coleridge and Sara Hutchinson and the Asra Poems*, Routledge and Kegan Paul, 1955.

# Index

# INDEX